D1474334

Liberalism versus Postliberalism

AMERICAN ACADEMY OF RELIGION

ACADEMY SERIES

Series Editor

Aaron W. Hughes, University at Buffalo

A Publication Series of The American Academy of Religion and Oxford University Press

AMERICAN ACADEMY OF RELIGION

LIBERALISM VERSUS POSTLIBERALISM

The Great Divide in Twentieth-Century Theology

John Allan Knight

OXFORD
UNIVERSITY PRESS

OXFORD
UNIVERSITY PRESS

Oxford University Press is a department of the University of Oxford.
It furthers the University's objective of excellence in research, scholarship,
and education by publishing worldwide.

Oxford   New York
Auckland   Cape Town   Dar es Salaam   Hong Kong   Karachi
Kuala Lumpur   Madrid   Melbourne   Mexico City   Nairobi
New Delhi   Shanghai   Taipei   Toronto

With offices in
Argentina   Austria   Brazil   Chile   Czech Republic   France   Greece
Guatemala   Hungary   Italy   Japan   Poland   Portugal   Singapore
South Korea   Switzerland   Thailand   Turkey   Ukraine   Vietnam

Oxford is a registered trademark of Oxford University Press
in the UK and certain other countries.

Published in the United States of America by
Oxford University Press
198 Madison Avenue, New York, NY 10016

© Oxford University Press 2013

Library of Congress Cataloging-in-Publication Data
Knight, John Allan.
Liberalism versus postliberalism : the great divide in twentieth-century theology /
John Allan Knight.
    p. cm.
Includes bibliographical references (p.) and index.
ISBN 978-0-19-996938-8 (hardcover : alk. paper)   1. Postliberal theology.
2. Liberalism (Religion)   3. Theology—History—20th century.   I. Title.
BT83.595.K55 2013
230'.046—dc23
2012026759

ISBN 978-0-19-996938-8

9 8 7 6 5 4 3 2 1
Printed in the United States of America
on acid-free paper

To my mother,
Justine Knight

And to the memory of my father,
John Allan Knight, Sr.

CONTENTS

CONTENTS

ACKNOWLEDGMENTS

I am indebted to many people, whom I cannot adequately thank, for the assistance and support they provided me as I completed this project. My debt to David Tracy is especially deep. He has been a gracious and wise mentor and friend who introduced me to a practice of reading theological texts with generosity, care, and honesty. His careful and insightful reading of these chapters kept the project from going astray at many points. Chris Gamwell and Kathryn Tanner also provided wise advice and attentive readings that were not only insightful, but also generous and patient. Paul Griffiths and Josef Stern also provided resources that were crucial in the development of the analysis I present here. Still, of course, the book's characterization of the divide between liberalism and postliberalism is my own. Any shortcomings in the argument or misreadings of texts are my own responsibility and can only be the result of my failure to heed their sage advice.

I am indebted to other colleagues as well, especially Cass Fisher and Bill Wright, who generously read and commented on nearly every chapter. Their insight, friendship, and support not only improved the project substantially, but made it immensely more enjoyable as well. Stephen Gunter has been an especially important mentor, friend, and conversation partner over several decades. His encouragement, support, and wise advice has been formative, sustaining, and deeply enriching, and it was crucial to this project. Matt Boulton and Andrei Buckareff have been important conversation partners, whose insights and friendship have proven invaluable.

Earlier versions of portions of chapters 2 and 3 appeared in "Descriptivist Reference and the Return of Classical Theism," in *Models of God and Other Ultimate Realities*, ed. Jeanine Diller and Asa Kasher (Dordrecht: Springer, forthcoming 2013), © Springer 2013, all rights reserved. An earlier version of a section of chapter 4 appeared as a part of "Truth, Justified Belief, and the Nature of Religious Claims: Schubert Ogden's Transcendental Criterion of Credibility," *American Journal of Theology and Philosophy*

27 (Jan. 2006): 55–83. An earlier version of several sections of chapter 5 appeared as "The Barthian Heritage of Hans Frei," *Scottish Journal of Theology* 61:3 (Aug. 2008): 307–26. An earlier version of a section of chapter 9 appeared as a part of "Why Not Davidson? Neopragmatism in Religious Studies and the Coherence of Alternative Conceptual Schemes," *Journal of Religion* 88 (April 2008): 159–89, copyright © 2008 by The University of Chicago. I am grateful to Springer, the *American Journal of Theology and Philosophy*, the *Scottish Journal of Theology*, and the *Journal of Religion* for permission to reprint these materials here.

I am very grateful to my editors in this series and at Oxford. I am particularly grateful to Kimberly Conner, whose perceptive counsel and unfailing encouragement kept the project going, especially after the death of my father, when it could easily have fallen by the wayside. Aaron Hughes shepherded the manuscript through the review process with admirable professionalism and efficiency. Cynthia Read and her team at Oxford have been a true joy to work with. Lisbeth Redfield helped me through a myriad of details, and my copyeditor, Will Moore, has remarkable eyes for detail. No one will know as well as I how much they have improved the book. Finally, Sravanthi Sridharan oversaw the production process with professionalism and efficiency. My gratitude for these fine professionals is indeed deep.

Most importantly, I would like to thank my wife, Melody Knowles, whose love and support were manifested in a myriad of ways, including her patient and careful reading of each chapter and her helpful comments on each one. Truly the book would not have been completed without her. I would also like to thank my children, Ella and Johnny, who not only patiently allowed their dad to sit for hours in front of the computer, but also provided remarkable (though perhaps unwitting) insight into a number of issues. Finally, I would like to thank my mother and father, whose love and support over the decades made it possible for me to devote my life to exploring and reflecting on my most highly valued commitments. My father did not live to see this book, but he read earlier versions of much of it. His comments and encouragement meant the world to me. His memory lives for me on every page of the book and of course is present to me every day. It is to them that the book is dedicated.

Liberalism versus Postliberalism

Introduction

During the 1960s, Antony Flew published a book entitled, *God and Philosophy*.[1] In the book, he argued that no philosophical support for theology is possible because statements about God are meaningless. His argument relied on the falsifiability hypothesis—that any claim not empirically falsifiable cannot be assigned any meaning. And since theistic claims cannot be empirically falsified, they must be strictly meaningless and incapable of philosophical support. Shortly after its publication, Flew presented his argument in a public lecture at the University of Chicago. Schubert Ogden was assigned to respond, and his critique demonstrated that Flew's argument failed because the falsifiability thesis was self-referentially incoherent. Since the thesis itself is not empirically falsifiable, it failed to meet its own desiderata and must be considered meaningless. Flew's response was silence.[2] Since that day, Ogden has become known for the force of the philosophical arguments he brings to theology, and the falsifiability thesis soon was widely acknowledged (even by most of its former supporters) to be incoherent.

Yet the incisive and devastating nature of Ogden's critique (advanced by various philosophers as well) was a mixed blessing. There is more to the falsifiability thesis than first meets the eye, and this "more" can reveal a good deal about the nature of religious and theological claims and the kinds of arguments that can be used to support them. The falsifiability thesis rests on a particular understanding of language that it shares with liberal theology. If the conversation had lasted longer, it might have resulted in a realization that discrediting the falsifiability thesis also casts doubt on the understanding of language it presupposes. And this realization, in turn, might have led to a

---

1. Antony Flew, *God and Philosophy* (New York: Harcourt, Brace & World, 1966).
2. A report of this event was related to me in a conversation with Franklin Gamwell.

reexamination of the great divide in twentieth century theology—the divide over how to validate Christian theological claims, instigated by Karl Barth's revolt against his teachers, the great nineteenth-century liberal theologians like Harnack and Hermann and their mentors dating back to Schleiermacher.

The full Barthian revolt, of course, is commonly dated to the publication of the second edition of Barth's *Epistle to the Romans* in 1922. Since then, theology in the twentieth century has been characterized by turmoil that has not only shaken the foundations of the western Christian theological tradition, but indeed has questioned whether Christian theology ever had or needed any "foundations." Much of the turmoil has arisen out of theology's struggle with how to validate its claims, and much of that struggle has revolved around whether and to what extent the validation of theological claims must be a "foundational" enterprise. What kind of argument should count as a validation of theological claims? For theologians such as Barth and his followers, the only validation needed by any theological claim is a showing that it comports with God's self-revelation in Jesus Christ. On this view, to validate theological claims by appeal to any other criteria, including criteria that Christians and non-Christians alike could share, is to forsake the central Christian affirmation that "Jesus is Lord." Liberal theologians, on the other hand, argue that God's self-revelation in Christ cannot be the sole criterion of validation, because this yields only a determination of whether the claim under investigation is distinctively Christian, but cannot determine whether such a claim is true. On the liberal view, to determine the truth of theological claims, we need criteria that are either universally (or at least widely) accepted, or that can be rejected only on pain of self-contradiction.

This liberal/Barthian divide has shaped the contours of theology throughout the twentieth century. Of course, this is not to say that all theologians were equally interested in it. Theologians outside the Anglo-American Protestant context have not given nearly as much attention to this liberal/Barthian divide as those within it. Nonetheless, the tension between liberal and Barthian ways of doing theology pervades every stream of late twentieth-century theology, with each stream either taking sides (e.g., process theology siding with liberal theology, postliberal theology siding with Barth) or incorporating the tension within the stream. Methodologically, corollaries of the divide can be seen in debates within feminist theology, liberation theology, and black theology, among other strands. For example, many of the debates within feminist theology over essentialism are parallel to the liberal/Barthian debate over theological method. Anti-essentialist feminist theologians argue that there is no universal (or universalizable) "women's experience," even in the dimension of oppression, that can serve as a universal criterion of validation (even if the scope of such "universalizing" is restricted to feminist theology).[3] In contrast, these authors stress the diversity of women's experience in a way that is methodologically similar to the Barthian and postliberal emphasis on the particularity of claims about Jesus. And indeed, some anti-essentialist feminist theologians have used postliberal writers such as Lindbeck as a resource in theorizing a postmodern, particularist approach to feminist theology.[4] Many womanist theologians have distanced themselves from both feminist and black theologians on similar grounds, and other parallels can be cited.

This methodological divide can often seem intractable because each side has an important demand that the other side cannot meet. Liberal theologians are concerned about the truth of theological claims and seek a way of doing theology that can legitimate or validate such claims as being true. They insist on validating theological claims by reference to criteria that are general (i.e., that are not limited to particular fields of discourse), and argue that any theological claim that cannot meet such criteria is arbitrary. Barthian theologians, on the other hand, and especially Barth's postliberal heirs, are skeptical that any such criteria can be articulated. Indeed, they argue that any attempt to meet such criteria distorts the claims of Christianity. Liberals, then, insist on general criteria of meaning and validation, while Barthians insist on the particularity of claims, especially concerning Jesus. Neither side can meet the other's demands, and this inability constitutes the great divide in twentieth-century theology.

Because the disagreement is methodological in nature, the problem itself seems to rule out any agreement over any grounds or criteria that might adjudicate it. In such an environment, how can dialogue be fruitful? Surely one important step in any productive dialogue is to delineate as clearly as possible just where the parties disagree. Naturally, there are a number of disagreements between liberals and postliberals that will remain mostly ignored here. These include many of their substantive theological disagreements outside the context of method. In this book, I will focus on their philosophical disagreements, and even more specifically, their philosophical differences over language. A conviction motivating this book is that the reasons for this mutual paralysis can be displayed by examining the underlying understanding of religious language each side assumes. It is precisely their understandings of religious language that renders each side unable to meet the demands of the other. This is the primary task of this book—to analyze the

3. See, for example, Linell Elizabeth Cady, "Identity, Feminist Theory, and Theology," in *Horizons in Feminist Theology: Identity, Tradition, and Norms,* ed. Rebecca S. Chopp and Sheila Greeve Davaney (Minneapolis: Fortress Press, 1997), 18, 21; Emilie Townes, *Womanist Ethics and the Cultural Production of Evil* (New York: Palgrave Macmillan, 2006).
4. Cady, "Identity, Feminist Theory, and Theology," 27.

methodological divide between liberal and postliberal theologies. This analysis, in turn, suggests elements of a new, more adequate theological method.

One aspect of the liberal/postliberal divide that in my judgment needs fuller discussion is their linguistic disagreement. It would be possible, and indeed useful, to analyze this disagreement from any of several different perspectives, including phenomenological, pragmatic, or deconstructionist perspectives, among others. But one perspective that especially needs fuller discussion, and partly for that reason is particularly useful, is an analytic perspective. From this perspective, liberal theologians typically have very different views of the meaning and reference of religious and theological language from those who seek to follow Barth. The lack of attention to this issue is surprising, in my view, because such views are an essential part of theological method. A theological method may include a number of elements, but any theological method of whatever stripe must include some account of how to interpret a religious or theological claim and an account of how to assess and defend such a claim (or an explanation of why no such defense is necessary). Whether explicitly articulated or implicitly assumed, the presence and operation of such accounts can be detected in any theological method. Consequently, interpretation and assessment are unavoidable parts of any theological proposal. But *to interpret* a theological or religious claim just is to give its meaning. And giving its meaning involves, among other things, addressing the reference of its singular terms like "God," "Jesus," "Augustine's *De Civitate Dei*," etc.[5] *To assess* such a claim, one must determine whether the claim could be true, and whether and under what circumstances one would be justified in believing it. And *to defend* (or support or provide reasons for) such a claim is nothing other than to show that the claim can be true and that one is justified in believing or asserting it (or to describe the conditions under which one would be justified in doing so). Thus, four crucial methodological concepts of any theological method are meaning, reference, justification, and truth. Failure to be clear about such important concepts has surely contributed to the intractability of the divide between liberals and Barthians in the twentieth century. In the chapters that follow, I try to make as clear as possible the contours of the methodological disagreement between liberal and postliberal theologies by describing their differing views on linguistic meaning and reference and analyzing the relationship between these differences.

One helpful tool in elucidating these differences can be found in the challenge to theology issued by the falsification theorists in the middle of

---

5. On some accounts of meaning, like the later Wittgenstein's, the issue of reference dissolves, so that *determining* the reference of singular terms is unnecessary. But such accounts nevertheless *address* the issue of reference by giving reasons why it can be dissolved.

the twentieth century. In part I of the book I shall focus my discussion on describing liberal theology and the way the falsification challenge brought to the fore its understanding of religious and theological language. Liberal theology, of course, is a messy business, with many of its adherents sharing more differences than similarities. Indeed, Jeffrey Stout has questioned the utility of using the term "liberalism" at all.[6] Yet a number of theologians still identify themselves as liberal, and I think some shared themes or concerns can be identified. I'll try to do this in the first part of the book. Chapter 1 includes a very brief survey of three important figures in nineteenth-century liberal theology: Schleiermacher, Ritschl, and Harnack. Their work nicely illustrates three themes characteristic of liberal theology—a methodological turn to the subject, a serious interest in historical investigation, and a search for the essence of Christianity. These three concerns work together to yield a theological method that is essentially transcendental in the way it derives its basic concepts and validates its basic claims.

The falsification challenge presented a serious threat to liberal theology, as we'll see in chapter 2. The ground for the challenge was prepared by the mid-century consensus on meaning and reference assumed by all the parties to the debate (Wittgensteinians joined the debate later). I'll call this the "descriptivist" view of language, and it is a crucial assumption of John Wisdom's famous parable of the imaginary gardener. This parable provided Antony Flew with a basis for his linguistic argument against theism. Skeptics such as Flew and Wisdom challenged theologians to differentiate the referent of "God" from that of "an imaginary gardener." In chapter 3, we'll see that, in the later 1950s and 1960s, a number of prominent theologians and philosophers took the falsification challenge to be very serious. Many of the major theological journals, as well as journals devoted to philosophical theology or philosophy of religion, published essays regarding the controversy.[7] A number of prominent theologians and philosophers of religion either addressed Flew's challenge directly or discussed the most

6. See Jeffrey Stout, *Democracy and Tradition* (Princeton, N.J.: Princeton Univ. Press, 2004), esp. 130–35, 140–57.
7. See, for example, Alastair McKinnon, "Unfalsifiability and Religious Belief," *Canadian Journal of Theology* 12 (1966): 118–125; John Hick, "Theology and Verification," *Theology Today* 17:1 (April 1960): 12–31; Leroy T. Howe, "Theology and its Philosophical Commitments," *Scottish Journal of Theology* 24 (1971): 385–406; William J. Wainwright, "Religious Statements and the World," *Religious Studies* 2 (1966): 49–60; John MacDonald Smith, "Philosophy and God," *Church Quarterly Review* 168, no. 366 (Jan. 1967): 75–83; George Mavrodes, "God and Verification," *Canadian Journal of Theology* 10 (1964): 187–91; Trevor Winston, "God and the Verification Principle: Faith versus Verification," *Religion in Life* 32:1 (1963): 29–35; Schubert M. Ogden, "God and Philosophy: A Dialogue with Antony Flew," *Journal of Religion* 48 (1968): 161–81; Donald D. Evans, "Falsification and Belief," *Studies in Religion/Sciences Religieuses* 1 (1971): 249–50; and Dallas M. High,

prominent responses.[8] Seminary journals published articles discussing the controversy directly or reviewing books by the participants.[9] Several leading journals devoted entire issues to the controversy,[10] and a number of books appeared collecting essays relating to the controversy.[11] Monographs appeared as well,[12] and clergy and members of religious orders weighed in on the controversy, as well as scholars.[13]

From within the ranks of liberal theologians, the responses tended to be a version of one of two sorts. The first sort can be characterized as generally noncognitive, arguing that religious or theological utterances were never

"Belief, Falsification, and Wittgenstein," *International Journal for Philosophy of Religion* 3 (1972): 239–50.

8. See, for example, John Hick, "Theology and Verification," *Theology Today* 17:1 (April 1960): 12–31; James C. S. Wernham, "Eschatological Verification and Parontological Obfuscation," *Canadian Journal of Theology* 13 (1967): 50–56; Kai Nielsen, "Eschatological Verification," *Canadian Journal of Theology* 9 (1963): 271–81; Alastair McKinnon, *Falsification and Belief* (New York: Humanities Press, 1970); Thomas F. Torrance, "Article Review of *Falsification and Belief* by Alastair McKinnon," *Scottish Journal of Theology* 25 (1972): 435–53; Howard R. Burkle, "Counting Against and Counting Decisively Against," *Journal of Religion* 44 (1964): 223–29; Schubert M. Ogden, "God and Philosophy: A Dialogue with Antony Flew," *Journal of Religion* 48 (1968): 161–81; Schubert M. Ogden, "Falsification and Belief," *Religious Studies* 10 (1974): 21–43; and Frederick C. Copleston, "God and Philosophy," *Journal of Theological Studies* 18 (1967): 303–308.

9. See, for example, Diogenes Allen, "Review of Falsification and Belief by Alastair McKinnon," *Princeton Seminary Bulletin* 64 (1971): 102–103; John Franklin Miller III, "First Order Principles in Science and Religion," *Iliff Review* 28:1 (Dec. 1971): 47–58; Ralph G. Wilburn, "The Problem of Verification in Faith-Knowledge," *Lexington Theological Quarterly* 4:2 (1969): 33–45; and James Harry Cotton, "Questions, Interest, and Theological Inquiry," *McCormick Quarterly* 22:2 (Jan. 1969): 121–33.

10. *Religious Studies* and *Religion in Life* published issues focused primarily on the falsification controversy. *Church Quarterly Review* and the *Canadian Journal of Theology* both published a number of articles throughout the mid-1960s on the controversy. For representative articles, see Thomas McPherson, "The Falsification Challenge," *Religious Studies* 5:1 (Oct. 1969): 81–84; Frederick P. Ferré, "God and the Verification Principle: Verification, Faith, and Credulity," *Religion in Life* 32:1 (1963): 46–57; William Gordon Ross, "God and the Verification Principle: The Question of Verification," *Religion in Life* 32:1 (1963): 8–18; and Kai Nielsen, "God and Verification Again," *Canadian Journal of Theology* 11 (1965): 135–41.

11. See, for example, Ronald E. Santoni, ed., *Religious Language and the Problem of Religious Knowledge* (Bloomington: Indiana Univ. Press, 1968); Basil Mitchell, ed., *The Philosophy of Religion* (Oxford: Oxford Univ. Press, 1971); and Robert H. Ayers and William T. Blackstone, eds., *Religious Language and Knowledge* (Athens: Univ. of Georgia Press, 1972).

12. See, for example, Ian T. Ramsey, *Religious Language* (London: SCM-Canterbury Press, 1967), and Alastair McKinnon, *Falsification and Belief* (The Hague: Mouton, 1970).

13. See, for example, Trever Winston, "God and the Verification Principle: Faith Versus Justification," *Religion in Life* 32:1 (1963): 29–35; Anselm Atkins, O.C.S.O., "Religious Assertions and Doctrinal Development," *Theological Studies* 27:4 (1966): 523–52; John King-Farlow and William N. Christensen, "Faith—and Faith in Hypothesis," *Religious Studies* 7 (1971): 113–24.

straightforward assertions, though they may often seem to be. Instead, they are to be understood symbolically, or as expressions of an intention to follow a certain way of life, or as expressions of an internalized spiritual principle. R. M. Hare, for example, famously argued that religious statements are expressions of our *"bliks,"* or fundamental attitudes toward the world.[14] The second sort of response can be characterized as generally cognitive, arguing that some religious or theological utterances are indeed straightforward (and meaningful) assertions. Some argued that theological assertions could in principle be falsified, but that in fact they have not been (or at any rate not all of them). John Hick, for example, argued that statements about God could indeed be falsified or verified, but only eschatologically—that is, after we die.[15] Others argued that such assertions are meaningful because there are things that count as evidence against them, despite their invulnerability to *conclusive* empirical falsification. Basil Mitchell, for example, acknowledged that evil counts as evidence against the truth of the assertion that God exists and is omniscient, omnibenevolent, and omnipotent. Thus, such an assertion is meaningful as an assertion even though a theist may not be disposed to allow evil or suffering to count as decisive evidence against it.[16] Still others argued that God's necessary existence, derived from a transcendental analysis of human experience, met all the descriptivist requirements for successful reference.[17] Yet none of these responses challenged Flew on a crucial fundamental supposition—namely, that the descriptivist understanding of language was correct. Liberal theology, that is, assumed that if religious or theological assertions are to be meaningful, they must meet the descriptivist requirements described in chapter 2.

Liberal theology contains internal dynamics that allow an adequate response. What I call a "purified" liberal theology, described in chapter 4, nicely illustrates the central concerns and internal dynamics of liberal theology. Rudolf Bultmann, Alfred North Whitehead, and Charles Hartshorne are complementary figures in several ways. Bultmann offers a characteristically liberal way of analyzing human experience (existential analysis)

14. R. M. Hare, "Theology and Falsification," in *New Essays in Philosophical Theology,* ed. Antony Flew and Alasdair MacIntyre (London: SCM Press, 1955; repr., 1958), 99–103 (page references are to reprint edition).

15. John Hick, *Faith and Knowledge* (Ithaca, N.Y.: Cornell Univ. Press, 1957), and "Theology and Verification," *Theology Today* 17 (1960): 12–31.

16. Basil Mitchell, *New Essays in Philosophical Theology,* 103–105.

17. This is one way to read Schubert Ogden's title essay in Schubert M. Ogden, *The Reality of God and Other Essays* (New York: Harper & Row, 1966; 2d ed., Dallas, Tex.: Southern Univ. Press, 1992), 1–70.

and interpreting biblical texts (demythologization), while Whitehead and Hartshorne offer a liberal conception of God intended to survive Kant's objection to the concept of God used by Anselm in his ontological argument. As it happens, this conception of God is also perfectly suited to satisfying the requirements of descriptivist reference demanded by the falsification theorists. These three figures illustrate what Barth calls the anthropological starting point of liberal theology (despite the obviously metaphysical character of Whitehead's and Hartshorne's thought) and the affinities between descriptivist reference and liberal theological method. These thinkers provide a fitting background for a more extended consideration of Schubert Ogden, whose signal achievement was to integrate Bultmann's existential hermeneutics and analysis of human experience with Hartshorne's dipolar concept of God. Now, neither process metaphysics nor Bultmann's existential analysis, both of which pervade Ogden's theological writings, ever became a consensus position among theologians who classify themselves as liberal. Thus one might think that Ogden can't be a true representative of liberal theology. Indeed, the many differences among liberal theologians could make one despair of finding any adequate representative for them. Yet Ogden offers an articulation of the central concerns of liberal theological method whose clarity and consistency remain unsurpassed. For Ogden, theological claims must be validated by showing that they are both appropriate to the normative Christian witness—interpreted using Bultmann's existential hermeneutic—and credible to human existence. These commitments make Ogden an excellent representative of the liberal position in theology and highlight the relationship between liberal theological method and a descriptivist stance on the meaning and reference of religious language.

Part II looks at the other side of the great divide in twentieth-century theology, Barthian and postliberal theology. Chapter 5 features Barth's struggle to provide an alternative to liberal theological method. Yet my focus is not on Barth himself, but on the way he is read by postliberals, and especially Hans Frei's early analysis of Barth's break with liberalism. For Barth himself, what he called the anthropological starting point of liberal theology was its central and fatal problem. Frei sees this clearly (as have most of Barth's interpreters) and identifies three themes in Barth designed to move him away from any such anthropological starting point. First, ontology must take priority over epistemology. Theology must begin with ontological affirmations about God, as these affirmations are given in the Incarnation and the witnesses to it in the Bible. Frei himself will work out this theme in his own insistence on the priority of biblical narratives in theology. Second, theological method must be subordinate to and governed by these positive ontological statements about God. This implies, Barth thinks (at least on postliberal readings), that theology cannot be truly systematic but must remain ad hoc, because all true systematizing will be anthropologically and epistemologically driven. Frei himself will work out this theme in his insistence that theological method be subordinate to and governed by the realistic readings of the Gospel narratives and the portrait or revelation of God given in them. The third theme is that of interpretation; on Frei's reading of Barth, interpretive method must be governed by his methodological commitments and his ontological affirmations about God. These three Barthian themes can be construed as almost antitheses to the three liberal concerns worked out by nineteenth- and twentieth-century liberal theologians. Barth and his postliberal heirs clearly want to do theology in a thoroughly different way.

But postliberal theologians are not merely cheerleaders for Barth, and they seek to do much more than simply reiterate his pronouncements. In fact, at least on my reading, they have a distinct way of reading Barth, however much postliberal theologians may differ from each other (and there are, of course, significant differences). They seek instead to develop Barth's project further, and to do that they enlist allies that were largely unavailable to Barth. Chief among these allies is Ludwig Wittgenstein and the ordinary language philosophers he inspired, though other allies are enlisted as well, including Eric Auerbach and Clifford Geertz. Thus, one could analyze postliberal theology from a pragmatic or literary perspective (and other perspectives are possible, too), focusing on Auerbach, Geertz, or others. But for my purposes, Wittgenstein and ordinary language philosophy are most important, because it is here in my judgment that we find one of the most important differences between liberal and postliberal theology. Cryptically put, liberal theologians' views of language tend to follow those advanced by Frege, Russell, and the early Wittgenstein, while followers of Barth (most explicitly the narrative theologians) follow the later Wittgenstein, Ryle, and ordinary language philosophy, which I'll describe in chapter 6. Frege, Russell, and the early Wittgenstein (there are, of course, significant differences among these three, but they need not detain us at the moment) were most important in developing the "descriptivist" view of language. It includes a view of both meaning (how sentences and subsentential units acquire their meaning or sense) and reference (how words or expressions "refer" or point to objects in the world). On this view, each meaningful sentence (if it is not a tautology) *describes* a corresponding possible fact. If this possible fact is actual, the sentence is true; if not, it is false. In other words, a sentence acquires its meanings by virtue of its *truth conditions*. To ask what a sentence means, you must ask what facts must obtain for the sentence to be true. For sentence parts (other than logical terms), meaning is also acquired descriptively, and it is closely related to reference. For example, the meaning of a singular term is a descriptive sense that uniquely describes the singular object to which the term refers. Reference, that is, proceeds by description. Similarly, the meaning of a sentence predicate is a description that describes the subject S of the sentence just in case the predicate is true of S. Consider the claim, "God created the universe." For descriptivists, the terms "God," "created," and "universe" must have a unique descriptive sense in order to have meaning. If they do, and the sentence is well formed, then one can figure out *what must obtain* in order for the sentence to be true. And this *what-must-obtain* constitutes the sentence's truth conditions and, *eo ipso*, its meaning.

Postliberal theologians, on the other hand, tend to follow the views of the ordinary language philosophers like the later Wittgenstein and Gilbert Ryle. If descriptivism takes the basic function of language to be that of describing a picture of the world or some portion of it (some possible fact or "state of affairs"), ordinary language philosophers take this view to be mistaken. Thus, later in his career, Wittgenstein replaces the inquiry about truth conditions (or *what-must-obtain* for the sentence to be true) with two others: First, under what conditions may this sentence be appropriately asserted? Second, what role does our practice of asserting the sentence play in our lives? Thus, he will say, "Don't think, look!"—or, as Hans Frei paraphrases, "Don't ask for the meaning, ask for the use." Therefore, all that is required for a sentence to have meaning is that there be roughly specifiable circumstances under which it is legitimately assertable and that the language game which involves its assertion plays a role in our lives. This is essentially the ordinary language view, though of course there were differences among ordinary language philosophers.

The central burden of the book is to show that underlying the methodological differences between liberal and postliberal theology is this difference over the way religious and theological statements acquire meaning. Though Geertz was important as well, it was primarily Wittgenstein to whom George Lindbeck is indebted in developing his theories of religion and doctrine. And along with Auerbach, it was primarily Wittgenstein and Ryle that Frei utilized to advance his Barthian insistence on the primacy of the Gospel narratives and his resistance to any theory that serves as an a priori lens through which to view them. Throughout his work, Frei argues that the task of Christian theology cannot include apologetics, because apologetic argument inevitably distorts the distinctive Christian message. Instead, just as Wittgenstein had argued that philosophy must foreswear explanation and limit itself to description, Frei argues that Christian theology must limit its task to Christian self-description and its method to the kind of "thick description" articulated by Clifford Geertz. Thus, though Geertz's "thick description" provides Frei with a model for Christian self-description, it is Wittgenstein who drives him to it. So chapter 6 sets out the central theses that constitute the way Wittgenstein and ordinary language philosophers understand language and why they reject descriptivism.

Earlier postliberalism was developed by Hans Frei's work in the 1970s. More than any of Barth's followers (perhaps even Lindbeck), Frei illustrates why a Wittgensteinian understanding of the meaning of religious language is crucial to the success of Barth's project, at least in its postliberal form. Frei sought to extend Barth's critique of nineteenth-century liberal theology by utilizing resources available to him that were unavailable to Barth. These include a way of understanding the nature of biblical narratives that he learned from Eric Auerbach and a view of language that he learned from Ludwig Wittgenstein and Gilbert Ryle. In Frei's early work, described in chapter 7, his reliance on Wittgenstein can be seen in his magisterial critique of modern liberal theology in *The Eclipse of Biblical Narrative* and in his constructive proposal in *The Identity of Jesus Christ*. His critique of modern liberal theology is centered around a conviction that descriptivism ("meaning as reference," to use his phrase) is a basic theological and philosophical mistake. His constructive project seeks above all to give primacy to the depictions of Jesus' identity located in the narrative structure of the Gospels. He does this through an argument about the meaning of these narrative depictions.

What might be called the second phase of postliberal theology revolved around Frei's essays from the 1980s and Lindbeck's influential theories of religion and doctrine articulated in *The Nature of Doctrine*. During this second period, as I argue in chapter 8, the postliberal reliance on Wittgenstein and ordinary language philosophy comes into even clearer focus. In subsequent phases, their students developed postliberal theology to address broader and somewhat divergent areas of concern. Thus, we can see somewhat different emphases in the work, for example, of Stanley Hauerwas, George Hunsinger, William Placher, Kathryn Tanner, and others. But insofar as they are advancing a truly postliberal agenda, they are indeed seeking, in one way or another, to carry forward the program of Frei and Lindbeck. Thus, in analyzing postliberal theology, I will narrow my focus to Frei and Lindbeck because, in my view, their reliance on Wittgenstein and ordinary language philosophy, though widely acknowledged, needs a fuller discussion.

More specifically, Frei appropriates three themes from ordinary language philosophy. First, against descriptivism, ordinary language philosophers hold that the meaning of a word, phrase, or sentence is nothing more than its use in ordinary life. For his part, Frei stresses that the meaning of the biblical narratives derives from their use in the life of the Christian community. The second and third themes follow from the first. To hold that meaning is nothing more than ordinary use is to display a distinctly antitheoretical bias—that is (second), that theories typically do more harm than good in philosophy. This antitheoretical bias is instantiated in the Barthian prohibition on systematizing. Third, if meaning is nothing more than ordinary use, then no theory of reference is needed to determine the meaning of singular terms. Again, Frei is committed to this last theme, but he has misgivings about its implications for his ability to say that Christian claims are *true*. He holds to the position that reference is important to issues of truth or falsity, but irrelevant to meaning, and this leads him into quandaries. His efforts to address these lead to perplexities among his interpreters. The picture of Frei is, in the end, a picture of a thinker who seeks to be faithful to Barth's agenda but who sees no better ally than ordinary language philosophy and thus does not see a way to avoid its problems. The eighth chapter thus sets up the ninth chapter's argument that postliberal theology cannot meet the liberal demand for validation of Christian claims because its commitment to Wittgenstein causes confusion over truth.

Thus, liberal theologians effectively accepted descriptivist demands for the acceptable use of religious language, while postliberal theologians cast their lot with Wittgenstein and ordinary language philosophy. Yet by the time this alignment had begun to take shape, analytic philosophers had grown dissatisfied with the two options on meaning and reference they had bequeathed to theology. Increasingly, analytic philosophers began to see both descriptivism and ordinary language philosophy as unsupportable. The important mid-century work of Ruth Barcan Marcus, J. L. Austin, Peter Geach, and Keith Donnellan, and continuing with the watershed work of W.V.O. Quine, Paul Grice, Donald Davidson, John Searle, and Saul Kripke, revolutionized philosophical thinking on many issues in philosophy of language. The work of these thinkers is diverse indeed, but all can be characterized as responding to the growing dissatisfaction with the antitheoretical orientation of ordinary language philosophy. The limitations of ordinary language philosophy drew the attention of philosophers of language as a part of the realization of two distinct needs. The first was the realization that a theoretical understanding of linguistic meaning and reference was important after all, notwithstanding the biases of the ordinary language school, which had been prominent in the middle of the century. The second was the realization that a distinction needed to be drawn between semantic meaning (the set of meanings a word, phrase, or sentence *could* semantically express) and speech acts (the meaning a word, phrase, or sentence *actually has* in a particular utterance). Three developments growing out of the response to ordinary language philosophy are of particular importance to this study. First is Donald Davidson's 1967 article, "Truth and Meaning," which argued for deriving linguistic meaning from a theory of truth for a language. So influential was this article, along with other Davidson articles supporting the approach, that the descriptivist or truth-conditional view of meaning quickly became (once again) the dominant view. An important aspect of the dominance of the Davidsonian program is that it spurred the articulation of technical criticism of truth-conditional views of meaning. I take up one particularly powerful such criticism in chapter 9. The second development was Kripke's *Naming and Necessity*, which delivered a critique that most considered fatal to the descriptivist view of reference. Kripke's book had antecedents, but it brought home to a wide audience the need to develop a different understanding of reference that was more direct than the descriptivist view. The third important development was Searle's articulation, following Austin and others, of speech act theory. This theory, which built on Grice's distinction between utterance (semantic) meaning and utterer (speaker) meaning, allowed the development of theories of meaning-as-use that did not have the antitheoretical baggage associated with Wittgenstein and ordinary language philosophy. Drawing on these two distinct realizations and the developments growing out of them, in chapter 9 I describe what I take to be fundamental problems with both the descriptivist and ordinary language views of meaning and reference, relying primarily on the work of Saul Kripke, Scott Soames, and William Alston.

Unfortunately, by the time these developments became widely known within analytic philosophy, most theologians had come to view analytic philosophy as dry, technical, and lacking any potential contribution to theological discussions. Consequently, theologians had available only two real options for understanding the meaning and reference of religious and theological language. If the descriptivist view were correct, then the liberal method of validating theological claims would indeed be the only adequate way of validating such claims. On the other hand, if the ordinary language approach were correct, then, as Frei suggests, the task of theology would be limited to Christian self-description, and the kind of validation undertaken by liberal theology would be misguided. With the descriptivist and ordinary language approaches the only two available, it seemed that a theologian must simply make her choice.

Chapter 9, then, provides critical scrutiny of both the ordinary language and the descriptivist approaches to linguistic meaning and reference. It does this through an engagement with two prominent representatives of these differing views, Ludwig Wittgenstein and Donald Davidson. Wittgenstein's view suffers from serious problems in its supporting arguments such that the best that can be said of it is that it is too vague to be either defended or conclusively refuted. But any attempt to fix this problem will abandon its central antitheoretical stance. Davidson, in contrast, is sufficiently clear to allow what I take to be a fatal criticism of not only Davidson's but any attempt to derive the meaning of a sentence from its truth conditions.

The concluding chapter begins with some implications of these criticisms for liberal and postliberal theological method. Recall in general that a theological method, as I am construing it, is a method not only for constructing, but also for interpreting, assessing, and defending theological or religious claims. To interpret a theological or religious claim just is to give its meaning, and the role of reference is to pick out that about which the claim is being made. So meaning and reference are important in that they are the mechanisms through which religious or theological claims are made.

The best way to summarize the implications of the book's reflections on meaning and reference is through a series of hypothetical suppositions. First, suppose that liberal theology were correct in its assumption of a descriptivist view of language. If meaning were constituted (always and only) by truth conditions, then particularized claims of the kind postliberals insist upon could not be made, because the only statements that would be meaningful would be those that contain no indexicality and that have the same meaning on each occasion of utterance. And even if we could make such a view of meaning defensible through variables for time and place of utterance (contrary to the argument in chapter 9), we would still face the issue of referring to God. If the only way successfully to refer to God were by way of description, then one would have to validate theological claims in the way that liberals like Ogden do. That is, the central theological question would be as follows: What descriptive senses together uniquely pick out God? Theology would then proceed through reflection on these descriptive senses. But since meaningful theological statements would be entailments from statements about God's necessary characteristics, it is difficult to see how the kind of particularity Barth and his postliberal followers insist upon would be possible.

Second, suppose that postliberals were right to follow the ordinary language view of meaning and reference. If descriptive reference to God could not succeed, then Frei's critique of liberal theology could be glossed in such a way as to make it valid. Suppose that postliberals like Frei were right that the reference of referring expressions (especially reference to God) were irrelevant to the meaning of religious statements because the use of such statements in a form of life were the only relevant determinant of their meaning. If that were so, then giving an adequate account of the truth or justification of theological claims would be difficult in the extreme, and there would be good reason for theology to limit itself to self-description. If neither direct reference nor descriptivist reference to God were possible, then we might be able to validate claims about God or Jesus through the kind of thick description of the Christian form of life that Frei advocates. But in the end, it would be hard to deny that theological statements would always ultimately be about the experience of the church.

Third, suppose direct reference to God could succeed. If it could, then a liberal way of validating theological claims would not be not the only valid way, and the particularized claims for which postliberals advocate would be possible. If both descriptive and direct reference to God are possible, then the liberal project is possible, but so is another constructive project that might be labeled in some sense or other as Barthian or postliberal. The defining mark of this latter project is that it makes claims that, though they can be justified, are not justified by appeal to a dimension of experience claimed to be universal. Therefore, any move beyond the liberal/postliberal divide in theology will need to envision a more inclusive method that allows the project of natural theology to succeed and that allows more particularized claims to be epistemically justified. Consequently, the chapter closes by suggesting crucial elements of this method.

The concepts of meaning, reference, justification, and truth are the crucial methodological concepts in the way I chart the liberal/Barthian divide. To summarize cryptically, postliberals are right that meaning is constituted by use, but wrong that reference is irrelevant to meaning. And at least Frei and his sympathizers are too strong in their antisystematic bias. I thus follow William Alston's recent theory of sentence meaning in which the meaning of an utterance determines the reference of its referring expressions. In turn, though, such referring expressions make a contribution to the meaning of the speech act in which the sentence is uttered. And because I seek a method that is more inclusive than liberal or postliberal methods, I follow Saul Kripke, Alston, and others in arguing for a version of direct reference that also allows reference to proceed by description.

Because reference makes an important contribution to meaning, both natural theology and the kind of apologetic enterprise important to liberal theology are possible. At the same time, because it is possible to refer to God either by description or by direct reference, theology can justifiably make the kind of particularized claims emphasized by postliberal and other Barthian theologians. Thus views of meaning and reference can be articulated that allow for a more inclusive theological method than those of either liberal or postliberal theology.

A danger lurks, however. Any theological method that claims for itself the ability both to make (and justify) particularized claims and to engage in the kind of validation enterprise argued for by liberal theology risks the promotion of triumphalism or theological imperialism. This danger can be avoided, in my judgment, by careful attention to the distinction between truth and epistemic justification. Thus any theological method capable of moving beyond the liberal/postliberal divide should provide an account of what it means to say that a theological claim is true, and what it means to say that such a claim is justified. Here again, developments in analytic philosophy over the last fifty years, and especially over the last twenty, make it an extraordinarily fruitful conversation partner in developing theological accounts of truth and epistemic justification (or warrant). So in the concluding chapter, I'll suggest some lines of inquiry that appear to me particularly promising.

The task of this study, however, is not to outline a proposal on theological method. Instead, it merely provides one reading of what I take to be the most important differences between liberal and postliberal theology, in the hope that this reading can highlight elements I believe are crucial to any adequate theological method. Its purposes are to suggest avenues of further conversation on the elements of theological method and to suggest that recent developments in analytic philosophy can provide very fruitful conversation partners in this important enterprise.

PART ONE

*Liberal Theology and the
Falsification Challenge*

CHAPTER ONE

Liberal Theology in the Nineteenth and Early Twentieth Centuries

It was in the nineteenth century that liberal theology came into full flower. The dominant liberal theological tradition addressed a number of extremely thorny issues, and even the wrong turns taken by theologians represented important advances. From the beginning to the end of the century—while methods, theories, doctrines, and other developments were hotly contested and extensively debated—the liberal tradition's formulations of the task and method of theology were surprisingly congruent. As the century opened, the most important figure in theology (with the benefit of hindsight) was Friedrich Schleiermacher. As the century closed, Adolf von Harnack influenced the field more than any other, and in between was Albrecht Ritschl. Others, of course, were important and influential—for example, David Strauss, F. C. Baur, and Cardinal Newman, to name only a few—but Schleiermacher, Harnack, and Ritschl define the field in terms of liberal theological method. Their conceptions of the task and method of theology evidence an astonishing coherence given that their work spans the whole century.

Further, their work nicely illustrates three concerns or themes characteristic of liberal theology throughout the century: First is an intense interest in the believing subject. In philosophy, Kant's Copernican revolution reversed the order between mind and what it perceived. Before Kant, it was assumed (and explicitly held by Locke, Hume, and others) that in cognition the mind receives impressions passively from the real world. Kant proposed that objects adapt themselves to our mind. Therefore, the world is at least partially a creation of our own mind, and the fundamental task of philosophy is to show how our experience is grounded in certain a priori structures of subjectivity itself. Among theologians in the nineteenth century, this turn to the subject is perhaps most closely associated with the name of Schleiermacher.

Second is a rapidly growing interest in the concrete events of history. Claims about Jesus, for example, must be grounded or validated by an appeal to historical evidence. This emphasis comes through particularly clearly in Ritschl, but obviously also in Harnack and others. Intrinsic to this growing interest in historical research was a recognition that an unavoidable aspect to historical research, historical judgments, and historical narratives is *value*—that is, value judgments are unavoidably operative at every level of doing history.

Third is a search for the essence of Christianity. Harnack's popular *What is Christianity?* provides an excellent example of this third concern (as do the many "Lives" of Jesus that appeared later in the century in the wake of Strauss's groundbreaking study).

These three concerns are interrelated, and all play important roles in the work of the century's three most influential theologians. When these three concerns operate together, at least in the liberal tradition in theology, what they yield is a theological method that is basically transcendental in the way it derives its basic concepts.

A brief consideration of these three theologians provides a methodological background for the development of liberal theology in the twentieth century. I shall not argue that this is the best way to characterize all or even most of liberal theology in the nineteenth century, nor will I survey a large range of that century's theologians. Instead, I shall show how these concerns operate in three of the most important and influential theologians of the nineteenth century in order to provide a basis for asserting (in chapter 4) that twentieth-century liberal theologians such as Rudolf Bultmann and Schubert Ogden do indeed stand in the dominant tradition of liberal theology when it comes to method.

I. THE "FATHER" OF LIBERAL THEOLOGY: FRIEDRICH SCHLEIERMACHER

Friedrich Schleiermacher wrote during the heyday of the Romantic period (from about 1780 until the early 1830s) and exemplified many Romantic values. But the period should not be seen as a simple rejection of the Enlightenment. Instead, the Romantics tried to enlarge the vision of rationality, preferring a version of rationality that was neither an abstract rationalism nor a reductionistic empiricism. Experience was valued, but not in the way empiricism values it. Instead, it was the depth or intensity of experience that mattered to the Romantics; coupled with this was a new concern with the diversity of human life, a concern to give value to, and learn from, different points of view.[1]

The Enlightenment had been concerned to investigate nature, but the Romantic emphasis on the depth of experience led to a search for the ways that an infinite or eternal spirit has infused the depths of nature. There is in most of the Romantics a mystical sense of the unity of nature, and of humanity's fundamental oneness with it. The Romantics wanted an understanding of this fundamental unity, an understanding that surpassed rationalism, and they felt that such an understanding could give them a better understanding of both humanity and nature.[2]

These concerns can certainly be seen in Schleiermacher, and he is generally considered to be the most important Protestant theologian between Calvin and the neo-orthodox period inaugurated by Karl Barth. Clearly, his two major theological works are the most systematically rigorous statement of liberal Protestant theology and its interpretation of the Christian religion, at least prior to Barth. This is what made Schleiermacher the target of neo-orthodox attack; Barth and Emil Brunner trace the "dead end" in liberal theology to the "false start" begun by Schleiermacher.[3] Their critique was not universally accepted, and even Barth seems to have reconsidered later in his career. But whatever one thinks of their critique, Schleiermacher undoubtedly represents a crucial turning point in modern Protestant theology.

Schleiermacher's earliest major work, *On Religion: Speeches to its Cultured Despisers,* is directed to his friends at the salon of Henrietta Herz, in an attempt to convince them that they are more religious than they think, that what they view as unacceptable about religion is not true religion at all, but a distortion. They were accustomed to the view that religion consists of believing in a personal God and personal immortality, along with a certain code of behavior. They simply found that they were more interested in other things.[4]

Schleiermacher attempted to show them that those things in which they were most interested were precisely what religion could provide. In

---

1. James C. Livingston, *Modern Christian Thought,* vol. 1: *The Enlightenment and the Nineteenth Century,* 2nd ed. (Upper Saddle River, N.J.: Prentice Hall, 1997), 83–84.
2. Livingston, *Modern Christian Thought,* 84–86.
3. See Karl Barth, *Protestant Thought in the Nineteenth Century,* trans. Brian Cozens and John Bowden (Grand Rapids, Mich.: Wm. B. Eerdmans, 2002), 411–59. Originally published as *Die protestantische Theologie im 19. Jahrhundert* (Zurich: Theoligischer Verlag, 1947; repr., 1952).
4. Brian Gerrish, *Continuing the Reformation: Essays on Modern Religious Thought* (Chicago: Univ. of Chicago Press, 1993), 158.

actuality, religion is a "sensibility and taste for the infinite," a sense that makes the things they valued most even more deeply valuable. Religion is neither simply beliefs nor morals; yet it inspires the search for knowledge and "should accompany every human deed like a holy music...."[5] Instead, he says, religion is in "the slumbering seed of a better humanity"; in it can be found passion that is truly noble and truly related to nature.[6]

Schleiermacher's greatest breakthrough is usually judged to be his new interpretation of religion as primarily a matter of "feeling" (Gefühl) that originates in immediate self-consciousness.[7] This judgment has much to commend it, for prior to Schleiermacher, religion had been thought of primarily as either an intellectual exercise or a moral one. At the time, the two most important ways of thinking about God were the English Deists' conception of God as a machine-maker[8] and Kant's conception of God as a law-giver.[9] Schleiermacher objects to both of these.

The Deist conception makes it difficult if not impossible to distinguish religious discourse from scientific discourse. If one argues that nature can (or cannot) be conceived without God, Schleiermacher's rejoinder is that this has nothing to do with religion. For Schleiermacher the God of religion is not an item in some metaphysical scheme. The scientific way of knowing and talking about God treats God as finite, as the first cause among many. But this, he argues, is not the religious way of knowing and talking about God.

Likewise, Schleiermacher rejects any Kantian conception of religion as morality. Morality, he says, is concerned with humans, whereas religion is concerned with God. Morality is active—it concerns human action. In contrast, piety is passive—it involves submission to God's action. Morality presupposes freedom, but piety accepts necessity. For Schleiermacher, piety takes its place alongside science and morality as a necessary and irreducible third mode of existence. Without it, humanity would be incomplete.[10]

5. Friedrich Schleiermacher, On Religion: Speeches to its Cultured Despisers, trans. Richard Crouter (Cambridge: Cambridge Univ. Press, 1988; repr., 1994), 103 (page references are to reprint edition; hereafter Speeches). See also Gerrish, Continuing the Reformation, 158.

6. Schleiermacher, Speeches, 83.

7. Claude Welch, Protestant Thought in the Nineteenth Century, vol. 1: 1799–1870 (New Haven, Conn.: Yale Univ. Press, 1972), 68. See Schleiermacher, Speeches, 105–10.

8. William Paley, Natural Theology (New York: Harper & Brothers, 1845), 37–38, 40–42, 49–51, 82–83; selected passages reprinted in Philosophy of Religion: Selected Readings, 4th ed., ed. Michael Peterson, William Hasker, Bruce Reichenbach, and David Basinger (New York: Oxford Univ. Press, 2010), 212–14.

9. Kant located religion not in the intellect but in the moral will, and this placement led him to define (natural) religion as "the recognition of all our [moral] duties as divine commands" (Immanuel Kant, Die Religion innerhalb der Grenzen der blossen Vernunft, in Werke in sechs Bänden, Band 5 [Köln: Könemann, 1995], 182).

10. Schleiermacher, Speeches, 97–108, 130.

To find out what true religion is, Schleiermacher says that we must turn from the outward trappings of religion and descend to the innermost sanctuary of life. Thus, the proper method of studying religion is introspection on the content of consciousness. This introspection reveals a primitive unity of consciousness that exists before reflection has divided it into subject/object polarities. In this fleeting moment of introspection, there is no division between self and other. In this fleeting moment, we experience a unity with the world, and this unity awakens in us our point of contact with the infinite. Through his introspective analysis of religious experience, Schleiermacher comes to define religion as "the sensibility and taste for the infinite."[11] Religion is the feeling that all that moves us in feeling is one, so that our living and being is living and being through God. Religion, therefore, has to do with the infinite, rather than with the finite. Thus, in the first place, contemplating nature alone will not get us to an understanding of true religion. And, in the second, one's own inner life must be plumbed first, then transferred to the realm of nature. The universe portrays itself most truly, he says, through the inner life. So the introspection that opens up religion to us also illuminates nature, rather than vice versa.[12]

But what about traditional religious doctrines? Are they not crucial to religion? As a feeling person, Schleiermacher says, I can become an object for myself when I consider my own feelings. Therefore doctrines are religious, but they are not religion. Feeling is essential to religion, Schleiermacher argues, but reflection is not, though it is in a certain sense unavoidable. Doctrines or religious beliefs may seem to trespass on science (*Wissenschaft*), but in fact they are of a different order, one that is independent of science.[13] Schleiermacher here is clearly navigating between two ditches. On the one hand, he wants to avoid a theistic idea compounded of various attributes, which would conceive of God as a person like ourselves, a single extramundane deity.[14] On the other hand, he also wants to avoid a pantheistic idea in which God is the single unity exalted above all personalism.[15]

Almost all of Schleiermacher's critics accuse him of pantheism—and certainly he gives them ammunition by infusing his language with pantheistic metaphors. But in fact, for Schleiermacher, both traditional theism and pantheism are products of reflection. Therefore they are not part of

11. Schleiermacher, *Speeches*, 103.
12. Cf. Schleiermacher, *Speeches*, 116–18.
13. Cf. Schleiermacher's discussion of miracles (*Speeches*, 132–33).
14. So he says that immortality as the desire for personal persistence is the antithesis of religion. The loss of self is not a severe loss; what is to be desired is loss of life for God's sake (Schleiermacher, *Speeches*, 139–40).
15. Schleiermacher, *Speeches*, 134–38.

religion. Further, neither is a mirror of what the Deity really is in itself. The gap between feeling and reflection cannot be overcome, and thus both traditional theism and pantheism fall short. Neither traditional theism nor pantheism, Schleiermacher maintains, can give a scientific knowledge of God. But this is no problem for religion; what matters is the structure of the feeling or experience that produced them both.[16] Thus Schleiermacher insists that religion has its root in the human spirit. We cannot despise religion without also despising humanity; to leave out religion is to impoverish human life. Romantic despisers of religion are being quite inconsistent with Romanticism.

If religion is a universal human characteristic, how should we understand particular positive religion? Deists had argued that Christianity is true only insofar as it represented the core common to all religion. Thus, whatever was particular about it was superfluous. For Schleiermacher, this core, natural religion, is an armchair construct corresponding to no reality at all. This constructed "essence" of religion has nothing truly religious about it, Schleiermacher says, but is simply a mishmash of morals, metaphysics, and science.[17] What is indispensable to religion is individuality. Even though the religious feeling is common to all, it can only express itself in a plurality of historical realities. Positive religion arises by selecting one religious expression, which then becomes the center of the religion. The truly religious person must pitch her tent somewhere, for true religion always expresses itself in some concrete positive form.[18]

As for Christianity, its central theme is reconciliation.[19] Creation and redemption constitute an indivisible whole, so Jesus occupies the central place. He, Schleiermacher says, is the author of the noblest that has *yet* appeared in religion. We should admire Jesus neither for his (unoriginal) moral teaching nor for his character. Instead, we should admire the divine in Christ, which is the clarity with which he exhibited the idea of the mediator.[20] Notice how Schleiermacher reorients the Christological question. The problem is not how to reconcile the two natures (divine and human), but to answer the questions "What is the religious ideal?" and "How is it to be related to Christ?" This is similar to Kant's approach in *Religion Within the Limits of Reason Alone*. For Kant, the Son of God was the archetype of religious consciousness. This cannot be simply identified with Jesus, but in Christ it gains a public foothold and is exhibited. Schleiermacher proceeds

16. Schleiermacher, *Speeches*, 136–39 (cf. 197–99).
17. Schleiermacher, *Speeches*, 192–93.
18. Schleiermacher, *Speeches*, 195–200.
19. Schleiermacher, *Speeches*, 213.
20. Schleiermacher, *Speeches*, 218–19.

in a similar way: he identifies the Christian idea of mediation as the central religious ideal. The significance of Jesus is then constituted by how he exemplified this ideal. But Jesus is not just a moral example (as nearly all Schleiermacher's critics assumed); more than a mere example, Jesus actually mediates his own intimacy with God. Yet Jesus never claims to be the only mediator. Instead, he calls his disciples to be mediators in and through him. If Schleiermacher is right about the essence of religion and of Christianity, then what this means, he thinks, is that Christianity is not the only possible religion. And he makes this argument in theological terms, not purely logical ones. Nothing, he argues, is more irreligious or "un-Christian" than to seek uniformity. Thus, new forms of religion must come, whether they are inside or alongside Christianity.[21]

Next to his allegedly pantheistic notion of God, Schleiermacher's treatment of the relationship of Christianity to other religions is the most criticized element of his *Speeches*. But it is difficult to deny that Schleiermacher's approach to non-Christian religions represents a substantial advance. During Schleiermacher's lifetime, orthodox theologians still ignored or dismissed other religions. Rationalist thinkers, on the other hand, still ignored or dismissed historically particular features of both Christianity and other religions. But for Schleiermacher, the unique, historically particular aspects of religion were what was *most religious* about it. So he tries to provide a third alternative to dogmatic exclusivism and rationalistic reductionism. Then, in *The Christian Faith (Glaubenslehre)*, he appears to abandon this third alternative and return to a more orthodox understanding. He took pains to assert that the two works were harmonious, but few have been persuaded. Schleiermacher's theological method, on the other hand, does display an interesting consistency from his early to late works.

Schleiermacher's understanding of religion as feeling echoes his Moravian upbringing and, in its Pietist tones, is not completely new. But the nuance of Schleiermacher's articulation of the religious self-consciousness gave a new intellectual power to an essentially Pietist religiosity, opening up a new way of understanding religion—neither rationalism nor essentially moral theory, but an irreducible third, *Gefühl*. Schleiermacher understood religion, as given in immediate self-consciousness, to be universal. All of our experience presupposes a sense of dependence—on others, our environing world, and ultimately on God. To use contemporary terms rather than Schleiermacher's own, this understanding of religion can be described (loosely) as transcendental and therefore as capable of providing a ground, in the Kantian sense, for all our talk about God.

21. Schleiermacher, *Speeches*, 219–21.

The conventional reading of Schleiermacher, in fact, sees this new definition of religion as providing just such a ground. Talk about God, whatever else it may be, is thus always and simultaneously talk about human subjectivity. Schleiermacher himself provides a good basis for such a reading in the introduction to *The Christian Faith*. There, he acknowledges that the typical arrangement of a dogmatic work had been to set out a doctrine of God as a single unit at the beginning. Schleiermacher's *Christian Faith*, though, begins with no such unit. Instead, he begins by saying that "dogmatics is a theological discipline, and thus pertains solely to the Christian Church."[22] The place to begin, then, is to figure out just what a church is. So Schleiermacher states that, at least for Protestants, "a Church is nothing but a communion or association relating to religion or piety,"[23] which leads to a discussion of piety or religion. Schleiermacher's understanding of religion is transcendental in this sense. All human experience, Schleiermacher suggests, can be described as a kind of knowing, feeling, or doing. But although knowing, feeling, and doing can be distinguished, they can never be separated. Any doing, he says, can arise from a knowing only insofar as it is "mediated by a determination of self-consciousness."[24] Self-consciousness in turn has two elements, one of which is self-caused and the other of which is not, and these elements correspond (respectively) to the subject's activity and receptivity.[25] Determinations of self-consciousness that express receptivity are feelings of dependence, while those that express activity are feelings of freedom. But the kind of self-consciousness that accompanies an action, he says, is always related to a prior moment of receptivity. Thus only the feeling of dependence can be absolute, never the feeling of freedom. And religion or piety is precisely this feeling of absolute dependence. Yet the feeling of dependence, or at least absolute dependence, would not be recognizable as such without the feeling of freedom.

In the first instance God signifies for us simply that which is the co-determinant in this feeling and to which we trace our being in such a state; any further content of the idea of God must be evolved out of this signification. Now this is just what is principally meant by the formula which says that to feel oneself absolutely dependent and to be conscious of being in relation with God are one and the same thing, because absolute dependence is the fundamental relation which must include all others in itself.[26]

22. Friedrich Schleiermacher, *The Christian Faith*, 2d ed., ed. and trans. H. R. Mackintosh and J. S. Stewart (Edinburgh: T & T Clark, 1989), § 2.
23. Schleiermacher, *Christian Faith*, § 3.1.
24. Schleiermacher, *Christian Faith*, § 3.5.
25. Schleiermacher, *Christian Faith*, § 4.1
26. Schleiermacher, *Christian Faith*, § 4.1.

Schleiermacher then describes how the Christian experience of piety differs from other religions, and how it is related to the redemption accomplished by Jesus. Piety thus functions as a dogmatic limit in Schleiermacher, marking off dogmatics from both philosophy of religion and ethics. Dogmatics is never separate from these, just insofar as knowing and doing are never, for Schleiermacher, separate from feeling. So piety functions as a limit in the sense that dogmatics has as its only subject matter the reflection on Christian piety or Christian experience.[27]

More importantly, though, at least in terms of Schleiermacher's influence, this limitation of dogmatics to reflection on piety leads him to argue that dogmatic or doctrinal propositions are of three types: "descriptions of human states,...conceptions of divine attributes or modes of action, or...utterances regarding the constitution of the world...."[28] Of these three forms, the second and third are derivative from the first form, which is fundamental: "Hence we must declare the description of human states of mind to be the fundamental dogmatic form; while the propositions of the second and third forms are permissible only in so far as they can be developed out of propositions of the first form."[29]

This threefold typology of dogmatic propositions leads directly to the famous concluding section in the introduction, in which he states that all dogmatic theology must proceed on the basis of "the direct description of the religious affections themselves."[30] And this leads to Schleiermacher's answer to those readers who, after reading the introduction, wondered what had happened to his doctrine of God. He states, "The doctrine of God, as set forth in the totality of the divine attributes, can only be completed simultaneously with the whole system."[31] This is because dogmatic claims about divine attributes and modes of action "cannot be understood without previous knowledge" of "human soul-states"—that is, the religious affections.[32] It is this conclusion that led most of Schleiermacher's readers to conclude that his entire theological program was anthropologically driven. Epistemic access to God, that is, was possible only through a prior understanding of human subjectivity. Whether this is the best way to read Schleiermacher is certainly debatable, but it has been the most common

27. See Brian A. Gerrish, *The Old Protestantism and the New* (Chicago: Univ. of Chicago Press, 1982), 201–202.

28. Schleiermacher, *Christian Faith*, § 30.

29. Schleiermacher, *Christian Faith*, § 30.2. It is rooted in his understanding of knowledge (Gerrish, *Old Protestantism and the New*, 201).

30. Schleiermacher, *Christian Faith*, § 31.

31. Schleiermacher, *Christian Faith*, § 31.2.

32. Schleiermacher, *Christian Faith*, § 31.2.

reading at least since Barth.[33] This reading of Schleiermacher helped moti-
vate the great divide in theology in the twentieth century, for it was not
only Barth and the postliberals who read him this way; most liberals did
as well. And it is this method of grounding theological claims through an
appeal to human subjectivity that was characteristic of liberal theological
method in the twentieth century. But prior to that it found itself instantiated in Ritschl and Harnack as well.

II. LIBERAL THEOLOGY IN THE LATER NINETEENTH CENTURY: ALBRECHT RITSCHL

In the last few decades of the nineteenth century, advances were made in
the application of the historical-critical method both to biblical texts and
to the history of Christian doctrine. These advances imbued the intellectual climate with agnosticism regarding metaphysics and with excitement
regarding historical-critical research. In this climate, German intellectuals' mid-century enchantment with Hegelian idealism began to seem out-
dated. So they returned to Kantian critical philosophy, and this return
brought in its wake a revival of his position that the most important
aspect of religion is its moral aspect. They therefore subordinated speculative reason to moral reason (at least in religion) and, coupled with this,
focused increasingly on the empirical and the historical. Even our moral
judgments do not emerge in a vacuum, but are mediated to us through
our participation in a historical tradition and in social relationships.[34]

All these moves can be seen in Albrecht Ritschl and his followers.
Schleiermacher had been correct, they felt, in grounding religion in experience,
but now there was an even stronger emphasis given to the notion that Christian
experience can be appropriated only through particular historical events mediated through a community. Thus Protestant theologians not only returned to
Kant, but they also began to reemphasize the importance of historical sources.
This twofold emphasis became characteristic of followers of Ritschl.[35]

Although Ritschl agreed that religion was a matter of experience, he
rejected Schleiermacher's definition of religion as "the feeling of absolute

33. I myself follow Brian Gerrish in thinking this reading something of a misreading.
See Gerrish, *Tradition and the Modern World: Reformed Theology in the Nineteenth Century*
(Chicago: Univ. of Chicago Press, 1977), 13–48; and *Continuing the Reformation: Essays
on Modern Religious Thought* (Chicago: Univ. of Chicago Press, 1993), 147–77.
34. Livingston, *Modern Christian Thought*, 270–71. My reading here of Ritschl will
largely follow that of Livingston in *Modern Christian Thought* (270–81).
35. Livingston, *Modern Christian Thought*, 270–71.

dependence." First, Ritschl thought it a mistake for Schleiermacher to take the individual Christian's consciousness as the proper object of theology. This made theology too subjective, in Ritschl's view. Instead, the proper object of theology is historical—that is, the historical event of Jesus Christ and the Gospel message presented in the New Testament. The sole norm for assessing Christian doctrinal claims is that of the historical Jesus. Thus the task of the theologian is essentially historical. Theology's primary task is to explicate not the consciousness of either the individual Christian or the church, but rather the meaning of God's self-revelation, historically given in Jesus Christ and witnessed to in the New Testament. So Ritschl is a preeminent example of the second theme of nineteenth-century liberal theology—the concern for historical validation.[36]

Contrary to Schleiermacher, Ritschl held religion not to be a matter of intuition or feeling. It is, rather, entirely practical (in the Kantian sense). It is neither mystical feeling, nor metaphysics. Instead, religion is fundamentally "the experience of spiritual freedom," of being freed from natural necessities.[37] Humans are both natural and spiritual beings; this dual nature (natural and spiritual) creates a contradiction that can only be overcome through religion. Only God can guarantee the victory of the moral and spiritual life over the natural order. Ritschl thus interprets specifically Christian experience not in terms of any experience of dependence, but in terms of freedom and liberation.[38] For Ritschl, the Christian experience of God is not an experience primarily of dependence, but of liberation that comes through faith in God's grace. But that grace is mediated to faith historically (and uniquely) in Christ. Christian knowledge of God thus comes through a historically mediated faith in and experience of God.[39]

Ritschl agrees with Kant that we cannot know things in themselves, but we can know things through their qualities and effects on us and through our response to them. Consequently, there are no uninterpreted historical facts. Facts are always interpreted according to a system of worth or value. As concepts, facts and values can be distinguished, but they are always

36. Livingston, *Modern Christian Thought*, 272–73.
37. Albrecht Ritschl, *The Christian Doctrine of Justification and Reconciliation*, vol. 3, trans. H. R. Mackintosh and A. B. Macauley (Edinburgh, 1900), 199. The quoted phrase is Livingston's (*Modern Christian Thought*, 273).
38. Ritschl, *Justification and Reconciliation*, 199. See also Livingston, *Modern Christian Thought*, 273.
39. Ritschl, *Justification and Reconciliation*, 209–10. See also Claude Welch, *Protestant Thought in the Nineteenth Century*, vol. 2: *1870–1914* (New Haven, Conn.: Yale Univ. Press, 1985), 8–10; Livingston, *Modern Christian Thought*, 273.

inseparable. Consequently, God cannot be known in God's self, but only as God is revealed to us through God's effects on us. This means that God can be known only in God's worth or significance for us, as that worth or significance is experienced through a historically mediated faith.[40]

For Ritschl, this indissoluble relation between fact and value means that we cannot know the objects of religious or theological reflection in themselves, whether through metaphysical knowledge or through immediate intuition. But it also means that the norms of theological adequacy are derived neither from a phenomenological account of Christian consciousness (whether individual or corporate) nor from a transcendental analysis of pure reason. Rather, they are established through a critical reconstruction of the concrete events of history (phenomena). Yet the actual historical norm, Jesus Christ, is never simply given empirically from bare historical facts. Instead, it is inescapably a value judgment of faith. For Ritschl, our knowledge of God—or of Christ as a theological norm—is gained only through God's effects on us (and through the operation of our value judgments). But that's not all; our knowledge of the historical Jesus is mediated in the same way—through his effects on the Gospel writers and on us. For Ritschl, theology must recognize and maintain the mutual interdependence of historical-critical research and value judgments of faith. Faith is utterly necessary, but so is application of rigorous historical criticism. Ritschl thought that only such historical criticism could save theology from speculation and subjectivism. Rigorous historical criticism is necessary if theology is to avoid the errors that too often accompany excessive subjectivism; it is also necessary in order to preserve the continuity of Christian identity. Yet theology must be honest and acknowledge the impossibility of naively empirical historical reconstructions. Therefore Ritschl built his theological method around two distinct and interconnected necessities—the necessity of historical research into the events through which Christians assert that God has been revealed and the necessity of value judgments of faith as an inescapable part of any judgment about the results of any historical research program.[41]

Ritschl's method thus marked a distinct departure both from Schleiermacher on the one hand and Kant on the other. Claude Welch's

---

40. Ritschl, *Justification and Reconciliation*, 212. See also Livingston, *Modern Christian Thought*, 274.

41. Still, the necessity of accessing the historical Jesus through the witness of the church does not mean that he took an uncritical attitude toward the primitive traditions. Instead, all traditions must be judged by the historical figure presented by Christ's life. This means that all speculation concerning Christ's preexistence and post-historical existence must be checked by what we know about the historical figure. This applies to those supernatural events of the Gospels such as Christ's Virgin Birth, his miracles, and the Resurrection. For Ritschl, these traditions are not integral to any estimate of the

judgment is on the mark: Ritschl's "was thoroughly a *church* theology and *theological* history. The theologian speaks only as a member of the religious community; theology is that community's critical self-knowledge. Everything that is said about the originating event is from the standpoint of the community."[42] In his history of the nineteenth century, Barth recognizes Ritschl's departure from Schleiermacher precisely at the point of the importance of the historical figure of Jesus.[43] And Barth is not as directly negative in his judgment of Ritschl's method as he is of Schleiermacher's. Yet consider the points that (in the judgment of many) marked Ritschl's advance over both Schleiermacher and Kant—the inseparability of judgments of fact and of value and the hermeneutical interdependence of history and faith. These points meant that at the center of both hermeneutical judgments regarding the historical Jesus and the norms of doctrinal assessment was Ritschl's understanding of religious experience as an experience of value. And it was this that led postliberals like Hans Frei to read his theology as anthropologically driven. Thus, Frei says, Ritschl joins a host of others, from the seventeenth through the twentieth centuries, who "have all been agreed that one way or another the religious *meaningfulness* (as distinct from demonstration of the truth) of the claim [that Jesus Christ is the Redeemer] could, indeed must, be perspicuous through its relation to other accounts of general human experience."[44]

Many historians have noted that Ritschl's work is an important bridge between nineteenth- and twentieth-century theology. In my view, one crucial aspect of this bridge is his linkage between historical judgments and the experience of value. History is therefore crucial, and so is experience—but not empirical experience so much as the experience of value. In the twentieth century, in what I will call a "purified" liberal theology, we will see that Schubert Ogden works these elements—historical research and the experience of value—explicitly into his method of validating theological claims.

---

historical figure of Christ. It is at this point that the ambiguity of Ritschl's hermeneutic becomes clear. For Ritschl, the historical Jesus movement erred in seeking to derive the normative Jesus Christ solely from bare historical facts, yet he himself makes historical judgments as to what traditions concerning Jesus are normative for faith on the basis of the criterion of the "historical figure presented by His life" (*Christian Doctrine of Justification and Reconciliation*, 406, also quoted in Livingston, *Modern Christian Thought*, 276). Thus it seems that he wants to infer Christological normativity only from certain strata of the historical traditions.

42. Claude Welch, *Protestant Thought in the Nineteenth Century*, vol. 2: *1870–1914* (New Haven, Conn.: Yale Univ. Press, 1985), 14 (emphasis in original).

43. Barth, *Protestant Thought in the Nineteenth Century*, 644–47.

44. Hans W. Frei, *The Eclipse of Biblical Narrative: A Study in Eighteenth and Nineteenth Century Hermeneutics* (New Haven, Conn.: Yale Univ. Press, 1974), 128 (emphasis in original).

III. LIBERAL THEOLOGY AT THE TURN OF THE CENTURY: ADOLF VON HARNACK

Among the theologians upon whom Ritschl had the strongest influence, certainly one of the most important was Adolf von Harnack. The influence of Ritschl's concern for historical sources is obvious in Harnack. Equally influential, though, is Ritschl's understanding of the inseparability of historical judgments of fact and judgments of value. Harnack follows his mentor in this regard, and thus for Harnack a historical narrative always inevitably involves a series of value judgments. But this is not something to be regretted, Harnack maintains, because that history must bear significance for our present life. If it doesn't, he writes, it's not worthy of study.[45]

Harnack undertook his massive study of the history of dogma because he understood the changes and developments in Christian dogma to have significance for contemporary Christian life. The significance of the history of dogma consists in its ability to reveal that dogmas themselves are not part of the eternal essence of Christianity. Thus the study of dogma actually frees the church from its tyranny. And this is what Harnack felt that the church in his day badly needed—to be freed from an authoritarian spirit that developed from misuse of dogmas and that was a deviation from the Gospel. This does not imply that individual dogmas were deleterious or deviations from the Gospel. On the contrary, many were historically useful to prevent distortions of the Christian message. Put another way, they allowed Christianity to endure when times changed. "The history of the Church," he writes, "shows us in its very commencement that 'primitive Christianity' had to disappear in order that 'Christianity' might remain...."[46] This same process was repeated throughout the history of the church. But for Harnack this process makes it clear that dogmas are historically conditioned. Thus, once the historical conditions that made them necessary have passed, the need for the dogmas that accompany them passes as well.[47]

45. "We study history," he says, "in order to intervene in the course of history and we have a right and a duty to do so.... [W]ith respect to the past, the historian assumes the royal function of a judge, for in order to decide what of the past shall continue to be in effect and what must be done away with or transformed, the historian must judge like a king. Everything must be designed to furnish a preparation for the future" (Harnack, "Über die Sicherheit und Grenzen geschichtlicher Erkenntnis," in *Reden und Aufsätze*, 7 vols. [Giessen: Alfred Töpelmann, 1904–30], 4:7; quoted in Livingston, *Modern Christian Thought*, 287).

46. Adolf von Harnack, *What is Christianity?* (London, 1901; repr., New York: Harper & Brothers, 1957; 2d repr., Minneapolis: Fortress Press, 1986), 13–14 (page references are to second reprint edition).

47. Livingston, *Modern Christian Thought*, 287–88.

One corollary to this view of the history of Christian dogma is that Christianity is not identical with any particular historical form. Indeed, this is Harnack's view. But if this is the case, the question naturally arises, "What is it that gives Christianity a continuity of identity?" If Christianity is to remain a living religion, and one that is the same religion as its previous historical instantiations, then an answer to this question must be possible. Harnack articulated the issue like this: "[E]ither the Gospel is...identical with its earliest form, in which case it came with its time and has departed with it; or else it contains something which, under differing historical forms, is of permanent validity. The latter is the true view."[48] This "something" that is "of permanent validity" will be the essence of Christianity, and Harnack believed it could be identified and abstracted from the particular historical forms of Christianity. Harnack was hardly the only one to search for the essence of Christianity; indeed, it was a third theme of liberal theology in the nineteenth century. It is important to see that it arises quite naturally out of the concern for the historical sources of theology and biblical interpretation. Harnack's search for the essence of Christianity was certainly one of the most influential, and he pursues it in his most popular book, *What is Christianity?* Published at the turn of the century, it was immediately and widely influential, and many consider it to be the most elegant and powerful statement of Protestant liberal theology, at least in Harnack's own era.[49] The question Harnack pursues in the book is obvious from its title, and his answer is that "the Christian religion is something simple and sublime; it means one thing and one thing only: Eternal life in the midst of time, by the strength and under the eyes of God."[50] This answer is Harnack's (German Protestant) interpretation of the essence of Christianity; not surprisingly, he arrives at it historically. He does not share Strauss's extreme skepticism toward the historical Jesus, though of course he was sensitive and realistic about his sources and is rightly regarded as the most erudite historian of his era. The historian's task, he says, is inevitably interpretive, for she cannot help but make decisions about the relative importance not only of sources, but of the events themselves. Indeed, the historian of Christianity "is of necessity required not to cleave to words but to find out what is essential."[51] He gives more detail to his answer by summarizing Jesus' life and teaching under three themes: "the kingdom of

48. Harnack, *What is Christianity?* 13–14.
49. The historian James Livingston, for example, writes, "More than any other book it represented the spirit of Protestant Liberalism in the decades just prior to WWI" (Livingston, *Modern Christian Thought,* 290; see also 286).
50. Harnack, *What is Christianity?* 8.
51. Harnack, *What is Christianity?* 13.

God and its coming[,] ... God the father and the infinite value of the human soul," and "the higher righteousness and the commandment of love."[52] The reason Harnack is often said to be a "primitivist" is that after describing what he takes to be the permanently enduring essence of Christianity, he then gives a summary interpretation of the history the church, describing why he thinks both the Orthodox and Catholic traditions have turned away from it. Luther briefly revived a form of Christianity much closer to the original essence of the religion, but soon the Protestant churches followed their Catholic and Orthodox predecessors.

Harnack has an interesting relationship to the divide between liberals and postliberals in the twentieth century. In the early 1920s, after Barth broke with liberal theology and after the publication of the second edition of his *Epistle to the Romans,* Harnack was one of the most prominent defenders of the liberal tradition in Protestant theology; in fact, Harnack was among those whom Barth viewed as liberal theology's chief representatives. Yet two things make Harnack a complicated target: First, the most prominent question regarding religion in the nineteenth century in German academic circles was not "What is Christianity?" but rather "What is religion?" On my reading, in approaching this latter question, Harnack does not propound a general theory of human subjectivity and then work out a philosophical or scientific answer, studying particular religions such as Christianity only as species of the genus "religion." Instead, he begins with the question of what is Christianity in the hope that this "may ... also throw light by the way on the more comprehensive one, What is Religion, and what ought it to be to us?"[53] Second, the book bears striking differences from, as well as one striking resemblance to, Frei's own summary of the essence of Christianity in *The Identity of Jesus Christ.*[54] The resemblance is simply that both attempted to contribute to the search for the essence of Christianity. But whereas Harnack relied on the fruits of historical research, Frei relied on literary criticisms of the Gospels. And whereas for Harnack it is Jesus' teachings that are of primary importance, for Frei it is the depictions of Jesus' passion, death, and resurrection where the essence of Christianity is most clearly to be discovered. Barth and Frei both eventually came to see Schleiermacher as a more complicated target of Barthian critique than he initially appears to be. In my own judgment, the same can be said of Ritschl and Harnack,

52. Harnack, *What is Christianity?* 51.
53. Harnack, *What is Christianity?* 6.
54. Hans W. Frei, *The Identity of Jesus Christ: The Hermeneutical Bases of Dogmatic Theology* (Philadelphia: Fortress Press, 1975; repr., Eugene, Oreg.: Wipf & Stock, 1997) (page references are to reprint edition).

too, though neither Barth nor Frei, I think, would agree. Indeed, I do not think Frei would deem it important that Harnack thought that studying Christianity would illuminate the study of religion, rather than vice versa. Frei states, "It seemed to Harnack, as to many other liberal theologians at the time... that Christianity really illustrated the perfection, or the most complete embodiment, of the genre religion. Therefore, if you studied the Christian religion, you studied religion in principle."[55] And I think that Frei would draw a sharp distinction between the respective projects of Harnack's *What is Christianity?* and his own *The Identity of Jesus Christ*: For Harnack, Frei says, "the very notion of religion, including Christian religion, had... an intellectual or moral-spiritual essence. It was not really the kind of complex organism which had to be understood as a social and cultural artifact, a continuous and constantly recreated structure in its own right."[56] Frei acknowledges that Harnack played an important role in the University of Berlin's rejection of a proposal to transform its theology faculty into a faculty of the science of religion, and he also insisted on retaining pastoral education in the university as well. But Frei attributes this to a confusion on Harnack's part, arguing that his understanding of religion, and of Christianity in particular, actually pointed to the opposite position.[57]

IV. THEMES AS THE CENTURY TURNS

The three liberal theologians I have mentioned briefly in this chapter show a few things about liberal theology. Clearly, it is a project of remarkable nuance capable of addressing and using to its own ends insights and developments from a wide range of nontheological disciplines (if indeed there are such things). Further, this suppleness characteristic of liberal theology permitted an integration of the three themes mentioned at the beginning of this chapter—a focus on religious experience characteristic of modernity's turn to the subject, a deep concern for historical investigation of all theological claims (including a recognition that value judgments are an integral and unavoidable aspect of historical investigation), and a search for the essence of Christianity (as well as of religion).

Yet there was a danger lurking. As the Greek tragic poets saw so clearly, every virtue has not only a corresponding vice, but also the capability—in

55. Hans W. Frei, *Types of Christian Theology*, ed. George Hunsinger and William C. Placher (New Haven, Conn.: Yale Univ. Press, 1992), 116.
56. Frei, *Types of Christian Theology*, 117.
57. Frei, *Types of Christian Theology*, 116–18.

itself and *as a virtue*—to bring its bearer not only honor and happiness but also ruin. Nineteenth-century liberal theology's ability to address the characteristic concerns of the century and to integrate its achievements resulted in a theological dynamic that, in the view of many, would privilege epistemology over metaphysics (at least eventually). As we will see, this would be Frei's judgment. Whatever one thinks of his assessment of individual theologians, the point is sound. Indeed, prominent and influential strands of modern continental philosophy have exhibited this characteristic as well.

This kind of assessment of liberal theology can be seen as an inquiry into what a particular strand or tradition of theology (or a particular theologian) takes to be "first philosophy" (or whatever the theological equivalent might be). This is the kind of analysis most often used by neo-orthodox and postliberal theologians (and others) in their assessments of liberal theology. So one way to analyze the liberal/postliberal divide in theology is to ask how each tradition differs regarding the relative privileging of epistemology and metaphysics.

But this is not the only analytical question that might be asked regarding differences over theological method. Another question that might be asked is how liberals and postliberals differ over religious or theological language. That is the question I will try to answer in the chapters that follow. It is the question raised by the falsification challenge posed to theology in the middle of the twentieth century. And while many take that challenge to have been answered, in my own view it continues to have substantial analytical importance. It profoundly influenced the way the three themes in liberal theology that I've discussed in this chapter were developed by liberal theologians in the twentieth century, at least from the middle of the century onward. It also exerted a significant influence on the contours of the debate between liberal and postliberal theologians in the latter part of the twentieth century. So, before turning to the development of what I will call a "purified" liberal theology in the twentieth century, it will be useful to analyze the challenge issued by the falsification theorists.

CHAPTER TWO

The Falsification Challenge

As it entered the twentieth century, liberal theology was a complex and nuanced endeavor, no less so in its method than in its positive dogmatic pronouncements. Harnack himself, though he was one of those whom Barth had foremost in mind in declaring that liberal theology represented a "dead end," gave an analysis of Christianity as a particularized starting point for addressing the question, "What is religion?" As read by Barth, though, Harnack and other liberal theologians approached theological questions "from below," by beginning with human experience. Notwithstanding what is arguably his misreading of Harnack, Barth provides an acute insight into the method of liberal theology, as I shall argue in chapter 4. This anthropological starting point can be seen most clearly and consistently in Schubert Ogden. What Barth feared most was the specter of Feuerbach. On Barth's reading, Feuerbach presents a powerful case that theological pronouncements about God are no more than projections of the realities of human subjectivity onto a blank divine screen. In Barth's view, liberal theology's anthropological starting point deprived it of any meaningful response to Feuerbach.

Barth's fear of Feuerbach and the liberal response to this fear came to dominate the interpretation of the debate between liberals and Barthians in the twentieth century, at least at the level of theological method. Because of this, theology never really came to terms with another extremely interesting (though at times highly technical) critique coming from another quarter, a critique that resulted in the falsification debates that occurred in the middle of the century. The critics were, by and large, analytic philosophers who offered an argument potentially more devastating than any articulated by Feuerbach. When theologians make statements about God, Feuerbach argued, they are in fact taking (the best) attributes they perceive in humanity and projecting them onto a divine being that may or may not be real. But he never argued, at least not explicitly, that such statements were meaningless. He may not have felt that they were adequately supported by evidence or arguments, but at least they were intelligible, meaningful claims that could be debated. The falsification theorists went further than this. They argued that one could not even make sense of theological claims because claims about God could not be assigned any meaning at all. For these critics, the significance of a critique like Feuerbach's was that there was no way to identify the referent of the term "God." And because the referent of "God" remained indeterminate, statements about God remained strictly meaningless.

So in one sense it is a bit surprising that theological responses never really got to the bottom of the critique. One reason for this, I think, is that the critique came out of an ongoing analytic philosophical conversation that was (and remains) quite technical and daunting to outsiders. But another reason is more subtle. One conviction that motivated many liberal responses was the conviction that there is a close relationship between the way language is understood and the way beliefs or assertions are epistemically justified. And this relationship was clearly inferred by liberal theologians in their construals of the falsification critiques. Consequently, many theologians and philosophers of religion saw the falsification challenge as a straightforward application of the falsifiability principle to theological or religious statements. Responses, therefore, tended either to criticize the falsifiability principle or to analyze theological and religious language from the point of view of the later Wittgenstein. But the challenge posed by the falsification theorists ultimately relied less on the falsifiability thesis of logical positivism than on the descriptivist requirements specified by Bertrand Russell for successful reference. Russell's analysis of reference was certainly assumed by the logical positivists, but it did not entail the falsifiability thesis defended by the logical positivists. And indeed Russell's view of language remained the dominant view long after the demise of logical positivism as a viable philosophical project. So it's useful to describe the development of theories about reference and meaning in analytic philosophy in the years leading up to the falsification debates.

I. BACKGROUND: FREGE, RUSSELL, THE EARLY WITTGENSTEIN, AND THE DOMINANCE OF DESCRIPTIVISM

If liberal theologians saw a relationship between understandings of religious language and epistemology, it was certainly not unprecedented—for we can see this relationship in both Gottlob Frege and Bertrand

Russell (in different ways). Frege comes to discussions of language via his background in mathematics and logic, and when he speaks of "reference" what he has in mind primarily is a system of interpretation of sentences of formalized languages that will provide an account of the truth conditions of all sentences of the language.[1] The reference of a term is assigned when it is associated with something in the world—an object or set of objects, a relationship, a concept, etc. In such formalized languages, as soon as one assigns the references of each term in a sentence and defines its logical operators, one has thereby determined its truth value. For the purposes of establishing the rules of deduction for a formalized language, it doesn't matter how a term and its extralinguistic referent come to be associated with each other. But when it comes to understanding how the sentences of natural languages come to have the meaning they have, it is much more important. Here's why: When Frege talks about meaning, he is vague about what he has in mind. But essentially, the meaning of a sentence is what I understand when I understand a sentence. When you tell me that you had a potato for dinner, if I understand the sentence you spoke, what I understand is the *meaning* of that sentence. And this is the case for the components of the sentence, too. If I've understood you, then I know what you're talking about when you used the term "potato." But if so, then why isn't it the case that the meaning of the word "potato" is just its referent—the object it stands for?

Frege discusses this issue in his famous article, "On Sense and Reference."[2] If the meaning or sense of a referring term or expression were just its referent, then to understand the meaning of a term, I would have to know the identity of the object to which it referred. Furthermore, if two terms referred to the same object, I would have to know this if I could be said to know the meaning or sense of each of the terms. But this cannot be true. As Frege discusses in his famous example, I could tell you that I saw the Morning Star this morning, and that I saw the Evening Star last night. You and I can both know the meaning of the sentences I utter even if we don't (yet) know that "the Morning Star" and "the Evening Star" both refer to the same planet. And since we can know the meaning of the sentences without knowing that the two terms in question are coreferential, they must have different senses. Consequently, because they have different senses while having the

1. In these remarks on Frege, I will be following the excellent discussion of Michael Dummett, *Frege: Philosophy of Language,* 2d ed. (Cambridge, Mass.: Harvard Univ. Press, 1981), 90–109.
2. Gottlob Frege, "On Sense and Reference," trans. Max Black, *The Philosophical Review* 57 (1948): 207–30; reprinted in *Readings in the Philosophy of Language*, ed. Peter Ludlow (Cambridge, Mass.: MIT Press, 1997), 563–83 (page references are to reprint edition).

same referent, Frege concludes that even ordinary proper names have a sense that amounts to more than their having the particular referent that they have. Frege puts it this way: When we discovered that the Morning Star was actually the same planet as the Evening Star, this really was a discovery. We gained new information that we did not have before. But if the sense or meaning of "the Morning Star" and "the Evening Star" just consisted in the terms' having the referent that they have, there would be no way to account for the acquisition of this new information.[3] Frege realizes that his account of language will be misleading if it cannot reflect the discovery of the coreferentiality of two previously understood terms. And his account of language can reflect such a discovery, he concludes, *only* if it contains an understanding of the *sense* of a term that is broader than the term's referent.

So what is this something "more" than a term's referent that comprises its sense? This turns out to be fairly complicated, but a crucial element is that to know the sense of a term is to know some information that allows you to fix the referent of the term. Which particular bit of information is required is not always clear, and it will not always be the case that when you know the senses of two coreferential terms you will know that they are coreferential. There may be a good deal of information that allows you to fix the reference of a particular term or name, and each different sense that a term has will be associated with a particular way of fixing the referent of the term. So to know of Jeb Bush that he is the former governor of Florida is to know one sense of the name, "Jeb Bush"; to know that he is the brother of George W. Bush is to know another sense; and to know that he is the son of Barbara Bush is to know still another sense. And the information required to pick out the referent of the term is some kind of description. For my purposes, the crucial thing to remember is this: To know the sense of a singular term is to know some *descriptive sense* that enables you to pick out or fix the term's referent. And fixing the referents of the singular terms or referring expressions in a sentence is necessary if one is to judge the truth or falsity of the sentence in which they appear.[4]

---

3. Until now in this discussion of Frege, I have been using "meaning" and "sense" interchangeably with respect to singular terms. But in fact they are distinct concepts. Nonetheless, Frege is not clear about just how they differ from one another, and indeed he is vague about meaning in general. He spends much more time discussing the distinction between sense and reference. And it is this distinction that is important with respect to Frege.

4. According to Dummett, the importance of Frege's distinction lies in the connection between the sense of a term and the information the term provides: "In order to determine whether or not a sentence is true, it is enough to know the reference of the various constituent expressions; but, in order to know what information it conveys, we must know their sense" (Dummett, *Frege*, 104).

For Bertrand Russell, descriptions assume an even greater importance, and for many years, his view about reference was the dominant view in Anglo-American philosophy.[5] For purposes of understanding the falsification debates, two aspects of Russell's thought about reference are especially important—his basic epistemological commitments and his theory of descriptions.[6] I will discuss his theory of descriptions first and later describe his two basic epistemological concepts. Russell's theory of descriptions arose in connection with his rejection of the view that every object of thought must have some kind of being. On this view, things such as Santa Claus, the Great Pumpkin, or the current king of the United States must have some kind of being even though they don't exist. If they did not have some kind of being, there would be no propositions about them, and therefore we could not make any statements expressing such propositions. Such statements are called "negative existentials," examples of which include these: "The Great Pumpkin doesn't exist." "White crows don't exist." "There is no king of the United States." Russell himself in an early work argued for the view before later rejecting it.[7] As Scott Soames describes it, the argument in favor of things that don't exist goes something like this:

P1: A meaningful negative existential is a sentence in a subject-predicate form.

P2: A meaningful subject-predicate sentence is true if and only if each of its referring expressions refer to some object.

5. There are two ways in which the story of Russell on reference has been told. The first version has been popular with many, including Saul Kripke. On this version, philosophers focus on Russell's claim that most proper names are "disguised definite descriptions" (in the mind of the speaker). Philosophers telling this first version then identify this view with Frege's notion of "sense," and this combination yields something like a "Frege-Russell description theory" of the sense or meaning of a proper name. Others have thought this a bit odd, because Russell was a critic of Frege on proper names, and offered his own theory as an alternative to Frege. Such philosophers have thus provided an alternative story that focuses on Russell's (closely related) claim that the only truly referring names are "logically proper names." On this story, however, logically proper names only introduce the objects that they name. This is very close to Mill's view that the meaning of a name *just is* its referent object. This then is taken to be the precursor to the "new theory of reference" in which proper names are simply tags that refer to their referents, and have no *meaning* in themselves. Neither of these versions is the whole story, though the second is, I think, closer to the truth.

6. My discussion of Russell will, by and large, follow the excellent analysis of Scott Soames in *Philosophical Analysis in the Twentieth Century*, vol. 2: *The Dawn of Analysis* (Princeton, N.J.: Princeton Univ. Press, 2003), 93–131.

7. Bertrand Russell, *The Principles of Mathematics* (New York: Norton & Co., 1903; 2d ed., 1938); cf. Bertrand Russell, "On Denoting," *Mind* 14 (1905): 479–93, reprinted in *The Philosophy of Language*, 4th ed., ed. A. P. Martinich (New York: Oxford Univ. Press, 2001), 212–27 (page references are to reprint edition).

P3: There are no objects that don't exist.

C1: Meaningful negative existentials cannot be true.

C2: True, meaningful negative existentials don't exist.[8]

The problem, of course, is that the second conclusion, C2, if it is true (and it follows from the premises P1–P3), is self-contradictory. In his early work, Russell thought that P3 was incorrect. On this view, every conceivable object of thought has some kind of being—and can be said to exist in some sense—irrespective of whether it subsists as a typical physical object. Within a few years, though, he rejected the argument (and indeed started attributing it to Meinong).[9] What allowed him to reject this extreme view was his theory of descriptions and its distinction between logical form and grammatical form. Russell believed that every meaningful sentence has a grammatical form and expresses a proposition that has a logical form. Sometimes the grammatical form mirrors the logical form, but often it doesn't. And in the case of negative existential statements, the grammatical form of a sentence is different than the logical form of the proposition it expresses. So in the case of a sentence such as "White crows do not exist" the logical form of the proposition it expresses is something like this: "For every object x, either x is not a crow or x is not white."[10]

When it comes to what we normally think of as proper names, Russell's theory of descriptions yields a rather odd result. Recall that for Frege proper names can have more than one sense, and each sense is associated with a descriptive condition that allows someone who understands the name to pick out its referent object. Russell follows Frege here but extends Frege's thought further: Whenever I use a proper name, Russell argues, I always have in mind some description that will allow me to identify the referent of the name. Consequently, in every sentence in which a proper name is used, a description can be substituted for it. This substitution of descriptions for proper names allows Russell to resolve the problem of negative existentials. For Russell, the logical form of the proposition expressed by the sentence "Santa Claus does not exist" can be found by first substituting some description for Santa Claus, such as "the chubby man with the white beard that lives in the North Pole." Once we do that, Russell believes, we can see that the logical form of the proposition expressed by the sentence "Santa Claus does not exist" is something like this: "Everything is such that either it is not a chubby man with a white beard or it does not live in the North

---

8. Soames, *Dawn of Analysis*, 97.

9. Russell, "On Denoting." See Soames, *Dawn of Analysis*, 98.

10. See Soames, *Dawn of Analysis*, 107.

Pole." This resolves the problem because no referring term or expression has appeared in the subject of the sentence whose reference is to something that doesn't exist.

There is one more puzzle that leads Russell to his counterintuitive view that names of people are really disguised definite descriptions. This puzzle arises from the interaction between propositional attitude ascriptions (sentences that ascribe to a person an attitude toward a particular proposition—such as "John believed that it was raining outside") and the logical rule called "the substitutivity of identity." According to this rule, when two singular referring expressions are coreferential (they refer to the same thing), substituting one expression for the other in any sentence will never result in a change in truth value. But when this rule is applied to sentences containing propositional attitude ascriptions, it yields some puzzling results, and Russell describes these by means of a famous example in "On Denoting."

> Now George IV wished to know whether Scott was the author of *Waverley*; and in fact Scott *was* the author of *Waverley*. Hence we may substitute *Scott* for *the author of* 'Waverley', and thereby prove that George IV wished to know whether Scott was Scott. Yet an interest in the law of identity can hardly be attributed to the first gentleman of Europe.[11]

In other words, if we can substitute "Scott" for "the author of *Waverley*," then if it is true that George IV wondered whether Scott was the author of *Waverley*, then it is likewise true that he wondered whether Scott was Scott. But it seems certain that George IV could in fact wonder whether Scott was the author of *Waverley* without also wondering whether Scott was Scott. And if he could, then there must be something that prevents the application of the law of substitutivity of identity. And what prevents the application of the law is that neither "Scott" nor "the author of *Waverley*" is a *logically proper name*. Instead, they are disguised definite descriptions, and because they are, the law of substitutivity does not apply. In the case of "the author of *Waverley*," this seems to be intuitively correct. But Russell thinks that in order to resolve the problem, "Scott" must also be treated as a disguised definite description.[12] Now

11. Russell, "On Denoting," 215.
12. We might wonder why the law would apply at all, since "the author of *Waverley*" is pretty obviously a definite description. Soames explains this quite well; the problem does in fact arise when the description "the author of *Waverley*" has primary occurrence. In this case, the sentence is interpreted as "There was one and only one person who wrote *Waverley*, and George wondered whether he was Scott" (Soames, *Dawn of Analysis*, 120).

this example is puzzling for a variety of reasons, and Russell's description of it is unclear at a number of points.[13] But the lesson that Russell drew was that ordinary physical objects or persons can never be the referents of logically proper names. The only true referents of logically proper names are things about which I cannot possibly be mistaken—myself, my own thoughts or immediate sense data, the abstract concepts that are the meaning of logical terms, and the relations between them. With respect to everything else, whenever we talk about material entities, whether they are people or other objects, the language we use is descriptive; it does not name them directly.

More than anyone else, Russell secured the dominance of descriptivism in Anglo-American discussions of language prior to 1970. Not all descriptivists follow all of Russell's views slavishly, but at least during the period of the falsification controversies, they generally followed him in viewing names (or referring expressions) as the basic linguistic unit. Therefore the centerpiece of any descriptivist view of language must be a theory of how such names (or expressions) refer to objects in the world. What they have in common is the notion that a name is successful in referring to an object insofar as it stands for one or more definite descriptions that (either singly or together) uniquely describe the referent object.[14] That is, of the descriptions that a speaker takes to be satisfied by an object, the speaker takes one or some to belong uniquely to that object. If, however, no object uniquely satisfies the most important description(s), then the purported name does not refer. More specifically, this way of understanding reference was part of what Soames calls the "reigning conception of language." This reigning conception had several central presuppositions, including four that Soames describes as follows:

(i) The meaning of an expression is never identical with its referent. Rather, the meaning of a substantive, nonlogical term is a descriptive sense that provides necessary and sufficient conditions for determining its reference. For example, the meaning of a singular term is a descriptive condition satisfaction of which by an object is necessary and sufficient for the term to refer to the object, whereas the meaning of a predicate is a descriptive condition satisfaction of which by an object is necessary and sufficient for the predicate to be true of the object.

(ii) Understanding a term amounts to associating it with the correct descriptive sense. In the case of ordinary predicates in the common language, all speakers who understand them associate essentially the same sense with them. This

13. For a discussion of some of these puzzling issues, see Soames, *Dawn of Analysis*, 118–126.
14. On some such views, the constitutive description(s) just is(are) the meaning of the name.

is also true for some widely used ordinary proper names—such as *London*. However, for many proper names of less widely known individuals, the defining descriptive information, and hence the meaning associated with the name can be expected to vary from speaker to speaker.

(iii) Since the meaning of a word, as used by a speaker, is completely determined by the descriptive sense that the speaker mentally associated with it, meaning is transparent. If two words mean the same thing, then anyone who understands both should easily be able to figure that out by consulting the sense that he or she associates with them.

(iv) Further, since the meaning of a word, as used by a speaker, is completely determined by the descriptive sense that he or she mentally associates with it, the meaning of a word in the speaker's language is entirely dependent on factors internal to the speaker. The same is true for the beliefs that the speaker uses the word to express. External factors—like the speaker's relation to the environment, and to the community of other speakers—are relevant only insofar as they causally influence the factors internal to the speaker that determine the contents of his or her beliefs.[15]

These four positions adequately summarize the descriptivist view of language, and it was well established by the time the falsification controversy broke out in the middle of the century. By 1950, Strawson and other ordinary language philosophers, under the influence of Wittgenstein's intermediate and later thought, had begun to challenge Russell's views. Nonetheless, descriptivism remained the dominant view prior to 1970.[16]

Russell's descriptivist understanding of language would pose significant difficulties for theologians seeking philosophical defenses of their theological positions. But even more problematic was the closely related epistemological role played by descriptions in his account of knowledge. The combination of Russell's accounts of language and knowledge formed a unified program that made the theological situation urgent in the middle of the century.

The enhanced epistemological role Russell gives to descriptions, in turn, were part of his rebellion (along with that of G. E. Moore) against the absolute idealism prevalent at Cambridge when Moore and Russell were students. The idealists at Cambridge tended to take certain ways of thinking, rather than phenomenal experience, as the basic concepts of epistemology. For Russell, in contrast, the basic epistemological concept is that of

---

15. Scott Soames, *Reference and Description: The Case Against Two-Dimensionalism* (Princeton, N.J.: Princeton Univ. Press, 2005), 1–2.

16. The situation changed dramatically in 1970 with the publication of Saul Kripke's *Naming and Necessity*, (Cambridge, Mass.: Harvard Univ. Press, 1972; repr., 1999).

"acquaintance," which is not a way of thinking but an immediate presentation. Acquaintance is a momentary qualitative experience of sense data. To stand in a relationship of acquaintance is to stand in a *nonpropositional, immediate relation* to an object.[17] "Object" here apparently does not include physical objects, but only sense data; thus what we can know by acquaintance seems to correspond in many cases to what Locke would call simple ideas.[18] But knowledge by acquaintance is not limited to such simple ideas. "We have acquaintance with sense-data, with many universals, and possibly with ourselves, but not with physical objects or other minds."[19] Acquaintance is immediate knowledge—it is not mediated by a description or by any other conceptual apparatus. Because it is immediate, it is not by means of acquaintance that we know any other physical object in the world. Acquaintance thus stands in contrast to the second basic epistemological relation, that of description. "We have descriptive knowledge of an object when we know that it is the object having some property or properties with which we are acquainted; that is to say, when we know that the property or properties in question *belong to one object and no more*, we are said to have knowledge of that one object by description, whether or not we are acquainted with the object."[20] Obviously, for most of the important things we know, our knowledge is by description, and Russell therefore held that "common words, even proper names, are usually really descriptions."[21]

We can immediately see what Russell's view implies for the knowledge of God (and the knowledge of God was the focus of the falsification controversy). If it is only some universals, sense data, and possibly ourselves that we can know by acquaintance, then insofar as we can know anything of other beings, it can only be by description. And this applies a fortiori to God, who (at least as a rule) incites no sense data at all. More importantly, even to have descriptive knowledge of God we must meet stringent requirements. Specifically, to say that we have descriptive knowledge

17. "I say that I am *acquainted* with an object when I have a direct cognitive relation to that object, that is when I am directly aware of the object itself. When I speak of a cognitive relation here, I do not mean the sort of relation which constitutes judgement, but the sort which constitutes presentation" (Bertrand Russell, "Knowledge By Acquaintance and Knowledge by Description," *Proceedings of the Aristotelian Society* 11 [1910–11]: 108–28.)
18. "It will be seen that among the objects with which we are acquainted are not included physical objects (as opposed to sense-data), nor other people's minds" (Russell, "Knowledge By Acquaintance," 112).
19. Russell, "Knowledge By Acquaintance," 126.
20. Russell, "Knowledge By Acquaintance," 127 (emphasis added).
21. "Common words, even proper names, are usually really descriptions. That is to say, the thought in the mind of a person using a proper name correctly can generally only be expressed explicitly if we replace the proper name by a description" (Russell, "Knowledge By Acquaintance," 114).

of God, we must be able to specify one or more properties, with which we are acquainted, that belong *only* to God. Russell imposes a twofold requirement, therefore, on anyone who purports to have knowledge of God: first, there must be some property or properties that are unique to God, and, second, the alleged knower must have knowledge of that property or those properties by acquaintance. At least at first glance, this would seem to rule out properties, such as omnipotence, of which knowledge by acquaintance would be hard to acquire.

Further, in order to *refer* successfully to some object or being, we have to have some knowledge of the object to which we are attempting to refer. And, since we can know other beings only by description, in order even to refer successfully to God, we will have to satisfy Russell's two requirements for descriptive knowledge. This will mean that we must have knowledge of some descriptive condition that is both necessary and sufficient to pick out God as the unique referent of the term "God."

II. CHALLENGES TO THEOLOGY: JOHN WISDOM AND ANTONY FLEW

In this context, very little catalyst was needed to spark a philosophical attack on the concept of God that would have broad appeal. And this catalyst came in the form of a parable—John Wisdom's parable of an imaginary gardener in his essay "Gods," which appeared in the mid-1940s. In his essay, Wisdom is exploring the nature of religious belief. More specifically, Wisdom wants to know just what kind of belief a person has when she believes that God exists. Some beliefs are straightforward assertions that can be tested by experimentation. I believe, for example, that my wife is at home, and I can test that belief by calling my home phone to see if she answers. If she answers, she is indeed at home; if not, there is a very good chance that she is at least not in the house.

Some such beliefs are explanatory hypotheses that, if true, can account for a set of phenomena. I go to the doctor's office with cold-like symptoms, including a very sore throat. She looks in my mouth and sees that my throat and the back of my mouth are quite red. She forms the explanatory hypothesis that I have strep throat. If I do, this would explain the existence of my symptoms. She can test her hypothesis by experimentation—by swabbing my throat and sending the swab to the lab for a culture.

One way of thinking about belief in God is that it is an explanatory hypothesis that, if true, should be able to withstand experimental testing. Wisdom offers the story of the garden as a way to illustrate "how it is that an explanatory hypothesis, such as the existence of God, may start by being experimental and gradually become something quite different."[22] The story is as follows:

> Two people return to their long neglected garden and find among the weeds a few of the old plants surprisingly vigorous. One says to the other "It must be that a gardener has been coming and doing something about these plants." Upon enquiry they find that no neighbor has ever seen anyone at work in their garden. The first man says to the other "He must have worked while people slept." The other says "No, someone would have heard him and besides, anybody who cared about the plants would have kept down these weeds." The first man says "Look at the way these are arranged. There is purpose and a feeling for beauty here. I believe that someone comes, someone invisible to mortal eyes. I believe that the more carefully we look the more we shall find confirmation of this." They examine the garden ever so carefully and sometimes they come on new things suggesting that a gardener comes and sometimes they come on new things suggesting the contrary and even that a malicious person has been at work. Besides examining the garden carefully they also study what happens to gardens left without attention. Each learns all the other learns about this and about the garden. Consequently, when after all this, one says "I still believe a gardener comes" while the other says "I don't" their different words now reflect no difference as to what they have found in the garden, no difference as to what they would find in the garden if they looked further and no difference about how fast untended gardens fall into disorder.[23]

Wisdom argues that belief in the existence of the unnoticed gardener was at first an experimental hypothesis, but as the process of experimentation proceeded, it became clear that there was no observable fact about the garden about which the believer and the unbeliever disagreed. Their sole disagreement was about whether there was an unseen and unheard gardener. Wisdom's point in telling the story is not to persuade us to believe or not to believe in the existence of God. It is instead to argue that with some questions, including the question of whether God exists, we cannot adjudicate between rival answers through empirical investigation. Yet it is appropriate, he argues, to ask which of the rival answers is more reasonable. And we should not assume that the process of adjudication doesn't involve the discovery of new facts.[24] I will not characterize the rest of Wisdom's interesting

22. John Wisdom, "Gods," *Proceedings of the Aristotelian Society* 45 (1944–45): 185–206; quoted passage at 192.
23. Wisdom, "Gods," 191–92.
24. Wisdom, "Gods," 192, 196.

essay, except to note that he does not take answering the question of reasonableness to be a simple or straightforward inquiry. In addition, he thinks that one's answer to the question of the existence of God will typically involve some concomitant feeling toward the world, in the same way that along with the difference between the two friends disagreeing about the existence of an unnoticed gardener "goes a difference in how they feel towards the garden, in spite of the fact that neither expects anything of it which the other does not expect."[25] Wisdom's story, and the tentative conclusions he draws from it, was one of the primary instigators of the theology and falsification controversy that arose several years later and therefore features prominently in it. So let's turn directly to that controversy.

As I mentioned, I do not think that Wisdom's purpose in relating his story of the unnoticed gardener was to persuade his audience to conclude that the concept of God could not be distinguished from that of an imaginary gardener. Yet that was precisely the conclusion drawn by falsification theorists such as Antony Flew. In Flew's adaptation of Wisdom's story, the two friends (which Flew names the Believer and the Sceptic) undertake further empirical investigation using bloodhounds, electric fences, and other means, but there is no direct sign of the gardener.

> Yet still the believer is not convinced. 'But there is a gardener, invisible, intangible, insensible to electric shocks, a gardener who has no scent and makes no sound, a gardener who comes secretly to look after the garden which he loves.' At last the Sceptic despairs, 'But what remains of your original assertion? Just how does what you call an invisible, intangible, eternally elusive gardener differ from an imaginary gardener or even from no gardener at all?'[26]

What makes this parable so illuminating, Flew argues, is that it is typical of nearly all theological utterance. And what is typical about it is that the Believer will not allow any empirical fact that the friends are able to observe to count against his belief that a gardener exists. But just this feature, Flew concludes, means that the Believer's putative assertion that an invisible gardener exists and tends the garden is really no assertion at all. At least at first glance, this seems like a bizarre conclusion. If the Believer says that an invisible gardener tends the garden, he may be wrong, but surely he is at least making an assertion (*an invisible gardener tends the garden*), even if the assertion is incorrect. How could Flew deny this?

25. Wisdom, "Gods," 192, 201–206.
26. Antony Flew, "The University Discussion," in *New Essays in Philosophical Theology*, ed. Antony Flew and Alasdair MacIntyre (London: SCM Press, 1955, repr., 1958), 96 (page references are to reprint edition).

Flew argues that whenever we are asserting that a particular state of affairs obtains, we are simultaneously asserting that another state of affairs does not obtain. That is, when we assert that p, we simultaneously deny $\sim p$. Logically, that is, $p = \sim\sim p$. So far, so good. But Flew points out that to say that $p = \sim\sim p$ is not to say that $\sim\sim p$ is an entailment of p. Instead, it is an identical proposition—that is, the same proposition. So to assert p just is to assert $\sim\sim p$. Consequently, if there is no state of affairs that satisfies $\sim p$, then there is no state of affairs that satisfies p. In that case, to assert p is to assert nothing at all. As Flew puts it, "if there is nothing which a putative assertion denies then there is nothing which it asserts either: and so it is not really an assertion."[27] Again, so far so good.

At this point, though, let's notice that Flew makes a subtle assumption that the Believer is unlikely to share. Flew assumes that if there is no *observable state of affairs* that p denies, then there is no *state of affairs at all* that p denies. But whatever the Believer may assert about the gardener being invisible, surely there is at least one state of affairs that the Believer denies—namely, *that there is no gardener*. Whether a particular state of affairs can be verified or falsified may be germane to whether one should believe that the state of affairs obtains, but Flew goes further than this. For Flew, if an assertion cannot be falsified, then it does not really assert anything and is strictly meaningless. Flew argues that statements about God are very much like the Believer's statement about the invisible gardener. Theological utterances, he says, seem at first glance to be assertions, but since the theist will not allow any conceivable empirical observation to count decisively against them, such putative assertions are not really assertions at all, but are meaningless.

I'll have occasion later to point out fatal difficulties (well enough known by now) in this falsifiability thesis, but one that should have been obvious is that it's self-referentially incoherent. That is, the falsifiability thesis itself cannot be falsified. Given such obvious flaws, what could have led thinkers like Flew to adopt the thesis in the first place? The answer to that question is likely to be somewhat complicated, and it is likely that the causal story will vary from thinker to thinker. For my purposes, though, the important thing to note is that it is a relatively short distance from the descriptivist conception of language I described earlier to the falsifiability thesis. Recall that at the time Flew was adapting Wisdom's story of the gardener, the descriptivist understanding of language was, as Soames says, the "reigning conception of language." For descriptivists, the meaning of a referring expression is a description of the necessary and sufficient conditions for determining its reference. Similarly, the meaning of a predicate

27. Flew, "University Discussion," 98.

is a description of the necessary and sufficient conditions for the predicate to be true of the subject of the sentence. And finally, the meaning of a sentence is a description of the necessary and sufficient conditions that must obtain for the sentence to be true. When Flew argues that theistic statements do not count as assertions because the people who make them do not allow anything to count against them, what he's saying is that they fail to fulfill the descriptivist requirements for meaningful language use. His argument actually makes two claims, it seems to me. First (to adapt his language about the gardener), when he argues that theists cannot distinguish God from an imaginary god or no god at all, he's saying that theistic claims do not provide any set of descriptive conditions that will allow us to determine that "God" refers to God and not to anything else, such as an imaginary God.

Second, Flew is arguing that, even if reference to God could be established, theistic claims do not set out necessary and sufficient conditions that will allow us to test whether the claim is true of God or not. This, I think, is the point Flew is trying to make in the following example:

> Someone tells us that God loves us as a father loves his children.... But then we see a child dying of inoperable cancer of the throat. His earthly father is driven frantic...but his Heavenly Father reveals no obvious sign of concern. Some qualification is made—God's love is..."an inscrutable love", perhaps.... We are reassured again. But then perhaps we ask: what is this assurance of God's (appropriately qualified) love worth, what is this apparent guarantee really a guarantee against? Just what would have to happen not merely (morally and wrongly) to tempt but also (logically and rightly) to entitle us to say "God does not love us" or even "God does not exist"?[28]

There are at least two ways to interpret what Flew is saying here. Flew might have used the example to argue against the reasonableness of the belief that God loves us. On this interpretation, the lack of empirical evidence of God's concern deprives the belief in God's love of (at least some of) its epistemic justification. But this is not the way Flew uses the example. In Flew's usage, the example suggests that the qualifications made to the statement that God loves us (e.g., that it is inscrutable) in response to the lack of empirical evidence have eroded the statement to the point "that it was no longer an assertion at all."[29] And if it no longer counts as an assertion, that is because it cannot be assigned a meaning. In turn, it seems to me, the reason Flew thinks the statement lacks meaning is that it does

28. Flew, "University Discussion," 98–99.
29. Flew, "Theology and Falsification," 98.

not describe a set of conditions that must be satisfied for the statement to be a true one. It is this set of conditions that allows us to judge whether the statement is true or false, and Flew challenges his interlocutors to set these conditions out: "I therefore," he says, "put to the succeeding sympo-siasts the simple central questions, 'What would have to occur or to have occurred to constitute for you a disproof of the love of, or of the existence of, God?'"[30]

With these questions Flew challenged his theistic interlocutors to show that statements about God met the requirements for being meaningful statements. Theologians responded in a variety of ways, three of which are particularly instructive for understanding the divide between liberal and postliberal Barthian theology in the twentieth century. Two kinds of responses were typical of liberal theologians; a third type of response, a Wittgensteinian one, was much more radical in nature. In the later decades of the twentieth century, this more radical response came to characterize postliberal styles of theology.

30. Flew, "Theology and Falsification," 99.

CHAPTER THREE

The Liberal Response

In the later 1950s and 1960s, a number of prominent theologians and philosophers took the falsification challenge to be a very serious one. After all, if Flew was right, statements about God were either meaningless or conclusively falsified. So they formulated responses designed to show that religious and theological language was indeed meaningful. From within the ranks of liberal theologians, the responses tended to be versions of one of two sorts. The first sort can be characterized as noncognitive in nature. Noncognitive responses generally argued that religious or theological utterances were never straightforward assertions, though they may often seem to be. Instead, they are to be understood symbolically, or as expressions of an intention to follow a certain way of life, or as expressions of an internalized spiritual principle, or (as R. M. Hare famously dubbed them) as *"bliks."* The second sort of response can be characterized as generally cognitive in nature. Cognitive responses argued that some religious or theological utterances are indeed straightforward assertions and that they are indeed meaningful. Some argued that theological assertions could in principle be falsified, but that in fact they have not been (or at any rate not all of them). Others argued that such assertions are meaningful because there are things that count as evidence against them, despite their invulnerability to *conclusive* empirical falsification. Yet both sorts of responses failed to challenge Flew on a crucial fundamental supposition—namely, that the descriptivist understanding of language (in this case religious or theological language) was correct. Liberal theology, that is, assumed that if religious or theological language is to be meaningful, it must meet the descriptivist requirements described in the last chapter. We can see this through a brief look at the noncognitive response of R. M. Hare and the cognitive response of Basil Mitchell. It is also evident in the responses of I. M. Crombie and the later response of Schubert M. Ogden, which in my own view is among the most coherent and penetrating of the liberal responses. I shall spend much more time with Ogden because in the next chapter I shall be considering his theological method as paradigmatic of liberal theology. These responses differed significantly from each other, but one of the things liberal responses had in common was their assumption of a descriptivist view of religious and theological language. On this issue, as I will argue in part 2, postliberal theology fundamentally differentiates itself from liberal theology.

I. NONCOGNITIVE RESPONSES: RELIGIOUS STATEMENTS ARE NOT ASSERTIONS

A number of theologians and philosophers of religion seemed to agree with R. M. Hare, who confessed that, "on the ground marked out by Flew, he seems…to be completely victorious."[1] The kind of religious language Flew attacks (successfully in the view of Hare and other noncognitivists), Hare says, is language that propounds "some sort of *explanation,* as scientists are accustomed to use the word."[2] In other words, Hare takes it to be a mistake to regard religious statements as straightforward assertions. If that's what religious statements were, Hare says, they "would obviously be ludicrous."[3] Instead, Hare argues, religious statements are expressions of "*bliks.*" Other theologians followed Hare's interpretive strategy. R. B. Braithwaite, for example, interpreted religious statements as expressions of "behavior policies"; Don Cupitt argued that religious statements were expressions of "internalized spiritual principles"; and for Paul van Buren, after the death of God, religious statements can only be regarded as stories or parts of stories. Even Paul Tillich can arguably be considered something of a noncognitivist in arguing that religious statements must be understood symbolically.[4]

1. R. M. Hare, "Theology and Falsification," in *New Essays in Philosophical Theology,* ed. Antony Flew and Alasdair MacIntyre (London: SCM Press, 1955; repr., 1958), 99 (page references are to reprint edition).
2. Hare, "Theology and Falsification," 101.
3. Hare, "Theology and Falsification," 101.
4. R. B. Braithwaite, *An Empiricist's View of the Nature of Religious Belief* (Cambridge: Cambridge Univ. Press, 1955); Paul van Buren, "On Doing Theology," in *Talk of God,* ed. G. N. A. Vesey (London: Macmillan, 1969), 52–71; Braithwaite, *The Secular Meaning of the Gospel* (London: SCM Press, 1963), passim; Don Cupitt, *Taking Leave of God* (London: SCM Press, 1980), passim; Paul Tillich, "Religious Symbols and Our Knowledge of God," in *Philosophy of Religion,* ed. W. L. Rowe and W. J. Wainwright (New York: Harcourt Brace Jovanovich, 1973), 479–88. For these citations I am indebted to Kenneth Surin, *The Turnings of Darkness and Light: Essays in Philosophical and Systematic Theology* (Cambridge: Cambridge Univ. Press, 1989), 41, 248 n.3.

Of these noncognitivist responses, Hare's was perhaps the most famous. Hare believed that if Flew was right about just what religious statements or religious beliefs were, then Flew was right that they were either false or non-sensical. But, he argued, Flew misconstrued the nature of religious beliefs and the religious statements that express them. To explain what he took religious beliefs to be, Hare related an alternative parable to Wisdom's. In Hare's parable, a lunatic is convinced that all Oxford dons want to murder him. To dissuade him of this belief, his friends introduce him to the most cordial, kindly and respectable dons they can find. But no matter how kind and friendly each one is, and no matter his reputation, the lunatic responds that the don's demeanor, kind treatment of him, and reputation is only the don's attempt to deceive him. Every fact his friends relate about this or that don is interpreted by the lunatic as part of the don's cunning plot. The luna-tic allows nothing, in fact, to count as evidence against his theory about dons. But since nothing counts against the lunatic's theory, Flew's challenge to theologians should require him to conclude that the lunatic asserts noth-ing about dons and that therefore there is no difference between his beliefs about dons and the beliefs of most people about dons. But Hare took it to be obvious that there is a difference, and he calls "that in which we differ from this lunatic, our respective *bliks*."[5] He conceded that Flew had demonstrated that a *blik* is not an assertion (though he didn't say just why he thinks this), but he maintained that it was important to have the right *bliks*.

There are other kinds of *bliks*, of course, than *bliks* about Oxford dons. Hare has a *blik* about the reliability of his car (he judged its workings to be mostly reliable in the absence of evidence to the contrary), and a more gen-eral *blik* about the world that caused him to have confidence "in the future reliability of steel joints, in the continued ability of the road to support [his] car, and not gape beneath it revealing nothing below; in the general non-homicidal tendencies of dons"; etc. One's *blik* about the world, Hare argues, cannot be formulated as an assertion, but this does not mean that there are no differences between sensible *bliks* and ridiculous ones, or that one cannot judge between them.[6]

Religious beliefs, Hare argues, are *bliks*. More specifically, in Hare's account they seem to be *bliks* about the world as a whole. Hare describes the difference between a theistic *blik* and a nontheistic one by means of the following analogy: Let us say that Jessica has a *blik* about the world that causes her to have confidence that natural phenomena generally occur in accordance with some law-like regularity and will continue to do so in the

5. Hare, "Theology and Falsification," 100.
6. Hare, "Theology and Falsification," 100–101.

future. Bill, on the other hand, due to an unhealthy fascination with the writings of Hume and Derrida, has a *blik* about the world that causes him to believe that natural phenomena occur by random chance. The difference between Jessica's and Bill's respective *bliks*, Hare says, "is the sort of difference that there is between [the *bliks* of] those who really believe in God and [the *bliks* of] those who really disbelieve in him."[7] For Hare, then, a religious belief is a kind of fundamental attitude toward the world as a whole, and a religious statement is an expression of this attitude. Note, though, that Hare never departs from the descriptivist understanding of religious language that Flew presupposes. On Flew's account, for religious language to be meaningful it must describe some state of affairs, and this state of affairs must be empirically falsifiable. Hare never disputes this understanding of the meaning of religious language; indeed, his concession of the force of Flew's argument seems at least to indicate that he agrees with it. Instead, he argues that Flew has misunderstood the state of affairs that religious statements describe. Rather than describing God's attributes or actions in the world, they describe the *blik(s)* of their utterers. So, for example, when an aging Karl Barth was asked about the most important thing he had learned in his lifetime of theological study, Barth is reported to have responded, "Jesus loves me, this I know." On Hare's construal, rather than describing an act (loving) of the referent of "Jesus" (the resurrected Jesus) toward the referent of the indexical "me" (Barth), Barth's remark instead describes Barth's own *blik* about the world. Nonetheless, presupposed by both Flew and Hare is the notion that the meaning of Barth's assertion consists in some descriptive sense that provides conditions the satisfaction of which is a necessary and sufficient condition for the assertion to be true. Where Flew and Hare differ is over the descriptive sense provided by Barth's assertion.

II. COGNITIVE RESPONSES

A. Religious Statements Are Assertions, But Not Falsified

Another kind of response was put forward by Basil Mitchell, and it can be generally characterized as a cognitive response.[8] Mitchell disputes Flew's claim that a theist will not allow anything to count as evidence against his belief in God's existence. Mitchell counters that theists do in fact allow that

7. Hare, "Theology and Falsification," 102.
8. Basil Mitchell, "Theology and Falsification," in *New Essays in Philosophical Theology*, 103–105. See also Mitchell's "Introduction" to *Philosophy of Religion*, ed. Basil Mitchell (Oxford: Oxford Univ. Press, 1971), 2.

some observable phenomena count against their religious beliefs. A theist, for example, would indeed admit that the existence of at least some kinds of pain, or the suffering brought about by natural disasters, counts against the assertion that God loves us. But it does not count *decisively* against the assertion, and in the situation where the evidence is ambiguous, a theist—or at any rate a Christian—will allow her faith to commit her to trusting in God.[9]

Like Hare, Mitchell offers his own alternative parable, in which, in an occupied country during a war, a stranger meets with a member of the resistance. In the meeting the guerilla is deeply impressed with the stranger and is completely convinced of his commitment to the resistance. After this the guerilla never again has a private meeting with the stranger, but sees him in public places from time to time. Sometimes the stranger's actions appear to confirm the guerilla's conclusion that the stranger is on the side of the resistance; but sometimes they appear in conflict with the conclusion. Similarly, when the guerilla asks the stranger for help, sometimes he receives it but sometimes he does not. And when he doesn't, he can conclude either that the stranger is not on the side of the resistance after all or that he is on the side of the resistance but has some reason for withholding help. If the guerilla has sufficient faith in the stranger, he will maintain the latter conclusion. Yet some of the stranger's actions do count as evidence against the first conclusion. And if such evidence increases while the evidence for the stranger's commitment to the resistance dwindles, Mitchell admits that at some point the guerilla would be "just silly" to persist in his faith in the stranger. But just what that point is, Mitchell says, cannot be specified in advance. Religious beliefs, Mitchell says, are like the guerilla's beliefs about the stranger. "'God loves men' resembles 'the Stranger is on our side'...in not being conclusively falsifiable."[10] Yet this does not imply that nothing counts as evidence against it, and Mitchell admits that pain and suffering does count as such evidence. Yet the statement "God loves us" and others like it are not, Mitchell insists, "provisional hypotheses to be discarded" if sufficient evidence to the contrary is produced. On the other hand, they are not "vacuous formulae (expressing, perhaps, a desire for reassurance) to which experience makes no difference...." Instead, he says, they are "significant articles of faith."[11] But he doesn't make clear exactly what he means by this. One might think that Mitchell's position here implies (1) that religious statements are assertions, and (2) that there is articulable evidence that can count against them,

9. Mitchell, "Theology and Falsification," 103.
10. Mitchell, "Theology and Falsification," 105.
11. Mitchell, "Theology and Falsification," 105.

but (3) that, as "significant articles of faith," there is no evidence that could count *decisively* against them. He later clarified, however, that he regarded the positions of I. M. Crombie and John Hick[12] as fuller developments of his own position, in which, for example, not only does the occurrence of evil count against the assertion that "God loves us," but that "suffering that was utterly, eternally and irredeemably pointless" would count decisively against such an assertion.[13] Thus, although Mitchell disagrees with Flew's conclusion that theism is in fact falsified, he (at least implicitly) concedes that Flew has made a legitimate demand that religious assertions be given meaning by describing a set of conditions the fulfillment of which would make them true (and the failure of which would make them false).

So it seems to me that, on Mitchell's interpretation, Flew understands religious utterances to be provisional hypotheses, while Hare understands them to be "vacuous formulae." Mitchell agrees with Flew that religious statements "must be assertions," at least insofar as they appear to be assertions rather than, say, petitions.[14] If Mitchell's understanding of religious utterances differs from Flew's, it is certainly not clear to me just how they differ. But it is clear that Mitchell nowhere questions the descriptivist understanding of religious language shared by both Flew and Hare. For Mitchell, as for Flew and Hare, religious utterances describe states of affairs, and this descriptive sense constitutes their meaning, irrespective of whether such states of affairs obtain.

Christian theologians and philosophers of religion returned to Flew's challenge during the 1960s, and even into the early 1970s, which indicates that they were not entirely comfortable with the responses. This discomfort can be seen in the responses of I. M. Crombie, which were among the most sensitive to the philosophy-of-language issues motivating Flew's challenge. Crombie's first response, which was not originally part of the University Discussion of Flew's falsification challenge, was published along with contributions from Flew, Hare, Mitchell, and others in the influential volume edited by Flew and MacIntyre, *New Essays in Philosophical Theology*, published in 1955.[15] In his response, Crombie shows, at least on my reading, that he understands Flew's challenge and considers it a challenge that Christians should not attempt to evade. But he also admits that his own

12. I. M. Crombie, "The Possibility of Theological Statements," and John Hick, "Theology and Verification," in *The Philosophy of Religion,* ed. Basil Mitchell (New York: Oxford Univ. Press, 1971), 23–52 and 53–71, respectively.

13. Mitchell, "Introduction," 2.

14. Mitchell, "Theology and Falsification," 105.

15. I. M. Crombie, "Theology and Falsification," in *New Essays,* 109–30. I should note that his explorations on this subject are a deviation from his usual field of expertise, which was Plato.

exploratory remarks are not an adequate answer. He returned to the issue a few years later in an essay, "The Possibility of Theological Statements," for a volume edited by Mitchell; he subsequently revised this essay for another volume edited by Mitchell in 1971.[16] It will be helpful to consider this latter contribution to the discussion because it demonstrates the uneasiness felt by Christian theologians and philosophers with their own responses to Flew's challenge—or at least the uneasiness felt by those who thought that a "cognitive" response was required.

In Crombie's response, he begins by stating that "all that is necessary for an utterance to be a meaningful statement is that it should be governed by rules which specify what it is about, and what it asserts about it."[17] This statement is not remarkable in itself, but it shows Crombie's understanding that Flew's challenge is twofold. It challenges theists to show both that the word "God" can have a referent and that statements about God are meaningful. With respect to reference, he says, perplexities arise because "God" is used like a proper name ("God loves us" is used similarly to "Mom loves us"), yet is unlike all other proper names because its reference cannot be derived from acquaintance with the object it denotes. Theists speak of God as though God were an individual, but the characteristics that make others individuals don't apply to God. Individuals, Crombie says, are either known to us (or have been known to someone) or they uniquely satisfy some description. That is, Crombie (seemingly following Russell) takes reference to be fixed either by acquaintance or by description. But with respect to God, there are problems with both ways of fixing the reference of God. No one has ever been acquainted with God, Crombie says; and of the descriptions that are sometimes said to be satisfied uniquely by God, no one can say what it would be like to conform to one of them.[18]

In my judgment, Crombie summarizes the challenge accurately. But his response quickly becomes convoluted. He poses counterexamples to the requirement of acquaintance, such as abstractions or fictional characters, but concludes that they do not help. Abstractions such as "the average person" are subject to "reduction" (which seems to be a kind of Russellian analysis). And using the names of fictional characters such as Achilles as a kind of reference analogue for "God" plays right into the hands of Flew and other critics. Crombie takes a clue from two traditional characteristics

16. I. M. Crombie, "The Possibility of Theological Statements," in *Faith and Logic,* ed. Basil Mitchell (London: George Allen and Unwin, 1958), 31–67, revised and reprinted in *The Philosophy of Religion,* ed. Basil Mitchell (Oxford: Oxford Univ. Press, 1971), 23–52. Hereafter, references to this essay will be to the 1971 reprint edition.

17. Crombie, "Possibility of Theological Statements," 26.

18. Crombie, "Possibility of Theological Statements," 32.

of God. First, he says, God exists outside of space and time, and therefore the reference of "God" cannot be fixed by acquaintance or demonstration. Instead, it must be fixed by what he calls "a conception of the divine"; by this he seems to mean a description. But here again he is hampered by the traditional notion that God must be beyond our comprehension. God is said to be omniscient, for example, but "[o]mniscience is not infinite erudition, and what it is must be beyond our comprehension."[19] The task, then, of finding a description that could fix the reference of "God" is something like the task of describing the indescribable. Crombie thus settles on a conception of the divine that "is the notion of a complement which could fill in certain deficiencies in our experience, that could not be filled in by further experience or scientific theory-making; and its positive content is simply the idea of something (we know not what) which might supply those deficiencies."[20]

Crombie seems to anticipate the objection that he still has not given his conception of the divine much positive content, if any. So he suggests that we might be able to derive positive content for the concept of God by noting that our own self-experience can only be described with the aid of nonphysical concepts. If we can use such concepts meaningfully (as in a statement such as "She had such a sweet spirit about her"), then we should be able to conceive of a nonspatial being. Yet we remain unable to conceive of what it would be like to be God, he says, so the conception of the divine is, after all, "not a conception, but a hint of the possibility of something we cannot conceive, but which lies outside the range of possible conception *in a determinate direction*."[21]

This is about the best Crombie is able to do in discussing the *reference* of "God." His strategy for giving *meaning* to divine predicates is somewhat similar: To approach the meaning of terms such as "infinite," "omniscient," "omnipotent," and the like, when they are predicated of God, we must consider each term as one of a set of ordered pairs—e.g., "finite/infinite," "contingent/necessary," or "derivative/nonderivative." For each pair, when one term is predicated of God, the other will be predicated of the world. The meaning of the term predicated of God will then be discovered in a derivative way from the meaning of the paired term predicated of the world. Crombie does not get specific about how this derivation should go, but he acknowledges that it cannot be "by any normal kind of derivation."[22] The best we can do, he

19. Crombie, "Possibility of Theological Statements," 43.
20. Crombie, "Possibility of Theological Statements," 43.
21. Crombie, "Possibility of Theological Statements," 45 (emphasis in original).
22. Crombie, "Possibility of Theological Statements," 50.

says, is first to figure out the meaning of the paired term predicated of the world. The sentence containing this earthly predication, he says, will express "an intellectual dissatisfaction with the notion of this universe as a complete system, with, as a corollary, the notion of a being with which one could not be thus dissatisfied."[23] When we make statements ascribing properties like omnipotence to God, he says, such statements "stand for the abstract conception of the possibility of the removal of certain intellectual dissatisfactions which we may feel about the universe of common experience."[24] Crombie nowhere cites Thomas Aquinas, but the similarities to Thomas's *via analogia* are difficult to miss. He is not troubled about whether Thomas, by saying we cannot know God's essence, admits the inconceivability of God. Indeed, Crombie says straightforwardly that in his essay, "I have tried to define a sense in which we *can* mean inconceivables...."[25]

After this essay, Crombie returned to writing on ancient philosophy, his previous specialty. Yet it is clear that Crombie is not satisfied with the answer he attempted in the "The Possibility of Theological Statements"—he compares it to writing a sentence that doesn't quite convey the true meaning of what one wants to say, but without knowing how to improve it.[26] I get the sense Crombie views the falsification challenge as being very serious indeed, tries to respond to the heart of the challenge, but is unsatisfied with his response. Though he never formulates a more satisfying response (at least not in print), he does not admit that the critics have succeeded. Others were not so reticent.[27]

It seems evident, to me at any rate, that what Hare and Mitchell are primarily concerned about is the epistemic justification of religious claims. And they seem to have an intuition that the epistemic justification of such claims is somehow related to the way such claims acquire meaning. Yet this relation is not at all clear, and neither writer makes much of a philosophical effort to spell it out.[28] But there is at least one liberal theologian,

23. Crombie, "Possibility of Theological Statements," 50.
24. Crombie, "Possibility of Theological Statements," 52.
25. Crombie, "Possibility of Theological Statements," 51 (emphasis in original).
26. Crombie, "Possibility of Theological Statements," 51.
27. See, for example, R. B. Braithwaite, *An Empiricist's View of the Nature of Religious Belief*; Paul M. van Buren, *The Secular Meaning of the Gospel* (New York: Macmillan, 1963; repr., 1965) (page references are to reprint edition).
28. As Braithwaite puts it: "[T]he primary question becomes, not whether a religious statement such as that a personal God created the world is true or false, but how it could be known to be true or false. Unless this latter question can be answered, the religious statement has no ascertainable meaning.... Meaning is not logically prior to the possibility of verification: we do not first learn the meaning of a statement, and afterwards consider what would make us call it true or false; the two understandings are one and indivisible" (*Empiricist's View of Religious Belief*, 2–3).

Schubert M. Ogden, who is quite clear about his own method and who at the same time addresses the question of religious language. He does this both in the context of the theology and falsification controversy and in the context of his own disagreement with D. Z. Phillips, a philosopher and theologian who is an ardent follower of the later Wittgenstein.

B. Religious Statements Are Transcendental Assertions

For theologians like Thomas Altizer and Paul van Buren, the attempt to refashion Christian theology so as to take adequate account of the non-existence of God may have seemed to be the only intellectually honest response to a challenge they thought insurmountable. To others, though, like Schubert Ogden, such an attempt was an exercise in futility. "However absurd talking about God might be," he says, "it could never be so obviously absurd as talking of Christian faith without God."[29]

Like the other liberal theologians we have considered, Ogden accepts the basic descriptivist approach to language presupposed by Flew. Unlike the others, though, he is confident that theology can meet Flew's challenge;[30]

29. Schubert M. Ogden, *The Reality of God and Other Essays* (New York: Harper & Row, 1966; repr., Dallas, Tex.: Southern Methodist Univ. Press, 1992), 14 (page references are to reprint edition).

30. Though his concerns do not run in precisely the same directions as mine, I am indebted to Mark McLeod for the collection of sources and synthesis of Ogden's various comments and thoughts on religious language. See Mark S. McLeod, "Schubert Ogden on Truth, Meaningfulness, and Religious Language," *American Journal of Theology and Philosophy* 9 (Summer 1988): 195–207. On McLeod's reading, Ogden uses "empirical" in three senses: (1) a positivistic sense, (2) a sense that includes both sensuous and nonsensuous experience, and (3) a Whiteheadian sense in which every experience includes an experience of both ourselves and another, of value, and of the whole (or of Deity) (McLeod, "Schubert Ogden on Truth," 197–98). These three senses of experience correspond to three kinds of claims: (1) factual claims, (2) contingent existential claims, and (3) necessary existential claims. Each kind of claim, McLeod argues, has its own test of meaningfulness. Factual claims acquire meaning positivistically (presumably through truth conditions). Contingent existential claims, he says, are falsifiable by conceivable, nonsensuous experience. McLeod does not say, however, just how this goes, or how it is distinguishable from acquiring meaning through truth conditions. So far as I can see, such statements also acquire meaning through truth conditions; but those truth conditions are of a different sort. Necessary existential claims are falsifiable only by showing that they are confused or self-contradictory. "Accordingly, whenever one shows a particular assertion to be meaningful, one also shows it to be true" (McLeod, "Schubert Ogden on Truth," 200). This just means that such statements acquire meaning through their truth conditions as well. Consequently, though the three types of claims may have different ways of testing their truth and meaning, they all acquire meaning the same way—through their truth conditions.

thus, Ogden doesn't hesitate to take religious language to acquire meaning in the descriptive manner we have been discussing.[31]

In a very early essay, Ogden conceived the theologian's task as that of a translator, translating the church's confessions into the language and conceptualities of her own day. "What is needed in theology," he argued, "is a thoroughgoing attempt to translate the meaning of the church's confession into the terms in which contemporary men [sic] either do or can most readily understand their life as persons."[32] On this definition, from a postliberal point of view, language functions as a bearer of concepts. Ogden's understanding of theology's task implies that there were certain prelinguistic ideas or notions formulated in the past, which now need to be reformulated using different language. But this reformulation need not change the meaning of the idea. And if different language can express the same idea, then it is the idea itself that gives meaning to the language, insofar as the language points to it. To use the vocabulary of descriptivism that we have been using, we can restate Ogden's position as follows: The theological confession formulated by theologians in the past described a set of conditions the satisfaction of which is necessary and sufficient for the confessions to be true. The theologian's task is to use contemporary language to describe that same set of conditions. Contemporary confessions acquire meaning in the same way as the classical ones. Their meaning consists in the descriptive senses that set out conditions the satisfaction of which is necessary and sufficient for the confessions to be true.

This understanding of language is shared by Antony Flew, and Ogden's response to Flew at least implicitly accepts it.[33] Ogden construes Flew's

31. When postliberals describe this stance, they will say that descriptivists understand language to acquire meaning "referentially." That is, the meaning of an assertion is constituted by the conditions that must obtain for the assertion to be true. An assertion acquires meaning through its ability to point to, or refer, to these truth conditions. From the point of view of postliberals like Hans Frei and George Lindbeck, this means that, for Ogden, despite the importance of language as a part of human experience, the primordial human experience is prelinguistic. This experience can be articulated linguistically, but for this to happen, experience must be organized into some form of prelinguistic understanding or notion, which is then transported or borne by language. Language has meaning insofar as it can point to such a notion.

32. Schubert M. Ogden, "The Lordship of Jesus Christ: The Meaning of Our Affirmation," *Encounter* 21 (Autumn 1960): 408–22, 410.

33. Schubert M. Ogden, "God and Philosophy: A Discussion with Antony Flew," *Journal of Religion* 48 (April 1968): 161–68, 161. As Ogden construes this challenge, it is "to confront the theist with the following dilemma: 'To find something positive to say about his proposed God, that shall have sufficient determinate content to be both falsifiable in principle and interesting, while not at the same time actually being false'" (162, quoting Antony Flew, *God and Philosophy* [New York: Harcourt Brace & World, 1966], ch. 8, para. 27).

challenge as involving three assertions regarding theism. First, it cannot identify to what the concept of God applies; second, it cannot speak of God in terms of a valid analogy; third, God cannot be conceived as infinitely powerful, wise, and good and as also having a will that can be disobeyed, and even if God could be so conceived, the claim that God exists is refuted by the existence of evil in the world.[34] Let's note a couple of points regarding Ogden's use of language and experience.[35] First, Ogden distinguishes between "empirical" and "experiential," which is a broader term. On Ogden's usage, "'empirical' means applying through some but *not all* possible experience, while 'experiential' means applying through *at least some* possible experience, and perhaps all."[36] For Ogden, the claims of metaphysics apply not only through some, but through all possible experience. That is to say, such claims concern states of affairs that are either necessary or impossible. And the question of the existence of God, Ogden says, is a metaphysical question. This means, in Ogden's judgment, that if the concept of God is meaningful, no empirical argument could ever disprove the existence of God.[37] Stated in another way, "theistic argument, properly understood, is not at all a matter of generalization from instances, for the decisive reason that it is not an empirical or scientific kind of argument but is strictly conceptual or metaphysical."[38] Recall that Russell thought it possible to have knowledge by acquaintance with some universals (abstract concepts) and the relations between them. Such knowledge satisfies his requirement for successful reference—which in turn is required for meaning. When Ogden says that the question of the existence of God is a metaphysical question, he is also saying that answering the question asserts knowledge by acquaintance with abstract concepts and the relations between them. So, to use Russell's terms, Ogden takes Flew to be making a category mistake in failing to take account of knowledge by acquaintance.

In addition, after taking issue with the method of Flew's falsification test, Ogden argues that the constitutive assertions of Flew's atheistic position "are without clear experiential significance."[39] More specifically, Flew's position fails "sufficiently to relate its terms and assertions to the experience

34. Ogden, "God and Philosophy," 163.
35. I do not wish to give an analysis of Ogden's arguments against Flew, though they seem to me successful. Perhaps the most telling argument advanced by Ogden is that Flew's "falsification test," which for Flew spells the defeat of the concept of God, also defeats the claim that the universe exists (Ogden, "God and Philosophy," 169). Crombie had earlier made a similar remark, though he did not press the claim ("Possibility of Theological Statements," 36).
36. Ogden, "God and Philosophy," 172 (emphasis in original).
37. Ogden, "God and Philosophy," 172–73.
38. Ogden, "God and Philosophy," 175 n.16.
39. Ogden, "God and Philosophy," 174.

which *alone* gives them any sense."[40] The implication of a statement such as this, it seems to me, is that language gets its meaning or sense by its ability to point to or describe an experience, though that experience need not be empirical experience. The nonempirical experience Ogden has in mind here encompasses the transcendental conditions of the possibility of any and all experience. So long as the assertion provides a descriptive sense the satisfaction of which provides necessary and sufficient conditions for the assertion to be true, the assertion will be meaningful. And its meaning will be constituted by that descriptive sense. This requirement holds both for empirical claims and for claims involving abstract concepts as well. In speaking of Flew's notion of "order in the universe," Ogden argues that there must be some experience that gives the phrase meaning: "What, as Hume might ask, is the impression from which his idea of order is derived and by reference to which it must ultimately be shown to have such meaning as it has?"[41] Such an impression, then, or experience, is what gives meaning to an assertion, insofar as the assertion is capable of pointing to it by means of a description. Ogden's descriptivist position on language is not merely incidental or unintended or simply assumed. Instead, one of Ogden's principal criticisms of Flew depends on it: Flew argues that the "order in the universe" need not be explained by reference to a divine Orderer. On Ogden's view, if Flew's understanding of order has meaning, this can only be derived by reference to some experience. This experience, in turn, is less than adequately understood if it is not understood as an experience of God. Thus:

> [T]he only experience of which I have any inside experience, and *by reference to which, therefore, my idea of order finally has whatever meaning it has,* is the order exhibited by my own occasions of experience as a self or person. Consequently, when I try to conceive what might be meant by speaking of "cosmic order," I find that I have no success at all unless I conceive of a *cosmic experience* and that in having this conception I already have everything of the theistic idea but the name. Flew's position, by contrast, seems to me to have the defect of non-theistic positions generally in that it makes use of ultimate conceptions such as order without sufficiently attending to the meaning actually given them by experience.[42]

40. Ogden, "God and Philosophy," 175 (emphasis added).
41. Ogden, "God and Philosophy," 175. This is the kind of question that fundamental or philosophical theology should ask. "Hence the *reductio ad absurdam* character of all the theistic arguments, which, if they succeed, leave theism as the only reasonable position, because the non-theistic alternatives are shown to be absurd, experience furnishing no coherent meaning for them" (175 n.16).
42. Ogden, "God and Philosophy," 176 (emphasis added). Shortly thereafter, Ogden again affirms that "the very meaning of the word ['order' is]...given...through experience...." (176).

The problem with Flew's position, on Ogden's view, is that its language lacks meaning because of its inability to give an adequate description of an experience that could imbue it with meaning. More precisely, the experience to which it points is more accurately described as in some sense an experience of God. This is what I take Ogden to mean when he says that the terms of Flew's affirmation of a cosmic order "are insufficiently analyzed in relation to our experience."[43]

This understanding of language is apparent in a contemporaneous essay in which Ogden argues that empirical theology has a bright future.[44] The best way to construe empirical theology, according to Ogden, is as that theological enterprise which appeals solely to experience (our common human experience) to justify its claims. He asserts that the problem of how to engage in empirical theology in a way that is fitting and appropriate to the witness of the Christian scriptures can be approached or formulated in explicitly linguistic terms. In this case, theology concerns the proper use of religious or theological language. In using such religious or theological language, Ogden assumes that a valid objection to any theological argument is that it relinquishes "the certainty that experience alone is able to provide as to the meaning and truth of any of our assertions."[45] Once again, this is no incidental assertion, but rather an important assumption of Ogden's argument. Ogden argues for empirical theology from two premises: First, God is both universally transcendent and universally immanent; thus, "if anything at all can be experienced, whether as actual or as merely possible, God, too, must be experienced as its necessary ground."[46] Second, human beings are "radically free and responsible."[47] These two premises are intrinsically related and are crucial for both the truth and meaning of the most basic Christian theological claims. "If God were not somehow experienced by us in our experience of anything whatever, ... [then the Christian faith in God] could neither be true nor have any consistent meaning. Likewise, unless every man were in the position to verify the claims of faith in terms of his own experience, he could not bear the responsibility for his existence...."[48] For Ogden,

---

43. Ogden, "God and Philosophy," 176.
44. Schubert M. Ogden, "Present Prospects for Empirical Theology," in *The Future of Empirical Theology*, ed. Bernard Meland (Chicago: Univ. of Chicago Press, 1969), 65–88.
45. Ogden, "Present Prospects for Empirical Theology," 71.
46. Ogden, "Present Prospects for Empirical Theology," 73.
47. Ogden, "Present Prospects for Empirical Theology," 73.
48. Ogden, "Present Prospects for Empirical Theology," 74–75.

then, experience serves two functions theologically. First, it provides the criterion for assessing the truth not only of empirical claims, but of metaphysical claims as well. This, of course, means that experience is broader than the experience of our senses, and includes what Alfred North Whitehead called nonsensuous experience.[49] Second, experience gives meaning to the language in which assertions are formulated, by serving as the referents to which such assertions point. In turn, it is by means of their descriptive senses that assertions point to, or refer to, their referents. Again, this second function also requires an understanding of language that takes account of its ability to point to or describe not only sensory experience but also what Ogden calls "nonsensuous experience" as well. Elsewhere he is explicit about this: "I hold that it is this complex experience of existence—of myself, others and the whole—which is the experience out of which all religious language arises and to which it properly refers."[50]

With this basic understanding in view, Ogden sums up well the problem of an adequate understanding of experience. If empirical theology seeks to talk about God without an understanding of nonsensuous experience that includes an experience of God, it has difficulty talking about God at all. "If he [the theologian] takes the course of insisting on empirical verification of his assertions, he has two main possibilities: either he must refer the word 'God' to some merely creaturely reality or process of interaction, or else he must deny it all reference whatever by construing its meaning as wholly noncognitive."[51] To escape this dilemma, he argues, empirical theology must adopt an understanding of experience similar to that of Whitehead—an understanding according to which all human experience includes an experience of self, other fellow creatures, and "of the infinite

49. See Ogden, "Present Prospects for Empirical Theology," 78–82. Ogden differentiates two types of empirical theology on the basis that one type does, and the other does not, limit experience to sensory experience.

50. Schubert M. Ogden, "How Does God Function in Human Life?" in *Theology in Crisis: A Colloquium on the Credibility of "God,"* ed. Charles Hartshorne and Schubert M. Ogden (New Concord, Oh.: Muskingham College, 1967), 34–35, (quoted in David R. Mason, "Selfhood, Transcendence and the Experience of God," *Modern Theology* 3 (July 1987): 293–314, 305). Note that in the quotation in the text, the notion of reference is a bit more explicit than the corresponding passage from Schubert M. Ogden, "How Does God Function in Human Life," *Christianity and Crisis* 27 (May 15, 1967): 105–108: "This complex experience of existence—of myself, others and the whole—is the experience out of which all religious language arises and in terms of which it must be understood." Nonetheless, here, too, Ogden says that religious language "is the language in which we express and refer to our own existence as selves related to others and to the whole" (106).

51. Ogden, "Present Prospects for Empirical Theology," 80.

whole in which we are all included as somehow one."[52] This understanding of experience allows Ogden to argue that assertions about God can be verified or falsified by reference to experience.[53] In addition, language about God gets its meaning by pointing to or describing aspects of our experience. The function of religious or theological language, in Ogden's view, "is to re-present symbolically, or at least at the level of full self-consciousness, this underlying sense of ourselves and others as of transcendent worth."[54] Ogden's requirement of experiential verification means that these symbolic re-presentations provide the descriptive senses the satisfaction of which provides the necessary and sufficient conditions for the truth of the assertions. And the meanings of the assertions are constituted by their descriptive senses.

After his debate with Antony Flew was largely over, Ogden returned to the issue of religious language in response to a proposal by Alastair McKinnon that sought to address the charges surrounding the alleged unfalsifiability of religious claims.[55] McKinnon proposes that when the different functions of language are properly distinguished, the charges appear spurious. On his proposal, the same claim can function in one or more of three different ways. The first is an "assertional" use, in which it makes a

52. Ogden, "Present Prospects for Empirical Theology," 85. On Ogden's view, Whitehead's "contribution to theological reflection may well lie less in the conceptuality provided by his imposing metaphysical system than in the understanding of experience of which that system is but the explication" (81). This is not the only important aspect to Whitehead's understanding of experience, for Ogden. It is also important to understand experience as being not only of existence or being, but also of value. "Our enjoyment of actuality," Whitehead asserts, "is a realization of worth, good or bad. It is a value-experience" (Alfred North Whitehead, *Modes of Thought* [New York: Macmillan & Co., 1936], 159; quoted by Ogden, "Present Prospects for Empirical Theology," 84).

53. This expansion of experience beyond sensory experience is central to Ogden's response to Flew's continuing assertion of the falsification challenge. Further, it implies a corresponding expansion of the kinds of assertions that are meaningful by reference to experience. More specifically, it implies "not only that the class of factual assertions is smaller than the class of *meaningful* assertions, but also that it is smaller than the class of meaningful *existential* assertions" (Schubert M. Ogden, ""Theology and Falsification" in Retrospect': A Reply," in *The Logic of God: Theology and Verification*, ed. Malcolm L. Diamond and Thomas V. Litzenburg [Indianapolis, Ind.: Bobbs-Merrill, 1975], 290–96, 293).

54. Ogden, "Present Prospects for Empirical Theology," 86.

55. Schubert M. Ogden, "Falsification and Belief," *Religious Studies* 10 (1974): 21–43. At this point Ogden is clearly aware of the discussion of Wittgenstein's later proposals by philosophers of language: "With the general shift in philosophy from 'verificational' to 'functional' analysis, the earlier positivistic account of science, based as it was strictly on the model of empirical generalization, has been exposed as seriously deficient" (22, citing Frederick Ferré, "Science and the Death of 'God'," in *Science and Religion: New Perspectives on the Dialogue* (New York: Harper & Row, 1968), 134–56. McKinnon's proposal is elucidated in Alastair McKinnon, *Falsification and Belief* (The Hague: Mouton, 1970).

straightforward factual claim. The second is a "self-instructional use," in which a sentence is really not making any claim at all, but is a heuristic device to help one understand other claims. The final use is not strictly a scientific use, but is a "meta-use" or "ontological-linguistic" use of a claim. Although this use is also heuristic, a sentence used in this way does make a claim about reality (i.e., it asserts a fact), but not a straightforward, empirical claim. Instead, on this third use, such claims are necessary claims that could not possibly be false. I should clarify at this point that, although this is the way McKinnon puts the matter, on Ogden's construal the necessity McKinnon intends is merely hypothetical, because in McKinnon's view "existence is never necessary."[56] In any event, sentences used in the first way are subject to the falsifiability requirement, but those used in the second or third ways are not.[57]

In addition to minor problems, Ogden sees two serious issues with McKinnon's proposal. First, because McKinnon's use of "necessity" in his third use is a strictly hypothetical necessity (on Ogden's reading), God's own existence must be strictly contingent. Without saying (in this article) exactly why this is a problem,[58] Ogden does not see how "God" could have any referent at all if it purports to refer to a contingent being. His argument seems to be that if God's existence is contingent, positing God as the creator of the universe (everything that exists except God) provides no more explanatory power than simply regarding the universe itself as ultimately brute.[59] Second, Ogden finds McKinnon's asserted similarity of science and Christianity (as "essentially interpretive activities") unpersuasive.[60] These two issues are related to what Ogden takes to be a more fundamental flaw, namely, "that [for McKinnon] the God of Christian faith must be in all respects a mere fact, simply one more contingent existent in addition to all the others."[61] For Ogden, however, God's existence must be strictly

56. Ogden, "Falsification and Belief," 27 (quoting McKinnon, *Falsification and Belief*, 86).
57. Ogden, "Falsification and Belief," 24–27.
58. That is, Ogden does not reiterate here the arguments previously made in "The Reality of God." (See chapter 4 in this volume.)
59. Ogden, "Falsification and Belief," 30. For a contrary argument on this point, see Richard Swinburne, *The Existence of God*, rev. ed. (Oxford: Clarendon Press, 1991) pp. 70–115.
60. Ogden, "Falsification and Belief," 31 (quoting McKinnon, *Falsification and Belief*, 21). It also seems to be the result of McKinnon's failure to take adequate account of the actual uses of Christian religious language. Unfortunately, however, Ogden does not develop this criticism, but simply refers to William A. Christian's distinction between a religion's "doctrinal propositions" and its "basic proposal." See William A. Christian, *Meaning and Truth in Religion* (Princeton, N.J.: Princeton Univ. Press, 1964), cited by Ogden, "Falsification and Belief," 32.
61. Ogden, "Falsification and Belief," 36.

necessary (though his actuality must be conceived as contingent), and this means that religion and science are fundamentally different: "Thus, whereas the cognitive claims of science proper, as distinct from such 'meta-claims' as it presupposes, are all merely factual, and hence factually falsifiable, the foundational claims of religion are quite beyond factual falsification, being the nonfactual or strictly metaphysical type of cognitive claims."[62]

Nonetheless, Ogden is consistent here with his earlier view that the notion of falsification is not entirely irrelevant to religious or theological claims. But falsification cannot proceed by reference solely to empirical experience, for human experience is broader than empirical experience. This in turn permits Ogden to distinguish between factual and empirical falsification (and falsifiability).[63] "Any claim may be said to be factually falsifiable if there are some at least conceivable facts that would render it false. But whether any such claim is also empirically falsifiable is, I maintain, another and independent question."[64] Among other reasons, this is because there is more to experience than empirical experience. In addition to empirical experience, Ogden maintains that human beings perceive themselves through an "inner, nonsensuous perception." Through this nonsensuous perceptual faculty, human beings perceive their own existence "as mutually related to others and to the inclusive whole of reality as such."[65] For Ogden, it is through this perceptual faculty that we perceive what is metaphysically necessary, including, to use Russell's terms, abstract concepts and the relations between them. Yet through this faculty we also perceive some things, including our own existence, that are mere facts. Thus, those putative facts that we do perceive, as well as claims flowing from them, are factually falsifiable, though they may not be empirically falsifiable. Ogden's term for this kind of nonempirical falsifiability is

---

62. Ogden, "Falsification and Belief," 38. Ogden points out that this by no means implies that religion and science are totally dissimilar, nor that one cannot speak of both as ongoing interpretive activities (39).

63. Ogden's terms here are confusing. When speaking of experience, Ogden is here using "empirical" in its typical, "scientific" usage, and not in the expanded usage for which he argued in "Present Prospects for Empirical Theology," discussed above. Nonetheless, when speaking of "empirical falsifiability," which he contrasts with "factual falsifiability," he means falsifiability not only through "external sense perception of ourselves and the world," which he calls "empirical experience," but also through our nonsensuous or "existential" experience of our own existence ("Falsification and Belief," 40). The confusion is illustrated well by a paragraph in which Ogden sets out to distinguish those claims subject to factual falsifiability from those subject to empirical falsifiability. Those subject to empirical falsifiability include claims that are "*existentially*, rather than empirically falsifiable...." (40 [emphasis in original]).

64. Ogden, "Falsification and Belief," 40.

65. Ogden, "Falsification and Belief," 40.

"existential" falsifiability, because the experience on which such claims are based "is our nonsensuous experience of our own existence rather than such experience as we have through our senses."[66] Still, Ogden's basic position on language seems not to have changed—that is, religious or theological language acquires its meaning by its ability to point to or describe something in our experience (though importantly expanded beyond sensory experience) to which it refers.

Ogden returned to the problem of religious language in a discussion of the Wittgensteinian philosopher of religion D. Z. Phillips.[67] In this article he reiterates his position that "the class of factual assertions is smaller than the class of meaningful assertions... [and] also smaller than the class of meaningful existential assertions."[68] He also reiterates his position that the statement "God exists," if possibly true, is necessarily true and thus one of a class of strictly metaphysical assertions, which, though they could never be falsified, must be verified by any and all experience.[69]

Ogden's own response to Flew's falsification challenge, which he recapitulates in this article, is only one of what Ogden takes to be two principal ways of responding. The other principal way of responding is "well represented in the writings of D. Z. Phillips...."[70] For Phillips, following (the later) Wittgenstein, language can acquire meaning only by its use within a particular form of life. This is the case with all language, including the language of truth and falsity. Consequently, not only the meaning but also the truth of the claim "God exists" can be determined only within the context of a religious form of life, because "the way in which we decide

66. Ogden, "Falsification and Belief," 40. Thus, "a claim is properly spoken of as 'existential' only if, in addition to asserting existence, the warrant for it is in the nonsensuous, as distinct from the merely sensuous, aspect of our experience" (41 n.1). One important example of a kind of claim that is subject to factual falsifiability but not empirical falsifiability is a mythical or mythological claim. Properly demythologized, such claims, though not empirical, are existential claims, claims about "the primal fact of our own existence in its authentic possibility," and thus are subject to factual falsifiability, though not empirical falsifiability (41). Myths "cannot be exhaustively interpreted in strictly metaphysical terms, since such terms pertain solely to *factuality*, as distinct from particular fact. Myth is in its own way the assertion of fact, even though, in spite of its empirical form, the only fact of which it intends to speak is the primal fact of our own existence in its authentic possibility, which includes, of course, the world and God as well in their factual aspect" (41 n.2).

67. Schubert M. Ogden, "Linguistic Analysis and Theology," *Theologische Zeitschrift* 33 (Sept.–Oct. 1977): 318–25.

68. Ogden, "Linguistic Analysis and Theology," 321.

69. Ogden, "Linguistic Analysis and Theology," 321–22.

70. Ogden, "Linguistic Analysis and Theology," 322. Ogden cites D. Z. Phillips's works *The Concept of Prayer* (New York: Seabury Press, 1981) and *Faith and Philosophical Inquiry* (London: Routledge & Keegan Paul, 1970).

whether something exists or not...varies systematically with the context in question."[71] On Phillips's view, it is philosophically arbitrary (it is "arbitrary linguistic legislation") to claim that the criteria of meaning appropriate for natural science is also appropriate to religion. To this extent, both Ogden and Phillips agree that the falsifiability requirement is arbitrary, at least so long as it requires empirical falsifiability.[72]

They disagree, however, about the reason for judging the falsifiability requirement to be arbitrary. For Phillips, the falsifiability requirement is arbitrary because it ignores the actual use of religious language in favor of legislating a normative use claimed to be valid irrespective of context. That is, Flew sets up the falsifiability requirement as the only way in which language can acquire meaning, irrespective of the language game in which it is used—he sets up, in other words, a "general justification." Ogden takes issue with Phillips on this point. Ogden takes Phillips's challenge to any "general justification" to assert that "actual use alone is a sufficient warrant for inferring proper use."[73] Ogden cannot agree. On the contrary, he argues, the criteria for determining the meaning and truth of Christian claims cannot be simply that of the Christian community's actual use of its claims. Instead, such criteria must be "generally accessible." These generally accessible criteria in turn restrict the possible proper uses of language. The range of possible meanings which a community may give to the language of its assertions, in other words, are restricted by "generally accessible criteria of meaning and truth...if they are to be allowed the general validity that they commonly claim."[74]

Against Phillips, therefore, Ogden defends the demand for "a general justification of religious or theological statements."[75] This general justification, however, cannot be the demand for empirical falsifiability demanded by Flew. Nonetheless, Ogden thinks it important to defend this demand for a general justification "because it is characteristic of religious

71. Phillips, *The Concept of Prayer*, 22 (quoted by Ogden, "Linguistic Analysis and Theology," 322).
72. Ogden, "Linguistic Analysis and Theology," 322.
73. Ogden, "Linguistic Analysis and Theology," 323.
74. Ogden, "Linguistic Analysis and Theology," 323.
75. Ogden, "Linguistic Analysis and Theology," 324. It must be said at this point that Ogden does not seem to see the force of the later Wittgenstein's critique of what Ogden and Phillips call a "general justification," perhaps because Ogden reads Wittgenstein through Phillips. For Ogden, words get their meaning by reference to some fact given in human experience. What Ogden does not acknowledge in this article is that for the later Wittgenstein, there is no such fact. Consequently, he dismisses Phillips as fideistic. It is not entirely clear whether this dismissal is based on Ogden's view that Phillips begs the question of justification, or on the view that Phillips's position involves a performative self-contradiction.

and theological statements that they tacitly or openly claim to be the kind of statements that need to be generally justified, i.e., they claim to be existential assertions or truth-claims."[76] Because they are truth-claims (i.e., they claim to be true), religious and theological assertions presuppose some criteria of truth—that is, some justification. And because they are existential, or transcendental, they require a general justification.[77]

This is as much as Ogden says in this article on linguistic meaning.[78] I think we can infer, however, Ogden's position on the meaning of religious or theological assertions. Theological assertions require a general justification because they presuppose some criterion of truth. This criterion of truth, in turn, sets the necessary and sufficient conditions that must be met for religious or theological assertions to be true. And it is these same conditions that are provided by the descriptive sense of the assertion; in turn, it is precisely these same conditions that give such assertions their meaning. That is to say, a sentence gets its meaning by reference to a descriptive sense the satisfaction of which constitutes necessary and sufficient conditions for it to be true. Less technically, the meaning of a sentence or assertion is constituted by its truth conditions. To ask what a sentence means, you must ask what facts must obtain for the sentence to be true. On this Ogden seems to agree with Flew, against Phillips. The truth conditions of scientific claims differ from those of religious or theological statements, but only because human experience itself is similarly differentiated.[79] That is, there is a nonsensuous aspect to human experience. And just as sensory experience provides the truth

76. Ogden, "Linguistic Analysis and Theology," 324.
77. Ogden, "Linguistic Analysis and Theology," 324.
78. This needs to be qualified as follows: Ogden says that religious or theological claims require a general justification for the additional reason that different religious traditions make conflicting truth-claims that cannot all be true, and that nonreligious ways of believing also make claims that contradict those of religious claims. Then he makes the following curious claim: "Consequently, my position is that there must be a general justification of religious or theological claims and that there cannot be any such justification unless there can be (1) a justification of religion as such as true and (2) a justification of any and all particular religious claims as true" ("Linguistic Analysis and Theology," 324). He does not further elucidate this position, and it seems on the face of it at least to stand in tension with his repeated insistence there is no such thing as religion in general or religion as such.
79. Ogden states, "I have expressly stated my agreement with Phillips that the criteria relevant to the justification of religion are in both respects radically different from those relevant to the justification of science. The point, however, is that, on my position, that very difference is a completely general difference, in the sense that it is a difference manifesting itself in human experience as such, in the experience of every man and woman, not only in the experience of those who are religious in a certain way or happen to be engaged in a particular scientific inquiry" ("Linguistic Analysis and Theology," 325).

conditions that imbue scientific statements with their meaning, our nonsensuous experience provides the truth conditions that imbue religious or theological assertions with their meaning.[80]

To sum up briefly, Ogden's view is that the ultimate criterion for judging the truth or falsity of any claim at all is human experience. Clearly, he differs with Flew and other falsification theorists about what comprises human experience. Still, human experience remains the criterion for judging the truth or adequacy of theological claims (and all other claims as well). To say this is also to say that human experience provides the truth conditions of an assertion. These truth conditions consist of the necessary and sufficient conditions for determining the referent of the subject term of the assertion, as well as necessary and sufficient conditions that must be satisfied for the predicate of the assertion to be true of the subject. These conditions are specified by the descriptive senses provided by the language of the assertion. We can therefore say that, for Ogden, these truth conditions imbue the assertion with its meaning.[81] And they do this by means of a description.

80. After 1977, Ogden did not again write as directly on the subject of language. Nonetheless, his subsequent writings do presuppose the positions he formulated in his engagements with falsification theorists such as Antony Flew. In *Doing Theology Today* (Valley Forge, Pa.: Trinity Press, 1996), for example, Ogden asserts that in the second (hermeneutical) phase of the theological task, the interpretive task (interpreting the formally normative Christian witness) that is required in order for the norm of appropriateness to be specified is "exactly what is also required" to specify the norm of credibility (14). That can only be the case if the interpretation of the meaning of the normative witness just is the specification of its truth conditions. This is because the norm of credibility sets out the conditions that must be met before a theological claim can be judged true. Thus, Ogden says that the normative witness "must be critically interpreted in concepts and terms in which this question today can be rightly asked and answered" (14). When Ogden describes the meaning of positions he opposes, he does so in terms of their truth conditions. In *The Point of Christology*, for example, in describing the meaning of revisionary Christologies' claims about Jesus, Ogden says that "it is of the innermost act of Jesus' own subjectivity that revisionary christologies presume to speak in specifying the truth conditions of the christological assertion" (70). In the chapter "A Priori Christology and Experience," in *Doing Theology Today*, Ogden specifies the meaning of his own "a priori christology" explicitly in terms of its truth conditions, which he constructs with an explicit view toward their experiential verification: "The a priori christology I have in mind stipulates the following as the conditions that need to be fulfilled in order to assert truly of anyone what christology asserts or implies about Jesus" (136). Recall here that it is *common* human experience that Ogden calls upon to verify religious claims. Thus his method of verification is transcendental, not empirical. See Schubert M. Ogden, "Response," *The Perkins School of Theology Journal* 26 (Winter 1973): 45–57, esp. 55.
81. Having said all this, it must be admitted that inferring Ogden's position on linguistic meaning, when he has not articulated one explicitly, is somewhat hazardous.

And to summarize specifically with respect to descriptivist reference, recall that Flew's point reflects a descriptivist view of reference. His position is that theists are not able to identify a descriptive sense to the term "God" that would pick out one being or object (God) and no others, not even imaginary others. Ogden, as we have seen, responds to Flew directly, but does not object to Flew's descriptivist understanding of reference.[82] Instead, he accepts this view of reference and undertakes to identify a descriptive condition that is necessary and sufficient to pick out God and no other object. This is one of the objectives in his argument for the reality of God. As I will describe in the next chapter, it is through this argument that Ogden identifies God. In his argument for the reality of God, he argues that human beings cannot avoid asserting that their actions, and indeed their very lives, are worthwhile or valuable. The experience of value, then, is a constitutive and undeniable part of human experience. Humans cannot avoid having confidence in the final worth of our existence, and this confidence Ogden calls faith. In Ogden's view this unavoidable faith must have an "objective ground in reality." The function of the term "God," Ogden writes, is to refer to the objective ground in reality itself of this unavoidable faith.[83] God, then, is the being that meets the description *the objective ground in reality of human persons' unavoidable faith in the worth of their lives,* and Ogden holds that God is the only being that meets this identifying description. Ogden is intending to show here that no imaginary God or mere idea of God could satisfy this descriptive sense. Consequently, he believes he has met Flew's challenge and has identified a descriptive sense of the term "God" that provides necessary and sufficient conditions for the term "God" to refer to God.

Another indication that Ogden accepts this descriptivist understanding of reference is his endorsement of parts of William A. Christian's

It might be possible, for example, to argue that Ogden would defend the position that truth conditions are necessary but not sufficient to imbue assertive sentences with meaning (and he might take nonassertives to be another matter altogether). In a private conversation, in fact, he has indicated that he takes nonassertives to be a different, or at least a more complicated, matter. He might also, for example, want a communication community to play some role in the establishment of linguistic meaning. He has given some indication of a move in this direction by his approving references to Habermas and Apel. See *Doing Theology Today*, ix. My own interests, however, are less exegetical than constructive and analytical. What I hope to show is what I take to be the relationship between truth-conditional or referential theories of meaning and the kind of transcendental method Ogden pursues.

82. Perhaps this is because, among other things, Flew simply assumes the view rather than arguing for it.
83. Ogden, *Reality of God,* 37.

description of religious language,[84] for Christian seems to accept a descriptivist view of reference. On Christian's view, when a person makes an assertion about God, in order for that assertion to be a truth-claim, the logical subject of her assertion must successfully refer to God. And for the reference to God to be successful, the person making the assertion "must do two things: (i) he must adduce some fact or other as a starting point for his reference and (ii) he must, by employing some interpretative category, connect this fact with the logical subject of this proposal."[85] On Christian's view, in other words, any successful reference must successfully identify a descriptive condition necessary and sufficient to pick out the referent of the referring expression.[86] On my reading, therefore, Ogden's use of

84. I am not arguing here that Ogden endorses or follows Christian's articulation in any straightforward way. Indeed, Ogden's relationship with Christian is not simple. In *The Reality of God,* the only citation of Christian comes in a footnote in which Ogden applauds him for "rightly insist[ing] on analyzing the logic of religious language in the context of 'a general logic of inquiry....'" (34 n.55, quoting William A. Christian, *Meaning and Truth in Religion* [Princeton, N.J.: Princeton Univ. Press, 1964], 3). But he criticizes Christian for "fail[ing] to see that the religious sort of question is not simply parallel or co-ordinate to the scientific and moral sorts, but, since it is related to them as a sort of limiting question, is also fundamental to them" (Ogden, *Reality of God,* 34 n.55). Thus Ogden prefers Toulmin's description of religious questions to Christian's. Elsewhere, however, he cites Christian with approval. For example, Ogden states that his (Ogden's) articulation of the "existential question" is what Christian calls a "basic supposition" of Christian faith (Ogden, *Point of Christology,* 30; Ogden, *Doing Theology Today,* 101). Though this point is somewhat ancillary to the question of reference, the passage Ogden cites does display a descriptivist understanding of reference. See Christian, *Meaning and Truth in Religion,* 84–88. Ogden also cites Christian somewhat more generally with approval in his discussion of the theology and falsification debates. See, for example, Ogden, "Falsification and Belief," 32–33. Ogden's citation of Christian in his own discussions of religious language indicates his awareness of Christian's views on language, including his views on reference, which were the prevailing views at the time. Though he distinguishes himself from Christian regarding religious claims as limiting claims, he does not take issue with Christian's view of reference. This does not indicate any straightforward adoption of Christian's views on reference. But it is evidence supporting my reading of Ogden's own writings as assuming a descriptivist view of reference.

85. William A. Christian, "Truth-Claims in Religion," *Journal of Religion* 42 (1962): 52–62, reprinted in *Religious Language and the Problem of Religious Knowledge,* 67–82, at 77 (page references are to reprint edition). Christian reiterates these criteria for successful reference in *Meaning and Truth in Religion,* 28–31.

86. In a later publication, Christian differentiates several different modes of referring. In each mode, he argues that if it is objected that a particular referring expression does not succeed in its reference, the person using the expression must meet the challenge. And the way he describes meeting the various challenges to various forms of reference can be characterized as arguing that the expression in question satisfies a particular descriptive sense or senses. On my reading, therefore, all these modes of referring are ways of meeting the requirements of successful reference Christian has previously set

Christian supports the position that Ogden assumes a descriptivist view of reference.[87]

During the formative years of Ogden's theological career, and in particular when he was developing his argument for the reality of God, a descriptivist understanding of both meaning and reference was dominant. So it would be reasonable to expect that an assumption of this understanding of reference could be detected in his writings. And indeed I think it can be: one can see it particularly clearly in his reference to God, his most important reference. As I will argue in the next chapter, Ogden is as good a representative of the liberal tradition in theology as one could ask for. In my judgment, therefore, descriptivism regarding religious language is a fundamentally important part of liberal theological method. In the next chapter, then, I shall examine the method of what I'll call a "purified" liberal theology in the twentieth century.

out, and are therefore ways of identifying a descriptive condition necessary and sufficient to pick out the referent of the referring expression. See Christian, *Meaning and Truth in Religion*, 185–209.

87. At this point, however, we should note an oddity about Ogden's endorsement of Christian's view of language. When Ogden cites Christian, it is to endorse his distinction between "doctrinal propositions" and "basic religious proposals," and he does not mention either Christian's view of reference or his four conditions that must apply for a religious proposal to be a proposal for belief. On Christian's view, a religious proposal must (1) be capable of self-consistent formulation, (2) be liable to significant disagreement, (3) permit a reference to its logical subject, and (4) permit some support for the assignment of its predicate to its subject. As Christian explains it, the second condition rules out claims that cannot coherently be denied (i.e., claims that are necessarily true). But if my reading of Ogden is correct, he takes his basic proposal about God's boundless love to be transcendentally validated and therefore necessarily true. In Christian's view, this means that the proposal "has no significant consequences" (Christian, "Truth-Claims in Religion," 69). Yet Christian himself expresses doubts about this conclusion, asserting that much more attention needs to be given to the following question: "Are there any basic religious proposals to which the second condition above (that they be liable to significant disagreement) somehow fails to apply, perhaps because they express 'necessary truths' or in some other way" (81).

CHAPTER FOUR

A Purified Liberal Theology

A number of prominent liberal theologians responded to the falsification challenge of Antony Flew. By and large, these responses accepted the descriptivist approach to language (meaning and reference) assumed by Flew. This was for good reason, for this descriptivist understanding of language is a crucial assumption of the methodological orientation of liberal theology. In other words, if the descriptivist approach to language is correct, then the methodological orientation of liberal theology is an appropriate one to pursue. I use the phrase "methodological orientation" because liberal theologians differ from one another in various elements of their methods, and yet they share a common orientation that consists of some core commitments. Generally speaking, these core commitments are the three themes I identified in the second chapter on liberal theology in the nineteenth century.

No one to my knowledge is as clear in articulating these core commitments, nor as consistent in following them, as Schubert M. Ogden. So in this chapter I will consider his theological method as a paradigmatic example of liberal theology: In Ogden's adoption of Alfred North Whitehead's "reformed subjectivist principle" and his characterization of religious or theological claims as existential, we will see in a clear methodological way the turn to the subject established in liberal theology by (at least) Schleiermacher. We will also see a clear historical concern in his search for a criterion of appropriateness. And, as in Harnack, we will see a concern for the "essence" of Christianity embodied in Ogden's concepts of God and of religion. So in many respects, despite the wide diversity apparent within liberal theology, I take Ogden to be about as paradigmatic of it as one can get.

Ogden is an ideal candidate for considering the relationship between descriptivist views of language and theological method for two reasons.

First is his clarity and consistency; second is the fact that he forged his most important (from the viewpoint of the relationship of language and method) methodological commitments during the late 1950s and the 1960s. These are crucial years for my investigation because they came after the impact of the falsification challenge had been widely felt, yet before Saul Kripke's assault on descriptivism in language in his ground-breaking *Naming and Necessity* in 1970.[1] Consequently, while Ogden articulates a clear and consistent liberal vision, he does so under the constraints of the reign of descriptivism in philosophy of language. If there is a close relationship between descriptivism and liberal theology's central methodological commitments, the theologian whose writings we would expect to reflect that relationship most clearly is Schubert Ogden.

In an article published prior to his dissertation, Ogden argues that the proper task of the theologian is "to present a new critico-constructive statement of the meaning of the Christian faith that will enable the church to speak to the exigencies of the immediate historical situation."[2] What this means is that the theologian must "translate" the meaning of the church's confession into the language and thought forms of her own day.[3] And no matter what part of the church's confession the theologian attempts to translate, as part of this explication or translation, she will have to answer two central questions: "What does it mean to say that Jesus is the Christ?" and "Is this statement about Jesus true?"

The falsification controversy forced Ogden to develop his theological method with an eye toward meeting descriptivist requirements. So when a theologian answers these two central questions about Jesus, those answers must provide a descriptive sense that allows us to fix the reference of "Jesus" and must describe the necessary and sufficient conditions for those statements about Jesus to be true. Further, insofar as answers to the two central questions about Jesus also make a claim about Jesus' relation to God, they must provide a descriptive sense that allows us to fix the reference of "God" as well as providing truth conditions for

1. Saul A. Kripke, *Naming and Necessity* (Cambridge, Mass.: Harvard Univ. Press, 1972; repr., 1999).
2. This is true not only for the systematic theologian, but also for the historical or the practical theologian; indeed, for any theologian *qua* theologian (Schubert M. Ogden, "The Lordship of Jesus Christ: The Meaning of Our Affirmation," *Encounter* 21 [Autumn 1960]: 408–22; 408–409).
3. "What is needed in theology, therefore, is a thoroughgoing attempt to translate the meaning of the church's confession into the terms in which contemporary men either do or can most readily understand their life as persons" (Ogden, "Lordship of Jesus Christ," 410).

the answers. Ogden met this challenge by admitting the requirement of experiential verification but broadening the notion of experience to include not only empirical experience but also the nonsensuous or existential aspect of experience.

In considering Ogden's method in more detail, I would expect to find that Ogden interprets Christian claims about Jesus in terms that can be verified by reference to (nonsensuous or existential) human experience. This will allow such claims about Jesus to contain a descriptive sense that provides necessary and sufficient conditions for the claims to be true. And, indeed, this is exactly what can be seen in his use of Rudolf Bultmann's method of demythologization and existential analysis. Further, I would expect Ogden's concept of God to include a descriptive sense that provides conditions the satisfaction of which is necessary and sufficient to allow us to fix the (unique) referent of "God." Once again, this is exactly what one finds in Ogden's use of the analysis of human experience and the dipolar concept of God articulated by Whitehead and Charles Hartshorne.

Therefore, in this chapter I will first describe Bultmann's method of existential analysis and his demythologizing interpretation of the New Testament's claims about Jesus. Next I will consider the contributions of Whitehead and Hartshorne. Whitehead provides the understanding of human experience needed to provide a descriptive sense that will allow the reference of "God" to be fixed. Hartshorne provides a complementary concept of God that allows us to fix the reference of the term "God" through a description of the nonsensuous aspect of human experience. If these descriptivist conditions are met in the way Ogden seeks to meet them, we might also expect him to be able to provide a transcendental argument for the reality of God through the nonsensuous aspect of human experience. Once again, this is exactly what we find. And this transcendental argument for God's reality provides the grounding for Ogden's signal achievement: Demonstrating that an existential interpretation of the New Testament claims about Jesus could be seamlessly integrated with a concept of God provided by process theology.

I. A LIBERAL THEOLOGICAL HERMENEUTIC: RUDOLF BULTMANN'S METHOD OF DEMYTHOLOGIZATION

Ogden's articulation of the theologian's task, and especially the problems with religious language raised in the falsification controversy, convinced him of the extraordinary significance of Rudolf Bultmann's contribution to twentieth-century theology.[4] This is because Bultmann had seen that the central questions facing Christian theologians had become problematic as a result of new modes of thought that had arisen in modernity. Ogden agrees: The church's "task of reinterpreting the mythological conceptuality in which the previous generations of believers had expressed the common faith" has become more important since the Enlightenment, because the Enlightenment itself and the scientific advances it inaugurated problematized the traditional reinterpretations.[5] Since the Enlightenment, modern women and men have come to possess a scientific view of the world, whereas the picture of the world shared by all the biblical writers was mythological. But a mythological view of the world is no longer credible to modern women and men. Consequently, because the message of the Gospel confronts us in a conceptual form that is mythological, the message itself "seems unintelligible, incredible, and irrelevant."[6] What was therefore needed in order to make the message intelligible, credible, and relevant was a method of "demythologization," which of course was the most famous contribution of Rudolf Bultmann.

By "mythological," Bultmann means a manner of thought in which phenomena or events in the world are given supernatural explanations. A mirage in the desert, for example, might be mythologically explained as a trick of Zeus. This kind of explanation, Bultmann says, "objectifies the transcendent and thus makes it immanent."[7] On Ogden's reading, Bultmann understands myth to perform three functions.[8] First, it objectifies the reality to which it refers and brings this reality into the subject-object polarity necessary for theoretical apprehension. Myth's objectifying function attempts to reduce transcendent power to simply another object, however powerful, in the spatio-temporal world. Second, myth performs an etiological function, attempting to give explanations for events or phenomena that cannot (at least presently) be otherwise explained. Thus it functions as a primitive form of science. Finally, myth

---

4. Schubert M. Ogden, *Christ Without Myth: A Study Based on the Theology of Rudolf Bultmann* (New York: Harper, 1961; 2d ed, Dallas, Tex.: Southern Methodist Univ. Press, 1991), 18 (page references are to 2d edition). In one of his first published articles, Ogden states that it is Bultmann who has given the outline of an adequate answer to the problem of the mythological language used by the Bible (Schubert M. Ogden, "The Debate on 'Demythologizing,'" *Journal of Bible and Religion* 27 [Jan. 1959]: 17–27, 20).

5. Ogden, "The Debate on 'Demythologizing,'" 18–19.

6. Ogden, *Christ Without Myth*, 24.

7. This is Ogden's translation. Rudolf Bultmann, "Der Mythos objektiviert das Jenseits zum Diesseits," in *Kerygma und Mythos*, ed. H. W. Bartsch, vol. 2 (Hamburg: Herbert Reich-Evangelischer Verlag, 1952), 184; quoted in Ogden, *Christ Without Myth*, 25.

8. Ogden, *Christ Without Myth*, 25–27.

takes a narrative form, a kind of second-dimension history alongside the history of ordinary events. For Bultmann (and Ogden), the New Testament is mythological in the sense that it displays these three functions or aspects of myth.[9]

Each of these mythological functions, however, has lost its persuasive power. Its objectifying function has lost its credibility because we now understand, Bultmann argues (and Ogden agrees), that the reality to which myths refer is not an "object" but a transcendent power. In addition, myth's etiological and narrative functions have been superseded by natural and historical science. Consequently, as a result of the New Testament's mythological picture of the world, the New Testament can no longer be accepted *tout court* by modern women and men. This is because modern women and men are committed to a scientific picture of the world, a picture in which the world is a "closed" totality. Natural laws of cause and effect are confined to agents within our natural world, and any explanation of phenomena that appeals to a "supernatural" causal agent (i.e., "miracles") is ruled out in advance. This is not an arbitrary procedure, but is necessary to preserve the idea of a causal order, which in turn is necessary for any adequate scientific understanding of the world and, indeed, for any adequate understanding of ourselves. Thus, the criticism of the New Testament as mythological arises *necessarily* out of the modern situation. As a result, it must be seriously addressed by theology.[10]

We should not think, however, that only peripheral miracle stories are compromised by their mythological orientation. Instead, *everything* in the New Testament is suspect insofar as it (1) cannot be established through historical-critical research or (2) presents human beings as susceptible to divine or supernatural agency independent of their own volition. This presents the fundamental problem that throughout the entirety of the New Testament the salvation event itself, the central proclamation of the New Testament, is consistently depicted in mythological terms. Moreover, Bultmann can find no nonarbitrary criteria for deciding which miracle stories to accept and which to reject. As a result, Bultmann feels that the theologian is faced with the choice either of accepting the mythological

9. There have been critics of Bultmann's treatment of myth, but Ogden believes their criticisms to be misguided. Most important for Ogden is John Macquarrie, *Myth in the New Testament* (London: SCM Press, 1952). Ogden argues against Macquarrie on pages 29–31.

10. "The only criticism that can be relevant for theology is the one that arises with necessity out of the situation of modern man" (Rudolf Bultmann, *Kerygma und Mythos*, vol. 1, 2d ed., ed. H. W. Bartsch [Hamburg: Herbert Reich-Evangelischer Verlag, 1951], 19; quoted in Ogden, *Christ Without Myth*, 31–32).

worldview of the New Testament in its entirety or of rejecting it in its entirety.[11] As we have noted, however, it is no longer possible for modern women and men to accept such a mythological picture of the world. The only credible solutions, therefore, are either to reject the New Testament or to interpret it in a "demythologized" way.

If the choices are as radical as Bultmann has suggested, however, why not simply give up the theological project altogether? What warrant is there for engaging in a demythologizing interpretation? For Bultmann, such an interpretation is warranted if and only if the New Testament kerygma itself calls for it. And it does, Bultmann argues, for two principal reasons: First, by its very nature, myth does not seek to render a scientific explanation of the world, but to express or advocate a way in which human beings do or should understand themselves in relation to their world. That is, the most basic purpose of myth is not so much to put forward an understanding of the objective world as to express an understanding of human existence, a human self-understanding. Second, the New Testament itself already contains an implicit criticism of its own conceptual mythology. Several factors lead Bultmann to this conclusion, the most important of which is the fact that the New Testament contains a fundamental conceptual contradiction regarding the nature of human existence. On the one hand, the fate of human beings seems determined by supernatural powers beyond our control; on the other hand, human beings are called to a decision concerning their own fate.[12] But we cannot have it both ways, in Bultmann's view— either we are fated by events beyond our control or we are responsible. And the controlling picture is one of God calling human beings to decide whether they will live in love for God or not. Thus, Bultmann concludes, it is incumbent on Christian theologians to render the New Testament's proclamation in a demythologized form that is both understandable and believable to modern women and men.

So understood, demythologization was the central project of nineteenth-century liberal theologians such as Ritschl and Harnack. Both Bultmann and Ogden, however, view the traditional liberal project as having severe shortcomings. Indeed, in the work of such nineteenth-century theologians, "the kerygma itself was actually eliminated."[13] Bultmann's

---

11. Ogden, *Christ Without Myth*, 37–38.

12. Bultmann, *Kerygma und Mythos*, vol. 1, 23, quoted in Ogden, *Christ Without Myth*, 40. Other factors include the unintegrated and sometimes contradictory nature of the New Testament's mythical assertions, and the fact that the New Testament itself already carries out a rudimentary program of demythologization (Ogden, *Christ Without Myth*, 40–41).

13. Ogden, *Christ Without Myth*, 42.

task, then—a task Ogden takes up—is to carry out the aim of liberal theology without compromising the kerygma. Although earlier liberal theology shared Bultmann's aim of translating the kerygma into a credible modern form, its failure consisted in the fact that the form used by the earlier liberals was structurally similar to the mythological form used in the New Testament. That is, the problem with the New Testament's mythologizing form is that it attempts to objectify both the being of God and God's call to human beings. But God's call, according to Bultmann, is not made in an objectifying mode. Instead, it is an existential call.

To explain this, Bultmann deploys the existential analysis described by Martin Heidegger in his groundbreaking *Sein und Zeit*.[14] It will be useful, then, to describe briefly two distinctions used by Heidegger in his existential analysis of human existence. The first is the distinction between inauthenticity and authenticity. This distinction relates to the way we exist with others. In most of our everyday life, we are inauthentic (*uneigentlich*)—we allow others to set our priorities, we adopt their ways of thinking, we adopt their ways of interacting with others, etc. Thus inauthenticity is essentially a way that I have not made my own (*eigen*); it is *uneigentlich*. But this inauthentic way hides itself, and we call others "Others" to hide our essential belonging to them. Yet these "others" are not any particular person or persons, for *any* other can play the needed role. So who is the "other" that dictates the inauthentic way? It is "not this one and not that one, not one oneself and not a few and not the sum of them all. The 'Who' is the neuter, *das Man*."[15] In contrast, the authentic (*eigentlich*) self is the self that has been "expressly [*eigens*] seized."[16] Because the authentic self has been dispersed into *Das Man*, it must first find itself.[17] It must become aware of its own possibilities, the most important of which is not existing at all. Thus the most important characteristic of the authentic self is awareness of its own finitude and thus of its fundamental temporality.

---

14. Martin Heidegger, *Sein und Zeit* (Tübingen: Max Niemeyer Verlag, 1927; repr., 1993) (page references are to reprint edition). English translation: *Being and Time*, trans. John Macquarrie and Edward Robinson (New York: Harper & Row, Publishers, 1962). Without denying the importance of Heidegger for Bultmann's thought, Ogden claims (along with Barth) that the "main lines" of Bultmann's dialectical thought were in place before he attempted to deploy Heideggerian concepts. Indeed, Ogden states that Heidegger simply gave Bultmann "a more conceptually precise way of stating the same dialectic which was the chief defining characteristic" of Bultmann's dialectical theology (Ogden, "The Debate on 'Demythologizing,'" 22).

15. Heidegger, *Sein und Zeit*, 126.

16. Heidegger, *Sein und Zeit*, 129.

17. Heidegger, *Sein und Zeit*, 129.

The second crucial distinction is that between *Vorhandenheit* and *Zuhandenheit*.[18] We see an object as *vorhanden* when we see it as simply there, taking up space and available for scientific analysis. Its primary characteristic is, in Descartes' terms, extension. For Heidegger, however, our primordial experience of entities in the world is not as *vorhanden*, but as *zuhanden*, as an "instrument," a *Zeug*, I can use to accomplish some goal. *Dasein*'s (for my purposes, it is fine to understand Heidegger's use of *Dasein* simply as "human being" or "person") experience of entities within the world is oriented toward the future, into which Dasein projects itself. Seeing entities as *vorhanden*, as objects of theoretical inquiry, is not an invalid way of seeing them, but it is derivative. A scientist studying quarks may see them as *vorhanden*; nonetheless, they are at the same time *Zeugen* she uses to get paid. Her mode of being in relationship to them will change from time to time.

This primacy of *Zuhandenheit* implies that the Cartesian attitude of *sine cura* (approaching intellectual problems objectively, or "without care") is not our primordial way of relating to the world. Thus, when Heidegger describes the world, and what it means to be a world (*die Weltlichkeit der Welt*), he does so in terms of *Zuhandenheit*. The "world" is not the sum total of objects (whose chief characteristic is extension) on hand (*vorhanden*). The world is the totality of the web of relationships of *Zeugen* viewed as *zuhanden*.[19] To be human is to structure this web of relationships according to our own goals and projects. Thus the most human characteristic is not a theoretical stance of *sine cura*, but is precisely the opposite, *Sorge* (care).

To return to Bultmann, it is easy to see the importance of Heidegger's analytical distinctions for Bultmann's project. The meaning of religious texts is never simply a *vorhanden* or theoretical one, but always carries an

18. There are no really good translations of these terms. *Vorhanden* in its most common meaning is "on hand" or "available" or, of items in a store, "in stock." Yet it no longer has the connotation of nearness, and stars in a distant galaxy can be said to be *vorhanden* to an astronomer with a telescope. *Zuhanden* has the sense of "handy," and the example Heidegger uses is that of tools at a workbench. They are *zuhanden* if they are on the bench ready for use and not put away in a box somewhere.

19. Thus, in a sense, the world is a construct of Dasein. This does not mean that the entities in the world would not exist if no human existed. They would exist, but not as a "world." When Heidegger talks about the "forgetfulness of Being," he means that the modern philosophical tradition has forgotten every other way of being in the world other than that of *Vorhandenheit*. It has forgotten them in the sense that it ascribes no ontological significance to them. Descartes' methodology, which was to begin with the *cogito*, and doubt the existence of everything else until it could be demonstrated, set up a problem that could not be solved. The tradition's fascination with this problem caused it to forget that there were other, more primordial modes of being than the one with which Descartes began.

existentiell meaning as its primary one. Religious texts present us with a picture of the kind of person we ought to become, and then ask whether we will choose to become such a person. As a religious text, the question that the New Testament presents to women and men is an *existentiell* question, a question presented not in a *vorhanden* manner, but in a *zuhanden* manner. At every moment of our lives, we must choose our own destiny, structuring our "world" accordingly. We must choose who we will become, by choosing whether to live in an authentic manner or in an inauthentic one.

Bultmann holds that the possibility of choosing an authentic existence has become possible because of a particular event—the event of Jesus Christ. Bultmann explicitly holds that there was no such possibility before Christ.[20] Nonetheless, Bultmann seeks to affirm that the Easter event was not a *vorhanden* historical event (*"kein historisches Ereignis"*).[21] Instead, its reality is one in which God graciously presents us with the possibility of and demand for reorienting our *zuhanden* world, for re-creating the significance of everything and everyone in our world. This possibility, precisely as one that presents itself in terms of significance, of *Zuhandenheit*, is not open to historical scrutiny.[22] Further, it is precisely because of the *zuhanden* nature of the possibility opened up by the Christ event that Bultmann says that to speak of God's act (and thus of the Resurrection) is also to speak of my own existence.[23] In the end, then, the reason Bultmann holds that the New Testament itself authorizes and demands demythologization is not at all that his theological method makes insufficient room for faith. On the contrary, the reason for the New Testament's demand is precisely that any act of God will always present us with a demand for faith.

Whatever Bultmann's own concerns, his method of demythologization plays an extremely important role in Ogden's liberal project. I have been arguing that Ogden accepts Flew's demand for experiential verification, but broadens the understanding of experience to include nonsensuous experience. What demythologization provides is a way of understanding—that is, *interpreting*—the central claims of Christianity so that they are susceptible

---

20. "The New Testament affirms not only that faith, as the attitude of new and genuine life, is first present after a certain time—faith was 'revealed' and 'has come' (Gal. 3:23, 25)—for that could simply be a statement about cultural history (*Geistesgeschichte*), but that it has first become a *possibility* after a certain time, namely, as the result of an *occurrence*, the occurrence of Christ" (Bultmann, *Kerygma und Mythos*, vol. 1, 31; quoted in *Christ Without Myth*, 65 [emphasis in original]).

21. Bultmann, *Kerygma und Mythos*, vol. 2, 104; Ogden, *Christ Without Myth*, 87.

22. Note the contrast here to the rise of faith in the Resurrection, which historians can discover (assuming adequate evidence).

23. No act of God, therefore, is open to historical scrutiny (Bultmann, "Der Mythos," 196; Ogden, *Christ Without Myth*, 92).

to experiential verification. The demand for faith in God is a demand for authentic existence; and the resurrection of Jesus is a kind of symbolic claim that such an existence is possible. For Bultmann and Ogden, theological claims about God, or about the identity of Jesus Christ, are always existential claims. As such, the descriptive senses associated with such claims are derived from elements of (nonsensuous) human experience. As a result, they are subject to (nonsensuous) experiential verification—that is, these descriptive senses articulate descriptive conditions the satisfaction of which is necessary and sufficient for the predicates of such claims to be true of the subject of the claims. And whether they are in fact satisfied can be determined by (nonsensuous) experiential verification. In the next section, I will argue that Ogden derives the descriptive sense required for the successful reference of "God" in a similar way—by beginning with a transcendental analysis of human subjectivity, which will reveal the structure of nonsensuous human experience.

II. A LIBERAL CONCEPT OF GOD: PROCESS THEOLOGY

Following Alfred North Whitehead, Ogden insists that theology as well as metaphysics must begin with an analysis of human subjectivity.[24] Here we can see modernity's turn to the subject most clearly. The problem with traditional metaphysics, on Ogden's view, is that it begins with an analysis of objects of ordinary perception, and then constructs interpretive metaphysical categories in terms of such objects.[25] When we do this, however, we assume in advance that real objects, insofar as they are real in themselves, are independent of other objects for their existence. This sets up a host of philosophical problems that Ogden takes to be insoluble if one begins with this Cartesian starting point. Beginning with human subjectivity, on the other hand, solves a host of mid-century problems by ensuring that one will be able to provide descriptive senses that are adequate to permit successful reference of singular terms and meaningful predicates. In particular, Ogden takes this kind of beginning to permit successful reference to God (neoclassically construed) and meaningful predications of attributes to God.

24. It "requires that we take as the experiential basis of all our most fundamental concepts the primal phenomenon of our own existence as experiencing subjects or selves" (Ogden, *Reality of God*, 57).
25. To put this in Heideggerian terms, it begins with a *vorhanden* analysis of objects instead of a *zuhanden* one. It assumes that the dimension of *Vorhandenheit* is the primordial dimension of our experience, when the truly primordial dimension of our experience is that of *Zuhandenheit*.

A. The Understanding of Human Experience Needed to Validate the Concept of God: Alfred North Whitehead

Ogden begins this way because, following Whitehead, he has adopted the "reformed subjectivist principle."[26] In a discussion of Descartes, Whitehead articulates his crucial insight as the principle "that the whole universe consists of elements disclosed in the analysis of the experiences of subjects."[27] That insight, often described as the modern turn to the subject, Whitehead calls the "subjectivist principle" (and sometimes "the subjectivist bias"). But, according to Whitehead, Descartes immediately assumed that his turn to the subject implied the further principle (which I will call the "corrupted subjectivist principle"): "that the datum in the act of experience can be adequately analysed purely in terms of universals."[28] In Whitehead's view, this further principle is not only unwarranted but should be rejected outright. The difficulty with the corrupted subjectivist principle is that it takes an object like *a gray stone* to be one of the primordial objects (and a corresponding assertion, such as *The stone is gray*, to be one of the primordial facts) from which metaphysics is to begin its analysis.[29] In Whitehead's view, however, the combination of the (accepted) turn to the subject and the corrupted subjectivist principle yields a conception of experience as exclusively sense experience, and a construal of the mind's role in sense experience as thoroughly passive (recall Locke's description of the mind as a blank piece of paper). In Whitehead's terms, the corrupted subjectivist

26. Ogden discusses this principle in a paper on Bernard Lonergan delivered at the International Lonergan Congress in 1970 (Schubert M. Ogden, "Lonergan and the Subjectivist Principle," in *Language, Truth and Meaning: Papers from the International Lonergan Congress 1970*, ed. Philip McShane (Notre Dame, Ind.: Univ. of Notre Dame Press, 1972), 218–35). In this paper, Ogden quotes with approval the opening lines of Lonergan's *Insight*: "Thoroughly understand what it is to understand, and not only will you understand the broad lines of all there is to be understood but you will possess a fixed base, an invariant pattern, opening upon all further developments of understanding" (Bernard Lonergan, *Insight* [New York: Philosophical Library, 1970], xxx; quoted by Ogden in "Lonergan and the Subjectivist Principle," 218). This statement, on Ogden's reading, constitutes an affirmation of the subjectivist principle.

27. Alfred North Whitehead, *Process and Reality: An Essay in Cosmology* (New York: Macmillan, 1929), 239.

28. Whitehead, *Process and Reality*, 252.

29. Alfred North Whitehead, *Process and Reality: An Essay in Cosmology*, Corrected ed., ed. David Ray Griffin and Donald W. Sherburne (New York: Macmillan, 1978), 158–59. Note that such an experience—that is, an experience of a gray stone—is a conscious experience. Far from being primordial, Whitehead holds that "consciousness arises in a late derivative phase of complex integrations [i.e., experiences].... Thus those elements of our experience which stand out clearly and distinctly in our consciousness are not its basic facts; they are the derivative modifications which arise in the process (162).

principle leads to the conclusion that all experience occurs in the mode of "presentational immediacy," and ignores experiencing in the mode of "causal efficacy."[30] This corrupted construal of experience, Whitehead argues, leads ultimately to skepticism, as Hume saw.

Instead, Whitehead advocates a "reformed subjectivist principle," which "fully accepts Descartes' discovery that subjective experiencing is the primary metaphysical situation which is presented to metaphysics for analysis."[31] But the "reformed" subjectivist principle rejects the notion that experience reveals only universals; instead, Whitehead argues that experience reveals actual entities as well.[32] Therefore, *The stone is gray* describes not a primordial metaphysical fact but instead a derivative abstraction.[33] Consequently, Whitehead argues for a notion of perception, or sense experience, as occurring in three modes: First is humanity's primary form of consciousness, the mode of "causal efficacy." It is a vague, inarticulate, and crude mode of perception, but it is present in all perception. It is the vague awareness that the objects of all our perceptions, and therefore of our very selves, are dependent upon, and indeed constituted by, the stream of actual events that comprise their causal story. Second is the mode of "presentational immediacy," which roughly speaking is the mode of immediate contemporary sensory perception. The final mode is the more advanced, mixed mode that Whitehead calls "symbolic reference." It is an interpretive compound of the two more primitive modes.

Ordinary experience, therefore, is an advanced interpretive integration in the mode of symbolic reference and the more primitive modes of causal efficacy and presentational immediacy. A perception of a gray stone, for example, is always structured so as to contain an awareness that the stone is a persisting entity with both a past and an efficacious future. In this latter mode, the mode of symbolic reference, an element of originative creative

30. Whitehead, *Process and Reality,* 151–53.
31. Whitehead, *Process and Reality,* 160.
32. We may be tempted to think that an actual entity is a mid-sized physical object such as a rock. But we must resist such a temptation, keeping in mind that Whitehead (and Ogden, following him) rejects "substance" metaphysics in favor of "event" metaphysics. An actual entity, which Whitehead also calls an actual occasion, is an event of becoming or process. It lasts for only an instant, and it is the unity in which the perishing occasions of the past are unified in a self-creative, novel present. Actual entities, therefore, "are the final real things of which the world is made up. There is no going behind actual entities to find anything more real" (Whitehead, *Process and Reality,* 18; see also 212–13).
33. "Accordingly, the notion 'This stone as gray' is a derivative abstraction, necessary indeed as an element in the description of the fundamental experiential feeling, but delusive as a metaphysical starting-point" (Whitehead, *Process and Reality,* 160).

freedom is introduced, and error is possible.[34] Because of the creative freedom inherent in the mode of symbolic reference, the subjective form is
freely determined by the subject, and the subject itself is constituted by
the integration of its prehensions. Subjective forms, therefore, introduce
the factor of valuation, as the subject relativizes each prehension vis-à-vis
all its other prehensions according to its overall subjective aim or purpose.
This relativization is in fact a valuation, and therefore every experience,
Whitehead argues, is an experience of value.[35]

If we begin with an analysis of human subjectivity, of ourselves *as selves*,
we find that what it means to be a self is to be social, relational, and temporal.
To exist independently of any other reality, whatever that might mean (if it
could mean anything), is not to exist as a self.[36] To be a self is to exist socially,
to be constituted (at least partially) by one's embeddedness in a social matrix.
The most intimate social matrix constitutive of my world is my own body,
with all the symbiotic relationships between and among its organs and the
organisms living in it. Through my body I also affect, and am affected by, the
larger societies beyond myself.[37] I cannot help but be related to these societies, and my existence as a self is constituted by these relations.

Being a human subject, or a self, is not only social; it is also temporal.
I experience myself only as an "ever-changing sequence of occasions of
experience," each of which I integrate with memories of past occasions
and anticipations of future ones. This integration is always inescapably
free and creative. The myriad of memories I freely arrange into a hierarchy
of significance; and out of the range of possible futures, I choose those
at which I will aim through an interplay of desire, significance, and perceived possibility. Thus, each occasion of my experience as a self is integrated with past and future into a new occasion of experience that is an

34. Whitehead, *Process and Reality*, 168–73. Whitehead's term for the perception of a
gray stone is "prehension," and a prehension, he says, always has three elements: the
prehending subject, the prehended datum, and the subjective form (this is *how* the
subject prehends the datum).

35. Whitehead, *Process and Reality*, 240–41.

36. "Whatever else the self is, it is hardly a substance which, in Descartes' phrase,
'requires nothing but itself in order to exist,' nor is it altogether without intrinsic temporal structure." Schubert M. Ogden, *The Reality of God and Other Essays* (New York:
Harper & Row, 1966; 2d ed., Dallas, Tex.: Southern Methodist Univ. Press, 1992),
1–70, quotation at 57 (quoting Descartes, *Principles of Philosophy*, in *The Philosophical
Works of Descartes*, vol. 1, trans. E. S. Haldane and G. R. T. Ross [Cambridge: Cambridge
Univ. Press, 1911], 239).

37. One could envision the societies to which I am related as a series of concentric
circles, of which the innermost is my body, and the outermost would be the entire universe. At each moment, then, I would be related to every occasion of experience that
has occurred up to that moment (to most, of course, I am related only very remotely).
But I am not internally related to any moment after my death.

experience of my self insofar as it is a freely and creatively chosen "new whole of significance."[38] As Ogden puts it, "Selecting from the heritage of the already actual and the wealth of possibility awaiting realization, I freely fashion myself in creative interaction with a universe of others who also are not dead but alive."[39] And because this fashioning creates a "new whole of significance," Ogden (following Whitehead) understands it as a valuation as well.

So far, then, Ogden has an understanding of human subjectivity that interprets every human experience as *(inter alia)* an experience of significance or value. He has a method of interpreting Christian theological claims as *(inter alia)* claims about existential significance. This will give him the experiential elements he needs to derive descriptive senses that can be associated with predicates of theological claims. All he needs now is to provide a descriptive sense that allows successful reference for the term "God." And this he will find in his appropriation of Charles Hartshorne's dipolar concept of God, and in his own transcendental argument for God's necessary existence through the unavoidable reality of faith.

B. The Dipolar Concept of God: Charles Hartshorne

Ogden's early thoughts on Hartshorne's *The Logic of Perfection* provide a foundation on which he will build his later reflections on the nature of religion and theology and how to go about demythologizing central Christian affirmations.[40] In this text (as in others), Hartshorne gives a central place to the ontological argument for God's existence, for it is this argument that provides the clue for answering Hartshorne's question: "How can religious experience or awareness achieve rational consciousness?"[41] For Hartshorne, Anselm's discovery consisted in his recognition of the unique logical status of the concept of "God," or "perfection." Because of its unique status, its existence can never be contingent; thus, God (or perfection) "either could not possibly exist, or it exists necessarily."[42] For both Hartshorne and Ogden, this means that God as classically conceived (by Aquinas, for example, on Ogden's reading, but many others as well) could not possibly exist. Thus

38. Ogden, *Reality of God*, 58.
39. Ogden, *Reality of God*, 58.
40. Schubert M. Ogden, "Theology and Philosophy: A New Phase of the Discussion," *Journal of Religion* 44 (Jan. 1964): 1–16. Charles Hartshorne, *The Logic of Perfection and Other Essays in Neoclassical Metaphysics* (La Salle, Ill.: Open Court, 1962).
41. Ogden, "Theology and Philosophy," 4–5.
42. Hartshorne, *The Logic of Perfection*, 61; quoted in Ogden, "Theology and Philosophy," 6.

theology needs a new "neoclassical" conception of God.[43] Equally important for Ogden's own development, however, is Hartshorne's concurrence
with Karl Barth that at some point in the ontological argument an appeal
to "faith" must be made.[44] Yet the faith to which Hartshorne, and Ogden
following him, appeal is much more general than specifically Christian
faith.[45] It is a "common faith" that is to some extent shared by all human
beings necessarily.[46] If this faith is necessary, then to deny it will involve
one in self-contradiction. This "common faith" Ogden describes as the basic
confidence in the significance of our existence that is presupposed in any
and all thought or action whatever.[47] Further, this means that the question
of the existence of God is necessarily involved in any proper understanding
of ourselves as human beings. Ogden quotes Hartshorne as follows:

> All proofs for God depend upon conceptions which derive their meaning from God
> himself. They are merely ways of making clear that we already and once for all
> believe in God, though not always with clearness and consistency. With no belief
> in God no belief could be arrived at; but the question at issue is as to the compara-
> tive self-knowledge of 'believers' and 'unbelievers.' Both employ ultimate concep-
> tions which unbelievers tend (or so it seems to believers) to leave unanalyzed.[48]

43. Langdon Gilkey, for one, doubts that this is a real need. First, Gilkey believes that
Ogden and other process theologians misinterpret Aquinas himself. Second, Gilkey
believes that "what process philosophers call 'classical theism' is a strange, hodgepodge
that bears little historical scrutiny." Third, whatever following this "hodgepodge"
might have acquired, Gilkey believes that "neither of the recently dominant forms of
religion in America, Protestant Evangelicalism and Protestant Liberalism, have had the
remotest relation to these traditional Hellenistic conceptions of God...." (Langdon
Gilkey, "A Theology in Process: Schubert Ogden's Developing Theology," Interpretation
21 [Oct. 1967]: 447–59, 449). Nor has this "classical metaphysical view of God had
any discernible influence on Hegel, Schleiermacher, Ritschl, Barth, Brunner, or the
Niebuhrs" (450). For a defense of the claim that "classical theism" accurately represents
Aquinas's understanding of God, see Philip E. Devenish, "Postliberal Process Theology:
A Rejoinder to Burrell," Theological Studies 43 (Summer 1982): 504–13, 505–507. For a
defense of God's eternity as conceived by Aquinas, see William J. Hill, "The Historicity
of God," Theological Studies 45 (June 1984): 320–33.
44. See Karl Barth, Fides Quaerens Intellectum: Anselm's Proof of the Existence of God in
the Context of his Theological Scheme, 2nd ed., trans. Ian W. Robertson (London: SCM
Press, 1960).
45. Hartshorne, The Logic of Perfection, 111–14; Ogden, "Theology and Philosophy," 9.
46. On Ted Peters's reading, "faith is universal. It belongs to the human condition as
such. Christian faith is one version of, or, better, one form of witness to, this universal
human faith" ("The Theological Method of Schubert Ogden," Dialog 29 [Spring 1990]:
125–34, 130).
47. As Ted Peters describes it, "Ogden holds that human faith is general animal faith
with self-consciousness added" ("Theological Method of Schubert Ogden," 130).
48. Charles Hartshorne, Man's Vision of God and the Logic of Theism (New York: Harper
& Brothers, 1941), 174–75; quoted by Ogden, "Theology and Philosophy," 12.

The problem, then, is how to conceive a God that is both independent of anything else in respect to its existence and at the same time genuinely related to my life. To do this, Ogden endorses Hartshorne's "dipolar" conception of God.[49] On this conception, God has two poles, an absolute pole and a relative pole. The relative pole is the more inclusive pole, in that God is really internally related to every other entity.[50] Moreover, God is internally related to every instant in the life of every creature, in the sense that God is really affected by every event in the life of all God's creatures.[51] In this sense God is supremely, or unsurpassingly, relative. The absolute pole describes the fact that God is "absolute relativity." That is to say, God is related to all God's creatures absolutely; God's internal relatedness to reality is not a contingent fact, but is an absolute fact that nothing could possibly change.[52] But this absolute pole is a formal or abstract one, which is "simply the abstract structure or identifying principle of his eminent relativity."[53] God, therefore, is dipolar—"at once supremely relative and supremely absolute."[54]

Ogden takes this dipolar conception of God to be coherent and to be amenable to his argument for God's necessary existence. The necessity of God's existence is what Ogden will need to fulfill the requirements for

49. See Charles Hartshorne and William L. Reese, *Philosophers Speak of God* (Chicago: Univ. of Chicago Press, 1953); Ogden, *The Reality of God*, 47–48. See also Charles Hartshorne, *The Divine Relativity: A Social Conception of God* (New Haven, Conn.: Yale Univ. Press, 1948).

50. We can describe the difference between external and internal relations as follows. To put matters crudely, process thought holds that who I am at any given moment is constituted by my creative integration of all the moments (at least all those of which I am aware, but probably others, too) that preceded this given moment; I am internally related to those prior moments, and to all those who existed during at least part of those prior moments. Thus, I am internally related to someone, like Abraham Lincoln, who existed before me. This is because at every moment of my life I am creatively integrating, to whatever large or miniscule extent, the events that constituted Lincoln's life. Lincoln, however, is externally related to me, because, since he is dead, he is no longer engaging in acts of creative integration.

51. This is Ogden's principle point of departure from those characteristics attributed to God by what he terms "classical theism." These attributes—"pure actuality, immutability, impassivity, aseity, immateriality, etc.—all entail an unqualified negation of real internal relationship to anything beyond his own wholly absolute being" (Ogden, *Reality of God*, 48–49).

52. In contrast, while our relatedness to *some* set of events is necessary, our relatedness to any particular actual occasions is contingent. God, on the other hand, is necessarily, or absolutely, related to any and all existent beings. "[J]ust because God is the eminently relative One, there is also a sense in which he is strictly absolute. His being related to all others is itself relative to nothing, but is the absolute ground of any and all real relationships, whether his own or those of his creatures" (Ogden, *Reality of God*, 60).

53. Ogden, *Reality of God*, 65.

54. Ogden, *Reality of God*, 48.

successful (descriptivist) reference. Concomitantly, this argument is also central to Ogden's theological method.

III. A CONSISTENT LIBERAL THEOLOGICAL METHOD: SCHUBERT M. OGDEN

To recapitulate briefly, from his early writings, Ogden has argued that the theologian's task is to "translate" the meaning of the Christian faith into the language and thought forms of her own day.[55] Such an exercise in translation presupposes "the correlation of the Christian witness of faith and human existence...."[56] Precisely because of the correlational structure of theology, the theologian will have to answer two central questions: "What does it mean to say that Jesus is the Christ?" and "Is this statement about Jesus true?" These two (roughly formed) questions are essentially those asked by Ogden through his two criteria of theological adequacy.[57] Theological claims must be *appropriate* to Jesus Christ, and *credible* to common human experience and reason. Ogden never moves away from these two norms, although he does deepen his reflections on them and provide them with more detailed and nuanced expression.[58] Ogden has always maintained that these two norms of systematic theology are "logically independent and mutually irreducible.[59] Note, however, that these are critical norms, while the theologian's task

55. Schubert M. Ogden, "The Lordship of Jesus Christ," *Encounter* 21 (Autumn 1960): 408–22, esp. 410.

56. Ogden, "What is Theology?" *Journal of Religion* 52 (1972): 22–40; reprinted in *On Theology* (San Francisco: Harper & Row, 1986; 2d ed., Dallas, Tex.: Southern Methodist Univ. Press, 1992), 1–21, 3.

57. Ogden, "What is Theology?" 4.

58. In his latest work, Ogden states that Christian witness always makes or implies two claims to validity, which it is the theologian's task to validate. The claims of Christian witness must be adequate to its content and fitting to its situation. This latter, fittingness requirement is a task of practical theology, while the task of systematic theology is to determine whether Christian claims are adequate to its content. This latter requirement of adequacy is then articulated in terms of two separate requirements of being appropriate to Jesus Christ and credible to common human experience and reason—Ogden's dual criteria of adequacy (Schubert M. Ogden, "Toward Bearing Witness," *Religious Studies Review* 23 [1997]: 337–40, 338).

59. Schubert M. Ogden, *Doing Theology Today* (Valley Forge, Pa.: Trinity Press, 1996), 9. Gerard Loughlin argues that this is not the case at all. On Loughlin's view, Ogden's norm of appropriateness is overdetermined by the norm of credibility. "What is the central criterion for determining the kind of story that should be told by the Christian community about Jesus? Simply, the story of Jesus that accords with the Christian's present self-understanding" ("On Telling the Story of Jesus," *Theology* 87 [Summer 1984]: 323–29, 329).

is both critical and constructive. This means that his method needs two parts—a critical and a constructive part.[60] Nonetheless, a theologian's constructive work must obviously satisfy the critical norms used to assess any theological claim. Thus the critical and constructive tasks are closely related.

A. Ogden's Constructive Method: Where to Begin and How to Go About Constructive Theology

In his latest work, Ogden describes the theologian's task as occurring in three phases.[61] The first phase is a historical phase, whose task it is to identify the formally normative witness that can validate theological claims as being appropriate to Jesus Christ. The second phase is a hermeneutical phase, in which the normative witness is interpreted existentially as the answer to the question of the meaning of ultimate reality for human beings.[62] The third phase is a philosophical phase, in which the theologian is to evaluate critically theological claims so as to determine whether they are credible to human existence. Putting the matter this way makes clear that the credibility claims made by theological statements are claims to existential credibility. Consequently, to assess such claims, a theologian must "determine both in principle and in fact what is to count as the truth about human existence."[63] In each phase the theologian appeals to secular standards. But the activity involved in the third phase in particular is thoroughly secular (not secularistic), inasmuch as it appeals only to common human experience and reason—i.e., to those aspects of human existence that any woman or man would experience simply by virtue of being human.

For Ogden, theological claims must be appropriate to Jesus Christ, and to be validated as such, a theologian must determine the criterion

60. Cf. Ogden, "What is Theology?" 6: "Insofar as a theological statement is adequate, and thus both appropriate and credible, it is at once dogmatic and apologetic, as well as critical and constructive."
61. Ogden, *Doing Theology Today*, 13–17.
62. I should note that one can distinguish between an interpretive task of articulating what the normative witness *meant* to its earliest (or earlier) purveyors (or hearers) and that of articulating what it *means* for us today. It is not clear whether Ogden thinks it important to distinguish between these two tasks and whether he would see both as belonging to the same phase. The important point, however, is that in the hermeneutic phase the theologian is to critically interpret the meaning of the normative witness so that what that witness meant in expressing itself as it did is now so formulated that the same meaning is again expressed.
63. Ogden, *Doing Theology Today*, 15.

for such validation. That is, the theologian must determine what is to count as the "formally normative witness." Ogden distinguishes between a witness that is formally normative from one that is "substantially normative." A substantially normative witness may validate some, but not all, theological claims as being appropriate to Jesus Christ. Still, a substantially normative witness will agree with all other appropriate witnesses. A formally normative witness, on the other hand, can validate the appropriateness of all theological claims, in that all theological claims must agree with it if they are to be appropriate to Jesus Christ. In the first phase of theological reflection, then, the theologian must determine what is the formally normative witness. We will see in the next section that it is the original apostolic witness, or the "Jesus-kerygma" that Ogden takes to be the formally normative or authorizing witness to Jesus Christ.[64] We should note, however, that determining the identity of this formally normative witness is a secular activity in that the norms of historical criticism and investigation must guide the theologian's determination of the formal norm.[65] More fundamentally, identifying the formally normative witness presupposes philosophy and philosophical theology. This is because identifying the formally normative witness requires understanding it, which involves interpreting it, and interpretation depends on a philosophical activity.[66]

In the second phase, Ogden interprets the formally normative witness as an answer to the existential question of the meaning of ultimate reality for us. He derives this answer from his argument for the existence of God. And it is this argument that will provide him with the descriptive sense he needs for successful reference of the term "God." Briefly, the argument is structured as follows. To begin with, in every exercise of freedom, we inescapably affirm a self-understanding as a good one. That is, every act affirms the goodness or significance of our existence. Our existence makes an ultimate difference and is thus ultimately good. This goodness we affirm is one that no event in the future has the power to deny. And the best explanation for this ultimate goodness is theism. Ogden's apologetic for Christian faith, then, or at least for theism, begins with the attempt to show that faith in

---

64. Ogden, *Doing Theology Today*, 13.
65. Ogden, *Doing Theology Today*, 11–12.
66. On Ogden's view, "because understanding witness also requires interpreting it, historical theology itself is already dependent on philosophy and philosophical theology. This is so because to interpret what is thought and spoken in one set of concepts and terms always requires another set in which to interpret it" (Ogden, *Doing Theology Today*, 14). I will describe in more detail just how Ogden identifies this formally normative Christian witness in the next section.

God is unavoidable.[67] Indeed, it is an *existential*, an intrinsic and transcendental aspect of human existence. Thus, Ogden's apologetic begins with an analysis of human existence.

For Ogden, acceptance of the reformed subjectivist principle implies two things above all else. First, it implies that "the primary object of philosophical reflection is my own existence as an experiencing self and that, therefore, philosophy's only proper task and method is integral reflective self-understanding."[68] Second, it implies that every human experience is an experience of value. I'll discuss this second implication later.

When Ogden says that the primary object of philosophical reflection is my existence as an experiencing subject, this is because every human act, whatever else it involves, is an act not only of understanding, but also of self-understanding.[69] Ogden does not mean by this that everything he does is done with some conscious understanding of its significance. We all do many things throughout the day without giving it a second thought. We breathe, digest food, put one foot in front of another when walking, misplace our keys, etc. Instead, he means that every act, insofar as it is characteristically human, implies an understanding of ourselves in relation to others and the whole of reality, including God.[70] If I take my daughter kayaking, or have dinner with a friend, or go to a museum, or buy a hot dog at a hot dog stand, all these activities make implicit assertions about how I understanding myself in relation to some other or others, and the whole of reality, regardless of whether I consciously believe such assertions or even think about them.[71]

Following both Lonergan and Whitehead, then, Ogden also maintains that the object and task of philosophy is self-understanding, or

67. As mentioned above, we may say that Ogden's starting point is the insight Anselm achieved through the ontological argument. The uniqueness of the concept of an infinite being implies that if God exists, God exists necessarily. That is, God's existence is either necessary or impossible. This means that if God does exist, we necessarily experience God in every experience that is so much as possible. Indeed, Ogden himself states that "there is a sound basis for the traditional formula in which theology is succinctly defined as *fides quaerens intellectum*" (Ogden, "What is Theology?" 2).

68. Ogden, "Lonergan and the Subjectivist Principle," 225.

69. Ogden, "The Task of Philosophical Theology," in *On Theology* (San Francisco: Harper & Row, 1986; 2d ed., Dallas, Tex.: Southern Methodist Univ. Press, 1992), 69–93, 70.

70. A host of philosophical issues may arise here regarding just what acts Ogden considers characteristically human. What about eating, digesting food, or breathing (etc.)? Ogden never addresses himself (in print at least) to such issues, and, so far as I can see, resolution of all (or any) such issues is not necessary to granting his point about implied self-understanding.

71. This is what I take Ogden to mean when he says that understanding itself is much broader than the "fully reflective understanding properly sought by philosophy...." ("Lonergan and the Subjectivist Principle," 225).

understanding what it means to understand. This means that human existence, although it is a contingent existence, has a unique primacy for Ogden. Although "it is certainly not constitutive of reality as such, God alone being the individual who is that, it is constitutive of our *understanding* of reality."[72] For Ogden, our everyday life in the world is a mode of understanding.[73] Thus, we need to distinguish between existential understanding and reflective understanding. Existential understanding is that understanding of ourselves, God, and the rest of reality that is implied by the lives we actually live and the actions in which we actually engage. At a fundamental level, this existential understanding must be that our lives are lived in basic faith in the worth of our existence. This basic faith, because it is a necessary truth about human existence, is constitutive of human existence as such.[74] Reflective understanding, in contrast, is that understanding in which our existential understanding is "re-presented in an express, thematic, and conceptually precise way."[75] The primary goal of philosophy, he says, and at least one important goal of theology is to bring our existential self-understanding into reflective consciousness. Both philosophy and theology seek an increasing congruence between existential and reflective self-understanding.

We are now in a position to see that the second phase of theological reflection, the hermeneutical phase, is grounded in Ogden's embrace of Whitehead's reformed subjectivist principle. The formally normative Christian witness, that is, must be interpreted in terms of human existence. More specifically, it must be interpreted in terms of the meaning or worth of human existence. This means that the formally normative Christian witness must be articulated as an answer to "the existential question about the meaning of ultimate reality for us."[76] The method theology should use to accomplish this task, as we have seen, is the existentialist interpretation Ogden has appropriated from Bultmann and Heidegger.

Above all Ogden draws two consequences from his embrace of Whitehead's reformed subjectivist principle. The first is that the primary philosophical task is to reflect on human self-understanding. The second is that human experience is always an experience of value, and this experience of value seems to have two aspects. On the one hand, following Whitehead, human experience always involves a valuation by the human subject of the objects

---

72. Ogden, "Falsification and Belief," *Religious Studies* 10 (1974): 21–43, quotation at 41 (emphasis in original).
73. Ogden, "Task of Philosophical Theology," 69–93, 70.
74. Ogden, "Task of Philosophical Theology," 71.
75. Ogden, "Task of Philosophical Theology," 71.
76. Ogden, *Doing Theology Today*, 14.

of our experience. On the other hand, every human action implies its own worth or value. This does not mean, of course, that I consciously consider every action I take to be worthwhile. Suppose, for example, I am addicted to a video game, and instead of working on this book (or playing with my children, doing housework, etc.) as I believe I should be, I find I am unable to refrain from playing this game for two or three hours every day. Even though I consciously believe my game-playing to be anything but worthwhile, the very act of playing itself contradicts any claim that the action is not worth doing. Any action at all, in other words, always carries an *implicit* claim by the actor that she considers the action to be worthwhile.

The third phase of theological reflection is its most explicitly philosophical phase, in which the principal objective is to establish the second criterion necessary to validate theological claims.[77] If theology is to reflect critically on Christian witness, it must reflect on both the explicit and implicit claims made by that witness. In Ogden's view, "Any witness at all makes or implies the claim to be adequate, and hence makes or implies the further claims to be credible as well as appropriate."[78] This second criterion is "both in principle and in fact what is to count as the truth about human existence."[79] What is to count here is not any and all truths about human existence, but the truth about the meaning of ultimate reality for us. Thus it is the existential truth about human existence. Again, following the reformed subjectivist principle, Ogden argues that this existential truth is given only through what he calls "common human experience."

Ogden's account of "common human experience" is as follows. Because understanding and value are elements or structures of *every* experience, they are constitutive of *common* human experience. And because Ogden construes human experience as having *a priori elements* of understanding and value, he is able to derive an answer to "the existential question" transcendentally. Recall that the existential question is constructed from elements of understanding and value. It asks about the meaning or significance of ultimate reality for us; or more specifically, "how we are to understand ourselves and others in relation to the whole if ours is to be an authentic existence."[80] Ogden's answer is as follows. Because every human

---

77. Ted Peters has expressed the distinction between the two norms as a distinction between meaning and truth. On Peters's reading, "appropriateness to Scripture has to do with meaning, and credibility has to do with truth" ("The Theological Method of Schubert Ogden," 125–34).

78. Ogden, *Doing Theology Today*, 18.

79. Ogden, *Doing Theology Today*, 15.

80. Schubert M. Ogden, *Is There Only One True Religion or Are There Many?* (Dallas, Tex.: Southern Methodist Univ. Press, 1992), 6.

action asserts (at least implicitly) its own worth, it is impossible, Ogden believes, for human beings to avoid continually asserting that their actions, and therefore their very lives, are worthwhile or valuable. If this is so, he believes, humans can't help asserting that human life itself is ultimately worthwhile. This is what Ogden calls our "basic faith" in the worth of our lives. And since we all necessarily have such a basic faith, Ogden argues that such unavoidable faith must have an objective ground in reality. This ground is God, in Ogden's view, and God must therefore be such as to validate our basic faith in the worth of our lives. Ogden argues that God's being the ground of our basic faith entails that God is constituted by God's boundless love for all of humanity. Every religious claim, therefore, must, at a minimum, be consistent with an understanding of oneself and all others as equally the object of God's boundless love. The authentic answer, then, to the existential question of the meaning or significance of ultimate reality for us is that I must live so as to re-present the fact that ultimate reality (God) so loves us as to guarantee the worth or significance of our lives.[81] This understanding of God's boundless love, then, is the criterion Ogden uses to determine whether religious claims are credible to human existence. And, in my view, Ogden has derived his criterion of credibility solely from a transcendental analysis of human experience.[82]

This transcendental argument for God's existence does precisely what Ogden needs it to do in order to respond adequately to Flew. Because the argument is grounded in human subjectivity, it derives the elements of a descriptive sense for "God" directly from human experience. And because God is the ground of the value or significance of every human act, which necessarily asserts its own significance, God's existence must be necessary.

81. Schubert M. Ogden, "The Reality of God," in *The Reality of God and Other Essays* (New York: Harper & Row, 1966; 2d ed., Dallas, Tex.: Southern Methodist Univ. Press, 1992), 1–70, esp. 37.

82. I should point out that not all of Ogden's interpreters view the criterion of credibility as a transcendental criterion. See, for example, Paul J. Griffiths, "How Epistemology Matters to Theology," *Journal of Religion* 79 (1999): 1–18. Griffiths interprets the criterion of credibility as he does because of Ogden's use of it to argue against positions with which he (Ogden) disagrees (15). Griffiths is certainly correct that the way Ogden uses the principle argumentatively does at times obscure a proper interpretation of it. Nonetheless, in my judgment, it would be more plausible to argue that Ogden does not always use the criterion appropriately than to argue that his use of it implies that he does not intend it to be a transcendental criterion. Moreover, the most sympathetic of Ogden's commentators also interpret the principle of credibility as transcendental. See, for example, Franklin I. Gamwell, "On the Theology of Schubert M. Ogden," *Religious Studies Review* 23:4 (Oct. 1997): 333–37; Philip E. Devenish and George L. Goodwin, "Christian Faith and the First Commandment: The Theology of Schubert Ogden," in *Witness and Existence: Essays in Honor of Schubert M. Ogden*, ed. Devenish and Goodwin (Chicago: Univ. of Chicago Press, 1989), 1–39.

Thus, the descriptive sense that Ogden associates with the term "God"—something like "the ground of our unavoidable faith in the value of our lives"—can be associated only with God and nothing else. Ogden has thus associated the term "God" with a descriptive sense that articulates a set of conditions the satisfaction of which is necessary and sufficient for the term to refer to God and nothing else. And because of the way in which those conditions were derived, we can have (to use Russell's vocabulary) knowledge by acquaintance that they are in fact satisfied. Consequently, Ogden has satisfied Russell's conditions for successful reference.

B. Ogden's Critical Method I: The Norm of Appropriateness

So far, I have discussed the way in which Ogden takes the term "God" to successfully refer to God and the way in which he takes claims made about God to be imbued with meaning. But that can't be the end of the story. Once we have made meaningful claims about God, those claims must be assessed. And Ogden does this through his dual criteria of adequacy. To critically sustain a theological claim, a Christian theologian must establish (or at least argue) that the claim is both appropriate to Jesus Christ and credible to common human experience and reason. But what does it mean to say that a theological claim must be appropriate to Jesus Christ? First and foremost, of course, it means that theological claims must be consistent with the life and teachings of Jesus. Yet Jesus' teachings themselves, as well as claims about his life, must be meaningful. And this means, at least if we accept descriptivist requirements (as Ogden does), Jesus' teachings and claims about his life must be associated with the kinds of descriptive senses I have described above. This will require that Jesus' teachings and claims about his life be interpreted in a particular way. And we should expect that Ogden will interpret those teachings and claims in terms of significance or value. This will allow the referring expressions in those teachings and claims to refer successfully and the predicates to acquire meaning in the descriptivist way. When we look at Ogden's norm or criterion of appropriateness, this is precisely how he interprets it. So let's look at Ogden's interpretation in more detail.

For both Bultmann and Ogden, to say that a theological claim must be appropriate to Jesus Christ is not to say that the claims of the Bible are simply to be restated in a contemporary language. The claims of the Christian scriptures must be demythologized, but this is called for by scripture itself, because the Gospel proclamation is not made in an objectifying mode, but is an existential proclamation. In an essay from 1971, Ogden states that the sense of the norm of appropriateness is that "it represents the same

understanding of faith as is expressed in the 'datum discourse' of normative Christian witness."[83] This seems to say nothing more than that a claim
must be appropriate to a demythologized interpretation of Christian scriptures. Still, this is not all there is to say about how to use the scriptures.
Ogden realizes that there is no uncontested interpretation of Christian
scriptures, even those that claim to be demythologizing interpretations.
Interpretations may differ from one historical period to another, and also
within a given period.[84] In 1976, Ogden provided an attempt to show how
scripture could be used in elucidating the norm of appropriateness. In "The
Authority of Scripture for Theology,"[85] Ogden investigates whether there is
a sense in which the canon of scripture can be said to be the sole primary
authority for Christian theology.[86] He concludes that scripture can be used
to adjudicate only whether a theological claim is appropriate, not whether
it is credible. In the course of the essay, Ogden discusses just what constraints should be imposed on the use of scripture. And this discussion sets
him squarely in the tradition of Ritschlian liberal theology.

First, following Hans von Campenhausen, Ogden holds that the history
of the canon itself must be taken into account in using scripture as a norm
for theology.[87] That is, "canon" itself is an ambiguous term, and to be understood rightly, it must be remembered that the canon as we have it was the
product of the experience of the church. It was the result of the church's
attempt "to control all putative authorities in relation to the primal source
of all authority in Christ himself."[88] But since the church is not infallible,
the canon itself must remain open to revision. This means that the most

83. Ogden, "What is Theology?" 4.
84. He says that "the two criteria of theological adequacy are situation-dependent as
well as situation-invariant in what they require. Although in one aspect their requirements are always the same, in another they are constantly different, contingent on the
possibilities and limitations of different historical situations. In general, their requirements in a situation are most likely to be discerned through intensive discussion with
its best secular knowledge—in the case of appropriateness, the knowledge of history;
in the case of credibility, that of philosophy and the special sciences as well as the various arts" (Ogden, "What is Theology?" 6).
85. Ogden, "The Authority of Scripture for Theology," Interpretation 30 (1976):
242–61; reprinted in On Theology (San Francisco: Harper & Row, 1986; 2d ed., Dallas,
Tex.: Southern Methodist Univ. Press, 1992), 45–68.
86. In the course of this investigation, Ogden maintains that the traditional Protestant
cry of sola scriptura is no longer defensible. There is a consensus among New Testament
scholars, with whom Ogden agrees, that scripture is itself tradition. Thus, "there is no
sense, finally, in which the canon of scripture is the primary authority for Christian
theology any more than for Christian faith and witness" (Ogden, "The Authority of
Scripture for Theology," 46).
87. Ogden, "The Authority of Scripture for Theology," 52, citing Hans Freiherr von
Campenhausen, Die Entstehung der christlichen Bibel (Tübingen: J. C. B. Mohr, 1968).
88. Ogden, "The Authority of Scripture for Theology," 53–54.

proper sense of "canon" is not the collection of writings that constitute the Christian Bible, but whatever is in those writings that is "authorized by Christ through the church's continuing experience under the guidance of the Holy Spirit."[89]

This leads to the second point, which is to realize that the primary criterion of the church in selecting the canon was that of "apostolicity"—that is, whether the text in question could claim apostolic authorship. But the church never simply accepted claims to apostolicity at face value. It drew on considerations that today we would consider historical, but in some circumstances it also drew on questions of content. If apostolicity was in question, the church considered a text's content. If the content of a book under consideration conformed to that of others already considered apostolic, this was evidence for its apostolicity as well. This is circular to some extent, but as long as there was some consensus that *some* text could claim apostolic authorship, the circularity problem could avoid being vicious. Now, however, the majority of historical critics agree that no New Testament text can credibly claim apostolic authorship. This does not mean that the scriptural texts are no longer authoritative, but it does require a reassessment of their authority. For Willi Marxsen, whose analysis Ogden follows to a large extent, this requires the frank admission that the Catholic option of "scripture and tradition" is a more adequate and consistent alternative than the Protestant option of *sola scriptura*. For Ogden, however, these do not exhaust the alternatives. Instead, a reassessment of scriptural authority could and should proceed on the basis of the same criterion of apostolicity used by the early church. That is, the original witness of Christ's apostles is the originating witness that constituted the apostolic church, and this witness is the primary norm for the theological authority of scripture. What is needed, therefore, is to identify this witness by means of "our present historical methods and knowledge," and to reassess the authority of the scriptures according to the criterion of this historically identified witness.[90]

Consequently, the theological authority of the New Testament is a derived authority. To show that a theological claim is appropriate to Jesus Christ, it is not sufficient to show that it is warranted by scripture. Instead, a theological claim must be shown to be authorized by the original witness

89. Ogden, "The Authority of Scripture for Theology," 54.
90. Ogden, "The Authority of Scripture for Theology," 59. This criterion of apostolicity means not only temporal but also material proximity to the original apostolic witness (60). Thus, the Gospel of John can be viewed as closer to the witness to Christ than the earlier synoptics in that it may be closer *materially*, though not temporally, to the original and originating apostolic witness.

of the apostles, as rendered by a historical-critical reconstruction. This original witness must be reconstructed only from "the earliest layer of the synoptic tradition."[91] With respect to the Hebrew Bible or Christian Old Testament, its authority has been generally understood by Protestant theologians to be controlled by the witness of the New Testament. This needs to be revised, in Ogden's view, so that its authority must now be controlled not by the New Testament writings, but by the original apostolic witness. In addition, because it is now generally agreed that the Old Testament writings and prophecies did not explicitly point to Christ in the way that the early church seemed to think, its authority must be constricted further. For Ogden, "the Old Testament writings document the particular linguistic form of the question of human existence—more exactly, of the ultimate meaning of human existence—to which the Jesus-kerygma presents itself as the answer."[92] That is, the Old Testament provides the concepts, linguistic forms, and presuppositions in which the original apostolic witness is expressed.[93]

Ogden revisited the norm of appropriateness to Jesus Christ in *The Point of Christology*, published in 1982.[94] In this important work, Ogden spends a good deal of time talking about (not surprisingly) the *point* of Christian reflection on Christ, because he thinks so much of Christology *misses* the point. On Ogden's view, both traditional and revisionary Christologies have taken the point of Christology to be an empirical-historical point, concerned entirely with the being of Jesus as this being existed in the past. Ogden, however, maintains that the point of Christology is entirely an existential point, concerned with the meaning or significance of Jesus here and now in the present.[95] Because it missed the point of Christology, traditional Christology has never been able to give a consistent account of the "two natures" of Christ asserted at Chalcedon. Traditional theology has never been able to articulate consistently what the claim that Christ has two

91. Ogden, "The Authority of Scripture for Theology," 64. Ogden says that this is the same layer or strata of tradition referred to by Marxsen as the "Jesus-kerygma" as distinct from the "Christ-kerygma" (64). See Willi Marxsen, *Das Neue Testament als Buch der Kirche* (Gütersloh: Gütersloher Verlagshaus Gerd Mohn, 1968), 108–109, 111.

92. Ogden, "The Authority of Scripture for Theology," 66–67, citing Rudolf Bultmann, *Theologie des Neuen Testaments* (Tübingen: J. C. B. Mohr, 1948–1953).

93. Ogden, "The Authority of Scripture for Theology," 67–68.

94. Schubert M. Ogden, *The Point of Christology* (San Francisco: Harper & Row, 1982; 2d ed., Dallas, Tex.: Southern Methodist Univ. Press, 1982).

95. Ogden, *Point of Christology*, 41. In the frontispiece to the book, Ogden quotes Luther's *Tractatus de libertate christiana*: "It is not enough nor is it Christian, to preach the works, life, and words of Christ as historical facts,... rather ought Christ to be preached to the end that faith in him may be established, that he may not only be Christ, but be Christ for you and me...."

natures means.[96] The reason, Ogden believes, is that traditional theology has used the conceptual assumptions of classical metaphysics. The inadequacy of traditional Christological accounts has given rise to "revisionary" approaches to Christology that seek to accomplish two tasks. First, these efforts attempt to demythologize the traditional accounts of Christ's two natures in a consistent way. Second, they attempt to provide an alternative conceptuality within which one can fully make the point of Christology without mythology. But these accounts have also been problematic because although they try to offer more adequate answers than traditional accounts, they assume the conceptualities in which traditional Christologies pose the question about Christ. This results in an inadequate conceptual framework in which revisionary Christologies attempt to provide an answer. So Ogden wants to explain clearly how his own account of the point of Christology differs from revisionary approaches to Christology. This difference will be apparent in the question, and in both the subject and the predicate of the answer given by revisionary Christologies, on the one hand, and on the other hand by Ogden's answer to the question about Christ.

Both Ogden and the revisionary consensus ask "Who is Jesus?" But when the revisionary consensus asks this question, they are asking an *empirical*-historical question about the being of Jesus-in-himself. Ogden, in contrast, asks an *existential*-historical question about the meaning (or significance) of Jesus *for us*. This difference in what is understood by the question will naturally result in a different understanding of the subject of the answer. For the revisionary consensus, the subject of the answer is the empirical-historical Jesus, whereas for Ogden, the subject of the answer to the question about Christ is the existential-historical Jesus. This difference is not simply a matter of arbitrary preference. Instead, Ogden thinks that if the subject of our Christological assertions is the empirical-historical Jesus, we are in deep trouble, because the empirical-historical Jesus is completely inaccessible to us.[97]

96. In the opinion of some commentators, Ogden is not able to do this, either. Eugene TeSelle, for example, argues that Ogden has "nothing but a high christology" in which Jesus' humanity "remains a matter of indifference or is at best of only marginal significance" (TeSelle, review of *The Point of Christology* by Schubert M. Ogden, *Religious Studies Review* 9 [July 1983]: 227–33, 229).

97. Eugene TeSelle agrees with Ogden that Jesus' inner life remains inaccessible to us, but believes that Ogden "overshoots badly" in his uncompromising rejection of any claim regarding the empirical-historical Jesus. TeSelle argues that it is possible to gain a reasonably accurate empirical-historical picture of Jesus' public activity and proclamation (TeSelle, review of *The Point of Christology*, 228). Gerard Loughlin, on the other hand, argues that the existential-historical Jesus can have no more support in the earliest historic witnesses than the empirical-historical Jesus ("On Telling the Story of Jesus," *Theology* 87 [Summer 1984]: 323–29, 327).

On Ogden's reading, those involved in the original quest of the historical Jesus assumed that the criterion for justifying Christological assertions
was the human figure of Jesus, rather than either the scriptural assertions
about him or the traditions of the church. As the quest proceeded, however, it became increasingly clear that Jesus had made no claim about his
own significance. He had made no Christological claims for himself. Thus
Harnack was famously compelled to conclude, "Not the Son, but only the
Father, is included in the gospel as Jesus proclaimed it."[98] The problem
here is obvious: if the empirical-historical Jesus is the sole criterion of the
appropriateness of Christological claims, then Jesus' silence means that
the church should be silent as well.[99]

The problem intensified in the years following World War I, when form
critics such as Bultmann and Martin Dibelius argued that even the claims
made by the earliest traditions about Jesus were not historical in nature.
These traditions constituted a witness to the (then) present significance
of Jesus rather than a historical judgment about the (recent) past being of
Jesus. Thus, if the empirical-historical Jesus was to be the sole norm for
Christology, this norm would have to be historically reconstructed from
non-historical texts. No such reconstruction, however, could yield any
certainty about what claims were actually spoken by Jesus. Indeed, the
possibility of any reliable detailed reconstruction was thrown into serious
question. Bultmann himself recognized, however, that the gospel did not
confront its hearer with a demand for an opinion regarding a historical
judgment. Instead, the gospel's demand is existential, confronting its hearer
with a decision of faith. To demand proof in the form of historical reconstruction was therefore not only unnecessary, but also illegitimate.[100]

As in his earlier essays, at this point Ogden finds particularly useful
Willi Marxsen's distinction between the "Christ-kerygma" of Paul and
John, which Bultmann had taken to be the real Christological norm, and
the "Jesus-kerygma" of the earliest parts of the synoptic tradition. Because
the Jesus-kerygma is accessible to historical-critical analysis of the synoptics, something of both the old and new quests of the historical Jesus

---

98. Ogden, *Point of Christology*, 45 (quoting Adolf von Harnack, *Das Wesen des
Christentums* [Stuttgart: Ehrenfried Klotz Verlag, 1950], 86).

99. Liberal theologians thus proclaimed that only the "religion *of* Jesus," not the
"religion *about* Jesus" is normative for the church (Ogden, *Point of Christology*, 45). This
point seems to problematize Loughlin's critique. See Loughlin, "On Telling the Story,"
327–28. Traditionalists, however, despite their strenuous objections to the findings
of these liberal theologians and biblical scholars, never questioned the underlying
assumption that the sole criterion for christological claims was the empirical-historical
Jesus.

100. Ogden, *Point of Christology*, 47–48.

can be preserved.[101] Marxsen accepts the distinction, made by Käsemann, Ebeling and others, between using empirical-historical inquiry to establish the *truth* of the kerygma and using it to establish the *authority* of the kerygma as Christian. Following Marxsen, Ogden affirms that the latter procedure is appropriate, while the former is not. In any event, no matter how close our investigation of sources take us to the historical Jesus, these sources will remain kerygma. Thus, "all we can ever hope to talk about is not what Jesus said and did, but what Jesus was *heard* to have said and *seen* to have done by those on whose experience and memory of him we are utterly dependent."[102] This would be the case for any historical figure, at least one who left no writings of her own. While this might not pose a problem in principle for some figures, it does pose an insurmountable problem when, as in the case of Jesus, the overriding concern of all our sources is to provide a witness of faith rather than a historical report. Thus, Ogden argues that Marxsen's position—"that no christological formulation can be theologically justified that cannot claim support in the historical Jesus"[103]—would leave us in the position of being able to justify no Christological claim whatever.[104]

On Ogden's view, however, we are not left in this position because no quest for the historical Jesus is necessary, regardless of whether it might ever be possible. The reason this is so is that the subject of Christological assertions is not the "empirical-historical Jesus," but is instead the "existential-historical Jesus." This means that the referent of "Jesus" in any Christological assertion is not simply a historical figure named Jesus, but

101. "If Marxsen was right, one could agree with Kähler and Bultmann that the norm of christology is indeed provided by the witness to Christ in the Bible or in the kerygma, rather than by the historical Jesus, even while maintaining more clearly than either of them had done that it is not the Christ-kerygma of Paul and John that constitutes this norm, but rather the Jesus-kerygma accessible through critical analysis of the synoptic gospels. To this extent at least something in the quest of the historical Jesus, old and new, could also be preserved and re-expressed" (Ogden, *Point of Christology*, 51).

102. Ogden, *Point of Christology*, 53 (emphasis in original). Gerard Loughlin makes the point that since "what Jesus was heard to have said and seen to have done" is to be constructed from the same texts and other historical data as is "what Jesus said and did," one should be no more difficult to construct than the other ("On Telling the Story," 327). Loughlin's critique does not address the genre of the texts, but only their mythological nature.

103. Ogden, *Point of Christology*, 52 (citing Marxsen, *Der Exeget als Theologe, Vorträge zum Neuen Testament*, 2d ed. [Gütersloh: Gütersloher Verlagshaus Gerd Mohn], 112, 149, 257).

104. On Ogden's view, "there can never be any distinction with respect to evidence, and in this sense any operational distinction, between Jesus as he actually was and Jesus as he is represented in the earliest stratum of witness that can now be reconstructed from the synoptic gospels" (*Point of Christology*, 55).

it is the living Christ who confronts us here and now with the demand of faith.[105] Consequently, the norm of appropriateness cannot have the character of an empirical-historical norm, but must instead have the character of an existential-historical norm. That is, the norm of appropriateness is not constituted by what Jesus actually said or did, but instead by the significance that his actions and words had for those who encountered him. At least this is the case with respect to the application of the norm to the constitutive Christological assertion. This is so precisely because the New Testament authors represent the significance of Jesus as having its root not only in his own words and actions, but in the fact that through them it was God who was and is still speaking and acting. That is, the assertions about Jesus in the New Testament are assertions "about Jesus as the decisive re-presentation of God...."[106] Thus, though we may not have access to the empirical-historical Jesus, it is the existential-historical Jesus that is the true norm of our Christological assertions. Whatever our empirical limitations, we do have access to the existential-historical Jesus precisely because our earliest sources are witness of faith.[107] Ogden's position here does not imply that historical inquiry is not important. Instead, the object of historical inquiry is not the historical Jesus, but the earliest Christian witness to him. It is this witness that constitutes the norm of appropriateness.[108] As one commentator has nicely summarized it, the norm is

105. It is "the one whom we already know most certainly through the same apostolic witness as well as all other witnesses of faith insofar as they are conformed to the witness of the apostles" (Ogden, *Point of Christology*, 57).

106. Ogden, *Point of Christology*, 59.

107. Ogden at times seems to imply that no empirical-historical claims about Jesus are relevant or important at all—for example, when he argues against moderates who assume that "christological formulations can be justified as appropriate only insofar as at least some empirical-historical claims about Jesus can be shown to be true" (*Point of Christology*, 60). But he is not arguing for such a strong claim. What he is arguing is simply that because the subject of the christological assertion is the existential-historical Jesus (the significance of Jesus for us), and because therefore the norm of appropriateness is an existential-historical one, whether Jesus himself made any claims about his own decisive significance, whether implicit or explicit, is theologically irrelevant (60–61).

108. Ogden, *Point of Christology*, 62–63. Charles Blaisdell argues that this construction of the norm of appropriateness is structurally similar to Plato's elaboration of the Forms in Book X of the *Republic*. On Blaisdell's reading, "There are three modes or levels of being—the Form, the object which imitates and participates in the Form, and a second object which imitates an appearance of the first object" ("The Christian Norm: In Response to Williamson and Ogden," *Process Studies* 16 [Fall 1987]: 169–73, 172). Ogden's construal of a norm is parallel in that "the Form is the Christ-event, and craftspeople and their productions are the 'apostolic witness' to that Form. Theologians then stand in the place of the artists for their works are founded on the productions of the apostolic witnesses (craftspeople)" (Blaisdell, "Christian Norm," 170).

established by "the empirical-historical rediscovery of the apostolic witness to the existential-historical Jesus."[109]

In Ogden's view both traditional Christologies and the revisionary consensus have assumed that the question about Jesus is an empirical-historical question, rather than an existential-historical one. As a result, the subject of their answers were empirical-historical. Ogden also argues that the predicates of their answers were empirical-historical, as well. For this reason, Ogden argues that the predicate of an adequate Christological assertion cannot be that either of traditional Christologies or of the revisionary consensus.[110] The revisionary Christologies assert that Jesus is the Christ only if he himself, as a human person, fully actualized the possibility of authentic self-understanding. The criterion, then, of whether Jesus is the Christ is Jesus' own personal relation to God. For the revisionary consensus, Jesus is who he is only because he consistently understood his own existence in the authentic way we are called to understand our own existence.[111]

There are several significant problems with this approach, as Ogden points out. Most obviously, revisionary Christologies require an understanding of the empirical-historical Jesus. As we have seen, however, Ogden takes the empirical-historical Jesus to be inaccessible. An even more serious problem is that the revisionary approach requires an understanding of the subjective consciousness of Jesus' own self-understanding. That is, what is normative for the revisionary Christologies is the faith of Jesus himself, understood as a model for our own.[112] In this usage, "faith" has at least two senses. First is the objective content of faith; that is, the propositions in which one believes. The second sense is the subjective or more existential faith by which one believes. This second sense can be understood broadly or more strictly. Used more broadly, it refers to the active moment of responding to God's love through good works. Used more strictly, it refers to the innermost act of trusting in God and being loyal to God's love. When the revisionary Christologies specify the truth conditions of Christological assertions, they are using the strict usage of the second sense of faith—the innermost act of trusting in God's love.[113]

Ogden has already pointed out the problem with recovering the historical Jesus. But even if one could get to the empirical-historical Jesus, one would face two more difficulties, in Ogden's view. First, to satisfy the truth

109. Jeffrey Carlson, "Ogden's 'Appropriateness' and Religious Plurality," *Modern Theology* 6 (Oct. 1989): 15–28.
110. Ogden, *Point of Christology*, 64.
111. Ogden, *Point of Christology*, 65–66.
112. Ogden, *Point of Christology*, 67.
113. Ogden, *Point of Christology*, 68–70.

conditions of the revisionary Christologies, one would need access to every moment of Jesus' subjectivity. Even for people now living whom we know most intimately, such continuous and unimpeded access is unavailable. The second difficulty is a corollary of the first. There is no historical source that could possibly tell us that there was no point in the entire life of Jesus when his self-understanding was inauthentic.[114] Furthermore, the sources that we have make no attempt to relate to us the second (subjective) sense of Jesus' faith.[115] Even those that imply some claim about Jesus' own faith are better interpreted as existential-historical statements, rather than empirical-historical statements.[116] Further, when viewed as metaphysical claims, the various Christologies of the New Testament seem contradictory. Thus, we should not try to understand the New Testament claims either as empirical-historical claims or as metaphysical claims.[117] Rather than empirical-historical or metaphysical claims, the honorific titles of Jesus in the New Testament, without exception, are claims about, first, the identity of God who authorizes our authentic self-understanding, and second, the decisive re-presentation of God that we see in Jesus.[118] Viewed in this way, the New Testament texts are consistent in their existential-historical claims about Jesus.[119]

It is in this sense that Ogden's rejection of "constitutive" Christologies should be understood. New Testament claims about Jesus should not be viewed as constitutive metaphysical claims. To be understood in such a metaphysical sense, Ogden believes that they would need to be judged against the norm of Jesus' own self-understanding. That is, a metaphysical statement about the being of Jesus in himself would need to be authorized by Jesus' own belief and claim about his own being. But, as we have seen, no historical source could possibly grant access to such an authorizing self-consciousness. This means that consistency with Jesus' self-understanding cannot be a necessary condition for the truth of Christological claims. But it also means that such

114. Ogden, *Point of Christology*, 70–71.
115. Drawing on Bultmann, Ogden states that "neither do the gospels speak of Jesus' own faith nor does the kerygma make any reference to Jesus' faith." Ogden, *Point of Christology*, 73.
116. Ogden, *Point of Christology*, 73–75.
117. "There can be little question that, when these [New Testament] christologies think and speak of Jesus as Son of God, they are so far from making the same metaphysical claim later made by the councils of Nicaea and Chalcedon that they may as well mean that Jesus is a human being whom God has appointed as that he is a divine being who has become man" (Ogden, *Point of Christology*, 76).
118. Ogden, *Point of Christology*, 75.
119. The New Testament Christologies are consistent in claiming that Jesus is "the decisive re-presentation of God, through whom God's own gift and demand become fully explicit, thereby authorizing our authentic understanding of ourselves" (Ogden, *Point of Christology*, 76).

consistency cannot be a sufficient condition, either. If the criterion were Jesus' self-understanding, the most that could be claimed for him would be that he is the primary authority of Christian faith and witness. Yet the New Testament writers claim that he is not only the primary authority, but the explicit primal source of all authority.[120] To authorize this claim, Jesus must be understood as the decisive re-presentation of God; God, then, is the implicit primal source of authority, and Christ is the explicit primal source that authorizes the authentic self-understanding.[121] Thus, "the only necessary and, therefore, the sufficient condition of any such assertion is that the meaning of ultimate reality for us that is always already presented implicitly in our very existence be just that meaning of God for us that is re-presented explicitly through Jesus."[122]

On Ogden's view, the truth conditions for Christological claims have two aspects. First, there is a metaphysical aspect. Jesus is truthfully said to be the Christ "if, but only if, the ultimate reality that implicitly authorizes the authentic understanding of our existence is the one who is explicitly revealed through Jesus to be God."[123] This condition can be satisfied only by a properly metaphysical inquiry into the structure of reality itself.[124] Second, this truth condition has a moral aspect. Appropriate Christological claims about Jesus are true

> if, but only if, the understanding of our existence that is implicitly authorized by what is ultimately real is the self-understanding that is explicitly authorized through Jesus as faith in God. In this aspect, the condition of the christological assertion can also be known to be satisfied through properly moral inquiry into how one is to act in relation to one's fellow beings.[125]

Thus, Ogden states explicitly that the truth conditions of any Christological claim are to be determined through a twofold investigation: a metaphysical investigation into the structure of reality, and a moral investigation into how human beings should act toward each other. This may seem to imply that such truth conditions could be deduced ahistorically from metaphysical and moral premises.[126] But Ogden does not intend to imply such a position.

---

120. Ogden, *Point of Christology*, 79.
121. Ogden, *Point of Christology*, 78–79.
122. Ogden, *Point of Christology*, 82.
123. Ogden, *Point of Christology*, 82.
124. Ogden, *Point of Christology*, 82–83.
125. Ogden, *Point of Christology*, 83.
126. Ogden can leave this impression through statements such as this: "I understand it to belong to the very essence of the Christian witness to attest that the fundamental option for salvation that is decisively re-presented solely through Jesus is also implicitly presented to every human being as soon and as long as he or she exists humanly at all" (Ogden, *Point of Christology*, 84).

Instead, there must be a third aspect to the investigation, a historical aspect, because the Christological question could not have arisen at all except on the basis of a *particular* experience of Jesus.[127] Thus, although the norm is an existential-historical norm, there is an empirical-historical aspect to the inquiry required to discover what the norm is. But the object of this empirical-historical inquiry is not the being of Jesus in himself, but is limited to the earliest witness to Jesus; more specifically, the earliest witness to the meaning and significance of Jesus.[128] In Ogden's articulation of the norm of appropriateness, we can see at least two, if not all three themes of nineteenth century liberal theology clearly operative. Not only is Ogden concerned to be faithful to the historical sources regarding Jesus, but also to articulate the norm in a way that is faithful to the reformed subjectivist principle.

To recapitulate briefly, Ogden has argued that the question about Christ is an existential-historical question. Thus, the subject of any adequate answer to the question must be an existential-historical one concerning the meaning of Jesus for us. Likewise, the predicate of any adequate answer must also be existential-historical. And they must be derived or found in a nontraditional canon. But even this nontraditional canon must be interpreted. And Ogden's interpretation is an existential-historical investigation into the significance of Jesus for us. The criterion of appropriateness, then, is constituted by Ogden's answer to the existential-historical question about Jesus. For Ogden, the significance of Jesus for us lies in his re-presentation of God's boundless love for us. It is this love that provides the ground for the value of all our actions. Thus, the descriptive senses associated with claims about Jesus and his relationship to God (as existentially interpreted) are derived from elements of human experience itself. Consequently, "God" will successfully refer in the way described in the last section, and we can "know by acquaintance" whether the conditions articulated by those descriptive senses are satisfied or not.

127. Charles Blaisdell sees this historical aspect of Ogden's norm of appropriateness as introducing a contradiction. For Blaisdell, no historically particular event can provide an absolute, trans-historical truth condition. "In other words, Ogden's concept of a norm for Christianity entails that it function as an absolute, even though it is a relative historical event" (Blaisdell, "Christian Norm," 171). Blaisdell's critique at this point rests on his failure to recognize Ogden's distinction between the norm of credibility and the norm of appropriateness. Unlike the norm of appropriateness, the norm of credibility is constituted transcendentally, and thus not subject to Blaisdell's critique.

128. Ogden, *Point of Christology*, 84–85.

C. Ogden's Critical Method II: The Norm of Credibility

After a theological claim has been determined to be appropriate to Jesus Christ, Ogden maintains that we must still determine whether it is credible to common human experience and reason. This second requirement is in recognition of the fact that those Christians making theological claims intend to assert that the claims are not only distinctly Christian, but also true. Ogden's way of asking whether such claims are in fact true is to ask whether they are credible to common human experience and reason.[129] Given what I have said so far, we can expect that Ogden will interpret theological claims existentially—i.e., in terms of significance or value. Because, as we have seen, understanding and value are constitutive elements of common human experience, we should expect to find Ogden using these elements to assess (existentially interpreted) theological claims. And this is precisely what we find.

Although one can discern a consistent trajectory of Ogden's use of the norm of credibility, his phrasing of the norm has varied a bit. In the early 1970s, he argued that the credibility of a claim was established by "the meaning and truth universally established with human existence."[130] A few years later, the definition sounded (though he may not have intended it to be) slightly more empirical,[131] but by the middle 1980s, he would clarify

---

129. "In this sense, the achievement of a systematic theology that is credible as well as appropriate is a validation of the claim of the Christian witness to re-present the truth of human existence." Ogden, *On Theology*, 1–21, 11. On the construal of Philip Devenish, the norm of credibility operates by comparing the Christian experience of Jesus with the "'universally human experience of the gift and demand of authentic existence.'" Philip E. Devenish, "Postliberal Process Theology: A Rejoinder to Burrell," *Theological Studies* 43 (Summer 1982): 504–13, 512 (citing Ogden, *The Reality of God*, 78). This experience, however, is "in a certain sense a *recognition* of 'the truth disclosed at least implicitly in human existence as such.'" Devenish, "Postliberal Process Theology," 512 (emphasis in original) (citing Schubert M. Ogden, "Sources of Religious Authority in Liberal Protestantism," *Journal of the American Academy of Religion* 44 [Sept. 1976]: 403–16, 406).

130. Schubert M. Ogden, "What is Theology," *Journal of Religion* 52 (1972), 22–40, 25.

131. To be credible, a claim had to be judged credible by the "universally human experience of the gift and demand of authentic existence," which in turn is "determined only by critically interpreting the whole history of human culture and religion." "Sources of Religious Authority in Liberal Protestantism," *Journal of the American Academy of Religion* 44 (1976), 403–16, 412 n.12, 415–16. Statements such as these caused at least one commentator to conclude that Ogden's use of experience is misleading, implying some kind of empirical claim while Ogden intended "a very specific philosophical interpretation of experience...." Owen C. Thomas, "Theology and Experience," *Harvard Theological Review* 78:1–2 (1985): 179–201, 186.

that theology's claims are "not subject to any strictly empirical mode of verification."[132] In light of such statements, I interpret his latest statements, such as that theological claims can be judged to be credible (or not) by reference to "existential truth" that is "given only through common human experience" as a transcendental criterion, and not an "empirical" criterion strictly construed.[133] In other words, "common human experience" refers to whatever is common to *any and all* experiences or acts of thought.[134]

This means that assessing the credibility of theological claims is and must be a philosophical task.[135] For Ogden, theological claims cannot be judged credible (or not) through any appeal to either scripture or tradition or any other kind of authority. Instead, the norm of credibility requires that the credibility of theological claims be assessed by appeal to human reason alone. Thus, this philosophical aspect of theology is and must be a thoroughly secular undertaking.[136] For Ogden, the great achievement of the Enlightenment, and one that must not be discarded, is "the consistent

132. Schubert M. Ogden, "The Experience of God: Critical Reflections on Hartshorne's Theory of Analogy," in *Existence and Actuality: Conversations with Charles Hartshorne*, ed. John B. Cobb, Jr., and Franklin I. Gamwell (Chicago: Univ. of Chicago Press, 1984), 16–37, 18.

133. Ogden, *Doing Theology Today*, 16. As noted, Owen Thomas also interprets "experience" in Ogden's norm of credibility as referring "not to the actual experience of modern people as they themselves interpret it, but to a quite specific interpretation of it" (Thomas, "Theology and Experience," 186). Later in the same article, Thomas says that Ogden's understanding of experience is less actual experiences than "an alleged transcendental analysis of experience or of the conditions of the possibility of all experience, or to various specific philosophical analyses and constructions of experience" (Thomas, "Theology and Experience," 192).

134. Still, there is a sense in which the norm is empirical, if that term is construed more broadly, because the norm works by testing whether claims can be verified by reference to experience (including both sensuous and nonsensuous experience). Thus, Ted Peters argues that "the ultimate court of appeal in maters of truth is common human experience and reasoned reflection upon that experience. It is this criterion which makes Ogden's method an empirical rather than an authoritative one" ("Theological Method of Schubert Ogden," 125–34, 128).

135. Christian systematic theology "has an essential philosophical aspect insofar as the claim of Christian witness to be adequate to its content also comprises the further claim that it is credible to human existence, practically as well as theoretically" (Schubert M. Ogden, "The Nature and State of Theological Scholarship and Research," *Theological Education* 24 [Autumn 1987]: 120–31, 125).

136. "In its philosophical aspect, in which it validates this further claim of Christian witness to be credible, systematic theology necessarily presupposes philosophical theology as an independent secular, or nontheological, discipline. In fact, unless philosophical theology were thus independent of Christian theology, it could not be the critical reflection that systematic theology requires in order to validate the claim of Christian witness to be credible as well as appropriate" (Ogden, "Nature and State of Theological Scholarship and Research," 120–31, 125).

affirmation of the unique authority of human reason over all other putative authorities."[137] If human reason is to have this unique authority, it must be because there is a common aspect to the experience of all human beings, simply by virtue of their being human, to which reason can refer or appeal in validating claims. "No matter what the claim is or who the claimant may be, whether or not it is valid can be determined only by critically validating it; this means, finally, only by discourse or argument somehow grounded in our common experience simply as human beings."[138]

For Ogden, the norm of credibility must be construed in this Enlightenment fashion because of the essential nature of religious claims.[139] All religious assertions at least imply "a claim to unique authority." Any religious assertion can contain such a claim to authority only because it also claims to be true, and this truth-claim is identical in kind to the truth-claims of any and all assertions. That is, religious assertions by their nature claim to be true, "and true not in some utterly different sense from that in which anything else is true, but in essentially the same sense, in that it, too, can be verified in some way or other by common human experience and reason. Far from denying reason's unique authority, then, a religion implicitly affirms it."[140]

During the middle 1970s, Ogden's engagement with liberation theology deepened his understanding of the norm of credibility. The ideology critique pressed forcefully by thinkers such as Gustavo Gutierrez and Jon

137. Schubert M. Ogden, "The Enlightenment is Not Over," in *Knowledge and Belief in America*, ed. William M. Shea and Peter A. Huff (Cambridge: Cambridge Univ. Press, 1995), 321–27, 322. Human reason, for Ogden, is "our capacity not only to make or imply various kinds of claims to validity but also, and above all, to validate critically all such claims as and when they become problematic by appropriate kinds of discourse or argument involving appeal in one way or another to common human experience" (Ogden, "The Enlightenment is Not Over.")

138. Ogden, "The Enlightenment is Not Over," 322–23. On Ogden's assessment, the achievement of F. D. Maurice was that he recognized precisely this point. Maurice understood, that is, that "the immediate object of theological reflection is the Christian witness of faith while the only criteria of theological statements, as regards their meaning and truth, are those established with human existence as such, and thus our own experience and reason simply as men" (Schubert M. Ogden, "The Reformation that We Want," *Anglican Theological Review* 54 [Oct. 1972]: 260–73, 262).

139. Religion, in Ogden's view, is "neither simply a metaphysics nor simply an ethics, [but] it is in a peculiar way both." This means that "religion is at once an understanding of the ultimate reality of self, others, and the whole and an understanding of our own possibilities of existing and acting in relation to this ultimate reality" (Schubert M. Ogden, *Faith and Freedom: Toward a Theology of Liberation* [Nashville, Tenn.: Abingdon Press, 1979; rev. ed. 1989], 32).

140. Ogden, "The Enlightenment is Not Over," 326. That is, a religion "affirms both the right and the responsibility of reason to validate critically all claims to validity, including its own claims to truth and unique authority" (326–27).

Sobrino convinced Ogden that he needed to think more deeply about the moral aspect of the norm of credibility.[141] Thus Ogden's interaction with liberation theology allowed him to clarify his own definition of Christian faith in terms of *freedom*. Indeed, he says that "faith is the existence of freedom." Christian faith particularly is and must be "a way of understanding and acting *in* freedom and *for* it."[142] This means that faith must be both liberated and liberating.[143]

Ogden's interaction with liberation theology, then, helped him to give an even more distinctly modern cast to what he meant by faith. He had long talked about it as an authentic self-understanding. In *Faith and Freedom* he clarifies that the central defining principle of faith as authentic self-understanding is freedom. Faith is "existence in freedom—freedom *from* all things and *for* all things."[144] Ogden, as we have seen, has attempted

141. This did not, however, occur in his initial engagement with liberation theology. Instead, Ogden's first engagement with liberation theology helped him to clarify the way in which the notion of freedom was fundamental to his own theological method. *Faith and Freedom*, his first sustained contribution to liberation theology, was published in 1979. Liberation theology, with its call for liberation of oppressed peoples, can be seen as in some sense complementary to Ogden's own effort to forge a thoroughly modern vision of theology that takes seriously the autonomy of human reason. Still, Ogden did not believe that most liberation theologians had succeeded in their task. One of the ways they had failed, in Ogden's opinion, was by having an overly restrictive or provincial understanding of the various and subtle ways in which not only human beings, but other creatures as well, are kept in bondage. In Ogden's view, there were four points at which liberation theologies typically failed. First, he viewed them by and large as more witness than theology. Second, though they had rightly focused on the existential meaning of God for us, they had given insufficient attention, in Ogden's view, to the metaphysical being of God in itself. Third, they had not adequately distinguished between two different though related forms of liberation (redemption and emancipation). The fourth point is the one related in the text. See Ogden, *Faith and Freedom*, 30–35. Later in this text, Ogden elaborates this fourth point, arguing that liberation theologies are inadequate insofar as they ignore the bondage of non-human creatures and their need for liberation from exploitation (Ogden, *Faith and Freedom*, 107–108). This text has been criticized from a variety of angles. James Cone feels that Ogden's understanding of common human experience is not common at all, but is essentially limited to the experience of North American white men (James Cone, review of *Faith and Freedom* by Schubert Ogden, *Union Seminary Quarterly Review* 35 [Spring-Summer 1980]: 296–300). Ted Peters believes that liberation theology's first point of failure on Ogden's account is unfair. Even on Ogden's own construal of theology, he argues, a number of writers (e.g., Cone, Letty Russell, and Gustavo Gutiérrez) are in fact doing theology rather than only witness (Ted Peters, review of *Faith and Freedom* by Schubert Ogden, *Interpretation* 35 [Jan. 1981]: 78–82).

142. Ogden, *Faith and Freedom*, 42–43. For Ogden, "faith understood as an existence in utter trust in God's love and utter loyalty to God's cause as they are decisively revealed in Christ can only be an existence in freedom...." (47).

143. Ogden, *Faith and Freedom*, 55.

144. Ogden, *Faith and Freedom*, 55. It is at this point that Ogden feels his own style of doing theology can make a contribution to liberation theology. Some critics view

to integrate Heidegger's and Bultmann's existential interpretation of human existence with the metaphysics of Hartshorne's philosophical theology. And the organizing principle of Hartshorne's process metaphysics is the principle of freedom. As Ogden puts it, "one of the ways—and, in my opinion, the most adequate way—of describing what process metaphysics is all about is to say that it is the metaphysics that takes 'freedom' as its key concept."[145] If this is the case, then freedom is the most fundamental aspect of all reality. Indeed, Ogden states that "even the least actual thing must bear at least some likeness to the eminent freedom of God...."[146] Because Ogden sees freedom as so fundamental to the metaphysical structure of reality, he seeks to make his theological method consistent with this metaphysical vision. Thus the characteristically modern vision of the autonomy of reason is the touchstone of Ogden's theological method. It is his initial engagement with liberation theology that helps him to articulate the connection between method and metaphysics in terms of freedom. In this work, he concludes that the real bondage of theology is when it is bound to remain the rationalization of positions already taken instead of critical reflection on their meaning and truth from the standpoint of human experience and reason.[147]

It was not until after the publication of *Faith and Freedom* that Ogden was able to incorporate the message of the liberation theologians into his own work. In 1980, in an article in *The Christian Century*, Ogden stated that issues of justice needed to be incorporated into his theological method.[148] By 1980, it had become "clear to [him] that what is required if theology

---

Ogden's contribution to liberation theology in a more negative light. Anselm Min, for example, argues that the poor, as victims of systemic injustice, "embody and suffer in their own life situation the universal human crisis of the time" (Anselm K. Min, "Praxis and Theology in Recent Debates," *Scottish Journal of Theology* 39 [1986]: 529–49, 545–46). Thus, he argues, the transcendental role fulfilled by the horizon of the poor justifies the privileged epistemic position occupied by this horizon. As a result, to "demand transcendence of all particular group experiences and perspectives [as he takes Ogden to do] would be to deny the socio-historical origin of human knowledge and revert to the ahistorical conception of human perspectives which is not without its own—although hidden—ideological content and consequence" (547).

145. Ogden, *Faith and Freedom*, 61. Indeed, process metaphysics "differs from every other because of the consistent and thoroughgoing way in which it generalizes the key concept of freedom" (61).

146. Ogden, *Faith and Freedom*, 114. Recall Descartes' theory of error, expressed in the *Meditations*, in which he describes the will, precisely because it is free, as the most perfect (and most like God) of all human faculties.

147. "Because the real root of theology's historic bondage is the underlying conception of its task as, in effect, the rationalization of positions already taken, the only way in which it can be emancipated is by reconceiving its task, instead, as critical reflection on such positions." Ogden, *Faith and Freedom*, 122.

148. Schubert M. Ogden, "Faith and Freedom: How My Mind Has Changed," *The Christian Century* 97 (Dec. 17, 1980): 1241–44.

is to deal satisfactorily with the issues of action and justice ... is a theological method comprising thoroughgoing de-ideologizing and political interpretation."[149] In his important work, *The Point of Christology*, which appeared two years later, Ogden did indeed attempt to integrate the gist of the liberation theologians' message into his own method. As we have already seen, in this work, Ogden maintains that to ask about the credibility of a claim is to ask about its truth conditions. There, with respect to claims about Jesus, Ogden states that

> The only condition of truthfully asserting it [a claim about Jesus] is satisfied if the God whose gift and demand are made fully explicit through Jesus is indeed what is ultimately real and if the possibility of faith in this God that Jesus explicitly authorizes is indeed our authentic possibility as human beings.[150]

This means that there is both a moral and a metaphysical aspect to the norm of credibility. And by now Ogden is clear that the central element of both aspects is that of freedom. The history of modern theology in the West, as Ogden reads it, has been determined by the modern quest for freedom and the secular culture that is the outcome and instrument of it. The two crucial features of this quest are the rise of modern science and technology and of the modern historical consciousness. These two features mean that now any appeal to authority can have only a strictly provisional validity.[151]

Unfortunately, however, the modern quest for freedom has not given social or economic benefits to the overwhelming majority of human beings in the world. The static class divisions of premodern and early modern times have not been removed, but generally only transformed into dynamic ones. In response, Christianity has not always adopted a prophetic role, but has often allowed itself to be used to provide legitimation for these divisions. This, in turn, has negative ramifications for the credibility of its message.[152] Consequently, if the Christian message is to be framed in terms of this modern quest for freedom, this quest must be seen not only as freedom from ignorance, but also as freedom from want and oppression. Thus, just as in earlier writings Ogden stated that the norm of credibility has a metaphysical and a moral aspect, here he says that it must have two prongs. Christian theological claims must be

---

149. Ogden, "Faith and Freedom: How My Mind Has Changed," 1242.
150. Ogden, *Point of Christology*, 87–88.
151. Ogden, *Point of Christology*, 89–90.
152. Ogden, *Point of Christology*, 92.

theoretically credible; and they must be practically credible in the face of the contemporary quest for justice. Theoretical credibility requires (negatively) demythologizing, or (positively) existentialist interpretation, which I have discussed previously. Ogden uses the notion of practical credibility here to deepen the moral aspect of the norm of credibility in such a way as to give it important political elements. Practical credibility, then, has an analogous structure to theoretical credibility. It requires (negatively) "de-ideologizing," or (positively) political interpretation.[153]

By "de-ideologizing," Ogden means interpreting the meaning of Christology (and, by implication, other theological claims) so as to disengage it from the economic, social, political and cultural world whose injustices it is used to legitimate.[154] Ideology, in Ogden's definition, is "a more or less comprehensive understanding of human existence, of how to exist and act as a human being, that functions to justify the interests of a particular group or individual by representing these interests as the demands of disinterested justice."[155] That is, ideology provides its own criteria of rationalization that overdetermine the assessment of its own interests as just. Ogden believes that de-ideologizing is authorized by the New Testament precisely because it proclaims justice to be the sole criterion by which relations among human beings can be justified.[156] Negatively, de-ideologizing involves unmasking the dominant interests that seek to legitimate unjust economic, political, social or cultural structures through distorted criteria of rationalization. Positively, political interpretation is an explication "of the implications of the Christian witness for the specifically political aspect of moral responsibility."[157]

153. Ogden, *Point of Christology*, 93–94.
154. Ogden, *Point of Christology*, 94.
155. Ogden, *Point of Christology*, 94.
156. Ogden's articulation of this point could be refined a bit. He says that "the primary use of ideology in the New Testament is not to justify the interests of some human beings against the just interests of others, but rather to give concrete content to Christian moral responsibility by making clear that it has to do precisely with establishing justice in human relations" (Ogden, *Point of Christology*, 95 [citations omitted]). On my understanding, given Ogden's definition of ideology (which I judge not to be controversial), to give "content to Christian moral responsibility" in this way is not to use ideology at all. I have tried to express this understanding in the text.
157. Ogden, *Point of Christology*, 95.

IV. CONCLUDING REMARKS

Ogden's method of interpreting and validating theological claims can be characterized as existential and transcendental and quintessentially liberal.[158] These characteristics are displayed in his dual criteria of adequacy, and they are characterized by a concern for the three themes of liberal theology I identified in chapter one. The criterion of appropriateness to Jesus Christ is existential in that it is designed to answer the existential question of the meaning or significance of ultimate reality for us. The criterion of credibility is transcendental in that, in order to be valid, theological claims must be verified by common human experience and reason, and Ogden derives his articulation of common human experience through a transcendental analysis of the conditions of the possibility of any and all acts of human subjectivity.

Thus, Ogden understands properly interpreted theological claims, and the two criteria that he uses to assess them, to be (at least ultimately) existential and transcendental. Consequently, the descriptive senses associated with such claims are made up entirely of elements of human experience. Ogden's transcendental argument for God's existence proceeds from his transcendental analysis of human subjectivity and yields an understanding of God whose existence (unlike that of all others) is necessary. The descriptive sense Ogden associates with "God" is thus unique and picks out God alone as its referent. This allows him to meet the demands of Flew and others who ask how Ogden's God can be distinguished from an imaginary one or no God at all.

The descriptive senses associated with the predicates of theological claims are also, in Ogden's view, entirely existential and thus are derived from elements of human experience. To use Russell's terms, we can therefore have knowledge, either through acquaintance or through description, of whether the conditions described in those descriptive senses are satisfied or not. Therefore, in my own judgment, Ogden's construal of theological claims and his criteria for assessing them satisfy the descriptivist

---

158. The roots of Ogden's thought in process theology are deep and widely recognized. This alone would earn him a place squarely in the tradition of liberal theology. Indeed, as David Tracy once remarked (in conversation), process theology is the expression *par excellence* of the modern impulse in theology. Yet his mature, constructive program extends beyond the tradition of process metaphysics. His subtle integration of Bultmann's existential hermeneutics, Whitehead's analysis of subjectivity, Hartshorne's concept of God, and Lonergan's transcendental method was unique in liberal theology. It gives him a method that is as clear and coherent a statement of the central concerns of liberal theology as one could want.

demands of falsification theorists such as Flew. Further, because Ogden developed his theological method during a time roughly coincident with his extensive engagement with Flew, I think it reasonable to view his method (including its interpretation of theological claims) as being motivated to some significant extent by the descriptivist requirements presupposed by the falsification challenge. If we view those requirements as valid, then I think Ogden has done a good job of satisfying them. As we will see, however, there are good reasons for rejecting these requirements, and the descriptivist understandings of meaning and reference that go with them.

PART TWO

Postliberal Theology and Ordinary Language Philosophy

CHAPTER FIVE

The Barthian Project in Postliberal Perspective

The responses to the falsification controversy from liberal theologians by and large accepted the descriptivist understanding of language that was fundamental to the argument of the falsification theorists. Postliberals and Barthians might have expected as much, for in their view the biggest problem with liberal theology's method was its anthropological starting point. But this is precisely what descriptivism required of theology, particularly in its embodiment in the falsification theorists. By requiring reference to proceed by way of descriptions, and then requiring knowledge by acquaintance to be at the bottom of epistemic justification, the dominant empiricist currents in English language philosophy seemed to require such an anthropological starting point.

Both in the nineteenth and twentieth centuries, liberal theology has been a complex and nuanced endeavor, no less so in its method than in its positive dogmatic pronouncements. Harnack himself, though he was one of those Barth had foremost in mind in his declaration that liberal theology represented a "dead end," gave an analysis of Christianity as a particularized starting point for addressing the question "What is religion?" As he was read by Barth, though, Harnack and other liberal theologians approached theological questions "from below," by beginning with human experience. Whatever one thinks of this analysis, human experience and reason have clearly been important in liberal theology's method of validating theological claims. And this implies that Barth, notwithstanding what is arguably his misreading of Harnack, had an acute insight into the method of liberal theology. What Barth feared most was the specter of Ludwig Feuerbach. On Barth's reading, Feuerbach presents a powerful case that theological pronouncements about God are no more than projections of the realities of human subjectivity onto a blank divine screen. In Barth's view, liberal theology's anthropological starting point deprived it of any meaningful response to Feuerbach.

Barth's critique of liberal theology, as is well known, has been profoundly influential on postliberal theologians. In this chapter, I shall be less interested in Barth himself than in the way he has been read by postliberals. And in my view one of the best resources for understanding Barth's influence on postliberal theology is Hans Frei's doctoral dissertation, "The Doctrine of Revelation in the Thought of Karl Barth, 1909–1922: The Nature of Barth's Break with Liberalism," which he wrote under the direction of H. Richard Niebuhr.[1] It was completed in 1956, and it concerned the changes that Barth's theological method underwent as a result of his break with liberalism. As he wrote his dissertation, Frei became convinced that Barth's break with liberalism was the most important event in protestant theology in the modern period.[2] At the end of his life, Frei was working on a typology of Christian theological method. In it, Frei argues that Barth's method of doing theology is the type that is most defensible against deconstructionist critics. He was wary of deconstruction and feared that the kind of hermeneutic method practiced by David Tracy and Paul Ricoeur is vulnerable to it. These fears bear remarkable resemblances to Barth's fear of Feuerbach and Barth's belief that nineteenth-century liberal theology was vulnerable to Feuerbach's critique of theological claims about God. Fundamentally, Barth believed that theology must move away from an anthropological starting point if it is to avoid Feuerbach's critique. Frei believes that deconstructionist critique of hermeneutic theory (whose instantiation in theology Frei sees as the most prominent heir of modern liberal theology) is structurally very similar to that of Feuerbach. Consequently, he sees his own project as a continuation of Barth's.

Frei, George Lindbeck, and other postliberals, in their effort to continue Barth's project, enlist philosophical allies. Unlike liberal theologians, postliberals truly have rejected descriptivist requirements for meaning and successful

1. Hans Wilhelm Frei, "The Doctrine of Revelation in the Thought of Karl Barth, 1909–1922: The Nature of Barth's Break with Liberalism" (Ph.D. diss., Yale Univ., 1956). An edited version was published to commemorate the tenth anniversary of Frei's death. Hans W. Frei, "The Doctrine of Revelation in Karl Barth," in *Ten Year Commemoration of the Life of Hans Frei (1922–1988)*, ed. Giorgy Olegovich (New York: Semenenko Foundation, 1999), 103–87. An earlier version of the analysis I present in this chapter can be found in John Allan Knight, "The Barthian Heritage of Hans W. Frei," *Scottish Journal of Theology* 61:3 (Aug. 2008): 307–26.
2. "No more crucial event has taken place in modern Protestant theology than Karl Barth's break with liberalism" (Frei, "Doctrine of Revelation," iii).

reference. They do this through their adoption of Wittgenstein's perspective on the meaning of religious language and on the lack of any requirements for successful reference. Before getting to this, however, it is helpful to consider the most important themes in Barth's work from a postliberal perspective.

To summarize briefly, Frei elucidates three themes in Barth, all of which are designed to move Barth's theological thinking away from its anthropological starting point. First, as he makes his break from liberalism, Barth begins to emphasize the priority of ontology over epistemology.[3] In Barth's view, one of the things that made liberal theology subject to Feuerbach's critique was that it began with epistemological considerations, and then refused to make claims that could not meet its epistemic criteria. After the break, Barth insists that theology must begin with ontological affirmations about God, as these affirmations are given in the Incarnation and the testimony to it in the Bible. Frei makes a similar move in insisting on the priority of the biblical narrative in theology. The second theme is closely related to the first and concerns theological method. After the break, Barth insists that theological method must be subordinate to, and be governed by, positive ontological statements about God. It is easy to see that this insistence is derived from Barth's prioritizing of ontology over epistemology. It implies as well that theology cannot be truly systematic, because Barth believes that all true systematizing will be anthropologically and epistemologically driven. Frei likewise insists that theological method must be governed by the revelation of God given in the biblical narratives. The third theme concerns the interpretation of the biblical texts. Barth insists that interpretive method must be governed by his methodological commitments and his ontological affirmations about God.

I. THE PRIORITY BARTH GIVES TO ONTOLOGY OVER EPISTEMOLOGY

On Frei's reading, Barth's break with liberalism reversed the relation of ontology to epistemology. Before the break (i.e., prior to 1915), epistemology not only determined the agenda of theology, but was conceptually prior as well. During his liberal phase, Barth understood one of the theologian's most important tasks to be that of finding normative conceptions to express the experience of Christ. Frei views this task as fundamentally epistemological: it is concerned with "the possibility of knowing God and saying something significant about that 'knowledge.'"[4] Barth is

3. "Among other things, this [Barth's break with liberalism] means a total reversal of his understanding of theological epistemology" (Frei, "Doctrine of Revelation," 118).
4. Frei, "Doctrine of Revelation," 26, 30.

not as concerned, that is, with the fact or notion of revelation in itself as with the rational explication of revelatory experience.[5] This epistemological concern marks Barth as a liberal during this early period, as does his basic "relational" approach to the problem (an approach or method of *Ineinanderstellung*). There must be some mode or capacity in human beings, on this approach, that permits them to receive God's revelation.[6]

When Barth came to consider the question of God, however, Barth was haunted from the beginning by the ghost of Feuerbach. Barth takes there to be an obvious antinomy between the particular concrete encounter with God, which is an experience of positive or particular revelation, and the universal or transcendent nature of God. Even in his liberal period, or at least the latter part of it, Barth refuses to resolve this antinomy, because, among other things, he wants to resist Feuerbach's critique. This refusal leaves Barth with a dialectic in thought form that provides a continuity with his postliberal dialectical method.[7] In Frei's view, what is novel in Barth's break with liberalism is not, therefore, his dialectical method, but his "rejection of immediate experience as the source of faith."[8] Barth was also concerned, during the liberal period, with the primacy of God, and he rejects any notion of cooperation in which divine and human work constitute cooperating means toward grace. Before the break, he sees the method of *Ineinanderstellung* as preventing such cooperation. After the break, however, he comes to regard this method as a conceptualization of divine-human cooperation and therefore rejects it.[9]

Even after the break with liberalism, epistemology continued to have a strong influence on the direction of Barth's theology, in Frei's view, but its relation to ontology changes. During the most strongly dialectical period, ontology and epistemology seem to be collapsed into one another.[10] After the second edition of *Der Römerbrief*, however, ontology begins to assume a conceptual primacy. By the time of the book on Anselm, the conceptual primacy of ontology is largely accomplished. After the break, in other

---

5. Frei, "Doctrine of Revelation," 31.
6. See Frei, "Doctrine of Revelation," 42–48.
7. A related form of this dialectic can be seen in Barth's attempt to be Christocentric in the early period: "To Barth's thinking, the endeavor to be totally Christocentric and yet to think completely as a 'man of culture' is bound to result in a clash" (Frei, "Doctrine of Revelation," 69).
8. Frei, "Doctrine of Revelation," 63.
9. The method of *Ineinanderstellung* involves an attempt to depict the nature of God and God's redemptive activity toward humanity via an articulation of human capacity. It involves, that is, an anthropological orientation to theology in general and the doctrine of God in particular.
10. Frei, "Doctrine of Revelation," 199.

words, the basis of the knowledge of God does not lie in any immanent relation between human existence and God, nor in immediate experience or *Ineinanderstellung*. Instead, "The ground and possibility of knowledge of God lies within the nature of God as he reveals himself of his own free grace. Hence, the epistemological judgment of faith is *in ordo essendi* (which is also normative for the *ordo cognoscendi*) preceded by, and based on a judgment of objective, ontic reality—the reality of God."[11]

According to Frei, the priority of ontology is the result of Barth's engagement with the biblical realists.[12] For them, the activity of the Holy Spirit and scripture are correlated in the Word of God.[13] This is what enables Barth to assert the primacy of God's revealing activity even in the area of the knowledge of God.[14] This correlation of the Holy Spirit and scripture in the Word of God, a correlation that is carried out wholly by divine action, is the ground not only of our relationship with God, but also of our knowledge of God.[15] Barth's basic dogmatic plan, then, is as follows: "[T]he content of revelation is the Word of God; the objective ground and possibility of revelation is the Incarnation of the Word of God; the subjective actuality and possibility of revelation lies in the outpouring of the Holy Spirit."[16] This is what Frei calls Barth's radical realism, and it is characteristic of his break with liberalism. It is the avenue through which Barth attempts to avoid relationalism on the one hand and fundamentalism on the other. For his part, Frei will also attempt to navigate between two shoals: on the one hand, a liberal (anthropologically derived) scheme of understanding into which biblical texts must fit and, on the other, a fundamentalist literalism. In the later 1920s and 1930s, however,

11. Frei, "Doctrine of Revelation," 119 (citations omitted).
12. The most important of these seem to be J. C. Blumhardt and Hermann Kutter. It was biblical realism that allowed Barth to express his belief in the objective, literal truth of the events narrated in scripture, "without being tied thereby to a fundamentalist, literalist interpretation of these events" (Frei, "Doctrine of Revelation," 150–51; see also 148–67, 434–38).
13. In Frei's view, "the fundamental conviction in regard to theological theory of knowledge on the part of Biblical realists is the correlation of the Holy Spirit and Scripture in the Word of God" ("Doctrine of Revelation," 502).
14. "This, then, is the first and most important lesson which Barth learned from Biblical realism: in order to assert as normative (not only negatively but positively in dialectical fashion) that the concrete content of the limit placed on man, history, and nature is the self-revealing God, one must begin with God whose revelation is altogether founded in his freedom. Thus our relation to him is founded solely on his freedom to be for us in grace and revelation. To know this is to discover it in one source only—in Scripture" (Frei, "Doctrine of Revelation," 504).
15. "Here, then, is Barth's typical affirmation during this period, that the ground of the relationship with God and of the knowledge of this relationship is the correlation which lies totally within the action of God, in the correlation of Spirit and Scripture which is the Word of God." Frei, "The Doctrine of Revelation," 510.
16. Frei, "Doctrine of Revelation," 119 n.161.

Barth argues that in this correlating act of God, God becomes analogous to "that which it creates in the recipient: faith as obedience—including rational obedience."[17] Even this analogy, however, is grounded in the free activity of God, and it is this grounding in which Barth's assertion of the primacy of ontology over epistemology consists.[18]

II. BARTH'S SUBORDINATION OF METHOD TO POSITIVE STATEMENTS ABOUT GOD

The next theme that is important to Frei is that of theological method, and this theme has three sub-moments. The first is closely related to the primacy of ontology over epistemology. Despite this primacy of ontology, on Frei's reading, Barth's basic concern remains epistemological: How are we to understand (or come to rational belief about) the relation of humanity to God? Throughout his career, both before and after the break with liberalism, the relation of humanity to God has primacy—indeed, almost a kind of transcendental primacy—over all other human relations.[19] But the way Barth comes to understand this relation changes after the break. In the liberal period, the relation itself was primary; it could be extrapolated from anthropology. After the break, however, the relation can no longer be understood "from below." Humanity can never make its way to God. Knowledge of God can no longer come by inferring a relation to our creator on the basis of an understanding of creation or of human experience. That is, our epistemic access to God must be construed in light of the primacy of Barth's ontological affirmations about God. Methodologically, this means that the doctrine of revelation must move into the foreground and become asymmetrical.[20] As it does, the objective content of revelation becomes conceptually independent of and prior to understanding.[21] Searching for God along the path from the finite to the infinite is impossible, for all one sees is the "constantly receding limits of finitude." On the other hand, "if

17. Frei, "Doctrine of Revelation," 121.
18. Frei, "Doctrine of Revelation," 120–23.
19. "At all times Barth has firmly held to the conviction that we are always in the presence of something or someone not created, and that this relationship between creature or finite man and the infinite is the prime relation in and through which all other relations take place" (Frei, "Doctrine of Revelation," 108–109).
20. "In revelation, he comes to see, there is a priority of ontic affirmation over epistemological or noetic affirmation" (Frei, "Doctrine of Revelation," 565).
21. The issue with which theology must come to terms is "to see the originality of the infinite as the origin and goal of the finite, to see the path from the infinite to the finite, rather than the path from the finite to the infinite" (Frei, "Doctrine of Revelation," 111).

one sees the path from the infinite to the finite, one sees God in his relation to his creature.... But this path, this view of God in his relation to his creature is possible only for God himself."[22] Thus relationalism is impossible, because "there is no synthesis between the endeavor of man seeking to relate himself to God, and God's relating of himself to man."[23] In Frei's view, this constitutes Barth's break with liberalism: Barth no longer construes human experience as constituted by a relation between faith and its object such that an analysis of human experience as such can yield any knowledge of God.[24] So construed, this break means that the relation of humanity to God must be derivative from the doctrine of God.[25]

Barth's problem, then—his "enduring concern" after the liberal phase—is, as Frei puts it, to find "a proper understanding of the relation of God to man within a proper *doctrine of God*."[26] This will give him the clue to the proper theological method. The starting point for finding this understanding of God's relation to us is Jesus Christ. Thus Barth's Christocentricity carries forward from the liberal period throughout Barth's career. After the break, though, Christ is no longer conceptually a step along a path from humanity to God. Instead, the doctrine of the Incarnation is also derivative from the doctrine of God, and this, Frei argues, accounts for the growing importance of the doctrine of predestination in Barth's thought. Theology must be Christocentric simply because of God's act of predestination.[27] According to Frei, "The question about Jesus Christ is no longer, why is he and not someone else the actualizer of our religious experience? The issue instead is to find the eternal ground for Jesus Christ's incarnation within the objective ground of the relation of God to man."[28]

22. Frei, "Doctrine of Revelation," 111 (citation omitted).
23. Frei, "Doctrine of Revelation," 112.
24. "Barth breaks radically with his liberal past, because he refuses to acknowledge a relational nexus in which faith and its historical content meet in experience" (Frei, "Doctrine of Revelation," 113).
25. "Positively expressed, this means that the relationship of God to man is wholly grounded in God" (Frei, "Doctrine of Revelation," 115).
26. Frei, "Doctrine of Revelation," 126 (emphasis in original).
27. Frei, "The Doctrine of Revelation," 128–29. "Double predestination is the unique act of God in Jesus Christ...." (129).
28. Frei, "Doctrine of Revelation," 127. When Barth broke with liberalism, what he opposed most fundamentally was liberalism's "confusion or synthesis of Christocentric revelation with religion" (Frei, "Doctrine of Revelation," iv). To resist this, Barth attempted "to express the sovereignty of God in his self-revelation over the very means and the mode of reception of revelation" (iv). Frei argues that Barth had no choice but to try to express this notion of sovereignty through the available traditions, which were academic liberalism, biblical realism and skepticism (iv–vii). Through these conceptual traditions, or some combination of them, Barth sought "to found the doctrine of revelation solely upon the doctrine of God, and to do so without violating the freedom and subjectivity and spontaneity of man" (vii).

Frei's reading of Barth's writings on Christology outlined the following problem: "[I]s the relation in faith to Jesus Christ the clue to the understanding of faith, history and revelation? Or, is it conversely true that Jesus Christ is a fact understood from the prior perspective of a theological and/or philosophical system?"[29] After the break, Barth insists that any resolution of this issue must sharply distinguish between the divine and human dimensions. Frei asserts that one can do this in three ways: "by sheer proclamation, i.e., by the refusal to allow methodology to predominate; by 'dialectic' or by analogy."[30] Barth tried all these ways. He wrote the second edition of *Der Römerbrief* during a strongly dialectical period, and by the time of the book on Anselm he was using a doctrine of analogy. But throughout all his post-break changes, he sought to have his positive affirmations about God govern not only the content of his thought, but his method as well.

This refusal of primacy to method is the second sub-moment of Frei's concern with theological method in Barth. Even during his liberal period, Barth had stressed the primacy of God. He followed Schleiermacher during this period in refusing to see faith as independent of revelation. Thus, when Barth attempts to stress the "absolute priority, independence, and sovereignty" of God's grace, for Frei this means preeminently to work out both a theological method and an understanding of our knowledge of God in terms of God's priority, independence, and sovereignty.[31] After the break, this emphasis on the methodological priority of God eventually developed into a consistent doctrine of predestination.[32] There were other continuities as well, including Barth's Christocentricity. During the liberal period Barth saw Christology as the only content of theology, which must be expressed in a relational form. After the break, Christology remains the only content of theology, but it now becomes an eschatological notion giving content to the proper object of theology, the Word of God.[33]

29. Frei, "Doctrine of Revelation," 65–66. "Barth in his early days equates Christ with history and faith with experience...." (72). The question formulated by Frei and quoted in the text, it seems to me, anticipates Frei's understanding of the central problem not only of Christology, but of theological method.
30. Frei, "Doctrine of Revelation," 554–55.
31. Frei, "Doctrine of Revelation," 439.
32. Frei, "Doctrine of Revelation," 431–32. Further, on Frei's reading, Barth incorporates to a large degree the thought forms of German idealism, particularly as used by Hegel and Schleiermacher.
33. This does not change even after 1931, though at that point Barth no longer understood the Word of God dialectically, but through an analogy between grace and nature that "is based solely on the congruence of grace and nature given uniquely and miraculously in the Incarnation" (Frei, "Doctrine of Revelation," 433).

On Frei's view, Barth walks a fine line between two opposing dangers.[34] On the one hand, he could capitulate to the liberals by translating (or transliterating) the Word of God into his own conceptual forms. On the other, he could remain purely critical, making only dialectical statements, thus consigning theology to prolegomena that could never get beyond method to substantive content.[35] If he wanted to move past criticism to a constructive phase (i.e., positive knowledge of God), Frei poses his problem thus: How can we have any knowledge of God at all without, on the one hand, positing some immediate divine-human complementarity within human nature that survives the Fall or, on the other, relying on a supernatural revelation that sunders faith and reason?[36] To achieve positive knowledge of God while avoiding these twin sirens, Barth needs to subordinate theological method to the substantive content of his doctrine of God. But the problem is how to effect this subordination without falling back on a pre-rational (or supra-rational) supernatural revelation. It was his study of Anselm that provided Barth with the breakthrough that helped him address this question. But Barth reads Anselm much differently than does Hartshorne and Ogden. For Barth, Anselm regards faith as a call to cognitive understanding, through which we participate (in a limited way) in God's mode of being. Faith is not faith, therefore, unless it involves right belief. "Faith, he insists after Anselm, is relative to the 'Word of Christ,' and is reception, knowledge, affirmation of this Word."[37]

An important ingredient in Barth's methodological breakthrough, and one that exercises a pervasive influence on Frei, is that there can be no separation of form from content.[38] Thus, not only the content of theology, but the form as well must be brought under the lordship of Christ. Theological method cannot be prolegomena, but must be consistent with its substantive claims, especially its claims about God. In order to fulfill this intention, in Frei's view, Barth gave a leading role to the content of revelation and sought to have this content determine his method.[39] The content of revelation is concrete, undialectical, and prior to dialectic. Thus, dialectic cannot synthesize

34. Barth faced "diametrically opposed dangers at the same time in his radical realism" (Frei, "Doctrine of Revelation," 187).
35. Frei, "Doctrine of Revelation," 188.
36. Frei, "Doctrine of Revelation," 193.
37. Frei, "Doctrine of Revelation," 194.
38. Frei states that "content torn from its form is no longer the same" (Frei, "Doctrine of Revelation," 546).
39. "But one must go further and state that no conceptual content is 'given' in itself. Its meaning, on the contrary, consists in its relation to other judgments and (in principle) to the totality of thought content" (Frei, "Doctrine of Revelation," 109).

its formal and material elements.[40] Barth's breakthrough consists in the fact that "content, or rather the object, constantly dominates the thought-form in Barth's understanding. Hence, thought-form and the meaning of its content are never properly and systematically balanced in his thought."[41]

Finally (the third sub-moment of Barth's method), Frei is particularly interested in Barth's opposition to systematizing. Indeed, the place of his principal critique is in this area. After the break with liberalism, Barth continued to maintain some form of the continuing immediate presence of God to creation. Yet without some kind of relational complementarity—that is, in denying that anything about God can be read off creation—it is difficult to conceive God's immediate presence. So relationalism continued to influence Barth in that it kept epistemological concerns within Barth's field of vision. In addition, it kept Barth concerned with theological method. Barth insists that the objective content of revelation cannot be limited by predetermined epistemological limits. Thus Frei argues that the task that preoccupies Barth after the break is how to articulate "the manner in which the complete primacy, uniqueness, and subjecthood of God conditions from the very outset the manner in which we may know him."[42] Barth tries to accomplish this task by insisting that the Word of God is both the content of theology and the basis of theological method. But this insistence presents Barth with a problem: How can this insistence be made to cohere with the freedom, spontaneity, and subjectivity of human beings? Ultimately, Barth finds the answer to this question in the doctrine of double predestination. Through this doctrine, the free grace of God can be the basis of the freedom, spontaneity, and subjecthood of human beings.[43] Thus, our freedom is not grounded in any "given" relational complementarity through which God's freedom can be understood. Instead, it is the free act of God in speaking God's Word to us that funds both human subjectivity and our knowledge of the freedom and sovereignty of God. Thus revelation is based on the doctrine of God alone (through the doctrine of the Word of God), and natural theology is ruled out. In this way, Barth was able to assert the sovereignty of God not only over our destiny, but over our epistemic access to God as well. At the same time, if God is known only through God's freely spoken Word, theological method must be founded on this same doctrine

40. "There is thus a constant choice, an inconclusive dialogue between one type of language which, however inadequately, represents its object, and another type which is only a negative pointer to its object or subject and is more interested in indicating the distance between itself and its object" (Frei, "Doctrine of Revelation," 537).

41. Frei, "Doctrine of Revelation," 539.

42. Frei, "Doctrine of Revelation," 443.

43. Frei, "Doctrine of Revelation," 455.

of the Word of God, and in doing so Barth is able to assert the absolute primacy and sovereignty of God over theological method as well.[44]

This move has radical implications for theological method. It means that there can be no independent or objective standpoint from which to view the relation of Creator and creature. Further, any method that takes the free and sovereign grace as its sole focus cannot produce any theological system.[45] Theology must therefore remain critical, and cannot take a constructive turn.[46] "For dialectic is incapable of providing" positive theological content.[47] This is why, in Frei's view, Barth finally made the turn to the *analogia fidei*, and it is this analogy that enables him to defend his positive, constructive claims, as well as to provide more coherence to his thought. But it is precisely here that Frei believes he runs the greatest risk of betraying his insight that systematizing must be resisted. And it is here that Frei's appraisal of Barth takes its most critical turn:

> Under these circumstances Barth's protest—the only genuinely consistent and completely consequential protest in academic theological circles—against liberal relationalism was entirely justified. But it is not nearly as evident that Barth did not then stand in danger—a danger apparently not completely overcome—of systematizing in the opposite direction. Is it really possible to understand the knowledge of revelation, the correlation (if the negativity of dialectic can be called a correlation) of revelation and faith—solely on the ground of the doctrine of God or of revelation? Is this assertion not already too 'systematic'?[48]

III. BARTHIAN INTERPRETATION OF BIBLICAL TEXTS

The first two themes, then, that Frei takes from Barth are that epistemology must be subordinate to ontology and that this priority of ontology has implications for theological method. That is, method must be subordinate to a doctrine of God (i.e., our epistemic access to God can only be ascertained

---

44. Frei, "Doctrine of Revelation," 452–58. This dual foundation in the Word of God can tend to collapse ontology and epistemology, and in Frei's view this is what happens in the second edition of *Der Römerbrief* (460). The Word of God remains both the object and the means of knowledge (461). It is not until Barth turns to a positive doctrine of analogy that he is able to prevent the collapse of epistemology and ontology and to reassert the primacy of ontology.

45. "He wanted to emphasize the primacy of objective intention and norms over methodological considerations without committing himself thereby to a system; for he thought, then as well as subsequently, that a theological "system" is a contradiction in terms" (547).

46. Frei, "Doctrine of Revelation," 462–63.

47. Frei, "Doctrine of Revelation," 499.

48. Frei, "Doctrine of Revelation," 566–67.

on the basis of our positive ontological affirmations about God), and any systematizing must be ruled out. The third theme I wish to highlight from Frei's initial work on Barth is that of interpretation. On Frei's reading, Barth works hard to make interpretive method consistent with his substantive claims. That is, interpretive method must be governed by the methodological commitments discussed above: the primacy and priority of God's free, initiating gracious act; the impossibility of any knowledge of God in the absence of such an divine act; and the resistance to systematizing. These commitments make the reader of scripture dependent on the guidance of the Spirit as the author of scripture in order to understand the revelation that occurs through scripture. This implies, importantly, that the meaning of the scriptural texts cannot consist in their referential function. If it did, in Frei's view, the reader would have to have some knowledge of the referent to which the text refers, as well as the referential intent of the author. But this kind of knowledge is precisely what the methodological commitment to the priority of the free, initiating divine act rules out.[49] And this just means that any correlation between the "word"—the scriptural text— and the Word of God that the scriptural text reveals cannot be systematic, but must remain ad hoc.[50]

Barth's method has its price, though, in Frei's view, and the price is paid in the areas of theological anthropology and human understanding. As the doctrine of revelation gradually evolves after the second edition of *Der Römerbrief*, any understanding of human nature in Barth becomes

49. Frei states this insight as follows: "Barth discovered that the object, revelation or the Word in the Scripture, is never understood except through the guidance of the author. In fact one must put the matter more strongly than that: the Word is not understood except through the author's letter. To assume that for an understanding of the author's objective intention, his words or concepts have but 'symbolic' meaning, that they are as remote from the object as they are near to it, that they deflect to the same extent that they reflect meaning, is to assume an independent position from that of the author toward the object of his own intention. One assumes then that he has prior knowledge of that which is also the author's objective intention. But just this is impossible, especially in the case of Scripture: it is simply true that we do need the letter of Scripture to tell us of revelation. We have no independent information of this normative object" (Frei, "Doctrine of Revelation," 542).

50. "But the relation between the 'word' and the Word of God is paradoxical. It goes without saying that there is no *systematic* coincidence between them. The fact that they do become correlated is due to the non-dialectical, free activity of God in his Word" (Frei, "Doctrine of Revelation," 543). This failure of systematization also means that there is no direct or immediate presence of the Spirit to the reader, and possibly not to Paul, either: "The Spirit is not then directly or immediately present to both Paul and commentator, nor do the thoughts of Paul and of the commentator merge into each other in a timeless dimension of truth above history. There is no 'merging,' there is only pointing from each to the other, from Paul to the Spirit to the commentator; from the Spirit to Paul to the commentator" (545).

derivative from Barth's Christology.[51] Frei expresses this problem thus: "The inability to grant, unsystematically but concretely, positive content to human nature derives in large part from the fact that revelation and the doctrine of God form the ground of all doctrine, and that Jesus Christ is the sole content of that doctrine, so that everything beside him, especially in separation and 'over against' him, appears to be abstract."[52] Frei himself attempts to avoid this problem through his articulation of narrative identity. This understanding of identity allows him to retain the methodological primacy of ontological affirmations about God while giving concrete, unsystematic content to human nature. The divine revelation, theology's starting point, is given primarily through a narrative depiction of Jesus' identity, and any understanding of human nature must also derive from the concrete narrative identity of particular human beings.

IV. CONCLUDING REMARKS

These three themes in Barth's work remained important insights for postliberal theologians like Frei and his colleague George Lindbeck—the subordination of epistemology to ontology, theological method, and interpretation. If Barth's own project in theology, and in particular his turn away from liberalism, is a project worth continuing, then there must be some way of describing just what was theologically wrong with the modern or liberal turn in Protestant theology. Neither Frei nor Lindbeck were content to use Barth's own descriptions, and in order to carry on Barth's project in their own characteristic way, Frei and Lindbeck use two important resources of which Barth seemed to be unaware. At least by the 1960s, Frei begins to read the later Wittgenstein and the ordinary language philosophers, especially Gilbert Ryle. Lindbeck reads them, too, and develops views on the nature of both religion and doctrine that are heavily dependent on the later

---

51. "The doctrine of revelation gradually evolves after the second edition of *Der Römerbrief*, and true to indications already present in that period it has positive content even though that content must be dialectically presented for the most part. But there is no such positive content as a counter-part in a doctrine of man. With regard to the doctrine of God and of revelation (the two tend to merge in the dialectical period) systematization and abstractness are guarded against successfully, and the positive, purely objective intention shines through with eminent success. This is not nearly so true of the doctrine of man and of human understanding, which tend to be sublated" (Frei, "Doctrine of Revelation," 568). Consequently, in Frei's view, "even though he later denies, in his understanding of the doctrine of man, any coalescence between Christology and anthropology, it is only in the light of Christology that any and all content of anthropology may be understood" (569–70 [citations omitted]).
52. Frei, "Doctrine of Revelation," 571.

Wittgenstein. Second, Frei reads Erich Auerbach's remarkable book, *Mimesis* (1953), in which Auerbach contrasts the ancient narratives of the Hebrew Bible to the Homeric narratives, especially the *Odyssey*. Auerbach is arguably more influential on Frei than on Lindbeck, but their reading of these authors convinces them that behind the liberal turn in theology lay at least two mistaken assumptions. First, modern liberal theologians were in large part motivated by an apologetic impulse to justify or defend the claims of Christian theology to Western intellectuals that were increasingly skeptical of these claims. One of the reasons this apologetic effort or impulse was mistaken, Frei argues, was that it does not do justice to the nature of the biblical stories on which such claims are based. The apologetic impulse, that is, ignores the "tyrannical" nature of the biblical stories. In Lindbeck's view, this apologetic effort ignores Wittgenstein's insight that religious or theological statements, including doctrines, derive whatever meaning they have from their use in a language game or form of life. It therefore assumes a kind of foundationalism that is no longer tenable. Second, modern liberal theologians assumed a referential theory of meaning by which not only words, but sentences and indeed the stories themselves, have meaning only insofar as they are able to "refer" or point to entities outside the text itself. Frei takes this understanding of meaning to be contrary to the nature of the biblical stories themselves, as well as being indefensible in its own terms. That is, it assumes the kind of descriptivism that I have discussed in part I. Just as liberal theology presupposes a descriptivist approach to religious and theological language, postliberal theology is, at least in the versions of both Frei and Lindbeck, heavily dependent on the linguistic analysis of the later Wittgenstein and ordinary language philosophy. In their rejection of descriptivism, ordinary language philosophers will develop their own understanding of how language acquires meaning (though at least Wittgenstein would have denied that he was articulating any *theory* of meaning at all) that does away with the need for any theory (or even a view) of reference altogether. And though the ordinary language philosophers provide important allies to postliberal theologians in their critique of liberal theology, their views on the dispensability of reference will give postliberal theologians fits.

CHAPTER SIX

Allies for Barth's Heirs

Wittgenstein and Ordinary Language Philosophy

At least according to Barth and his postliberal heirs, the biggest problem with liberal theology's method was its anthropological starting point. But this is precisely what descriptivism required of theology (and of all other disciplines, really), specifically in its embodiment in the falsification theorists. The theology and falsification controversy, rather than bringing some new challenge to theology, simply made clear that the dominant empiricist currents in English language philosophy seemed to require such an anthropological starting point. In fact, one way to view descriptivism is to see it as the expression in philosophy of language of the empiricist currents dominant in Anglo-American philosophy in the middle of the twentieth century. By analogy, one way to view liberal theology—and, as we have seen, this is the way Schubert Ogden, viewed it—is as quintessentially the theological expression of what Whitehead called the "reformed subjectivist principle." This means in turn, or so I have argued, that descriptivism is at the heart of the method of liberal theology. And if that is the case, then rejecting the method of liberal theology (or at least rejecting it on the grounds that Barth and his postliberal followers do) requires a rejection of the descriptivist understanding of language that is at its heart. This is precisely and explicitly what postliberal theologians like Frei and Lindbeck do. They turn to the later Wittgenstein and those ordinary language philosophers, like Gilbert Ryle, whom the later Wittgenstein influenced. In his later years, Wittgenstein abandoned the project of the *Tractatus Logico-Philosophicus* on which he had embarked in his earlier years as both a follower and a critic of Russell. It will be helpful to describe briefly the project of the *Tractatus* in order to understand Wittgenstein's later thoughts on why the *Tractatus* was misguided and what the proper approach to language should be. Understanding Wittgenstein's later rejection of the *Tractatus* will require some remarks about Wittgenstein's later reflections on following a rule and the relevance of these reflections for his later understanding of linguistic meaning. Wittgenstein's later understanding of meaning inspired Ryle's writings on meaning and identity. And all these philosophical reflections provide crucial allies to postliberal development of Barth's project.

I. WITTGENSTEIN'S *TRACTATUS LOGICO-PHILOSOPHICUS*

The *Tractatus Logico-Philosophicus* (1922) is Wittgenstein's early work in which he demonstrates both that he is working under the influence of Russell and that he wants to depart from Russell's views in several respects, including the understanding of metaphysical simples and other matters.[1] Here, I want to focus on the understanding of linguistic meaning that is put forward in the *Tractatus*.[2] First, Wittgenstein asserts that there are two sorts of sentences, the most basic of which are atomic sentences. Such sentences, Wittgenstein says, provide a picture of logically possible facts or states of affairs. How are they able to do this? They do it by structuring the collection of logically proper names that the sentence contains. Logically proper names are the simplest type of linguistic expression; these names name or refer to an object, and this object constitutes the meaning of the name. Thus we can represent an atomic sentence by *a O b*, in which the object named or referred to by *a* is over, or on top of, the object named or referred to by *b*. Wittgenstein says that the atomic sentence *a O b* and the state of affairs it pictures or describes share a common form, which he calls a logical form. There is nothing intrinsic about the words used in the sentence *a O b* that causes them to refer to the objects that are their referents, and there is nothing about the sentence *a O b* that causes it to share the logical form of the state of affairs in which the referent of *a* is on top of the referent of *b*. The association of the terms and sentences with their referents is simply a matter of linguistic convention.

---

1. Ludwig Wittgenstein, *Tractatus Logico-Philosophicus*, trans. C. K. Ogden (London: Routledge & Keegan Paul, Ltd., 1922; repr., London: Routledge, 1990).
2. In this summary of the theory of meaning expressed in the *Tractatus*, I am following the excellent account of Scott Soames in *Philosophical Analysis in the Twentieth Century*, vol. 1: *The Dawn of Analysis* (Princeton, N.J.: Princeton Univ. Press, 2003), 215–20 (hereafter *Dawn of Analysis*).

When Wittgenstein says that an atomic sentence represents or refers to a logically possible fact or state of affairs, he does not mean that possible facts or possible states of affairs are entities with some kind of existence that is weaker than that of actual facts or states of affairs. Consequently, for such a sentence to be meaningful is not for it to refer to or represent some entity that constitutes its meaning. Instead, an atomic sentence is meaningful if and only if the objects named in the sentence could possibly have been arranged the way the names of those objects are arranged in the sentence. Wittgenstein calls the theory of meaning articulated in the *Tractatus* a "picture" theory of meaning, because on this view the meaning of a sentence is constituted by the picture it constructs of a possible state of affairs. The possible arrangement of objects described in the atomic sentence constitutes the meaning of the sentence. In this sense the understanding of meaning in the *Tractatus* is a *descriptivist* understanding. It is also a *truth-conditional* theory of meaning in the following sense: Each atomic sentence has a corresponding possible fact. If this possible fact obtains, the sentence is true; if not, it is not. To know what a sentence means, you must know what facts must obtain for the sentence to be true. What this means is that a sentence acquires its meanings by reference to its *truth conditions*.

Because his theory is a truth-conditional one, Wittgenstein needs to have a view about truth. He does, and it's one that is entirely expected. In the *Tractatus,* he takes an atomic sentence to be true just in case it describes an atomic fact. The sentence will describe an atomic fact if and only if the objects named in the sentence are actually arranged in the way described by the sentence. As for the second kind of sentences—nonatomic sentences— their truth or falsity will always be derived from the truth or falsity of atomic sentences. This is because there are no nonatomic facts for nonatomic sentences to describe. Instead, the only kind of facts that exist are atomic facts. Therefore, to be meaningful sentences, nonatomic sentences can only be truth-functional compounds of atomic sentences. As a result, the truth or falsity of a meaningful nonatomic sentence will be determined automatically by the truth values of its component atomic sentences. There is, of course, more to say about the way in which Wittgenstein derived nonatomic sentences from atomic sentences.[3] Nonetheless, what I have said so far suffices to give a general picture of Wittgenstein's early view of meaning. I should just recall two significant features of the Tractarian theory

3. For example, Wittgenstein developed a system of logic that used a generalized notion of a truth-function operator, and eliminated quantifiers as separate operators. Soames, *Dawn of Analysis,* 220–21.

of meaning. First, it is a *descriptivist* theory in the sense I have been using the term so far. Second, we can call it a *referential* theory in that it holds the meaning of an atomic sentence to be constituted by the possible fact or state of affairs to which the sentence refers. In the next chapter I will discuss Hans Frei's criticism of liberal theology's *referential* view of the meaning of both biblical texts and theological claims. In using this term, Frei intends to say, I believe, that the view of meaning presupposed by the liberal theologians he criticizes closely resembles the view expressed in the *Tractatus*. Postliberal theologians like Frei will reject this understanding of meaning, as eventually did Wittgenstein himself.

II. WITTGENSTEIN'S *PHILOSOPHICAL INVESTIGATIONS*

In what Wittgenstein called his earlier "picture" theory of language, the meaning of a sentence is constituted by the picture it constructs of a possible state of affairs. Early in his career, Wittgenstein believed that this "picture theory" presupposed that the logical structure of language "mirrors" the structure of reality. But after publishing the *Tractatus*, Wittgenstein gradually came to believe that it is impossible to demonstrate that language mirrors reality sufficiently to make a descriptivist (or truth-conditional or referential) theory of meaning defensible. So in the *Philosophical Investigations* (1953), Wittgenstein describes why he has rejected his former view and has come to believe that a good deal of language is not descriptive or referential, and that even the parts that do have referential or descriptive functions are not completely referential or descriptive.[4] Consequently, language cannot acquire its meaning from its ability to describe or refer to some part or aspect of the world. Instead, language gets its meaning from the role(s) it plays in an agreed pattern of usage that structures some significant and intelligible part of our lives.

He begins the *Investigations* with an example in which he sends someone to the grocery store with a slip of paper with "five red apples" written on it. The grocer opens a drawer marked "apples," looks up the word "red" in a color table, and recites the numbers one through five. For each number he recites, he takes out an apple corresponding to the color in the table. Then, Wittgenstein says, one might ask, "'But how does he know where and how

4. Ludwig Wittgenstein, *Philosophical Investigations*, 3d ed., trans. G. E. M. Anscombe (Englewood Cliffs, N.J.: Prentice-Hall, n.d.). Here again, I am following the excellent discussion of Scott Soames in *Philosophical Analysis in the Twentieth Century*, vol. 2: *The Age of Meaning* (Princeton, N.J.: Princeton Univ. Press, 2003), 3–27 (hereafter *Age of Meaning*).

he is to look up the word "red" and what he is to do with the word "five"?'—Well, I assume that he acts as I have described. Explanations come to an end somewhere.—But what is the meaning of the word 'five'?—No such thing was in question here, only how the word 'five' is used."[5] At the beginning of the *Investigations*, then, Wittgenstein redirects his discussion of meaning away from the way words or sentences can refer to parts of the world and toward a discussion of actions. In this example, to understand the meaning of the phrase "five red apples" is to understand what to do when you see them in some particular situation. Here the meaning of "five red apples" is not constituted by the phrase's ability to refer to five objects in the world that are red apples, but it is the role that the phrase plays, or the use that it performs, in some particular form of life—in this case, grocery shopping.

After this example of grocery shopping, Wittgenstein uses other examples drawn from the interactions between a builder and his assistant. In these examples, sentences (often consisting of one or two words) are not used to describe anything, but are primarily used to give orders. He then describes a number of other examples designed to undercut the notion that the primary use of language is to state a fact, to describe a state of affairs, or to predicate a property of some object. In these examples, the most important use of language is to coordinate words and actions. In the case of the builder and his assistant, the only purpose of the language they use in speaking to each other is to facilitate their interactions so that they can accomplish their purposes.[6]

On reading some of Wittgenstein's examples, we might be tempted to think that he has made his point that large parts of language are not used descriptively or referentially. But wouldn't he allow that some uses of language are straightforwardly referential? Suppose, for example, I point to my shoe and say, "This is a shoe." Even here, Wittgenstein argues that it's not so simple. Even an ostensive definition such as this example requires a number of background assumptions in order to serve its purpose. Am I pointing at a shoe, or at my foot? For the sentence to work you need to know that I'm pointing at my shoe, and you also need to know what part or aspect of the shoe I'm trying to point out. Am I pointing at the whole shoe, or the shoelace, or the sole, or the tongue, or some other part? Am I indicating its color, or its height, or that it's not a sandal, etc.? But Wittgenstein's point is not only that background assumptions are necessary in order for the sentence to be understood. These background assumptions can only be understood when we have already understood a good deal of the language

5. Wittgenstein, *Philosophical Investigations*, § 1.
6. Wittgenstein, *Philosophical Investigations*, § 2, 6–21.

in which the sentence is spoken. Now an ostensive definition would seem to be the most obvious case in which language acquires meaning referentially or descriptively. But if we have to understand a good deal of language before we can understand even an ostensive definition, Wittgenstein says, then sentences cannot acquire their meanings, at least not primarily, through their ability to describe or refer to some possible state of affairs.[7]

Wittgenstein argues that the meaning of what we think of as ordinary proper names, such as "Excalibur" or "Pam Jones," cannot be their referents. Consider the sentence, "Excalibur has a sharp blade." If Excalibur is broken to bits, it no longer exists. If it does not exist, he says, then no object corresponds to the name "Excalibur." Therefore, if the meaning of a name is its referent, Wittgenstein says, then "Excalibur" has no meaning, and the sentence "Excalibur has a sharp blade" is nonsensical as well. He makes a similar argument regarding an individual who has died. If Mr. N.N. has died, then there is no longer anything corresponding to the name "Mr. N.N." Again, Wittgenstein says, if the meaning of a name is its referent, then the name "Mr. N.N." has no meaning, and the sentence "Mr. N.N. has died" is nonsensical as well.[8]

After going through many different uses to which language can be put, Wittgenstein says that there is no single thing that is common to all uses of language. That is, there is no essence of language or language use. Instead, he says, various different uses of language may be (and usually are) related to one another in many different ways. It is in this context that Wittgenstein says that different uses of language can bear "family resemblances" to one another. The most famous example that Wittgenstein uses is the word "game." There are many different practices that we call "games" of one kind or another. He says, "I mean board-games, card-games, ball-games, Olympic games, and so on. What is common to them all?—Don't say: 'There *must* be something common, or they would not be called "games"'—but *look and see* whether there is anything common to all.—For if you look at them you will not see something that is common to *all,* but similarities, relationships, and a whole series of them at that."[9] And to describe these similarities, he says, he can think of no better expression than "family resemblances." The

7. Wittgenstein, *Philosophical Investigations,* § 26–32. See Soames, *Age of Meaning,* 6–8.
8. Wittgenstein, *Philosophical Investigations,* § 39–40. See Soames, *Age of Meaning,* 11–12. It is not clear that Wittgenstein's argument really establishes that the meaning of a proper name can't be its referent. See Soames, *Age of Meaning,* 13–15. See also Soames, *Beyond Rigidity: The Unfinished Semantic Agenda of Naming and Necessity* (New York: Oxford Univ. Press, 2002), chapter 3; Nathan Salmon, "Existence," in *Philosophical Perspectives,* vol. 1, *Metaphysics* (Atascadero, Calif.: Ridgeview, 1987), 49–108; and Salmon, "Nonexistence," *Noûs* 32 (1998): 277–319; these sources are cited in Soames, *Age of Meaning,* 15 n.8.
9. Wittgenstein, *Philosophical Investigations,* § 66.

practices represented by the word "games" form a "family," he says, and bear family resemblances to one another.[10] Because of this, no descriptivist understanding of meaning is sufficient to account for the meaning of words like "game."

The same holds true for ordinary proper names. Even if we ignore the fact that more than one individual can (and usually do) bear the same name, there won't be any single description, or disjunctive group of descriptions, that a language user must associate with a name in order to use it competently. Further, there won't be any such description, or disjunctive group of descriptions, that refers uniquely to a single individual (at least not usually).[11] And the description(s) I have in mind when I use a name are likely to differ from one instance of use to another. So he says, "I use the name 'N' without a *fixed* meaning."[12] But this does not detract from the usefulness of the name. According to Scott Soames, Wittgenstein's thoughts on names imply that when I use a name what I thereby convey is largely vague and inexact. But this is quite consonant with the overall picture the *Investigations* paints of ordinary language as being perfectly meaningful (because nevertheless useful) even when it is vague and inexact.[13] I'll make one final point about Wittgenstein's discussion of names, especially in section 79. His discussion is not sufficient to give us a full-blown theory of the meaning of names. Thus, Soames argues that there are three ways to extend Wittgenstein's comments into an adequate theory. The first way focuses on the fact that the meaning of a name will differ from speaker to speaker and from one occasion of utterance to another. Still, there are a group of descriptions associated with the name, and the referent must satisfy some number of them for the name to refer. As Soames puts it, the meaning of a name for a particular speaker "is given by a vague description—*the unique individual x who satisfies a sufficient number of the following descriptive claims: x is F, x is G, and so on.*"[14] This is the view associated with John Searle.[15] The second way to extend Wittgenstein's remarks focuses on the fact that *what a speaker means* by an expression at some given occasion of utterance is distinct from *what the expression itself means.* While the speaker that uses a name typically associates a name with some description or set of descriptions, the meaning of the name or expression itself frequently will not be

10. Wittgenstein, *Philosophical Investigations,* § 67.
11. Wittgenstein, *Philosophical Investigations,* § 79.
12. Wittgenstein, *Philosophical Investigations,* § 79.
13. Soames, *Age of Meaning,* 19.
14. Soames, *Age of Meaning,* 20. There are several versions of this theory, each of which has problems, in Soames's view (20–21).
15. John Searle, "Proper Names," *Mind* 67 (1958): 166–73.

associated with any description or group of description that uniquely picks out the referent of the name. The third way of extending Wittgenstein's remarks proceeds like the second way, but adds that the meaning of the name itself (in a language) just is its referent. Soames thinks that this is the correct view, but acknowledges that Wittgenstein himself would have resisted it.[16] Each of these ways of extending Wittgenstein's remarks toward an adequate theory represents an advance over Wittgenstein himself, but we should note that one of the reasons Wittgenstein would have resisted them is precisely that they represent an advance *toward a theory*. One of the most striking things about the *Investigations* is the antitheoretical sentiment that is on display there. And this antitheoretical sentiment will be shared by the ordinary language philosophers for whom Wittgenstein is so influential.

Wittgenstein's central arguments in his critique of the *Tractatus*'s descriptivism consist in four important points.[17] First, the crucial element in linguistic meaning is the coordination of language use with action. That is, the use of language to facilitate actions or practices is conceptually primary, and it is prior to using language to name or describe things. Second, precisely because this coordination of language use with action is primary, language users must have some skill at it before they will be able to engage in associating names or descriptive predicates with objects in the world. Third, different instances of naming, referring, and describing will not always be the same kind of activity. Thus, the use of names or other expressions will carry different meanings both when used in different contexts and when used for different linguistic purposes. Fourth, descriptivists are wrong to try to explain linguistic competence through the association of expressions with objects. Instead, substantial linguistic competence must already be in place before a speaker will be able to associate an expression with an object. In other words, mastery of a language fundamentally has less to do with one's skill at associating expressions with objects in the world than with one's skill at using a set of social practices to coordinate one's actions with those of others.[18]

The last aspect of the *Investigations* I need to mention briefly is Wittgenstein's remarks on following a rule. In the *Investigations* Wittgenstein rejects the notion that the meaning of a sentence (atomic or otherwise) consists in the possible fact or state of affairs that it describes. Now, he replaces the inquiry about possible facts with two others: First, under what

16. Soames, *Age of Meaning*, 21–23.
17. Here I am following Soames's useful summary in *Age of Meaning*, 23.
18. Soames, *Age of Meaning*, 23.

conditions may this sentence be appropriately asserted? Second, what role does our practice of asserting the sentence play in our lives?[19] Thus, he will say, "Don't think, look!" or, as Frei paraphrases, "Don't ask for the meaning, ask for the use."[20] This redirection that Wittgenstein effects in the *Investigations* is central to his rejection of the project of the *Tractatus*. If asking about meaning requires asking about truth conditions, then an assertion that a person means something by what she says is meaningless. But no such conclusion follows if we replace inquiries about truth conditions with those suggested in the *Investigations*. In that case, all that is required for a sentence to have meaning is that there be roughly specifiable circumstances under which it is legitimately assertable, and that the game that involves its assertion plays a role in our lives.

Of course, these specifiable circumstances, and the role that the assertion plays, can only be specified with reference to a community. They don't make sense as applied to a single individual considered in isolation. This is because to ask about the role that an assertion plays and the conditions under which it can play that role is to ask about what *rule* we follow in asserting it. But Wittgenstein argues that, considering a person in isolation, there is no fact about her in virtue of which we can tell in a given case whether she is following a rule or not. Thus, it is not possible to obey a rule "privately."[21] In contrast, to use Kripke's famous example, in a community, Jones can decide whether Smith means addition by "+" by determining whether Smith's answer to 68+57 is the same as the answer Jones is inclined to give.[22] If there are enough concrete cases in which the answer Smith gives agrees with the one that Jones is inclined to give, Jones can assert that by "+" Smith means addition.[23] A person will be deemed to be following a rule for using "+" when in enough cases her responses agree with those of (at least most of) the community. But note that deeming a person to be following a rule is always

19. This summary of Wittgenstein's thoughts in the *Investigations* is indebted to Saul Kripke, *Wittgenstein on Rules and Private Language* (Cambridge, Mass.: Harvard Univ. Press, 1982; repr., 2000). Kripke's "skeptical" interpretation of the *Investigations* is highly contested. See, for example, P. M. S. Hacker, *Wittgenstein: Connections and Controversies* (Oxford: Clarendon Press, 2001), 268–309. Nonetheless, though it seems that no interpretation of Wittgenstein goes uncontested in the literature, I take the general descriptions I am giving in this section to be *relatively* uncontroversial.

20. Hans W. Frei, "Theology and the Interpretation of Narrative," in *Theology and Narrative*, ed. George Hunsinger and William C. Placher (New York: Oxford Univ. Press, 1993), 104.

21. And consequently, as is well known, Wittgenstein rejects "private language."

22. See Kripke, *Wittgenstein on Rules and Private Language*, passim.

23. If in a community every person thought that every other person were not following the rule correctly, there would be little point to the practice. But in fact, communities do come to agreement on the meanings of very many words and sentences.

provisional. If a person begins to behave in a bizarre way, the community may deem her no longer to be following the rule.

Wittgenstein's discussion of following a rule contributes three components crucial to his understanding of linguistic meaning. First, the *agreement* of the community as to its practices is essential. The game of ascribing rules and concepts to each other would fall apart in the absence of such agreement. Second, the rules on which we agree, and the way in which they interact with our practices, constitute our *form of life*. For Wittgenstein, our form of life is just a given; it is a brute fact that must be simply accepted, and it is in the context of our form of life that the agreement of the community is enacted. Third, there must be *criteria* by which the community judges whether one of its members is following the rule in question. These criteria must be outward and observable; that is, they must be public criteria. They need not in all cases be exhaustively specifiable in advance. In practice, they are applied on an ad hoc basis. Thus, to ask about the meaning of a word or a sentence is to ask about the rules for using the word or sentence and about its usefulness in the community's form of life. On the other hand, to ask about the reference of a word or a sentence is to ask about its truth conditions, and Wittgenstein is convinced that truth conditions cannot yield meaning.

Wittgenstein's later thoughts on following a rule fit quite well with his critique of the project of the *Tractatus* and of descriptivism more generally. In the next chapter we'll see how these Wittgensteinian themes appear in postliberal critiques of liberal theology. For now, though, I want to turn to one of the leaders of the ordinary language school, Gilbert Ryle, who provided further and more accessible reflections on Wittgenstein's later work. He also extended Wittgenstein's thoughts on language to other philosophical issues like the concepts of mind and of personal identity. As we'll see in the next chapter, both Ryle's work on personal identity and his reading of Wittgenstein were influential in the development of postliberal theology.

III. GILBERT RYLE ON MEANING

Ryle's work in the theory of meaning contributes two fundamental insights that will become useful in Frei's work. Ryle argues that no referential theory of meaning is plausible and that an independently existing "third realm" of abstract objects (including meanings) is indefensible. In my judgment, one reason that meaning assumed such an important role for Frei is that it offers invaluable assistance in Frei's refusal (following Barth) to allow primacy to epistemology in theological method.

In carrying forward Barth's project of deriving theological method from the doctrine of God (which in turn is derived from the biblical witness to God's Incarnation in Jesus Christ), Frei must get past the thorny issue of circularity. If we begin with the biblical texts, are we not already using some version of understanding? If so, whatever notion of understanding we derive from the doctrine of God (which we derive from the biblical texts) will be overdetermined by the version of understanding through which we derived the doctrine of God in the first place. For Frei, this circularity can be avoided by attending to the notion of the meaning of the texts themselves. Ryle is useful precisely at this point, for he argues that there is some kind of (yet to be specified) relation between knowledge and meaning, because understanding, at least as it occurs in communication, already implies the notion of meaning.[24]

In Ryle's view, it was John Stuart Mill who provided the first influential modern discussion of the notion of meaning.[25] Mill made two assumptions that Ryle takes to be a false start. He supposed, first, that the meaning of sentences are merely compounds of the meaning of words; second, that words, or at least the vast majority of them, functioned like names. They get their meaning by their ability to point or refer to some object. Descriptive phrases functioned in this same way, as did most other sentence components. Meaning was thus assimilated to reference, and the referential function of names became the basic semantic function. Ryle saw several problematic consequences of Mill's assumptions.[26] First, most words are not nouns, and of those that are, many do not refer to particular entities. In the sentence, "Mom owns a dog," for example, on this referential understanding of meaning, "a dog" would simply mean the dog that Mom owns (i.e., its referent). But if that were so, then (supposing Mom's dog were named Hubert), the sentence "Hubert is a dog" would simply mean "Hubert is Hubert." To avoid this, many took "dog" to refer to some kind of entity, "namely, either the set or class of all actual and imaginable dogs, or the set of canine properties which they all share."[27] Moreover, collective

---

24. Gilbert Ryle, "Theory of Meaning," in *British Philosophy in the Mid-Century*, 2d ed., ed. C. A. Mace (London: George Allen and Unwin, 1966), 239–64. "The ideas of understanding, misunderstanding and failing to understand what is said already contain the notion of expressions having and lacking specifiable meanings" (239).

25. Ryle, "Theory of Meaning," 241. See John Stuart Mill, *System of Logic* (1843).

26. Ryle notes that the most problematic consequences were drawn by Mill's successors. Mill's distinction between connotation and denotation allowed him to avoid the worst consequences. On Ryle's reading, however, while Mill understood the meaning of a word or phrase to be its connotation, his successors interpreted him (wrongly in Ryle's view) as assimilating meaning to denotation (Ryle, "Theory of Meaning," 247–50).

27. Ryle, "Theory of Meaning," 250.

nouns (e.g., "all the pickup trucks in Texas") and even imaginary things such as centaurs must be ascribed some sort of reality in order for their names to have any meaning.[28] Thus, a referential understanding of meaning, in Ryle's view, depends on the existence of this "third realm" of logical or ideal entities.

This expansion of the "Platonic menagerie" (to borrow a phrase from Alvin Plantinga) was also supported by the sustained efforts of certain philosophers to specify the task of philosophy.[29] These efforts resulted in "Platonistic" arguments for a "third realm" of nonmental, nonmaterial entities that included concepts, numbers, propositions, etc. In Ryle's view, Edmund Husserl and Alexius Meinong in particular used the term "meanings" (*Bedeutungen*) to refer collectively to this third realm of logical or intentional objects.[30] For many, the characteristic task of philosophy and logic became that of investigating "meanings."[31] Later in this study I will suggest that Frei makes similar interpretive moves in his criticism of Paul Ricoeur and David Tracy. He reads them (not incorrectly) as being influenced by the phenomenological tradition that followed the lead of Husserl. When Ricoeur and Tracy speak of "modes of being-in-the-world," Frei interprets them in a way similar to Ryle's interpretation of Husserl. In Frei's view, such modes of being-in-the-world are intentional entities existing

28. It was collectives, on Ryle's account, that exposed the radical inadequacy of this understanding of meaning. Not only can objects be collected into classes, but classes themselves can be collected in the same way. "So now suppose I construct a class of all the classes that are not, as anyhow most classes are not, members of themselves. Will this class be one of its own members or not? If it embraces itself, this disqualifies it from being one of the things it is characterized as embracing; if it is not one of the things it embraces, this is just what qualifies it to be one among its own members" (Ryle, "Theory of Meaning," 252).

29. Ryle argues that these efforts proceeded along three lines. First was the effort on the part of thinkers like Frege to make mathematics independent of empiricism and psychologism. For this project to succeed, there must be a field of inquiry whose objects of study are neither material nor mental. These objects are "logical objects"—numbers, sets, classes, concepts, and the like. Second, the method of psychology became less introspective and *a priori* and more experimental and scientific (i.e., more like the natural sciences). This implied that mental process were properly studied experimentally and that epistemologists, moral philosophers and logicians studied something other than mental processes. Third, Brentano and his pupils (principally Meinong and Husserl) argued persuasively that mental or psychological processes don't proceed in a wholly self-contained way, but that such processes have objects, namely, intentional objects (Ryle, "Theory of Meaning," 258–60).

30. Ryle, "Theory of Meaning," 261. Identifying the third realm in this way seemed natural since, after all, thoughts and the nature of their objects are conveyed by words and sentences. "The 'accusatives' of my ideas and my judgings are the meanings of my words and my sentences" (261).

31. Ryle, "Theory of Meaning," 262.

in the "third realm"—entities strikingly similar to Ryle's interpretation of Husserlian "meanings."

In any event, Ryle argues that this Husserlian articulation of the task of philosophy set the stage for Wittgenstein's *Tractatus*, a treatise devoted not only to formal logic but also to describing the task of philosophy. Wittgenstein agreed that the task of philosophy was to elucidate or clarify the meaning of the expressions used by all who use language, but he argued that meanings cannot be entities which it is the job of language to denote.[32] To speak of meanings in this Platonic way is "nonsense," and therefore sentences cannot function like names. Instead, the meaning of an expression or sentence is better thought of as "a style of operation performed with it" or "the logic of [its] functioning."[33] Yet in the *Tractatus* Wittgenstein still understood the logical structure of sentences that made sense to be a "picture" of the structure of the states of affairs to which they refer, though this picture is not itself a separate entity. It wasn't until his later work that Wittgenstein concluded that this picture theory itself could not be defended. And this conclusion constitutes Wittgenstein's final decisive break with a referential notion of meaning. As I've discussed, for the later Wittgenstein, to know what a sentence means is simply to know how it may and may not be used in the performance of a language game.[34]

Ryle takes Wittgenstein to have established definitively that the notion of an independently existing "third realm" of concepts, propositions, numbers, sets, etc., is indefensible. Consequently, meanings are not themselves entities, and meaning therefore cannot be equivalent to reference. Insofar as sentences or expressions seem to contradict these fundamental insights, Ryle argues that they are "systematically misleading."[35] Ryle's reflections on systematically misleading expressions lead him to conclude that metaphysical statements having "reality" or "Being" as their subject are

32. Logical constants ("is," "not," "and," etc.), for example, do not stand for objects at all, though they do have meaning.

33. Ryle, "Theory of Meaning," 262–63. This account of the task of philosophy was widely persuasive, so that by the mid–twentieth century it had become customary to say that philosophical problems are linguistic problems (263).

34. Ryle, "Theory of Meaning," 255.

35. Gilbert Ryle, "Systematically Misleading Expressions," in *Logic and Language* (first series), ed. Antony Flew (Oxford: Basil Blackwell, 1963), 11–36. Such expressions are "couched in a syntactical form improper to the facts recorded and proper to facts of quite another logical form" (14). Statements such as *Courage is a virtue* may mislead us into thinking that there is some entity to which the word "courage" or "virtue" refer. Such statements can be restated in a form such as *Courageous persons are virtuous* (21). In Ryle's view, once we can see the systematically misleading nature of the expressions, however, we can also see that it is wrong to assume "that every statement gives in its syntax a clue to the logical form of the fact that it records" (17).

at best systematically misleading, and at worst meaningless.[36] In the next chapter I will point to the influential role Ryle's reflections on meaning and Platonic entities play in Frei's critique of liberal theology. Frei will argue that much of modern theology assumes precisely the kind of referential understanding of the meaning of biblical texts that Ryle calls a "monstrous howler."[37] As we will see in the next chapter, Frei argues that the kind of hermeneutics practiced by Ricoeur and Tracy assumes the kind of Platonic entities (in their case, modes of being-in-the-world) whose indefensibility Ryle takes Wittgenstein to have definitively established.

IV. GILBERT RYLE ON IDENTITY

What Frei learns from Ryle about the identity of a person or character is that a person's identity should not be thought of as some entity or "ghost in the machine" that exists "behind" a person's actions—actions that "manifest" this otherwise hidden, "true" self or identity. Ryle problematizes what he calls the dogma of the "ghost in the machine," or the "intellectualist legend" in the context of discussing the distinction between "knowing how" to perform some task and "knowing that" some proposition is true.[38] The distinction itself is neither remarkable nor problematic. But it often leads to a common (mis)understanding of identity—the dogma of the "ghost in the machine." Because many of our activities are the result of our first thinking about what to do and then doing it, some have assumed that underlying every activity is some kind of theorizing. Behind every instance, that is, of "knowing how" is at least some instance of "knowing that." And if human activity is viewed on the model of a machine, then this theorizing is conducted by the "ghost in the machine," or the mind.

Ryle takes this understanding of mind to be misconceived, because "there are many activities which directly display qualities of mind, yet are neither themselves intellectual operations nor yet effects of intellectual operations. Intelligent practice is not a step-child of theory. On the

36. "If I am right in this, then the conclusion follows, which I accept, that those metaphysical philosophers are the greatest sinners, who, as if they were saying something of importance, make 'Reality' or 'Being' the subject of their propositions, or 'real' the predicate. For at best what they say is systematically misleading, which is the one thing which a philosopher's propositions have no right to be; and at worst it is meaningless" (Ryle, "Systematically Misleading Expressions," 18).

37. See also Ryle, "Theory of Meaning," 243.

38. Gilbert Ryle, *The Concept of Mind* (London: Hutchinson, 1949; repr., Chicago: Univ. of Chicago Press, 1984), 27, 29; more generally, 25–61 (page references are to reprint edition).

contrary theorising is one practice amongst others and is itself intelligently or stupidly conducted."[39] The crucial objection to the "intellectualist legend" is based on the claim that theorizing is itself an activity. If such theorizing itself had to be an application of a prior bit of theorizing, which would in turn have to be an application of an even prior bit of theorizing, no activity could ever begin.[40]

This discrediting of the "intellectualist legend" implies that there are some activities that both display and require intelligence, but whose criteria of intelligent performance remain unformulated.[41] Thus it is not the case that every activity that is intelligently performed really involves two activities—the activity itself and a prior, "purely intellectual" activity such as thinking about the activity, planning its performance, etc. "When I do something intelligently, i.e., thinking what I am doing, I am doing one thing and not two."[42] Knowing how to perform some activity, then, such as sailing a thirty-foot sloop, need not require the ability to articulate in advance the rules or criteria for performing it well.[43] Nonetheless, though a person may lack the ability to formulate criteria for intelligently performing an activity that she knows how to perform, this does not imply that such a person would not be a good judge of whether another person is performing the activity in question intelligently or badly. If a person knows how to perform an activity, she will have some understanding of what it takes to perform it intelligently, though she might be unable to theorize about the causes or criteria of intelligent performance. That is, even though performing an activity intelligently is one activity and not two, "execution and understanding are merely different exercises of knowledge of the tricks of the same trade."[44]

Ryle is arguing that when we see a person acting intelligently (or stupidly), we are not observing *clues* to the working of that person's mind. Instead, we are observing the working of the person's mind.[45] This simply follows from Ryle's position that intellectual activity is not limited to theorizing done by a mind that exists behind the curtain of a person's body. In the next chapter, we'll see similar arguments at work in Frei's mature work, when he distinguishes

39. Ryle, *Concept of Mind*, 26.
40. Ryle, *Concept of Mind*, 30.
41. Ryle, *Concept of Mind*, 30.
42. Ryle, *Concept of Mind*, 32.
43. "Knowing *how*, then, is a disposition, but not a single-track disposition like a reflex or a habit. Its exercises are observances of rules or canons or the applications of criteria, but they are not tandem operations of theoretically avowing maxims and then putting them into practice" (Ryle, *Concept of Mind*, 46).
44. Ryle, *Concept of Mind*, 55.
45. Ryle, *Concept of Mind*, 58.

Christian theology as Christian self-description from philosophical theorizing about such Christian self-description.[46] Frei will argue that each are activities in their own right and need not depend on the other activity's formulation of criteria for intelligent performance. Further, in Frei's constructive work on the identity of Jesus Christ, he will argue that Jesus' identity consists in the actions he performs and the events that happen to him. It is not as though his "real" identity is a "ghost" that must be discovered behind such actions and events.

46. Frei does not mean to deny, of course, that a good deal of theorizing is already involved in Christian self-description. But he will argue that Christian self-description need not depend on prior philosophical theorizing to render it credible.

CHAPTER SEVEN

Earlier Postliberalism

Narrative Theology and Hans Frei's Synthesis

of Wittgenstein and Barth

B y the middle of the century, the theology and falsification controversy revealed that to fulfill their central methodological commitments, liberal theologians (at least most of them) felt they had to meet the descriptivist requirements for meaningful language use. Consequently, the most thoroughgoing way to reject the method of liberal theology would be to reject the descriptivist understanding of language that seemed to be at its heart. The most obvious allies to enlist in this project were the later Wittgenstein and the ordinary language philosophers whom he influenced, like Gilbert Ryle. And this was indeed the strategy of early postliberals like Hans Frei and George Lindbeck. This chapter will highlight the ways in which Frei's early work, at least on my reading, displays this strategy.

Hans Frei is probably the most important figure in the early development of postliberal theology, and his two major works, *The Eclipse of Biblical Narrative* (1974) and *The Identity of Jesus Christ* (1975) shaped the postliberal movement.[1] The former is Frei's extended interpretive narrative of what he takes to be liberal theology's "wrong turn." He analyzes this wrong turn

---

1. Perhaps more than anyone else, Frei is responsible for the development of what has come to be known as narrative or postliberal theology. Frei and George Lindbeck are often cited as the two most important influences on the development of narrative theology, but Lindbeck himself suggests that Frei was an important influence in the development of Lindbeck's most influential book. George A. Lindbeck, *The Nature of Doctrine: Religion and Theology in a Postliberal Age* (Philadelphia: Westminster Press, 1984), 12–13. See also William C. Placher, "Introduction," in Hans W. Frei, *Theology*

from the perspective of the way language acquires meaning. Prominent in his analysis is his critique of "meaning-as-reference" and his increasing receptivity to the idea that the Christian community as the "cultural-linguistic" context in which the Gospels are read is crucial for their meaning. Throughout his career, Frei maintains that the meaning of a biblical text must be distinguished from its reference. In his earlier work he argued that the meaning of the biblical texts was simply the depictions contained in them. Their meaning was located in the text itself and should not be understood referentially. The genre of biblical narratives was similar to that of realistic novels. Just as the sentences and paragraphs in realistic novels have meaning despite their failure to refer to some "real" (or extratextual) event, so the meaning of biblical narratives should not be thought of as being "located" in any extratextual events to which the narratives referred. This repeated theme in Frei's critical work is a key indicator of the extent of his reliance on Wittgenstein and ordinary language philosophy. Just as the later Wittgenstein came to view his earlier "picture theory" of language as a fundamental philosophical mistake, Frei argues that it is a fundamental theological mistake to think that the meaning of biblical narratives consists in their ability to refer to or describe some picture of reality.

The crucial factor in the meaning of the biblical texts in the earlier part of Frei's career was their narrative form. During the 1980s, however, Frei's understanding of the meaning of the biblical texts shifted somewhat, so that now it is the use of such texts in the life of the community that assumes the primacy previously held by the texts' narrative form. This shift (or development) in Frei's thought brings into clearer relief his reliance on Wittgenstein in his understanding of the meaning of the biblical texts. Among Frei's critics, it is not uncommon to see this shift (or development) as due to the influence of Frei's colleague, George Lindbeck. Yet not everyone agrees. In an important recent study of Frei, Jason Springs responds in three ways: First, he argues that Frei's shift toward the literal sense of scripture in his later work should not be thought of as a shift at all, but is rather a natural development. Second, Springs argues that whatever affinities toward Lindbeck's "cultural-linguistic" theory of religion

and *Narrative: Selected Essays*, ed. George Hunsinger and William C. Placher (New York: Oxford Univ. Press, 1993), 20 n.1. For a brief biographical sketch, see Placher, "Introduction," 3–25, esp. 4–5. For a fine account relating Frei's personal journey (based on Frei's publications, as well as extensive interviews) to his public theological proposals, see John F. Woolverton, "Hans W. Frei in Context: A Theological and Historical Memoir," *Anglican Theological Review* 79 (Summer 1997): 369–93. Another excellent biographical sketch can be found in Mike Higton, *Christ, Providence and History: Hans W. Frei's Public Theology* (London: T & T Clark, 2004), 15–20

Frei's later work exhibits, these are outweighed by the differences between them. Finally, Springs argues that however Wittgensteinian Lindbeck's theories of religion and doctrine may be, Frei was not a "card-carrying Wittgensteinian."[2]

One of the principal reasons Springs disagrees with those who see a distinct shift in Frei's later work is that Frei did not learn about Wittgenstein and ordinary language philosophy from Lindbeck; on the contrary, their influence was present in Frei's earlier work as well.[3] With this conclusion I wholeheartedly agree; indeed, Frei's early work, no less than his later work (though perhaps less obviously), displays a thoroughly Wittgensteinian character. The point at which I will disagree with Springs's fine treatment of Frei has to do with the extent of Frei's reliance on Wittgenstein.[4] No doubt Frei would agree that too heavy a reliance on any particular philosophical theory would compromise the Barthian nature of his project to an extent that would make him uncomfortable. And I would agree with Springs that Frei would not have *wanted* to see himself as a "card-carrying Wittgensteinian." Indeed, he made substantial efforts to distinguish his own position from at least some readings of Wittgenstein—those of D. Z. Phillips, for example. Yet despite the subtlety of Springs's defense, my own view is that Frei's efforts in this regard were not ultimately successful. And as I shall argue in the next chapter, though he may not have carried a Wittgensteinian card, Frei remained about as Wittgensteinian as any theologian who loves Wittgenstein could ask. But in developing postliberal theology, Frei relies not only on Barth and ordinary language philosophy, but also on the work of Erich Auerbach.[5] So we need to take a brief look at those aspects of Auerbach's work most influential on Frei.

---

2. Jason A. Springs, *Toward a Generous Orthodoxy: Prospects for Hans Frei's Postliberal Theology* (New York: Oxford Univ. Press, 2010), 50. Springs's exposition of Frei is one of the clearest that has appeared to date, and his interpretation is nuanced and erudite. Overall it is a work of exemplary scholarship.

3. Springs, *Toward a Generous Orthodoxy*, 42–50.

4. See my "Wittgenstein's Web: Hans Frei and the Meaning of Biblical Narratives," *Journal of Religion* (forthcoming).

5. In the preface to *The Eclipse of Biblical Narrative: A Study in Eighteenth and Nineteenth Century Hermeneutics* (New Haven, Conn.: Yale Univ. Press, 1974), Frei indicates that Barth, Eric Auerbach, and Gilbert Ryle were particularly important influences on the development of his thought. As Placher points out, others were influential as well, including H. Richard Niebuhr, who directed Frei's dissertation (Placher, "Introduction," 6). Woolverton also highlights the influence of Niebuhr in "Hans W. Frei in Context." In the case of Niebuhr in particular, Frei's theological relationship with him was complex, and Frei himself indicated in a conversation with Woolverton that when he joined the Yale faculty in 1957, he and Niebuhr "parted theologically" (Woolverton, "Hans W. Frei in Context," 389). See also Higton, *Christ, Providence and History*, 3.

I. BACKGROUND: ERICH AUERBACH

In Frei's judgment, "no student of the Bible has ever denied the power and aptness of the analysis of biblical passages and early Christian biblical interpretations in the first three chapters of *Mimesis*."[6] *Mimesis*'s famous introductory essay, "Odysseus' Scar" should suffice to indicate that Frei saw Auerbach as an ally in his effort to advance the Barthian subordination of theological method to the affirmations about God given in scripture.[7]

Auerbach describes two opposed types of literature represented by the Homeric poems and the canon of the Old Testament.[8] On Auerbach's account, the *Odyssey* and the other Homeric poems tell their stories by providing "a complete externalization of all the elements of the story."[9] Little is left in suspense, and the characters in the stories are everything they seem to be.[10] Characters' internal deliberations take place in full view of the reader, so that any intrigue on the part of the characters comes as no surprise to the reader. This externalization of the Homeric poems prevents

6. Frei, *Eclipse*, vii. Frei also cites two of Auerbach's works in an early paper on Barth read at a memorial colloquium on Barth held in 1969 at Yale Divinity School (Hans W. Frei, "Karl Barth—Theologian," in *Karl Barth and the Future of Theology: A Memorial Colloquium Held at the Yale Divinity School, January 28, 1969*, ed. David L. Dickerman (Yale Divinity School Association), 1–14, 28–29, 45–64; reprinted in *Reflection* 66:4 [May 1969]: 5–9; also reprinted in *Theology and Narrative*, 167–76; citing Erich Auerbach, *Dante: Poet of the Secular World* [Chicago: Univ. of Chicago Press, 1961], and "Scenes from the Drama of European Literature," in *From Time to Eternity: Essays on Dante's Divine Comedy*, ed. Thomas G. Berger [New Haven, Conn.: Yale Univ. Press, 1967], 118ff.). Placher and John David Dawson also note Auerbach's influence on Frei. See John David Dawson, "Figural Reading and the Fashioning of Christian Identity in Boyarin, Auerbach and Frei," *Modern Theology* 14 (April 1988): 181–96; Placher, "Introduction," 3–25.

7. Auerbach finished his magisterial *Mimesis* in 1945 and published it in Switzerland in 1946. Erich Auerbach, *Mimesis: The Representation of Reality in Western Literature*, trans. Willard R. Trask (Princeton, N.J.: Princeton Univ. Press, 1953; repr., 1991) (page references are to reprint edition). Auerbach believed that in the years leading up to and during World War II, a previously unified humanistic European culture was dissolving. *Mimesis* represents, among other things, Auerbach's chronicling of this cultural dissolution, as well as his criticism of it. The unity of European culture had been rooted for centuries in the Christian tradition of figural interpretation of the Bible. Pushed by anti-Semitism, however, (among other things) Europe no longer recognized the indebtedness of its secular cultural unity to this tradition. For a brief biographical sketch, see Dawson, "Figural Reading," 186–87.

8. These types are described in the famous introductory essay, "Odysseus' Scar," in Auerbach, *Mimesis*, 3–23.

9. Auerbach, *Mimesis*, 4.

10. Other commentators have noticed a "retarding element" in the poems, found in long digressions. Auerbach takes this element not to arise from any attempt at suspense or surprise, but instead from "the need of the Homeric style to leave nothing which it mentions half in darkness and unexternalized" (*Mimesis*, 5).

any distinction between foreground and background, so that the available present arises out of the depths of a more hidden past. Instead, "the Homeric style knows only a foreground, only a uniformly illuminated, uniformly objective present."[11]

Auerbach's second type of literature, that of the Bible, contrasts with the Homeric style on almost every level. Much of the characters in its stories are hidden from view. In the story of the binding of Isaac in Genesis 22, for example, we are told that God speaks to Abraham and instructs him to sacrifice his son Isaac. But we are not told where the interchange takes place, where Abraham is when he hears the instruction, or from where God delivers it. Perhaps most importantly, we know that God issues the instruction in order to test Abraham, but we are told nothing about God's reasons for this testing. Likewise, we are told very little about Abraham's journey— only that it took three days, that Abraham began the journey early in the morning, and that it ended at the place God told him. We are told only what we need to know in order for the text to have its intended effect.[12]

Because so many details about the characters are left untold, we are keenly aware of a hidden side of the story, a background that remains mysterious and creates suspense. At the same time, however, many characters are involved in numerous stories. This combination of the characters' histories and the paucity of detail in the stories create multiple layers and depth to their thoughts and feelings.

> Abraham's actions are explained not only by what is happening to him at the
> moment, nor yet only by his character (as Achilles' actions by his courage and his
> pride, and Odysseus' by his versatility and foresightedness), but by his previous
> history; he remembers, he is constantly conscious of, what God has promised
> him and what God has already accomplished for him—his soul is torn between
> desperate rebellion and hopeful expectation; his silent obedience is multilay-
> ered, has background.[13]

In contrast, the Homeric characters exist and act entirely in the present, a trait reflected in their delight with their physical existence in the world.

---

11. Auerbach, *Mimesis*, 7.
12. Auerbach, *Mimesis*, 7–10. According to Auerbach, this paucity of detail invites, indeed "demands," the symbolic readings it later received (10). About Isaac, we are told only that he is Abraham's only son and that Abraham loves him. "Only what we need to know about him as a personage in the action, here and now, is illuminated, so that it may become apparent how terrible Abraham's temptation is, and that God is fully aware of it" (10–11).
13. Auerbach, *Mimesis*, 12.

Thus it does not matter in the end whether the Homeric stories have any historical basis. Their purpose is to draw the reader or hearer out of her world into an alternative present in which the story itself can be enjoyed for its own sake.[14] The biblical stories, on the other hand, have a very different purpose, a purpose that is "tyrannical."[15] The biblical stories claim to be *true*; indeed, they claim to render the *only* true narrative of the history of humankind in its relation with the divine.[16]

The biblical stories, that is, comprise a universal history, both past and future, and anyone who wishes to be included in this all-inclusive history of significance must understand her own life in its terms. Moreover, this claim to being universal history generates its own history of interpretation. Because the story is universal, all subsequent events must be seen through the eyes of the story, and this requires interpretation.[17] Given the "tyrannical" purpose of scripture—producing a universal history of significance—the questions that occupy the historical critic and the form critic, though interesting, are ultimately beside the point, at least in terms of Auerbach's goal of providing opposed literary types. On Auerbach's account, the traditional elements from which the biblical stories were constructed are finally irrelevant to the universalizing thrust of the narratives. The narratives *as they now stand* claim to tell universal history and to overcome our reality with the only true one.[18]

If Auerbach is right about these narratives, the Barthian project of deriving a method from the scriptural revelation was demanded by the nature of the texts themselves. In his critique of liberal theology, Frei will argue that the liberal tradition does not recognize this tyrannical feature of biblical texts.

14. Auerbach, *Mimesis*, 13–14.
15. Auerbach, *Mimesis*, 14.
16. "The world of the Scripture stories is not satisfied with claiming to be a historically true reality—it insists that it is the only real world, is destined for autocracy. All other scenes, issues, and ordinances have no right to appear independently of it, and it is promised that all of them, the history of all mankind, will be given their due place within its frame, will be subordinated to it. The Scripture stories do not, like Homer's, court our favor, they do not flatter us that they may please us and enchant us—they seek to subject us, and if we refuse to be subjected we are rebels. . . . Far from seeking, like Homer, merely to make us forget our own reality for a few hours, [the biblical narrative] seeks to overcome our reality: we are to fit our own life into its world, feel ourselves to be elements in its structure of universal history" (Auerbach, *Mimesis*,14–15).
17. Auerbach, *Mimesis*, 15–16. In addition, the inclusion of a variety of genres within an overarching narrative provides an additional generative impulse to this history of interpretation (17–21).
18. Auerbach, *Mimesis*, 23.

II. FREI'S CRITIQUE OF LIBERAL THEOLOGY

Like Barth, Frei had tremendous respect for the great liberal thinkers of the eighteenth and nineteenth centuries, but nonetheless viewed the turn they brought about in Protestant theology as a mistake. Like Barth, Frei's own historical study of modern Protestant theology gave him a chance to develop his own way of doing theology in critical dialogue with a tradition of methodological opponents. But Frei had conceptual tools unavailable to Barth to help him analyze the great upheaval in Protestant theology that was largely completed by the time Schleiermacher and Strauss had finished their most important works. I have discussed the most formative of these tools. I now want to discuss how Frei used them in his analysis of the "wrong turn" he believed liberal Protestant theology to have made.

Frei's critique of liberal Protestant theology in the modern period correlates with his positive evaluation of the three Barthian themes mentioned above. In Frei's view, modern theology's wrong turn was accomplished via several culprits that play the role of recurrent villains in Frei's narrative. These villains are apologetics, the prominence of historical-critical investigation, and a twofold confusion regarding the meaning of biblical (and other) texts. This last villain was constituted by a confusion of meaning with reference and a derivation of the understanding of meaning from a (Lockean) theory of knowledge. These villains were mutually related and worked together to thwart any development of the three Barthian themes discussed in chapter 5.[19] Deriving a theory of the meaning of the biblical texts from a theory of knowledge, for example (or at least from Locke's theory of knowledge), disallows the Barthian projects of subordinating epistemology to ontology and of deriving interpretive method from a theological method that is itself derived from a doctrine of God. Apologetics, as well, tends to give primacy to epistemology and to prevent any subordination of theological method to positive ontological affirmations about God. At least on my reading, of the villains I've listed, Frei took the confusion regarding the meaning of biblical narratives to be the most fundamental, in the following sense. What Frei called "meaning-as-reference"—which I take to be equivalent to the descriptivism I've discussed in chapter 6, though he never described it as explicitly as I did there—in and of itself could thwart the development of the themes Frei identified in his study of Barth.

---

19. These themes are to prioritize ontology over epistemology, to have method determined by constructive content rather than vice versa (and the correlative resistance to systematizing), and to make interpretive method cohere with these other two commitments (a coherence that rules out a referential understanding of the meaning of the biblical texts).

Consequently, because a Wittgensteinian view of meaning-as-use was the only alternative available to Frei, the implication of Frei's discussions of the meaning of the biblical narratives is one that Frei's defenders will certainly contest (and in truth I think Frei would as well)—to be a consistent Barthian one must be a Wittgensteinian when it comes to language.[20]

A few crucial episodes in Frei's fascinating narrative will suffice to show the significance of the turn away from figural interpretation by eighteenth- and nineteenth-century theologians in Frei's view. In Frei's analysis, this turn constitutes a turn toward a descriptivist or referential understanding of the meaning of the biblical texts, and this is in Frei's view one thing that made the turn a mistake. In the next section, a reading of *The Identity of Jesus Christ*, Frei's own positive dogmatic contribution, will indicate how Frei thinks postcritical constructive work can be done in accordance with the three Barthian themes I've discussed and without assuming a descriptivist understanding of the meaning of the Gospel narratives.

Frei's discussion of the modern turn in Protestant theology draws heavily from the work of Barth, Auerbach, and Wittgenstein and ordinary language philosophy. If Barth's own project in theology, and in particular his turn away from liberalism, is a project worth continuing, then there must be some way of describing just what was theologically wrong with the modern or liberal turn in Protestant theology. Auerbach and ordinary language philosophy (along with Barth) provide Frei with the conceptual tools that he needs to describe the "category mistake" made by Protestant theology in its turn to liberalism. Central to Barth's project is the decision to take the Word of God as revealed in the Bible as the starting point in theology; prior to the modern turn, Frei argues, this had been done through figural interpretation of the Bible. Auerbach's account of the "tyrannical" demand of the biblical stories makes clear for Frei the stories' susceptibility to figural interpretation. And it is Ryle's critiques of the "ghost in the machine" and of the "Platonic menagerie," and Wittgenstein's and Ryle's critiques of descriptivism—or, as Frei calls it, a referential understanding of meaning—that provide Frei with the clues he needs to describe the mistake made by Protestant liberalism. In Frei's view, behind the liberal turn lay two assumptions that Frei deems mistaken. First, modern liberal theologians were in large part motivated by an apologetic impulse to justify or defend the claims of Christian theology to Western intellectuals that were increasingly skeptical of these claims. This impulse is clearly on display in

20. For a differing view, see Springs, *Toward a Generous Orthodoxy*.

Schleiermacher's *Speeches,* and Frei takes it to be characteristic of liberal theology. One of the reasons this apologetic effort or impulse was mistaken was that it does not do justice to the nature of the biblical stories on which such claims are based. The apologetic impulse, that is, ignores the "tyrannical" nature of the biblical stories. Second, modern liberal theologians assumed a referential theory of meaning by which not only words, but sentences and indeed the stories themselves, have meaning only insofar as they provide a descriptive sense that can "refer" or point to entities or states of affairs outside the text itself. Frei takes this understanding of meaning to be contrary to the nature of the biblical stories themselves, as well as being indefensible in its own terms.

Frei tells this story in *The Eclipse of Biblical Narrative.*[21] Frei's historical sketch of eighteenth- and (early) nineteenth-century hermeneutics proceeds under the following thesis:

> a realistic or history-like (though not necessarily historical) element is a feature, as obvious as it is important, of many of the biblical narratives that went into the making of Christian belief. It is a feature that can be highlighted by the appropriate analytical procedure and by no other, even if it may be difficult to describe the procedure—in contrast to the element itself.[22]

However such an "appropriate analytical procedure" might be formulated, in Frei's view it cannot have as a constituent part a referential or descriptivist understanding of meaning. Later in the chapter it should become evident that Frei takes such an understanding of meaning both to be inappropriate to narrative or "history-like" texts (i.e., incapable of adequately rendering their meaning) and to distort the biblical texts by failing to acknowledge their tyrannical nature.

Prior to the modern period, Christian preachers and theologians had envisioned the world as "formed by the sequence told by the biblical

---

21. Frei, *Eclipse.* George Schner has helpfully suggested that the book proceeds through three sections plus an introductory section. George P. Schner, "The Eclipse of Biblical Narrative: Analysis and Critique," *Modern Theology* 8 (April 1992): 149–72. Though I will follow Schner's delineation of sections, I will not follow his more detailed seven analytical "views." Another helpful reading of *The Eclipse* in the context of Frei's overall work is by Cyril O'Regan, "*De doctrina christiana* and Modern Hermeneutics," in *De doctrina Christiana: A Classic of Western Culture,* ed. Duane W. H. Arnold and Pamela Bright (Notre Dame, Ind.: Univ. of Notre Dame Press, 1995), 217–43. Unfortunately, O'Regan is not as clear as he could be about the distinction between reference and referential theories of meaning (or, to use Frei's term, "meaning-as-reference"). Schner is more clear on this distinction than O'Regan, but O'Regan's article remains useful otherwise.

22. Frei, *Eclipse,* 10.

stories."[23] On Frei's analysis, three features of this kind of reading were most important: First, if a biblical story were to be read literally, then it must have "referred to and described actual historical occurrences."[24] Second, if the world described by the biblical stories is one single world (i.e., one single temporal flow), then the stories must themselves tell one cumulative story. And the way the stories were joined together into a single cumulative story was by making the earlier stories figures or types of the later stories. In Frei's view, this kind of figural reading does not conflict with the literal sense, but is a natural extension of it. Third, since the biblical stories tell one cumulative story of the only real world, then these stories must also tell the story of each present age and the individuals in it. A Christian was to understand and to conduct her own life so that it made sense as a part of the single cumulative biblical story.[25]

This method of biblical interpretation was thus primarily a matter of the interpreter interpreting her own life and the world around her as a part of the world made accessible by the biblical narratives. During the eighteenth century, however, Frei argues that this mode of interpretation increasingly broke down, among both radical thinkers like Spinoza and conservatives like Johannes Cocceius and Johann Albrecht Bengel. For these thinkers, the "actual" historical world became detached from the world depicted in the Bible. Now, instead of making the world accessible, the biblical stories simply "verify" or provide evidence for these independently accessible events.[26]

As Frei puts it, the direction of interpretation now reversed itself. The principal interpretive question was no longer how to make my own life and experience of the world intelligible in terms of the biblical narratives. Instead, the primary question was whether the biblical texts (and whatever concepts may be derived from them) depict the "real" world as I otherwise apprehend it. A crucial implication of this new direction was that "whether or not the story is true history, its *meaning* is detachable from the specific story that sets it forth."[27] This detachability of meaning resulted in the literal reading of the stories being divided from and opposed to the figural reading, with the latter becoming increasingly "discredited both as a literary device and as a historical argument."[28] In its isolation from figural reading, the literal reading of a story now came to mean two things: first, grammatical and

23. Frei, *Eclipse*, 1.
24. Frei, *Eclipse*, 2.
25. Frei, *Eclipse*, 2–3.
26. Frei, *Eclipse*, 3–4.
27. Frei, *Eclipse*, 6 (emphasis in original).
28. Frei, *Eclipse*, 6.

lexical precision in estimating what a text meant to its original audience, which in turn implied a single meaning of statements; and, second, the coincidence of the description with the historical facts.[29]

The Eclipse of Biblical Narrative (1974), then, is "an investigation of the breakdown of realistic and figural interpretation of the biblical stories, and the reversal in the direction of interpretation."[30] In Frei's telling, interpreters even after the reversal continued to attend to the literal sense of the stories. But the literal sense came to mean the single meaning of a text, which was given by the event or reality to which the text referred. Nonetheless, all agreed that something more was necessary for interpretation, and that was "ideational meaning or religious significance."[31]

When modern interpreters turned away from figural interpretation, the crucial point was not that they denied any nonliteral meaning to the texts, but that their understanding of the literal meaning changed. Instead of being the literal depictions themselves, the meaning of the narrative was "located" in some extratextual event or idea to which the text referred. In Frei's view, this occurred because biblical scholars had available to them a method of investigating any historical reference contained in a text, but no literary method by which realistic narratives could be understood. Thus, the separation of story from its meaning occurred because scholars confused history-likeness (literal meaning) with historical likelihood (ostensive reference). As the story was separated from its meaning, the narrative itself went into "eclipse."[32]

For Frei, "realistic interpretation" means above all that the meaning of a story cannot be divorced from its actual telling. Even miraculous events are realistic if they are indispensable to the rendering of a particular character or plot. Thus, in a realistic story, the sublime or more serious elements mix inextricably with the more quotidian. The crucial point, though, is that in a realistic narrative, the locus of meaning is the narrative text itself.[33] Echoing Ryle, Frei argues that such narratives do not derive their meaning

29. Frei, *Eclipse*, 7. Under this new separation of literal and figural reading, the closest successor to literal reading became historical reconstruction, while the closest successor to figural reading became biblical theology (8).
30. Frei, *Eclipse*, 9.
31. Frei, *Eclipse*, 10.
32. Frei, *Eclipse*, 10–12, 16, 27. Frei's thesis about the causes of the eclipse (in distinction from the eclipse itself) have not gone unchallenged. Nicholas Wolterstorff, for example, thinks it more likely that alternatives to realistic interpretation were sought because of rising skepticism about the propositional content of the literal sense of an increasing number of parts of the biblical narratives (Wolterstorff, "Will Narrativity Work as Linchpin? Reflections on the Hermeneutic of Hans Frei," in *Relativism and Religion*, ed. Charles M. Lewis [London: Macmillan Press, 1995], 71–107, esp. 92–93).
33. Frei, *Eclipse*, 13–14.

from their reference to some reality or event outside the story. If they did, in Frei's view, realistic novels could have no meaning at all, because they depict events that have not occurred. Instead, their meaning is neither some event nor idea to which they refer, but is simply the depictions they contain.[34]

During the eighteenth century, first in England then in Germany, the meaning of the biblical narratives became distinguished from the narrative depictions themselves. Frei argues that in England, at the turn from the seventeenth to the eighteenth century, the most important technical theological development was the movement of revelation to the conceptual center of theology, which raised two issues. The first was philosophical: Is the notion of a historical revelation inherently rational or credible? And the second was historical: How likely is it that such a revelatory event has in fact taken place? From the beginning, the notion of a historical revelation revolved around Jesus Christ, and the factual questions centered on the miracles he performed. As it happened, all these questions were decided by reference to criteria external to and independent of the biblical stories themselves.[35]

In this context, in England in the early to mid-eighteenth century, Anthony Collins, a crucial figure to whom Frei devotes an entire chapter, was involved in a dispute over the role of the prophecies cited as evidence of Jesus' role as the Messiah. "The question was: Are the prophecies cited in evidence really applicable to the event they are supposed to demonstrate, and, if not, is there any reason to believe the Christian claim about Jesus?"[36] For Collins, Jesus' identity as the Messiah could be established only by his fulfillment of Old Testament prophecy.[37] Furthermore, for Jesus' birth and life to constitute a fulfillment of such prophecy, it must be a fulfillment of the literal sense of such prophecies.[38] The only

34. "Literal depiction constitutes and does not merely illustrate or point to the meaning of a narrative. . . ." (Frei, *Eclipse*, 27). One might object that sentences in realistic novels need only refer to conceivable states of affairs. But Frei would respond that such a possible state of affairs would then have to assume some kind of Platonic actuality, of which its description would be a mirror. Following Wittgenstein and Ryle, Frei would consider this to be nonsense.

35. Frei, *Eclipse*, 51–54.

36. Frei, *Eclipse*, 66.

37. Frei, *Eclipse*, 68. Collins was a follower of Locke, who had argued famously that Jesus' miracles validated his identity as the Son of God, and in consequence his claims as coming from God. See John Locke, *The Reasonableness of Christianity*, ed. John C. Higgins-Biddle (Oxford: Clarendon Press, 1999). For Collins, however, Jesus' miracles could never establish his identity as the Messiah, though lack of them could invalidate his Messianic identity (Frei, *Eclipse*, 68).

38. That is, the Old Testament prophecies of a Messiah must have had enough of the features of Jesus to provide sufficient evidence for a judgment that the Old Testament prophets had someone very like Jesus in mind.

other alternative was to interpret the prophecies nonliterally—that is, mystically or typologically. But Collins argued successfully that the rules for nonliteral interpretation applied by the New Testament authors when interpreting the Old Testament texts were either lost or nonsensical. Collins thereby eliminated all but two alternatives regarding the question of Jesus' status as the Messiah: One can take the prophecies literally, in which case they do not predict Jesus (contrary to the claims of their New Testament interpreters), or one can take them nonliterally, in which case their interpretation appears arbitrary or absurd.[39]

According to Frei, out of this debate emerged a general agreement that only those statements make sense that can be interpreted according to the rules of regular and natural use of language and thought.[40] In turning prophecy into prediction, Collins succeeded in identifying the literal sense of a text with its historical reference. But he did so in a way that was no longer compatible with figural interpretation: "A proposition is literal if it describes and refers to a state of affairs known or assumed on independent probable grounds to agree or disagree with the stated proposition."[41] This definition of the literal sense rules out any kind of figural interpretation and identifies the literal sense of a statement with its historical reference.[42] The meaning of biblical texts thus became constituted by their reference to independently verifiable (or falsifiable) fact claims.[43]

Frei describes two important moves that Collins made, which effectively located the meaning of texts outside their actual linguistic use. First, "he assigned the origin of specific meaning to the intention of the individual author."[44] This is an important step toward historical-critical interpretation.[45] Second, and most important for Frei, Collins argued

---

39. Frei, *Eclipse*, 67–70.
40. See Frei, *Eclipse*, 74–75.
41. Frei, *Eclipse*, 76.
42. Thus, Collins effected "the complete separation of literal and figurative (or typical) senses. Figurative meaning, hitherto naturally congruent with literal meaning, now became its opposite" (Frei, *Eclipse*, 76).
43. Collins's "(implicit) criterion for interpretation in this controversy about how biblical statements make sense was the same as that explicitly formulated by the early logical positivists some two hundred years later to cover all statements that are neither tautological nor emotive: the meaning of a statement is the method of its verification" (Frei, *Eclipse*, 77).
44. Frei, *Eclipse*, 78.
45. Collins's strategy of assimilating the meaning of the texts to authorial intention was "quite different from previous affirmations of the unity of intention with linguistic use. It is an important step in preparing the way for the practitioners of historical-critical method" (Frei, *Eclipse*, 78).

that the meaning of biblical texts must conform to Locke's epistemological principles.

> Most important of all, to Collins as to Locke there are finally only two kinds of ideas, those of sensation representing external substances and their qualities, and those of reflection by which we apprehend the operation of our own minds. Statements about empirical-historical events are obviously propositions derived from complex ideas of sensation. Indeed, all meaningful propositions that are not about ideas of reflection must refer to empirical states of affairs. In other words, the rational use of language is not only a matter of logical coherence but of externally received impressions or ideas to which words correspond. This fact underlies all else that Collins assumes. 'Meanings' are in effect propositions about the external world for him. Literal language is their only proper expression and, unlike the earlier orthodox literalism about the Bible, Collins's literalism describes things that have no intrinsic connection with the words except to dominate them as signs representing things we know.[46]

Fundamental to all of Collins's views, in other words, was an understanding of meaning-as-reference (a referential notion of meaning).[47] In Frei's view, Collins transformed "an argument over the meaning and interpretation of

---

46. Frei, *Eclipse*, 81.
47. Frei, *Eclipse*, 81. In Locke's and Collins's analysis, "only literal interpretation makes sense, because unlike typological interpretation it involves a ruled use of language. At the same time the meaning of words, particularly in statements of descriptive prediction, is so completely derived from sense experience of the external world that meaning turns out to be identical with verifiability or with likelihood based on past observation. The upshot of analyzing the ruled use of language is that meaning becomes identical with ostensive reference. The meaning of a statement is the spatiotemporal occurrence or state of affairs to which it refers" (78). More specifically, Collins derives four criteria of meaning from Locke. First, from Locke's assertion that knowledge is the agreement or disagreement of simple ideas, Collins concludes that any set of rules governing a nonliteral sense of language must be nonsensical, because they can never yield knowledge. Second, the "specific form of agreement between two statements expressing what is claimed to be the same idea must be that of identity" (82). Thus, no sentence could have both a nonliteral sense and a literal sense, because the two ideas to which the different senses would point would not, by definition, be identical. Consequently, though it would be possible to speak of a sentence having more than one possible meaning, any one of which *might* be the real meaning, it is nonsense to speak of a sentence having more than one *true* meaning. Third, to elaborate on the second criterion, regarding any sentence having as its subject matter some physical event, "in any description—retrospective, contemporaneous, or predictive—a person can have but one event or one kind of event in mind. A specific description has but one reference or one kind of reference, or, to put it another way, any proposition has but one meaning" (82). Fourth, since words derive their meaning from their reference to ideas, "verbal propositions are significant to the extent that they express clear and determinate ideas" (83).

biblical narratives . . . into one over the reference of those narratives."[48] That is, Collins shaped the terms of the debate such that the meaning of the narratives would now be understood referentially. Furthermore, "the ground rules for meaning-as-reference have now been drawn up."[49] First, the author of a text must be considered "wholly and ordinarily human" because his intention can only be discerned if it is governed by the rules of natural thought and language. No revelation can contravene such rules.[50] Second, all statements must be explained by the logical and grammatical rules governing all natural use of language.[51] Finally, the theory of meaning must conform to Lockean epistemological principles; and on those principles, the meaning of the biblical texts, if they are to make sense, must be governed by a referential theory of meaning.[52]

In Germany, also, during the eighteenth century the meaning of the biblical texts came to be constituted by their extralinguistic reference. In Germany, however, Frei argues that there was more of an emphasis on ideal "objects"—concepts, possible states of affairs, etc.—as being candidates for the meaning-giving referents of texts. Thus, in German thought on the meaning of the biblical texts, there were two strands of theological development, one of which spoke of meaning as the historical or ostensive referent and the other as ideal referent.

Here, according to Frei, the argument proceeded much as it had in England. A group of scholars whom Frei calls "Supernaturalists" argued the historical factuality of the biblical reports of miracles and fulfillment of prophecy.[53] For S. J. Baumgarten, for example, the biblical revelation

48. Frei, *Eclipse*, 84.
49. Frei, *Eclipse*, 84.
50. Frei, *Eclipse*, 84.
51. Frei, *Eclipse*, 84–85. Thus, "The meaning of scripture (Locke called it 'traditional revelation') cannot be conveyed, even if its original could have been received, except by ideas derived from those we already have. Whatever original revelation may have been, its communication has to be by way of propositions that make sense in the same way any others do" (83).
52. Collins thus laid all the groundwork needed for the ascendancy of the historical critical method, "granted only that the consideration of the author would expand beyond the notion of his intention to that of the specific cultural and historically limited setting that serves to explain his thought and writing. Given that expansion, the dominance of meaning-as-reference over the explicative sense of the text and the reintegration of the two by critical examination of the referent was all that was additionally needed as philosophical support for the triumph of historical-critical interpretation of biblical narratives" (Frei, *Eclipse*, 85). Statements must be interpreted in conformity with "the fact that ideas of sensation and the words expressing them, including statements about history, always represent states of affairs in the external world. That is to say, theory of meaning is equivalent to theory of knowledge, and to understand is identical with being able to distinguish between what is true and what is false" (Frei, *Eclipse*, 85; see also 78).
53. Frei, *Eclipse*, 87–88.

contained nothing contrary to reason, and thus should be interpreted using ordinary (rational and natural) analytical means. The historical referent of a text governed its explicative sense. Texts "make sense to the extent that they can be shown to refer, and refer faithfully, to these events."[54] In Frei's view, two emphases were emerging: First, there was an emphasis on authorial intent as the surest clue to the meaning of the narratives. Second, there was a clearly emerging referential or descriptivist understanding of meaning, in which the meaning of a biblical text is constituted by the facts to which it refers.[55]

The philosophical groundwork for the notion of meaning-as-ideal-reference was laid, in Frei's view, by Christian Wolff, whose influence in hermeneutics far outlasted the discrediting of his systematic philosophy and natural theology. Like Locke, Wolff held that meaning was governed by epistemological principles. For Wolff, a concept is rational or possible when it is the concept of a possible reality. Otherwise, it is merely empty words. Such rational or possible concepts can be the referents of sensible sentences, so long as they are truly rational or possible—that is, so long as they do not violate the principles of noncontradiction and sufficient reason.[56]

Frei argues that for Locke and Collins, meaning was constituted by ostensive reference. "Wolff's theory of meaning-as-reference, on the other hand, is ideal. The reality to which a concept or a word refers is the ideality of possibility underlying either an actual thing or a general truth."[57] Hermeneutic theorists later in the century regarded the biblical texts as having a *Sache* that could be understood as either a historical event ("meaning-as-ostensive-reference") or as an abstract religious teaching, whether dogma or general religious idea ("meaning-as-ideal-reference"). In either case, or in a mixture of the two, meaning is referential.[58] The influence of Wolff in Germany, and the debates over prophecy in England involving Collins meant that

> Explicative meaning was reference. Words referred to stable objects which were
> either space-time occurrences or didactic ideas, whether dogmatic or those of
> natural religion.... Everything conspired to confine explicative hermeneutics

54. Frei, *Eclipse*, 89; see also 91–92.
55. Frei, *Eclipse*, 91–93. "Locke's theories, refracted through such deist controversies as that on prophecy and through later supernaturalist and historical-critical exegesis, exemplified a massive scholarly movement for which there was a direct convergence of the meaning of biblical narrative with the shape of the events to which they refer" (93).
56. Frei, *Eclipse*, 96, 98–100. This understanding of meaning as referential makes meaning, in effect, "a function of knowing reality" (101).
57. Frei, *Eclipse*, 101.
58. Frei, *Eclipse*, 101.

to meaning as reference—to equate meaning with knowledge of potential or actual reality—and to make the primary reference historical rather than ideal.[59]

In the later part of the eighteenth century, Frei argues, biblical hermeneutics attempted to take full account of the explicative sense of the texts (via historical criticism) and their "deeper" religious sense (via religious interpretation). These disciplines were considered to be fully theoretical, with problems more technical than intrinsic. Explication and application were considered both congruent with each other and intrinsically unproblematic because, in Frei's view, both assumed a univocal use of language and a descriptivist or referential theory of meaning.[60] Unlike the English Deists, German scholars considered the Bible rich in religious truth, however unreliable it might be as an historical document. Here, too, it acquired this religious meaning referentially. Yet despite their assumptions about language, German scholars were confident of the compatibility of their skeptical historical judgments and their positive religious evaluation of the biblical texts.[61]

In Frei's opinion, the dual emphases on negative historical judgments and positive philosophical interpretations meant that biblical hermeneutics was "steadily and intimately related to religious and theological issues."[62] And the literature on the relation between biblical hermeneutics and theological issues was primarily apologetic.[63] In Frei's view, the two related quests of German Enlightenment theology—for a case for the reasonableness of Christianity and for a reduction of Christianity to the reasonable religion that was its real meaning—both implied that the Bible was both historically and religiously dispensable. But many theological writers were reluctant to come to that conclusion. Such writers can be distinguished by their answers to the following question: "Is the *religious* content of the Bible dependent on the historical factuality of the occurrences narrated in it?"[64]

59. Frei, *Eclipse*, 103.
60. Frei, *Eclipse*, 106–11.
61. Frei, *Eclipse*, 113–16. For German Enlightenment scholars, the Bible did not constitute, but exemplified, religious truth. Arguing that Reimarus's *Wolfenbüttel Fragments* need not disturb Christians, for example, Lessing stated that Christianity "'is not true because the Evangelists and Apostles taught it, but they taught it because it is true. The written traditions must be explained from its inner truth'" (115, quoting G. E. Lessing, "Gegensätze des Herausgebers," in *Gesammelte Werke*, ed. Paul Rilla [Berlin: Aufbau-Verlag, 1954–58], 7:813).
62. Frei, *Eclipse*, 116–17.
63. Frei, *Eclipse*, 117.
64. Frei, *Eclipse*, 118.

Frei distinguishes three answers to the question: Traditionalists answered affirmatively, Deists and rationalists negatively, and mediating theologians gave a qualified yes. But all understood the meaning of the biblical texts referentially, whether the referents were ideal or historical.[65] Those that took the referents of the biblical texts to be historical argued for the factuality and religious significance of the referenced events. Those who thought the literal meaning of the stories too unreasonable either argued that their true meanings were constituted by their ideal (and not ostensive) reference or admitted that their meaning was their ostensive reference. In the latter case the true referents of the stories were events reconstructed by historians, and it was these reconstructed events that were understood to have abiding meaningfulness.[66]

Importantly, Frei takes all these positions to be driven in two ways by apologetic concerns. Both scholars' understanding of *how* the biblical texts mean what they do, and the *actual* meanings ascribed to them, were formulated in such a way as to make them amenable to apologetic argument. Such formulations reversed the direction of interpretation and solidified the understanding of meaning-as-reference.[67] Instead of being the world into which the interpreters' lives must be fitted in order to make sense of their own lives, the biblical story could make sense only insofar as it could be made to cohere with their quotidian life in their current world. This interpretive reversal also eliminated the possibility of a truly narrative rendering of scripture.[68]

Apologetics, therefore, was inextricably intertwined with a descriptivist or referential understanding of the texts' meaning. But this is only part of Frei's story. The other part was played by historical critics, who were interested in the ostensive reference of the texts—either the events to which the texts directly refer, or to reconstructions that take their place.[69] Frei argues that the very method of historical criticism precludes narrative interpretation because it assumes that the meaning of the texts is their ostensive reference. Historical criticism requires such a descriptivist or referential theory of meaning because of its commitment to Lockean epistemological principles, which dictated that only claims whose meaning is constituted by their reference to clear and distinct

---

65. Frei, *Eclipse*, 118–19. By the latter part of the eighteenth century, "Explicative meaning . . . was taken to be either ostensive or ideal reference, so that these [biblical] stories too make sense by referring" (119).
66. Frei, *Eclipse*, 119–20.
67. Frei, *Eclipse*, 121–28.
68. Frei, *Eclipse*, 130, 133.
69. Frei, *Eclipse*, 134–35.

ideas can make sense.[70] Thus, "neither religious apologists nor historical critics were finally able to take proper and serious account of the narrative feature of the biblical stories."[71]

The assumption of a descriptivist or referential understanding of meaning, though it may seem highly abstract and technical, was in Frei's view of the greatest moment. This understanding had become established by the time of the appearance of the realistic novel in England and literary criticism of the Bible in Germany. Because both historical criticism and religious apologetics assumed such a strong form of this descriptivist understanding of meaning—such that only on such a view could the biblical texts make sense—the literary-critical tools used to analyze realistic literature could not be used to analyze the biblical texts precisely because such literature assumes another understanding of meaning.[72] In contrast to the development of the realistic novel, no matter what the theological views of biblical commentators,

> what the biblical narratives are all about is something other than their character
> as cumulatively or accretively articulated stories whose themes emerge into full
> shape only through the narrative rendering and deployment itself. The curious,
> unmarked frontier between history and realistic fiction allows easy transition if
> one's interest is the rendering and exploration of a temporal framework through

70. The upshot of the debate over prophecy, in Frei's view, "was the sharp logical distinction of historical judgment from explicative (in particular, literal) sense, and the immediate reintegration of the two things under the dominance of an understanding of meaning-as-ostensive-reference. This is the philosophical context of historical criticism. Clearly, historical-critical analysis can be no more sympathetic than religious apologetics to an interpretation of the narrative text for which the narrative shape, theme, and course are of the greatest interest because they constitute the story's meaning, an interpretation that is not governed, as historical procedure is bound to be, by a theory of meaning either as ostensive (or ideal) reference or as an extension of such reference. This is not to say of course that historical explanation is 'wrong.' It *is* to say, however, that the philosophical or conceptual apparatus, including the theory of meaning, underlying historical criticism of the gospel narratives tends to move it away from every explication of texts not directly governed by a referential theory of meaning or by the cognate identification of meaning with knowledge" (Frei, *Eclipse*, 135 [emphasis in original]). "Assumptions about the way statements and texts are to be understood are very much of a piece with general epistemology. Meaning is reference; statements if they are logically coherent refer to true or actual states of affairs which we know. Theory of meaning is virtually identical with theory of the knowledge of reality" (138).
71. Frei, *Eclipse*, 136.
72. "The situation in the study of the Bible was at one with a prevailing outlook in philosophy. . . . 'Meaning' involved the proper representation of reality in accurate description through clear and distinct ideas. Where this could not be done, the use of words threatened to become vaporous, unclear and indistinct, an ephemeral dream." Frei, *Eclipse*, 138–39.

their logically similar narrative structure, perhaps most of all in the case of the biblical stories where the question of fact or fiction is so problematical. But when prime interest is concentrated on the fact issue—and it could hardly be otherwise in eighteenth-century examination of the Bible—the unmarked frontier is no longer merely real. Now it becomes impenetrable; one is either on one side of it or the other, and the decision between them is the crucial issue.[73]

In Germany, scholars paid attention to the genre of literature in the Bible, but always as a part of historical criticism. Frei emphasizes that all proceeded under the assumption that the meaning of the biblical texts must be understood referentially if they are to make sense.[74]

Frei finds it surprising that German historicism did not precipitate any development of realistic literature in Germany. Frei sees several reasons for this failure. In addition to political factors, the principal reason seems to be "the enormous universalizing tendency" that reached its philosophical zenith in Hegel. In contrast, in England, which had developed a tradition of powerfully realistic novels, literary realism in biblical studies was co-opted by factual historical concerns. This phenomenon was observable in Germany as well, but the "universalizing tendency" Frei observes in German culture pervaded German historicism itself. Seen against the background of an assumption of meaning-as-reference, many commentators (including both rationalists and Pietists) attempted to hold together two often quite different meanings or references in the same story—an ostensive historical one and an idealistic one, though the idealistic referent is understood as itself historically developing spirit. The difficulty of keeping the two together, in Frei's view, resulted in most texts being given either a realistic (historical-factual) or idealistic interpretation, but not both. This categorizing of texts as one or the other precluded a realistic narrative reading of the texts. It was done largely with apologetic interests in view and resulted from the confusion of meaning and reference (among other things).[75]

Given this disjunctive interpretive tendency, it was not surprising that after Strauss had convinced a group of radicals that no plausible historical reconstruction could justify a doctrine of reconciliation, this group would view the true meaning of the gospel in the thoroughly secular way of Marx

73. Frei, *Eclipse*, 150.
74. Frei, *Eclipse*, 155–58. "In Germany also, biblical interpreters took for granted the identity of meaning with reference, historical or ideal, after the fashion of Locke's and Wolff's philosophies; and theory of meaning was equivalent to theory of knowledge" (155).
75. Frei, *Eclipse*, 213–20.

and Feuerbach.[76] In Frei's view, the appearance of the reinterpretations of religion by Marx and Feuerbach

> means that the reversal which started in the late seventeenth century has been fully effected. The elements of the story that figural interpretation had originally woven into one single narrative have now been transposed into another framework. Their meaning, detached from their narrative setting, is now their reference to some other story, some other world, some other context of interpretation.[77]

Strauss himself illustrates well the tension between ostensive and ideal reference, which comes to the surface after his *Life of Jesus* (1935) in the form of the effort to relate "faith" and "history." In Frei's view, all efforts to address the issue presuppose Strauss's setting of the problem:

> (1) Is the meaning (and therefore the truth) of the gospels necessarily connected with reliable historical knowledge of Jesus as uniquely related to God? (2) If one answers affirmatively, can one actually demonstrate that the most plausible historical explanation of the 'supernatural' elements in the accounts, the elements indicating the uniqueness of Jesus, is that they are factually probable?[78]

Strauss believed that the answer to both questions would turn out to be "no," and that the answer to the first question should be indexed to the answer to the second. If an account is impossible in principal to validate historically, this indicates that the referent (and thus the meaning) of the account was not to be considered ostensive or historical. Instead, as Frei observes, such accounts were to be judged as mythical, and "the clue to their meaning is rather to be found in their authors' consciousness, which was historically conditioned to the level of their cultural and religious context."[79] Nonetheless, Strauss still understood the authors' intentions to be literal, thus undercutting mediating positions. Subsequent Romantic mythophiles, more philosophically inclined, differed from Strauss in their understanding of myth. But they shared with him a disjunctive understanding of their interpretive options. The meaning of the biblical accounts is either their ostensive historical reference or the mythical spirit of the writers' age. No other option seemed available, and in either case, Frei argues, the meaning of the texts was understood referentially.[80]

76. Frei, *Eclipse*, 225.
77. Frei, *Eclipse*, 230.
78. Frei, *Eclipse*, 233.
79. Frei, *Eclipse*, 233.
80. Frei, *Eclipse*, 234–44.

At the turn of the eighteenth to nineteenth century, three distinct hermeneutic positions were available. The meaning of the biblical texts could be understood as their ostensive (i.e., historical) reference; as their ideal reference (to some ideal or universal truth); or as the consciousness they represented (the mythophile position).[81] On Frei's analysis, these options, along with the debate over miracles, presented theologians with a dilemma. On the one hand, one could acknowledge the natural, human origin and nature of the biblical writings. But then she must admit that they are not only fallible, but also unreliable and historically conditioned. Further, she must admit that any truth-claims made by them must be relative rather than absolute. On the other hand, one could follow the supernaturalists, asserting that the writings were inspired, factually reliable, and infallibly true.[82] This would require (1) showing that the putative facts to which they referred were at least plausible, (2) articulating criteria for determining which writings have their meanings constituted by their ostensive reference and which do not, and (3) demonstrating "the ostensive character or sense of a large and crucial segment of the writings, especially descriptions of divine intervention. . . ."[83]

Frei notes that the tasks of the supernaturalists proved too extreme for most. Moreover, the mythophiles provided a superior way to distinguish those writings that ostensively referred and those that did not, and also a superior answer to the related question of their "real" meaning if it was not their ostensive reference. Because all three positions construed the texts' meaning as "located" extratextually, the central hermeneutic task was somehow to connect the meaning of the texts with their words. The mythophiles proposed that the mythological consciousness exemplified by the author connects them, and this consciousness is accessible via historical understanding. This proposal proved more persuasive than its rivals.[84] Despite its popularity, however, the category of myth could not, in Frei's view, take adequate account of the character of the biblical narratives. Strauss had distinguished biblical "myths" from nonbiblical ones by observing that biblical myths are simple and realistic, while nonbiblical myths are embellished and "weird."[85] Yet Strauss used the same analytical tool (myth) to interpret both kinds of stories. He observed the

81. Frei, *Eclipse*, 256–65.
82. Frei, *Eclipse*, 267.
83. Frei, *Eclipse*, 268.
84. Frei, *Eclipse*, 268–69.
85. Frei, *Eclipse*, 275. As Frei notes, Strauss used other factors as well (275–76).

distinction, in other words, but could not account for it analytically.[86] And the reason that the single notion of myth could not handle this distinction is that nearly everyone assumed that the meaning of the text's words could not be located in their use in the stories. In turn, the deeper reasons for this mistake are Frei's familiar culprits: apologetics, preoccupation with factual investigation, confusion of meaning with reference, and deriving a theory of meaning from a theory of knowledge. But the crucial mistake, in Frei's view, is locating the meaning of a text outside the text itself.[87] This is particularly misleading in the case of realistic narratives like those in the Bible,[88] but Frei believes it to be a pervasive obstacle to understanding more generally because it presupposes a realm of Platonic entities. Quoting Ryle, Frei states: "An intention is an implicit action, an action an explicit intention; in the words of Gilbert Ryle, 'to perform intelligently is to do one thing and not two things.'"[89] Frei states that, if Ryle is right, it is unnecessary to posit some "mysterious realm of being and meaning . . . in order to discover what makes any intelligent action publicly or commonly available."[90]

In the hermeneutic shift in the early nineteenth century, exemplified best by Schleiermacher, Frei notes that the meaning of the term "hermeneutics" changed "from determination of the rules and principles of interpreting texts to inquiry into the nature of understanding discourse and what is manifest in it. . . ."[91] For Strauss, hermeneutics was concerned with assessing the subject matter of a text, whether it is accurate in what it alleges, and why it was written. In the nineteenth century, Frei argues, such issues remain hermeneutically important, but another question is added: "What, it was asked, are the principles involved in the rendering of the distinct mode of consciousness, the individual thoughts, the collective presuppositions and tendencies of given eras of the past?"[92] In order to get at this question, one needed a prior account of human understanding. One could only understand the consciousness of a past era relationally, as it were. In Kantian fashion, the consciousness of a past era could not be known in itself, but only through the interpreter's consciousness

86. Frei, *Eclipse*, 274–76. The mythophiles "had no category for dealing with the meaning of biblical narratives other than the disjunctive device that assigned either ostensive or mythical status to them" (274).
87. Frei, *Eclipse*, 277–79.
88. Frei, *Eclipse*, 281.
89. Frei, *Eclipse*, 281, quoting Gilbert Ryle, *The Concept of Mind* (London: Hutchinson, 1949; repr., Chicago: Univ. of Chicago Press, 1984), 40.
90. Frei, *Eclipse*, 281.
91. Frei, *Eclipse*, 282.
92. Frei, *Eclipse*, 285.

or understanding.[93] But the interpreter's understanding is to a large extent constituted by what it understands, and so understanding itself is a complex dialectic that is ineluctably linguistic.[94] Consequently, for Schleiermacher, there are two distinct moments to interpretation, which are inseparable though mutually irreducible. "The 'grammatical' moment in interpretation is directed toward understanding the discourse as a focus within a language as a whole, characterized by its relation to the total linguistic stock. The 'psychological' or 'technical' moment is directed toward understanding the discourse 'as a fact in the thinker.'"[95] The importance of empathy with the author was as important for Schleiermacher as it was for Herder, but Schleiermacher's understanding of the linguistic nature of thought kept grammatical interpretation of equal importance with psychological interpretation.[96]

Schleiermacher's conception of understanding not only highlights the distance between the present and the past, it also makes this distance a problem for self-understanding. As a result, Frei argues, application became a distinct and important *hermeneutical* issue for the first time.[97] The reason for application's hermeneutic importance is that meaning has now become ambiguous, hovering somewhere between the sense of a text, its subject matter, and its significance.[98] For Schleiermacher, the meaning of a text is neither its explicative sense, nor its subject matter (whether ostensive or ideal reference), nor both together. Instead, it is the dialectic between, on the one hand, the connection of all these with the spirit of the author and of his age and, on the other, the interpreter. The aim of interpretation is no longer "a fixed relation of unvarying subject matter and words"; instead, the "hermeneutical task reaches to the complex unitary source of discourse, whence conscious intentional idea, true sense, individual self-expression, and style all originate."[99] It was indeed a seismic shift that Schleiermacher brought about.

93. Both Hegel and Schleiermacher agreed "on the autonomous and (at least for Hegel) creative role of the interpreter (or to put it in a less individualistic mode: the role of 'spirit') in the task of interpretation. Whatever is to be understood is refracted through the interpreter's understanding so that hermeneutics now turns from the rules or guidelines for interpreting texts, which it had been hitherto (and was still to be for Strauss), to the theory of the process of knowing or understanding. The aim of hermeneutical procedure must be to answer the question: What does it mean to understand?" (Frei, *Eclipse*, 288).

94. Frei, *Eclipse*, 291–92, 300. "Language to Schleiermacher is something like a form of life (to use Wittgenstein's phrase), and life is tied to language" (293). For Schleiermacher, "no thought is accessible except as speech. . . ." (295).

95. Frei, *Eclipse*, 292 (quoting Schleiermacher, *Hermeneutik* [ed. Kimmerle], 80).

96. Frei, *Eclipse*, 295, 299–300.

97. Frei, *Eclipse*, 303–304.

98. Frei, *Eclipse*, 304.

99. Frei, *Eclipse*, 305.

Nonetheless, for all his innovation Schleiermacher did not, in Frei's view, account any better for the realistic character of the biblical narratives than his predecessors. Both Schleiermacher and Hegel reinforced the earlier tendency to locate the meaning of the texts in a subject matter external to the texts themselves, and to understand the text through this external subject matter. Once again, on Frei's reading, it was an apologetic impulse that led Schleiermacher to seek a universal hermeneutic method and to interpret all texts through it. In Frei's view, Schleiermacher's success depended on his specifying a coherent relation between psychological and grammatical interpretation, as well as his ability to describe the origin of discourse so that thought and speech or self-expression are coherently related. In Frei's judgment, Schleiermacher was successful on neither count. Consequently, the focus of meaning constantly shifted from the discourse as such to the consciousness expressed therein. In the Gospels, this turned out to be the consciousness of Jesus.[100]

The "hermeneutics of understanding" (as Frei calls it, whether in Schleiermacher's or Hegel's or some other version) had little in common with its predecessors. But what it did have in common was its location of the meaning of the biblical narratives outside the texts themselves. Its understanding of meaning was not as directly referential as its predecessors, but it was ultimately referential; a text acquired meaning through a descriptive sense that points to something else.[101] The most fundamental problem with this understanding of meaning, in Frei's opinion, is that it does not let the texts speak for themselves, much less acknowledge their tyrannical purpose. In fact, in Frei's view, to understand the meaning of a text—or at least the biblical narratives—in this way is *inevitably* to change its meaning:

> But most important in our general context is that the whole procedure—whether in the form that Schleiermacher and his later followers gave it or in that which Hegel and his followers gave it—simply undercuts all realistic narrative. As soon as one's perspective, i.e. the process of understanding itself, schematically sets the terms on which the text is to be interpreted, the meaning of the text is bound to be similar to the structure of understanding or 'linguisticality' or some other special structure of human self-and-other apprehension. What this does to narratives we have seen in the instance of Schleiermacher on the

100. Frei, *Eclipse*, 307–12, 320.
101. Frei, *Eclipse*, 316–23. "The meaning of the narrative is something other than the narrative shape itself. There is, for this whole point of view, simply no way of dealing with descriptive or narrative shape without shifting its meaning to a more profound stratum. The documents mean something other than what they say" (318).

death and resurrection of Jesus. Whatever cannot be ranged into this structure becomes meaningless, or at best forced back into it by way of a reinterpretation of its 'objectified' form. The text itself, not as self-expressions or 'word events,' but simply as the formal narrative shape of a story, cannot be the meaning or the subject matter of the narrative.[102]

It is difficult to overestimate the influence of Auerbach and ordinary language philosophy in Frei's assessment of the modern turn in Protestant theology. More specifically, in Frei's view it was a descriptivist understanding of the meaning of the biblical texts that kept Protestant theology on the wrong track until Barth. And it was the pervasiveness of this understanding that made it so difficult for Barth to articulate the break he wanted to achieve. The importance of this understanding of meaning for Frei is highlighted by the fact that his most substantial single work (by far), *The Eclipse of Biblical Narrative*, is devoted to charting the establishment of the hegemony of this understanding in modern theology. The importance Frei placed on "meaning-as-reference" is evidenced by the consistency with which he uses it to criticize modern Protestant theologians and biblical interpreters. Whether he is discussing Anthony Collins, supernaturalists, mythophiles such as D. F. Strauss, biblical theologians such as J. P. Gabler, Pietists or Wolffians, Ritschl or Harnack, Herder, Schleiermacher or Hegel, Frei emphasizes that their fundamental mistake was to take the meaning of the biblical narratives as constituted by some descriptive sense that can refer to some possible state of affairs.

When one considers the three themes in Barth's work that most impressed Frei in his formative dissertation, one can easily see why it was so important for Frei's own project to chart this understanding of the meaning of the biblical texts. On my reading, Frei takes all three Barthian themes that come through in his work on Barth to be undermined by the descriptivist or referential understanding of meaning that he analyzes in *The Eclipse of Biblical Narrative*. When meaning is located outside the texts themselves, Frei argues that the conditions and criteria of the meaning of such texts must be given by independently established epistemological principles. This is precisely what happens in the work of Anthony Collins, for whom the criteria and possibilities of the meaning of biblical texts are given by Lockean epistemological principles. The work of Collins figures so prominently in the narrative Frei tells in *The Eclipse of Biblical Narrative* because it established that epistemology must be prior to ontology in theological method—the establishment of a mistake as far as Barth and Frei are concerned.

102. Frei, *Eclipse*, 322–23.

Second, this priority of epistemology transformed all debate about the meaning of biblical texts into debates about their reference. This transformation was motivated by an apologetic impulse, beginning with referents that all should consider plausible, then arguing that such reasonable referents (whether historical, ideal, or located in Jesus' consciousness) are the real referents of the biblical stories. The meanings of such stories were articulated so as to make them amenable to apologetic argument, creating an ordered pair of meaning and understanding that were complementary and universally accessible. On Frei's telling, whether in an earlier Lockean form (such as that of Collins) or in a more sophisticated hermeneutic form (such as that of Schleiermacher), the fundamental duality of this ordered pair persisted. Such a systematic ordering gives priority to method over any positive affirmations about God. That is, in Frei's view, whatever the biblical texts may say about God, the meaning of such statements must be construed in conformity with this independently established ordered pair.

Finally, any interpretive method that has a referential understanding of meaning as a constituent part cannot be governed by the primacy and priority of God's free and initiating grace, because in Frei's view such a method assumes, rather than denies, epistemic access to God in the absence of such an initiating act. When the meaning of the biblical texts are held to consist in their reference to some extratextual reality, and when the conditions and criteria of that meaning are given in advance by a prior theory of understanding, it follows, on Frei's view, that the reader must already have some independent understanding of the reference of the texts if she is to understand their meaning. Interpretive method is therefore governed not by the priority of God's free and initiating grace, but rather by an independent theory of understanding. All of this overturns the "tyrannical" nature of the biblical narratives and makes them subordinate to the epistemological needs of apologetic argument. As I move now to Frei's constructive proposal, I hope it will become clear that he will attempt to instantiate all three of these Barthian themes by beginning with the Gospel narratives and by working with an understanding of their meaning that is decidedly nonreferential.

III. FREI'S CONSTRUCTIVE PROPOSAL

Frei's constructive work evidences a view of modern Christian theology consistent with *The Eclipse of Biblical Narrative*: modern theology has been animated by an apologetic aim, and its organizing principle has been anthropological.[103] Its content has been almost exclusively Christocentric, and it has been preoccupied with the project of arguing for the possibility (and truth) of claims about the revelation in Jesus Christ by means of an independently justifiable account of the human condition.[104] Contrary to Barth, then, modern Christian theology has prioritized epistemology over ontology,[105] and has attempted to understand humanity's relation to God through theological anthropology instead of through the doctrine of God. Thus theology is now confronted with two basic alternatives, one of which, following Barth, is nonapologetic and dogmatic, and the other of which, in the tradition of liberal theology, is essentially "a metaphysic or ontology in which Christology would play a peripheral role."[106] Frei, of course, opts for the Barthian option: "I believe that it is not the business of Christian theology to argue the *possibility* of Christian truth any more than the instantiation or *actuality* of that truth. The possibility follows logically as well as existentially from its actuality."[107] This situation, Frei argues, in which theology faces two opposed alternatives, means that the situation is ripe for another debate over the essence of Christianity.[108] Frei understands his dogmatic proposal to be a contribution to this debate.[109]

103. Frei's constructive proposals are set out primarily in three works that appeared between 1966 and 1975. In 1966, Frei published a long article in the *Christian Scholar* setting out a constructive proposal derived from the narrative depiction of Jesus' identity in the (mostly synoptic) Gospels. Hans W. Frei, "Theological Reflections on the Accounts of Jesus' Death and Resurrection," *Christian Scholar* 49 (Winter 1966): 263–306. The article is reprinted in Frei, *Theology and Narrative*, 45–93. Hereafter, page references to this article will be to the reprint edition. Frei's proposal was delivered in a lecture the following year at Harvard Divinity School and was further developed in a series entitled "The Mystery of the Presence of Jesus Christ," which appeared in the same year (1967) in *Crossroads*, an adult education magazine published by the Presbyterian Church (U.S.A.). The lecture is reprinted as "Remarks in Connection with a Theological Proposal," in Frei, *Theology and Narrative*, 26–44. Hereinafter, page references to this lecture will be to the reprint edition. This series was subsequently expanded and published in book form under the title, *The Identity of Jesus Christ: The Hermeneutical Bases of Dogmatic Theology* (Philadelphia: Fortress Press, 1975; repr., Eugene, Oreg.: Wipf & Stock, 1997) (page references are to reprint edition).

104. Frei, "Remarks," 29.

105. Despite the inconsistency of Frei's language in the 1967 lecture with that in his dissertation, I take this to be the meaning of this statement: "Theology, like philosophy, has been agitated by epistemological and ontological rather than metaphysical questions" (Frei, "Remarks," 28).

106. Frei, "Remarks," 27.

107. Frei, "Remarks," 30.

108. Frei, "Remarks," 31.

109. "My aim is to take a first step toward getting at the question: What is the essence of Christianity? My plea is that this be done in a nonperspectivist way if possible." Frei, "Remarks," 31.

In making this contribution, Frei attempts to carry out the objective that he sees Barth trying to achieve throughout his career, both in his dialectical period and in the period after Barth's book on Anselm—namely, to resist letting his method overdetermine his affirmations about God, but instead to let his positive affirmations about God govern his method.[110] Frei sees three clues to how he can accomplish this objective. First is Auerbach's contention that the biblical narratives are tyrannical in their purpose, that they seek to overcome our reality and to tell the only true narrative of the history of the divine-human relation. If Auerbach is right about the nature of the narratives, then in Frei's view any method that begins with an independently established anthropological scheme cannot be faithful to the nature of the biblical narratives. Thus, the place to begin in searching for the essence of Christianity is the biblical narratives themselves. And if theology is to be Christocentric, then it makes sense to begin with the synoptic Gospels.[111] The second and third clues come from Wittgenstein and Ryle and are closely related. These are their contentions: first, that descriptivism is indefensible (a contention for which Frei argues throughout *The Eclipse of Biblical Narrative*) and, second, that the "ghost in the machine" cannot be defended as an adequate understanding of the self.[112] In Frei's view, to take these second and third clues seriously requires two related positions. First, the identity of a person is not merely evidenced or symbolized by that person's actions and what happens to her; instead, such events are constitutive of her identity.[113] Second, the meaning of the Gospel narratives is not constituted by their reference to some independently existing series of events or state of affairs. Instead, their meaning must somehow be internal to the narratives themselves. When a narrative depicts some event or series of events, the "locus of meaning" is not the events to which the narratives refer, but the depictions themselves. Thus, as Frei is fond of saying, the texts "simply mean what they say." It is not essential to Frei's method that this understanding of meaning be universalized so that it is true of all

---

110. See Frei, *Identity*, 130–31. This is what Barth means when he says that theological method cannot be prolegomena but must be part of the subject matter of theology.

111. Frei, "Remarks," 32.

112. See Frei, "Remarks," 35.

113. Frei feels that what happens to a person has been left out of theological anthropology. "I can describe my response to my interpretation of and reaction to something done to me. But the interaction of character and circumstance is more than this. I become what I am also by what is done to me and becomes a determinative part of me—and that not only by my interpretation of, or reaction to, it" (Frei, "Remarks," 37). "A man is known precisely to the extent that he is what he does and what is done to him. . . . He is neither envisaged nor formed nor read as a private, inferred, hidden self for which action is merely symbolic" (36).

kinds of statements. Rather, Frei is saying only that the meaning of real-istic, history-like narratives is constituted not by any referential function, but rather by the depictions that the narratives convey.[114] In articulating his understanding of the identity of a character in a realistic narrative, Frei is trying both to avoid assuming a "ghost in the machine" and to be faithful to the way in which such narratives mean what they do.

If Frei is to be consistent with these "methodological" positions, in addressing the essence of Christianity he must seek a description of the identity of Jesus based on what Jesus does and on what happens to him as those events are depicted in the synoptic Gospels. The meaning of the Gospels' statements about Jesus are constituted by these depictions.

Frei does not object to the Christocentricity of liberal theology, for his own contribution to the question of the "essence" of Christianity is thor-oughly Christocentric. What troubles him is the way the Christocentricity of liberal theology expresses itself. Most liberal theologians, in Frei's view, exhibit a Christocentric orientation because they assume (not necessar-ily incorrectly) that the claims about Jesus made in the New Testament present modern readers with profound epistemological problems. Thus they approach the New Testament in the hope of answering the question, "How must the New Testament claims about Jesus be construed if they are to be even possible, much less plausible, to modern readers?" In Frei's view, such an approach limits the possible meanings of the New Testament narratives to those that can be defended by an independently formulated epistemological scheme. Frei believes that this typically modern approach to the New Testament claims about Jesus fails to do justice to the "tyranni-cal nature" of the New Testament narratives.[115] He takes his own approach to be more faithful to the character of the texts themselves. One should approach the texts so that their meaning emerges from the narratives themselves (instead of being a function of their reference to nontextual events), and then decide as a separate matter whether one will accept the claims that they make.[116]

When one lets the meaning of the narrative emerge from the texts themselves, one is better able to avoid assuming that the real identity of Jesus is a "ghost in the machine," because what the narratives provide are simply events in which Jesus acts intentionally and is acted upon by others. The primary way in which Jesus' identity is described in the text, in Frei's view, is an "intention-action" description. Keeping this kind of identity

114. In these limitations of Frei's remarks about meaning, his Barthian resistance to systematizing is apparent.
115. Frei, "Remarks," 40, 56–58.
116. Frei, "Remarks," 40.

description primary is Frei's way of avoiding the "intellectualist legend." But because Jesus' identity is continuous over time and over a large number of actions and events, intention-action description must be supplemented by a "subject-manifestation" description. When Frei does turn to the Gospel narratives, he finds that the identity of Jesus depicted there is that of *one who is present to his disciples*. But Jesus' presence is of a unique kind. Because his presence constitutes his identity, Frei argues that he cannot be conceived as not present: "Christian faith involves a unique affirmation about Jesus Christ, viz., not only that he is the presence of God but also that knowing his identity is identical with having him present or being in his presence."[117] Of course, one can think of Jesus of Nazareth as simply one who lived and died and is no longer present in any sense other than that in which any person who has died is present in the memory of those who knew or knew of her. But to think of Jesus this way, Frei argues, is not to think of *Jesus who is depicted in the Gospels* at all. It is instead to conceive of a different identity than the one depicted in the Gospel narratives and to ascribe this different identity to Jesus.

The Identity of Jesus Christ is Frei's most extended treatment of this unique claim, that to understand the identity of Jesus is to actually have him present. Because of the unique nature of Christ's presence, Frei says that it cannot be defined, but it can be described.[118] Frei takes Christ to be present in the Word and Sacraments, but "the fully personal use of 'presence,' when applied to Jesus Christ, is not qualified like the other two [i.e., presence in the sacraments and in the Word of God], but rather *completed* in a way that is beyond our imagining and conceiving."[119] Further, Frei takes this unique claim about Jesus' identity and presence to depend on the traditional claims about Christ's resurrection, ascension, and impartation of the Spirit, because "the unity of presence and identity must have a physical and temporal basis in his resurrection."[120]

117. Frei, *Identity*, 53.
118. Frei, *Identity*, 76–78.
119. Frei, *Identity*, 83. In Frei's view, "the term 'presence' also denoted symbolic, especially verbal, communication between human beings" (79). In this sense, Christ is communicatively present in the Word of God. "In both instances, Word and Sacrament, we have a hint that their use is not literal, but analogical, when applied to the presence of Jesus Christ" (79). Christ's presence in the sacraments, though it is a real presence, is not a physical presence. "Though it is the nearest thing we have to the physical presence of Christ, it is not identical with the latter" (79).
120. Frei, *Identity*, 86. As Frei puts it, "the claim that Christ is present, although signifying much more than certain attendant physical and historical claims, must have such assertions for its basis. One must, in short, say that he was raised from the dead, ascended on high, and from thence imparts his Spirit" (77).

But the very basis of Christ's presence, the Resurrection, poses a dilemma regarding whether to understand the Resurrection literally or symbolically. On the one hand, the "modern imagination" requires us to understand the Resurrection symbolically. If Christ's resurrection were a literal fact, then he would have an existence to which we could not aspire. In such a case, to speak of life "in Christ" would mean nothing to us here and now, but could only indicate a hope of some future life that we could not understand.[121] On the other hand, what is left out of the modern imagination's symbolic understanding of the Resurrection is Christ's *real* (more than symbolic) presence to the church.[122] But this real presence seems to imply that there are no terms for describing Christ's presence that are generally available. Frei articulates the dilemma in succinct terms as follows: First, "there is no precise parallel between the presence of Jesus Christ and the way we think of the presence of other persons and, secondly, that the use of imagination in regard to Jesus cannot adequately represent his presence to us as the resurrected Lord."[123] For Frei, this dilemma means that one cannot talk about Christ's presence without first describing Christ's identity.[124]

Frei forms his conception of identity in an attempt to perform two tasks. First, he wants to synthesize three principal characteristics: uniqueness, self-awareness, and moral agency.[125] Second, citing Ryle, Frei seeks to avoid the mistake of assuming a "ghost in the machine."[126] Thus, Frei will avoid

121. That is, Christ could not "share" his presence with us (Frei, *Identity*, 91).
122. "When the Christian speaks of Christ's presence, he means that Jesus *owns his own presence and yet turns and shares it with us.* Thus the Christian is forced to part company with the imaginative view discussed above, precisely because what is to him essential about Jesus is left out—his *real* presence. In contrast, Jesus, raised from the dead, is present to himself and therefore can and does share his *real* presence with us" (Frei, *Identity*, 91 [emphasis in original]).
123. Frei, *Identity*, 94.
124. Frei asserts that this danger of distortion may imply to some that we should reject the notion of "presence" with its notions of turning and sharing. "He cannot *turn* to us; he can only *share* with us what he no longer owns for turning. For his turning to us is accomplished only in *our* imagination or perhaps *our* moral decision. There is then a way of talking about the presence of Christ that is, for the Christian, not appropriate to the description of Christ's relation to the believer. It is that of talking about Christ's presence before talking about his identity, or trying directly and concretely in our talk to grasp the presence of Christ. What is grasped is empty space—the shadow of our own craving for full and perpetual presence" (Frei, *Identity*, 92). Rather than eschewing all talk of Christ's presence, Frei argues that such distortion may be avoided by beginning with Christ's identity, speaking of his presence only after articulating his identity: "the dilemma, in short, stems from the fact that we cannot reach the singular identity of Jesus Christ by starting simply with his presence. If we still insist on the total unity of presence and identity, as indeed we must, we must begin at the other end—with his identity" (94).
125. Frei, *Identity*, 95–97.
126. Frei, *Identity*, 99.

speaking of identity as some inner quality or state separable from its outer manifestations. Instead, the primary form of identity description Frei uses is that of "intention-action" description. An intentional action is one process, though one can distinguish between intentions and actions. Describing a person's intentional actions must be the primary form of identity description: "For a person is not merely illustrated, he is *constituted* by his particular intentional act at any given point in his life."[127] Still, Frei recognizes that some actions or sequences of actions are recognizably characteristic of a person's identity, while others stand in tension with that identity. Both sorts of actions or sequences must be gathered into a story comprising an intention-action description. On the other hand, we can obviously observe changes in a person's identity over time. Actions that are typical of a person's identity may later become atypical. Yet it is the same person, with the same identity, that persists through both earlier and later stages. To describe the unbroken continuity of a person's identity through its changes, Frei uses a "subject-manifestation" or "self-manifestation" description.[128]

Frei distinguishes his approach to identity from two others that he takes to be distorting. The first approach begins by "asking how a person in a story illuminates, or perhaps merely illustrates, this or that problem of our common existence."[129] Frei finds this approach inadequate because it overdetermines the kind of character one finds in a story.[130] A second approach adds a "depth dimension to the story's surface, which is actually a speculative *inference* from what is given in the story. . . ."[131] On this approach, the story becomes merely an exemplification of the characters' internal dispositions.[132] Frei argues that this approach also involves presuppositions that distort the identity of the characters in the story. Besides its disregard for Gilbert Ryle's warnings, this second approach assumes that the only actions that form a person's identity are those actions that the person herself intentionally performs. Frei sees no reason to make this assumption. In his view, "a person's story is not only the enactment of *his own* intentions or his own identity, but the enactment of others' intentions and even of unintended events as well as those not specifically intended."[133] The role of external events and unintended actions in the formation of a

127. Frei, *Identity*, 100.
128. Frei, *Identity*, 99–100.
129. Frei, *Identity*, 134.
130. Frei takes this approach to be exemplified by Bultmann and Tillich (Frei, *Identity*, 134–35).
131. Frei, *Identity*, 135.
132. Frei, *Identity*, 135.
133. Frei, *Identity*, 137; see also 135–37.

person's identity cannot be accounted for by purely descriptive categories. Thus, there can be no substitute for the narrative itself of a person's life, and this is no less true for Jesus than for anyone else.[134] "The identity of Jesus in that story is not given simply in his inner intention, in a kind of story behind the story. It is given, rather, in the enactment of his intentions. But even to say that much is not enough. Rather, his identity is given in the mysterious coincidence of his intentional action with circumstances partly initiated by him, partly devolving upon him."[135] Identity, therefore, has a certain elusive character, and even self-manifestation description can proceed only indirectly.[136]

Frei then proceeds to a substantive description of Jesus' identity, beginning with Jesus' enacted intention and then moving to his self-manifestation. In describing the enacted intention of Jesus, Frei summarizes: "In the New Testament story, Jesus is seen to enact the good of men on their behalf—or their salvation—in perfect obedience to God."[137] We cannot verify the "historical" Jesus' "true" intentions or motivations, but his *enacted* intentions in the narratives demonstrate his commitment to obeying God's will. As the narrative of Jesus' life moves forward, power and powerlessness coexist, and the story narrates a transition from power to powerlessness. It is this progression, Christ's identification with the guilty and their helplessness "provide the Gospel's story of salvation. Yet this helplessness is his power for the salvation of others."[138] This coexistence of power and powerlessness coheres nicely with the interaction between Jesus' own actions, or enacted intentions, and external circumstances. Jesus' identity is narrated in a threefold way: through the actions he himself initiates and undertakes, his response to circumstances, and the "sheer impingement" of circumstances on him.[139]

This Gospel narration focuses on Jesus' obedience to the mission given to him by God, and in contrast says little about his faith. By focusing on Jesus' obedience, the Gospels make the will of God an indispensable part of Jesus' identity. And by narrating his identity in the threefold way

134. Such categories "cannot describe how external events become ingredient in a person's identity directly, i.e., other than by his own response to them. All that one can do to describe a person in that situation of direct impact by circumstances upon him (and not as refracted through his own response) and how he becomes himself in and through these circumstances is simply to tell the story of the events" (Frei, *Identity*, 137–38).

135. Frei, *Identity*, 138.

136. Frei, *Identity*, 141.

137. Frei, *Identity*, 145.

138. Frei, *Identity*, 146–47.

139. Frei, *Identity*, 147.

mentioned above, the focus of the story is clearly Jesus in his unsubstitutable identity. Further, his identity is oriented toward carrying out the mission given him by God. At the same time, Jesus' obedience to God constitutes his love toward other persons. Yet Jesus' love for humanity is not some personal deportment or quality, but is "the specific vocation entailed by his mission of obedience to God."[140] The mission given by God to Jesus was his merciful, saving activity that entailed his giving his life for us.[141]

Jesus' unsubstitutable identity, to which obedience to God is indispensable, makes Jesus' life, death, and resurrection necessary to and constitutive of the salvation offered by God through him. The overall pattern of the narrative demonstrates a movement from power to powerlessness. The earlier portions of the narrative consist of self-contained stories demonstrating Jesus' power and authority. Beginning with the preparation for the Last Supper, however, the scenes in the narrative become much more integrated. From that point on, the narrative provides us with a sustained, unbroken story of Jesus' passion, death, and resurrection. The scene in the Garden of Gethsemane is also a crucial turning point in the story, from Jesus' power to his powerlessness. Yet Jesus' powerlessness is brought about at his own initiative as part of the mission to which he is obedient. Even during the arrest and crucifixion, Jesus' "abiding intention" is enacted so that the circumstances that constrain him work in the service of his intention to obey God.[142] After Gethsemane, circumstances that impinge upon Jesus from the "outside" become more important to the enactment of his identity. In Gethsemane, "with circumstances narrowed to the decisive point, it became part of his own free agency to enact the coincidence between his own decision and the developing events. From that coincidence would develop the crucial pattern of events in which his identity would be enacted."[143] This interaction of Jesus' own agency and "public circumstance" is the intention-action description of Jesus' identity.[144] As it is narrated, Jesus' laying down of power and authority and putting himself "helplessly" at the mercy of those who would kill him

140. Frei, *Identity*, 151; see also 148–51.

141. As Frei puts it, "the *referent* of Jesus' obedience is the will of God. . . . The *content* or meaning of that obedience is the pattern of merciful, saving activity. . . ." (Frei, *Identity*, 152 [emphasis in original]).

142. Frei, *Identity*, 150–53.

143. Frei, *Identity*, 154.

144. Intention-action description "locates the identity of an individual at the point at which his inward life, coming to outward expression, is linked with or meshes into the train of public circumstances. Such a description of Jesus' identity comes at the crucial point of his transition from authoritative power to helplessness" (Frei, *Identity*, 154).

is constitutive of his identity.[145] "To be obedient to God was to pour out his blood in behalf of men. Who, then, was Jesus? He was what he did, the man completely obedient to God in enacting the good of men on their behalf."[146]

If there is a transition from Jesus' power to powerlessness, to whom does the initiative or power to act pass? Clearly, it passes to historical forces, but God is somehow enacting the divine will in these forces. The narrative never reduces the divine will to any immanent historical telos, but it does present the divine will as working through historical forces, an interaction that becomes particularly congruent in Jesus' passion and death. Concomitantly with the convergence of intentions of God and Jesus' persecutors, however, Jesus' own intentions become increasingly identified with those of God. Nonetheless, a distinction always remains between Jesus and God. And despite the increasing identification of Jesus' and God's intentions, as Jesus' power makes the transition to powerlessness, the initiative passes from Jesus to God. As it does, God's own agency becomes increasingly dominant over Jesus', using historical forces as "secondary agents" and then finally dispensing with historical agents altogether in the Resurrection. The increasing dominance of God's initiative reaches its apex, then, in the Resurrection. Yet despite the increasing dominance of God's own activity, that activity remains hidden from view, and we see only its effects. It is this very pattern through which the narrative describes God's presence and action in Christ:

> In his passion and death the initiative of Jesus disappears more and more into that of God; but in the resurrection, where the initiative of God is finally and decisively climaxed and he alone is and can be active, the sole identity to mark the presence of that activity is Jesus. God remains hidden, and even reference to him is almost altogether lacking. Jesus of Nazareth, he and none other, marks the presence of the action of God.[147]

Because it is God acting in the Resurrection, if the Resurrection is to be an essential part of the identity of Jesus, it cannot consist solely in an intention-action description. Instead, in the Resurrection accounts, intention-action and self-manifestation descriptions work together. And in terms of the Resurrection itself, "God's deed in raising Jesus is actually

---

145. The transition from power to powerlessness is "made in the full consistency of the same identity carried from intention into action: Jesus was what he did and suffered, the one whose identity was enacted in his passion and death" (Frei, *Identity*, 155).
146. Frei, *Identity*, 152.
147. Frei, *Identity*, 160.

a deed in which the identity of Jesus is *manifested*, rather than being the achievement of a historical *occurrence*."[148] Yet the Resurrection is an enacted event, and indeed is the climax of the Gospel narrative. Thus it is not merely "the *manifestation* of his *identity*" but an event that enacts the intention of God.[149] And both the intention and the enactment are crucial to Jesus' identity. In Frei's view, treating the Resurrection accounts differently from those of the Passion and Crucifixion—say, treating the Crucifixion historically and the Resurrection mythologically—does violence to the literary character of the narratives. Frei is not surprised that conceptual schemes have arisen to deal with the Resurrection accounts. But he believes that such schemes should remain at the descriptive level, and not try to assume an explanatory role.[150] On my reading of Frei's position here, such explanatory attempts tend inevitably to remove the "locus of meaning" from the narrative itself and place it in some other realm, whether transcendental or historical or otherwise. But the Gospel narratives, in Frei's view, will not bear this descriptivist understanding of meaning. Instead, the texts must be so interpreted that their meaning arises from the narrative structure itself, not through its referential function. "However necessary as such *descriptive* schemes may be, they cannot provide *explanatory* theories for the narrative's claims and for the various patterns of meaning inherent in it, and inherent in it in such a manner that meaning cannot be detached from the narrative form."[151]

So far four patterns of meaning have emerged from Frei's intention-action description of Jesus' identity in the Gospels: Jesus' obedience, the coexistence of power and powerlessness, the transition from power to powerlessness, and the interrelation of Jesus' and God's intention and action.[152] After the intention-action description, Frei moves to a self-manifestation description.[153] On Frei's analysis, the Gospels narrate three stages in Jesus' life through which his identity is described: his infancy, his adult ministry, and the last stage of his life. In the infancy narratives, Jesus is not an

148. Frei, *Identity*, 162 (emphasis in original).
149. Frei, *Identity*, 162 (emphasis in original).
150. Frei, *Identity*, 161–63.
151. Frei, *Identity*, 163.
152. Frei, *Identity*, 164.
153. He contrasts the two as follows: Intention-action description "deals with a specific, enacted project of a person—a specific sequence in the perfection of its enactment from initial inception to completed execution." Self-manifestation description "tries to point to the continuity of a person's identity throughout the transitions brought about by his acts and life's events" (Frei, *Identity*, 165). In the context of the Gospel narratives, Frei understands the self-manifestation description of Jesus' identity as "the structuring of the Gospel story as a whole into a single developing series of stages in the identification of its persisting subject, Jesus of Nazareth" (164).

individual in his own right, but a representative figure that "is identified wholly in terms of the identity of the people of Israel."[154] In this stage there is no intention-action description, but the events surrounding his birth and infancy manifest his representative, stylized identity.

Jesus' baptism marks a transition in which he starts to become an individual in his own right. His identity still has a representative quality, but it is nonetheless different than in his infancy. After his baptism, the representative quality of Jesus' identity has less to do with summarizing Israel's past and more to do with God's direct and immediate, or imminently pending, rule over Israel. As the witness to or embodiment of the reign or kingdom of God, he is both a representative of Israel and an individual in his own right. As such, his identity is enacted and manifested in history, and historical questions about his life and ministry can now be raised that were not appropriate for the infancy narratives.[155] Such historical questions, however, seem much less important for Frei than for others. In Frei's estimation, figuring out how much is historically accurate is very speculative. More importantly, for Frei, "the meaning of these texts would remain the same, partially stylized and representative and partially focused on the history-like individual, whether or not they are historical."[156]

Although the first two stages are by no means unimportant, the last stage is most important for Frei's understanding of Jesus' identity.[157] This last stage is most clearly history-like, and is thought to be more historically accurate than the other two. The transition to the third stage is marked by the beginning of the journey of Jesus and his disciples to Jerusalem, and Jesus' prediction of the fate that awaited him there. During this stage, or at least at the beginning of it, Jesus' identity is still representative of the kingdom of God. "Nonetheless, that very identification now becomes increasingly problematical and tenuous."[158] In fact, in the last stage, all the representative qualities of Jesus' identity become problematic, and the story increasingly focuses on his singularity. We have seen already that during the Passion sequence, the initiative passes from Jesus to God as Jesus'

154. Frei, *Identity*, 165–66.
155. Frei, *Identity*, 168–69.
156. Frei, *Identity*, 169.
157. "The significantly unique identity of an individual, in this instance Jesus of Nazareth, is to be discerned by asking (1) where the bond between intention and action in his story is most clearly evident; and (2) where the direct bond between himself as individual subject and his outward self-manifestation is strongest and most clearly unitary in character." In the case of Jesus, "The answer to both questions is in the crucifixion-resurrection sequence." This is where he is "most of all himself" (Frei, "Theological Reflections," 46).
158. Frei, *Identity*, 170.

power passes into powerlessness. Yet this transfer of initiative and power clarifies the story's focus on Jesus' singularity rather than obscuring it.

> A fascinating feature of this narrative is that this increasing action of God does not detract in the slightest from the increasingly sharp focusing on Jesus' singularity. Further, it is in this interaction that Jesus' identity is clarified as the one unsubstitutable Jesus of Nazareth. Indeed, at the climactic point of the divine action, the resurrection, where God alone is active, it is Jesus alone who is manifest.[159]

The narrative's intention-action description of Jesus' identity comes to a climax in the Passion and Crucifixion; its self-manifestation description comes to a climax in the Resurrection and post-Resurrection appearances. Jesus' connection with symbolic features, which became ambiguous during the last stage of his life, are reestablished in the Resurrection and post-Resurrection appearances. In Frei's view, the narrative is structured so that all the components of Jesus' identity description are brought to fulfillment and to their clearest manifestation in the resurrected Jesus. The narrative is thus a structured whole, in which the representative identity manifest in the infancy narratives and in the accounts of Jesus' adult ministry are now climactically clarified in the historically singular, unsubstitutable person of Jesus. "At the end of the story, as at its beginning, there is full identity between Jesus and Israel. But whereas at the beginning it was the community that served to identify him, the reverse is now the case. He, Jesus, provides the community, as well as God's Kingdom and the stylized savior figure, with his identity."[160]

Frei's reading of the narrative, with its climax in the integrated accounts of the Resurrection, in Frei's view carries three broad implications. First, the Resurrection cannot be interpreted as a myth. In the

---

159. Frei, *Identity*, 171.
160. Frei, *Identity*, 172. At this point, Frei argues that a "subject-alienation" description is neither helpful nor applicable to an analysis of the narrative depiction of Jesus' identity. It seems to me that Frei believes such a descriptive device assumes a "ghost in the machine" understanding of identity and allows the story to mean what it does only referentially. "We must neither look for his identity in back of the story nor supply it from extraneous analytical schemes. It is evident that in the story Jesus' true being is not mysteriously hidden behind the action or within a supposedly distorted, 'objectified,' or 'mythological' self-manifestation. No. He is what he appeared to be—the Savior Jesus from Nazareth, who underwent 'all these things' and who is truly manifest as Jesus, the risen Christ. Such, it appears, is the story of Jesus in the Gospels. . . . Not only the substance of the claim that human beings are self-alienated in this world, but even the idea applied as a formal scheme for the description of human identity is inapplicable in connection with the Gospel story" (173).

Gospel narratives, Jesus' identity is manifest in its most singular and unsubstitutable way in the Resurrection. In contrast, were it a myth, the Resurrection would contain the least particular, and most universal, description of Jesus' identity. Thus, far from being a myth, it is "a demythologization of the dying-rising savior myth."[161] Second, the Passion-Crucifixion-Resurrection sequence must be the primary focus of both theological and historical assertions about Jesus, rather than Jesus' teaching ministry or sayings. "A Soteriology or Christology involving assertion of the indispensable uniqueness of Jesus cannot possibly make good on any claim that the person of the depicted Jesus is directly known from his teachings and that his final personal bearing and destiny in the story are but functions of these words."[162] More generally, if historical questions are to be investigated and religious content dependent on them, it will have to be in the Passion-Crucifixion-Resurrection sequence.[163] Third, throughout the narrative but particularly in the accounts of the Resurrection, fictional description and factual claims merge so completely that their very form makes a sort of quasi-ontological argument not only for the factuality of the Resurrection, but also for Jesus' continuing presence in the church. The fictional description, which renders Jesus' identity—an identity most clearly and singularly manifest in the Resurrection—merges with the factual claim that God resurrected him so that an understanding of Jesus' resurrection is necessary to an understanding of his identity.

> The narration is at once intensely serious and historical in intent and fictional in form, the common strand between them being the identification of the individual in his circumstances. To know *who* he is in connection with what took place is to know *that* he is. This is the climax of the story and its claim. What the accounts are saying, in effect, is that the being and identity of Jesus in the resurrection are such that his nonresurrection becomes inconceivable.[164]

Frei extends this argument so that grasping Jesus' identity not only requires *conceiving* of the Resurrection, but also requires *believing* that the Resurrection of Jesus occurred.[165] If we think of Jesus as one who has not

---

161. Frei, *Identity*, 174; see also Frei, "Theological Reflections," 82–83.
162. Frei, *Identity*, 176.
163. Frei, *Identity*, 177.
164. Frei, *Identity*, 178–79.
165. Frei explicitly reads the narratives as arguing that "to grasp what this identity, Jesus of Nazareth (which has been made directly accessible to us) is is to believe that he has been, in *fact*, raised from the dead" (Frei, *Identity*, 179).

been raised, we are not thinking of the Jesus whose identity is described in the Gospels.[166] "*That* he is and *who* he is . . . are one and the same thing. His identity is so unsubstitutable now through the event of resurrection that he can bring it to bear as the identifying clue for the community that becomes climactically focused through him."[167] Like the argument discovered by St. Anselm, on Frei's view this argument from Jesus' identity to his quasi-necessary presence is valid only in this one unique case. Nonetheless, Frei does not restate the argument in syllogistic form. It is a literary argument, and Frei seems to believe it cannot be so restated. Indeed, he asserts that explaining the transition from literary depiction to historical and religious affirmation is impossible.[168]

> This, then, is the identity of Jesus Christ. He is the man from Nazareth who redeemed men by his helplessness, in perfect obedience enacting their good in their behalf. As that same one, he was raised from the dead and manifested to be the redeemer. As that same one, Jesus the redeemer, he cannot *not* live, and to conceive of him as not living is to misunderstand who he is.[169]

In Frei's view, therefore, for a Christian not to believe in the Resurrection is rationally impossible. Yet he states that "whether one actually *believes* the resurrection is, of course, a wholly different matter."[170] Now what this means, it seems to me, is that the kind of transcendental method for which Ogden has argued is ruled out by the identity description of Jesus in the Gospels. Any method that begins with describing the conditions of the possibility of understanding or believing the Resurrection and then seeks to describe the Resurrection event in terms of those conditions will inevitably distort the identity of Jesus, in Frei's view. Such a method would yield an understanding of Christ's resurrection (and thus of his presence) for which belief in the factuality of that presence would not be essential. Any such method Frei would take to be motivated by apologetic concerns. For his part, Frei takes apologetic methods to involve a task he believes to be impossible: namely, to provide a rational bridge over the gap from unfaith to faith. But the crossing of this gap cannot be explained.[171] Thus, in Frei's view, theology must begin not with describing the possibilities of

---

166. "To think him dead is the equivalent of not thinking of him at all" (Frei, *Identity*, 180).
167. Frei, *Identity*, 181.
168. Frei, *Identity*, 180.
169. Frei, *Identity*, 182 (emphasis in original).
170. Frei, *Identity*, 183 (emphasis in original).
171. Frei, *Identity*, 183.

human subjectivity, but instead with the narrative of Jesus' life, death, and resurrection.

> Note that we do not ask: Is it possible? Is it demonstrable? How can we become persuaded of this difficult belief? Just these are the kinds of questions that would call for the dubious kind of bridging of the gap which we have avoided, between the believer with his formal question affirming and seeking to describe the presence of Christ and the unbeliever with his inability to presuppose or grasp that presence.[172]

So Jesus' identity, in Frei's view, cannot be abstracted from his presence. But neither can it be abstracted from the identity of God. The climax of the Gospel is "the full unity of the unsubstitutable individuality of Jesus with the presence of God."[173] Jesus' identity and presence, and its unity with the presence of God, are part of what Christians mean when they speak of the Holy Spirit. From now on, "we can no longer think of God except as we think of Jesus at the same time, nor of Jesus except by reference to God."[174] Frei has argued, as we have seen, that Jesus' identity is not correctly conceived if Jesus is conceived as not present. "This, however, does not mean that his presence can be directly grasped or conceived."[175] Instead, to speak of the Spirit is to speak of the fact that the presence of the complex unity, Jesus as God's presence, is indirect. We have also seen that, in Frei's view, one will not correctly conceive of Jesus' identity unless one *believes* him to be present. Referring to the Spirit is a Christian way of referring to this unity of factual affirmation and moral commitment. In every other instance, facts and moral attitudes are separate. But in "this one unique instance," knowing Jesus' identity, affirming his presence, and following his command to love one's neighbor are "one and the same thing."[176]

To speak of the Spirit is not only to speak of the unity of Jesus' identity with the presence of God, but also to speak of Jesus' continuing presence in

---

172. Frei, *Identity*, 182.
173. Frei, *Identity*, 186. "In short, to speak of the identity of *Jesus*, in which he is affirmed by the believer to be present, is also to speak of the presence of *God*" (186). In the final sequence of resurrection and resurrection appearances, Jesus' identity "is declared to be the complex unity of the unsubstitutable Jesus from Nazareth with the presence and action of God" (186).
174. Frei, *Identity*, 187.
175. Frei, *Identity*, 187.
176. Frei, *Identity*, 188. "Just as Christ's presence and identity cannot be conceived apart, factual affirmation of him and commitment to him cannot be conceived apart either, no matter how far or short a person may fall in practice in respect to the one or the other or both" (188).

and with the church. "The church is both a witness to that presence [of Jesus and God who is one with him] and the public and communal form the indirect presence of Christ now takes, in contrast to his direct presence in his earthly days."[177] If Jesus is present in and with the church, then the identity description of Jesus must analogously apply to the church. The continuing indirect presence of Christ is constituted by the Word and Sacrament, which in turn constitute the self-manifestation identity of the church. In the Word and Sacrament, Jesus' continuing presence in the church is temporally (Word) and spatially (Sacrament) manifest. But the identity of the church is analogous to, and not identical with, that of Jesus. In terms of intention-action description, just as Christ's identity had to be narrated, so does the church's. But there are at least two differences: First, the church must follow Christ at a distance rather than being a complete reiteration of Christ's identity. The church is to be a collective disciple, not a "Christ figure."[178] Second, the church's history is obviously not finished, nor is it a private history. It will be enacted in interaction with the world. Christ's presence to history "means that history is neither chaotic nor fated, but providentially ordered in the life, death, and resurrection of Jesus Christ, who is Lord of the past, the present, and the future."[179]

IV. CONCLUDING REMARKS

In *The Identity of Jesus Christ*, therefore, one can see clearly Frei's attempt to remain faithful to the central insights of his mentors. Following Barth, he seeks to begin biblically rather than apologetically. Instead of presenting an argument for belief in Christ's resurrection and presence that would be available to an unbeliever, he leaves intact the gap between faith and unfaith. Again following Barth, he prioritizes ontology over epistemology, arguing for a biblical literary kind of quasi-ontological argument for Jesus' continuing presence rather than beginning with epistemological conditions

177. Frei, *Identity*, 188–89. Frei also speaks of Christ's presence in the Word and Sacraments. The church, he says, "is constituted by the one (his presence, which must be spatially and temporally based—even though these bases are not identical with his presence) as well as by the other (his presence to the course of human history) and by their unity" (189). Thus, there must be spatial and temporal bases (Word and Sacrament) for Christ's presence, along with love for the world. "Of themselves and separately, the one (Sacrament or Word) is simply religious ritual and the other humane ideology, and the two have very little in common. The church is founded on and sets forth the unity of both only through the presence of Jesus Christ" (189).
178. Frei, *Identity*, 190–94.
179. Frei, *Identity*, 191.

and arguing that they are fulfilled. This argument itself is faithful to Auerbach's understanding that the biblical texts seek to overcome our reality with their own. This is precisely what happens in Frei's quasi-ontological argument. In his description of Jesus' identity, one can see his attempt to avoid what Ryle called the "ghost in the machine." On Frei's telling, Jesus' identity is constituted by his intentions and actions and by what happens to him, an identity that must be narrated rather than merely conceptually described. The overall movement of Frei's thought is (1) to begin with the narrative structure of the Gospels, (2) to provide a narratively structured description of the identity of Jesus, (3) to provide an argument from that very narrative structure for the truth of the central Gospel claims about God's own presence in Christ, and (4) to spin out nutshell accounts of the Word of God, the Sacraments, the Holy Spirit, and the church and its mission and ethical obligation. The book is a remarkably creative attempt to accomplish these objectives in a way that is faithful to the Barthian project described in chapter 5 (this volume).

Between the publication of *The Identity of Jesus Christ* in 1975 and his next major works, Frei's understanding of the meaning of the biblical narratives shifted or developed. Whether or not this development can be attributed to the influence of George Lindbeck's Wittgensteinian theory of the nature of religion and religious doctrines, it does bring into starker relief the extent of Frei's Wittgensteinian understanding of religious and theological language, or at least of the biblical narratives.

CHAPTER EIGHT

Postliberalism II

George Lindbeck and Frei's Later Work

If, in Frei's view, the narratives cannot get their meaning by referring to some nonlinguistic reality, then how do they acquire meaning? Frei's thinking on this issue shifted—from his early work, in which meaning is constituted by narrative form, to his later work, in which meaning is constituted by community usage.[1] This oversimplification, however, hides an important continuity in Frei's thought regarding meaning. From his earliest published work to his last, he opposed any descriptivist or referential understanding of the meaning of biblical narratives, and he was consistent in insisting that any understanding of their meaning take account of their narrative nature.[2]

In his early work, the role of the community in determining the meaning of biblical texts is certainly less prominent, and is arguably somewhat less important. Instead, the narrative form assumes prominence. In a 1967 lecture, he argued for "a reading in which the text itself is the

---

1. Though he doesn't describe it in just the way I do, Mike Higton has acknowledged a similar shift in Frei's theological focus from his early to his later work. Mike Higton, "Frei's Christology and Lindbeck's Cultural-Linguistic Theory," *Scottish Journal of Theology* 50:1 (1997): 83–85. For a contrary view, see Jason A. Springs, *Towards a Generous Orthodoxy: Prospects for Hans Frei's Postliberal Theology* (New York: Oxford Univ. Press, 2010).
2. He almost never mentions biblical texts that are not narrative in form. In addition, he always explicitly maintained that he was not intending to make universal pronouncements on the linguistic meaning of all assertions or uses of language. Instead, he always maintained that his statements on linguistic meaning were meant to apply only to the case of biblical (primarily Gospel) narratives.

meaning, the narrative form indispensable to the narrative's meaning."[3] In this lecture he states his early position on meaning in clear terms: in the case of biblical narratives, "[t]he formal structure of the narrative itself is the meaning."[4] In *The Identity of Jesus Christ*, he argues that the meaning of the Gospel narratives is simply the depictions they render.[5] In arguing that part of Jesus' identity in the narratives is his obedience to God, Frei asserts that the meaning of Jesus' obedience is not given by reference to something extratextual, whether truth conditions or otherwise. Instead, "[t]he *content* or pattern of that obedience is the pattern of merciful, saving activity."[6] In *The Eclipse of Biblical Narrative*, Frei continues to insist on the narrative structure as the linchpin of meaning. Here he argues that "realistic interpretation" requires that the meaning of a story cannot be divorced from its actual telling.[7] The crucial point, though, is that in a realistic narrative, the locus of meaning is the narrative text itself. Echoing Wittgenstein, Ryle, and ordinary language philosophy, Frei argues that such narratives do not derive their meaning from their reference to some reality or idea outside the story. Instead, their meaning is simply the depictions they contain. In other words, the meaning of the stories is constituted by their narrative structure.[8]

After publication of *The Eclipse of Biblical Narrative* in 1975, Frei's colleague, George Lindbeck, was working on *The Nature of Doctrine*, which was published in 1984. On the majority reading of Frei's later work, Lindbeck's influence can be seen in Frei's essays from the 1980s, in which his principal interest shifts to the "literal sense" of the biblical texts. This shift places more methodological importance on the community because the community is a much more important factor in determining what the literal

3. Hans W. Frei, "Remarks in Connection with a Theological Proposal," in Hans W. Frei, *Theology and Narrative: Selected Essays*, ed. George Hunsinger and William C. Placher (New York: Oxford Univ. Press, 1993), 26–44, quotation at 41.

4. Frei, "Remarks," 34. As I've indicated in chapter seven, Jason Springs has argued that the development of Frei's thought exhibits such strong continuity that it's misleading to speak of a "shift" at all. In my own view, Springs understates the amount of movement in Frei's position, though Springs quite rightly emphasizes the continuities. But however strong or weak the shift or development from Frei's earlier to his later position, for my purposes the important point for this chapter is that his later work is heavily reliant on a Wittgensteinian view of the meaning of religious and theological language. See my "Wittgenstein's Web: Hans Frei and the Meaning of Biblical Narratives," *Journal of Religion* (forthcoming).

5. Hans W. Frei, *The Identity of Jesus Christ: The Hermeneutical Bases of Dogmatic Theology* (Philadelphia: Fortress Press, 1975; repr., Eugene, Oreg.: Wipf & Stock, 1997), 61 (page references are to reprint edition).

6. Frei, *Identity*, 152 (emphasis in original).

7. Hans W. Frei, *The Eclipse of Biblical Narrative: A Study in Eighteenth and Nineteenth Century Hermeneutics* (New Haven, Conn.: Yale Univ. Press, 1974), 13–14.

8. Frei, *Eclipse*, 27.

sense of a text is than in specifying its genre or narrative form. Similarly, Lindbeck's rule theory of doctrine and religion provides a Wittgensteinian role for religious communities. Thus, at least according to the majority of interpreters, as Frei moved closer to Lindbeck in according a greater role to the community in establishing the meaning of biblical texts, he also moved to a position closer to the later Wittgenstein.

It is also possible to see Frei's later focus on the literal sense as a natural development of his position. This is Jason Springs's reading, and on this reading a concern for the literal sense and the role of the community was operative in Frei's early work as well. But what this means is that, on the one hand, Frei's reliance on Wittgenstein was an important feature of all his work and that, on the other, there are more differences between Frei and Lindbeck than is commonly supposed. Still, Wittgenstein exerts a powerful influence on both Frei and Lindbeck, however different (or similar) may be their appropriations of Wittgenstein's insights. Lindbeck's reliance on Wittgenstein is not difficult to detect, and in Frei's later work we will be able to see the increased transparency of his reliance on Wittgenstein.[9]

I. GEORGE LINDBECK ON RELIGIONS AND DOCTRINES

In Lindbeck's most influential book, *The Nature of Doctrine*,[10] he contrasts his theories of religion and doctrine with two others, which he calls "cognitive-propositionalist" and "experiential-expressivist."[11] On a cognitive-propositionalist view, doctrines function as propositional claims about states of affairs. Religions are sets of such truth-claims, and to be a member of a religion is to accept its truth-claims. On an experiential-expressivist view, doctrines are re-presentations of inner feelings, attitudes, or existential orientations, which are re-presented in symbol systems, narratives, etc. In themselves, doctrines are neither informative nor discursive, but are symbols of basic attitudes or orientations that we already have. Doctrines on this view are judged not primarily by

9. I think Frei would give a cautious agreement with this assessment. In 1967, he stated, "In regard to understanding, (remember: for this particular exegetical task!) I find myself influenced increasingly by Wittgenstein and J.L. Austin. . . ." Frei, "Remarks," 26–44, 33.

10. George A. Lindbeck, *The Nature of Doctrine: Religion and Theology in a Postliberal Age* (Philadelphia: Westminster Press, 1984).

11. The theories of doctrine and religion articulated in Lindbeck's book are designed to facilitate ecumenical and interreligious dialogue. His theory of doctrine is designed to allow doctrinal reconciliation without capitulation, and his theory of religion is designed to be religiously neutral.

whether they conform to some objective reality, but by how adequately they re-present this basic existential attitude or orientation. Religions in turn are expressions or symbolizations of a common or universal religious experience.[12]

Lindbeck takes both of these approaches to be inadequate, so he argues for a "cultural-linguistic" approach, using language and grammar as descriptive analogies.[13] Religions are like languages, he says, and doctrines are like grammar. Doctrines are not propositions describing states of affairs, but rules about how to make intelligible propositions. The experiential-expressivist approach, he argues, holds doctrines to be outer re-presentations of inner feelings or attitudes, while on the cultural-linguistic view, language shapes all experiences from the beginning, so there cannot be any experience that is not linguistically constituted.[14]

Lindbeck issues several caveats, two of which bear mentioning.[15] First, when he says an activity is linguistically constituted, he means constituted by a *particular* linguistic system. Therefore, there cannot be any such thing as religion in general, and, more generally, humans have incommensurable experiences. To speak of the religious quality of all experience, from a cultural-linguistic point of view, is to use language to which no meaning can ultimately be assigned. Second, Lindbeck says that religion is *like* a culture, not that it *is* a culture. Unlike a culture, it has a specifiable domain—namely, *that which is most important*. But precisely because their domain is that which is most important, religions are comprehensive interpretive schemes which themselves give a structure to all human experience and understanding of self and world. A religion functions similarly to language, which structures our thought and in fact

---

12. Lindbeck, *Nature of Doctrine*, 9–16. Lindbeck recognizes that some views, such as those of Rahner and Lonergan, often combine these two approaches, but Lindbeck subsumes them under one or the other approach (*Nature of Doctrine*).

13. As accounts of doctrines, he believes it is difficult for either cognitive-propositionalist or experiential-expressivist views to account for doctrinal reconciliation or change or development without capitulation. As accounts of religion, they are ill suited for interreligious dialogue (Lindbeck, *Nature of Doctrine*, 17–18). For a trenchant critique of Lindbeck's interpretation of those he takes to follow the experiential-expressivist view, as well as of Lindbeck's programmatic proposal, see David Tracy, "Lindbeck's New Program for Theology: A Reflection," *The Thomist*, 49:3 (July 1985): 460–72.

14. Lindbeck, *Nature of Doctrine*, 30, 33–34, 36, 48.

15. The other three are as follows. First, he means language to include any form of symbolic action that has a conventionalized meaning. Second, he doesn't mean that an action or its meaning is necessarily *exhausted* by its linguistic constitution. Third, we might engage in activities that are not linguistically constituted. But these activities are not distinctively human. That is, what it means to be human is to exist in a culture, to take part in a form of life that is regulated by a language game. Activities that are distinctively human, then, will be linguistically constituted.

makes thought possible. Religion makes possible descriptions of realities and formulations of beliefs, but always with reference to *that which is most important*.[16]

Comparing Lindbeck's three models in other than utilitarian terms is problematic, just as comparing the adequacy of two languages would be. Lindbeck argues that the best comparative criterion is that of categorial adequacy.[17] When a religion makes a truth-claim, the more its linguistic system allows it to specify what it means, the more adequate the religion will be as a system of cultural-linguistic categories. But the meaningfulness of these categories can only be judged in a religion-specific way. Christian categories may not be adequate to express the Buddhist concept of Nirvana, but they would not need to be. A religion needs only those concepts adequate to express its own claims, since there is no religious experience or core common to all. To say that a religion is categorially false means either that its claims cannot be conceptualized or that the concepts needed to express its claims cannot be articulated in an understandable way. Thus to say that a religion is categorially false would entail not that it is propositionally or expressively true *or* false, but meaningless.[18]

A doctrine, as Lindbeck construes it, is a communally authoritative teaching regarding beliefs and practices considered essential to the identity of the group. Adherence to these teachings is what constitutes being a faithful member of the community. Whether a community has official doctrines or not, there have to be one or more *operational* doctrines in order to identify the group as *this particular group*. Doctrine is therefore inescapable.[19] Lindbeck draws from this inescapability two implications for explaining doctrinal development or change. First, doctrinal change does not proceed from new experiences. Instead, doctrine changes in the same way that language changes; it results from dialectical interactions between the cultural-linguistic system and changing life situations the system schematizes.[20] Second, on Lindbeck's view, there can be no specifiable experience

16. Lindbeck, *Nature of Doctrine*, 32–34, 49. Note the similarity to Wittgenstein's construal of religion in Ludwig Wittgenstein, *Lectures and Conversations on Aesthetics, Psychology and Religious Belief*, ed. Cyril Barrett (Berkeley and Los Angeles: Univ. of California Press, n.d.), 53–72.

17. Lindbeck uses "truth" in three ways: "ontological" truth concerns whether a claim corresponds to reality; "intrasystematic" truth concerns the internal coherence of a set of claims; and "categorial" truth concerns the adequacy of the categories of a cultural-linguistic system (Lindbeck, *Nature of Doctrine*, 48, 64–66).

18. Lindbeck, *Nature of Doctrine*, 48–51.

19. Even those groups that try to eschew doctrine have as their identifying doctrine that they eschew (other) doctrines (Lindbeck, *Nature of Doctrine*, 74).

20. Lindbeck, *Nature of Doctrine*, 39.

that is truly universal.[21] He therefore argues that the cultural-linguistic approach is superior to its rivals not because it best expresses some common experience, but because it has a higher explanatory value; it explains, better than its rivals, what happens in doctrinal change.[22] Its superior explanatory power derives from its allowing a doctrine to remain (categorially) true even while theological formulations or understandings change. In order for a doctrine to stay the same while theological formulations vary, doctrines cannot be understood to make assertions about states of affairs. Instead, doctrines are rules about how to use religious language, or how to act religiously. They are second-order claims, or rules, about how to formulate first-order claims. These first-order claims do make claims about states of affairs, but doctrines, second-order claims, do not.[23]

Lindbeck understands the essential methodological difference between his cultural-linguistic approach and the experiential-expressivist approach to be that their starting points are different. Re-presentational views start with a feeling or experience of authentic or fundamental faith, which is then re-presented through the Bible and tradition. On Lindbeck's view, it is better to start with the Christian stories, which then shape and structure experience through doctrines. So an experience can be said to be Christian only insofar as it is shaped through the Christian stories, texts, and traditions, and interpreted through Christian doctrines. The advantage of this view of doctrine, in Lindbeck's view, is that it does not reify either experiences or truth-claims. These can change through time, while only the grammar (doctrine) remains constant.[24]

21. Lindbeck, *Nature of Doctrine*, 39–40, 78–9. Calvin's *sensus divinitatis*, Schleiermacher's feeling of absolute dependence, and Ogden's common human experience, seem to be impossible from this point of view. If there are aspects of experience that are universal, Lindbeck does not believe we have sufficient access to them to allow us to give a meaningful description of them. There is an apparent self-referential problem here. Lindbeck seems to take *non-universalizability* to be a universal characteristic of all human experience. Lindbeck does not address this issue.

22. Ultimately, though, there is no definitive way to decide which approach is the correct one (Lindbeck, *Nature of Doctrine*, 40–42).

23. Lindbeck, *Nature of Doctrine*, 79–80. Many doctrines can do double duty. *I believe in God the Father Almighty, maker of heaven and earth*, for example, is a double-duty doctrine. It operates as a first-order claim, stating that it is God who created heaven and earth. But this is not its *doctrinal* function. It functions as a doctrine by laying down a rule that when we talk about God, our language must not be inconsistent with the belief that God created heaven and earth. Our formulation of how God created heaven and earth might change over time, but the doctrine, the rule about how to speak, would remain the same. Our new understanding about how the world came into existence gets re-inscribed back into the linguistic world, the language game, of the biblical texts and the tradition, through the use of doctrines (79–80).

24. Lindbeck, *Nature of Doctrine*, 80–81.

On a rule theory, theological debates do not focus on criteria and whether a particular view meets the criteria. Instead, debates are broadened to cover the proper grammar, and to determine who are authoritative speakers of the language. Dogmatics focuses on specifying the meaning of the Christian faith intratextually. Theology more broadly construed reinscribes extrasystematic events within the system, using a modified version of typological or figural biblical interpretations. But Lindbeck does not understand the Christian story to explicate the "true" meaning of these extrasystematic events. Instead, for Christians these events are meaningless until they are absorbed into the broader Christian narrative.[25]

Lindbeck understands his approach to require abandonment of several modern commitments, notably including the assertion of the primacy of the historical-critical method over literary approaches to the Bible. On literary approaches, the search for the historical Jesus or for a philosophical validation of the possibility of the Resurrection becomes much less important. Instead, of paramount importance is the character of Jesus and his role in the plot of the Gospels and of the Bible as a whole. Like Frei, Lindbeck wants to avoid a theological method that begins with experience and then adjusts biblical interpretations and theological language to fit this experience. Instead, he insists that experience is linguistically constituted from the beginning, and he wants the language that constitutes it to be the language of the Christian story, because he believes one cannot change Christianity's language without changing Christianity.[26]

II. LINGUISTIC MEANING AND THE LITERAL SENSE IN FREI'S LATER ESSAYS

Lindbeck argues that first-order religious claims derive their meaning from their use in the community's religious life (its form of life), and this use is regulated by the grammatical rules (language games) known as doctrines. The community is given a similar role in Frei's shift in emphasis from the narrative form of scripture to its literal sense. Frei discusses his understanding of the literal sense and its importance for theology in a series

---

25. Lindbeck, *Nature of Doctrine*, 113–18.
26. Lindbeck, *Nature of Doctrine*, 119–26. Lindbeck realizes that his approach runs the risk of being construed as wholly relativistic, or fideistic. So far as I can see, he does not have a defense to these charges. Instead, he thinks a certain kind of fideism or relativism is unavoidable. The charges themselves, he believes, presuppose a desire for a foundation outside of all religions from which different religions can be compared and judged. But Lindbeck does not believe such a foundation is available (128–30).

of essays published or presented from 1982 until 1987. In "Theology and the Interpretation of Narrative: Some Hermeneutical Considerations,"[27] he argues that for centuries theology has proceeded in two forms or types, or at least in two contexts. In the first, theology is the "queen of the sciences," providing unity and purpose to all other disciplines. In this context, theology is discourse about God (*logos* about *theos*), and its initial and most important task, on Frei's construal, is to show how the word "God" and the concept it represents refers to a (indeed, the) Divine Being.[28] The concept itself can only be intelligible in the context of an overarching philosophical scheme. This is because philosophy is not only a discipline in its own right, but is in addition a foundational discipline, providing an all-fields-encompassing set of criteria that adjudicate what counts as meaningful language, rational belief, and knowledge.[29] Thus, reflection on religious phenomena or ideas must be grounded in a foundational philosophical theory. Frei takes the hermeneutics of Paul Ricoeur and David Tracy to be just such a theory. It sets our transcendental conditions of possibility within which the "fusion of horizons" that constitutes understanding a text can occur.[30] That is, it provides interpretation with truth conditions.

But if Wittgenstein is right, this project can never be successful, precisely because it assumes that the terms that constitute interpretation of a text are given meaning not by the community (the church), but by their transcendental truth conditions. Instead, Frei argues that a more excellent way (the second form or type) would be one that follows Wittgenstein and Clifford Geertz, seeking simply to describe how the church uses its theological language. It must do this because the church itself is language forming.[31] The concepts "meaning" and "understanding" are not defined in advance by reference to transcendentally established truth conditions, but arise out of their agreed use in the community. They are better seen as dependent on their context.[32] This does not imply that we can't talk about the meaning of biblical narratives, or of theological discourse. But it does mean that we can't do so in a context-neutral or language-independent way. To do this would be to ask about their truth conditions in isolation

27. Hans W. Frei, "Theology and the Interpretation of Narrative: Some Hermeneutical Considerations," in Frei, *Theology and Narrative*, 94–116.
28. Frei, "Theology and the Interpretation of Narrative," 95. One can see this explicitly in Schubert Ogden's essay, "The Reality of God," in Schubert M. Ogden, *The Reality of God and Other Essays* (New York: Harper & Row, 1966; repr., Dallas, Tex.: Southern Methodist Univ. Press, 1992, 1–70).
29. Frei, "Theology and the Interpretation of Narrative," 95.
30. Frei, "Theology and the Interpretation of Narrative," 101.
31. Frei, "Theology and the Interpretation of Narrative," 100.
32. Frei, "Theology and the Interpretation of Narrative," 101.

from the community. Meaning, understanding, and other philosophical constructs or concepts can be used, but they must be subordinated to Christian self-description. That is, what it means to understand a story or a text can only be determined by the use of such an understanding in the Christian form of life. The biblical narratives are to be understood in their literal sense, simply because this is the way the Christian community has used them in its form of life. And this form of life, so far as I can see, is ultimately brute.

As Frei argued in *The Eclipse of Biblical Narrative*, though, the "literal sense" can be construed in several different ways. So he distinguishes three versions of the literal sense, the last of which bears the strongest affinity to Frei's way of doing theology. "First, *sensus literalis* may describe the precise or fit enactment of the intention to say what comes to be in the text."[33] That is, the literal sense of a text is that sense in which the text is read as the expression or enactment of the author's intention. This authorial intent may be understood as either human or divine, or both. If a text is considered to have dual (divine and human) authorship, the "divine" literal sense (the text as enactment of divine intent) may be thought of as overlapping with other senses, such as figurative or typological senses. No such overlapping could occur, however, in regard to the intent of the human author. In Frei's view, this understanding of the literal sense as indexed to authorial intent has had the effect of inspiring both historical criticism (searching for the "real" intent of the human author) and fundamentalist bibliolatry and assertions of factual inerrancy.[34]

The second understanding of the literal sense "refers to the descriptive fit between *verbum* and *res*, sense and reference, signifier and signified, 'Sinn' and 'Bedeutung,' between grammatical/syntactical and conceptual sense, between the narrative sequence and what it renders descriptively."[35] On this understanding, the literal sense is just the meaning given by the

33. Frei, "Theology and the Interpretation of Narrative," 102.
34. Frei, "Theology and the Interpretation of Narrative," 102–103.
35. Frei, "Theology and the Interpretation of Narrative," 103. Note the allusion here to Frege's seminal essay, "Über Sinn und Bedeutung," *Zeitschrift für Philosophie und Philosophische Kritik* (1892): 100. The essay first appeared in translation in Gottlob Frege, "On Sense [Sinn] and Reference [Bedeutung]," trans. Max Black, *The Philosophical Review* 57 (1948): 207–30, reprinted in *Readings in the Philosophy of Language*, ed. Peter Ludlow (Cambridge, Mass.: MIT Press, 1997), 563–83. Although *Bedeutung* is most commonly translated "meaning," it is clear from the text of Frege's essay that "reference" is the better translation. Though other translations have appeared (see, e.g., "On Sense and Nominatum," trans. Herbert Feigl, in *Readings in Philosophical Analysis*, ed. Herbert Feigl and Wilfred Sellars [New York: Appleton-Century-Crofts, 1949], 85–102), most translators have followed Black's use of "reference." I am aware of no translation that uses "meaning."

depiction in the text itself. The project of identifying or describing the "real" nature or properties (or existence) of a text's extralinguistic referent is not a part of interpretation of the literal sense of the text. Instead, the referent is given to the interpreter "only under the depiction"—that is, linguistically in the narrative form of the text and nowhere else.[36] On my reading, this second understanding is the kind of narrative interpretation for which Frei had previously argued and that he thought had gone into eclipse in the modern period.

On the third understanding, "the *sensus literalis* is the way the text has generally been used in the community. It is the sense of the text in its sociolinguistic context—liturgical, pedagogical, polemical, and so on."[37] Like Lindbeck, Frei here cites Wittgenstein as inspiration for his articulation of this third understanding of the literal sense.[38] In the context of a religious community, the way a text is used in a community just is the teaching of the text that the community considers to be authoritative.[39] In the modern period, Frei argues, the literal sense of the biblical texts came to be their referentially understood meaning (the events to which they purported to refer). Yet it is not the referential understanding of their meaning that constituted this sense as their literal sense, but the judgment of the community that their extralinguistic reference was their authoritative teaching. Thus what makes a particular sense of a biblical text the "literal" sense is nothing other than the community's judgment (or the presupposition of certain of its actions) that this particular sense is authoritative. And a particular sense will be authoritative insofar as it enables the church to live out its mission.[40]

By 1982, Frei had moved from the second to the third understanding of the literal sense as the understanding he prefers. His preference for this third understanding was due to his belief that it is the understanding best suited to preserving Barth's aim of deriving theological method from the Word of God, rather than allowing an independently derived

36. "No further knowledge is needed," Frei writes, and "none is available" (Frei, "Theology and the Interpretation of Narrative," 104).

37. Frei, "Theology and the Interpretation of Narrative," 104.

38. "This is the setting in which it is appropriate to reach for that saying of Wittgenstein that has so often and wrongly been given the status of a general principle: 'Don't ask for the meaning; ask for the use'" (Frei, "Theology and the Interpretation of Narrative," 104). Frei also acknowledges being deeply indebted to Charles M. Wood, *The Formation of Christian Understanding* (Philadelphia: Westminster Press, 1981) (115 n.13).

39. Frei, "Theology and the Interpretation of Narrative," 105.

40. Frei, "Theology and the Interpretation of Narrative," 105–106. Frei cites Augustine, for example, who "understood the plain sense of Scripture to be that which conduces to faith, hope, and the twofold love of God and neighbor" (105, citing Augustine, *De Doctrina Christiana* I, 36, 40; II, 6, 8, 9, 14).

theological method to overdetermine an interpretation or understanding of the Word of God. Frei came to believe that the second understanding of the literal sense was susceptible to a charge of being subservient to an independently derived literary theory.[41] Frei's move to this third understanding reveals his commitment to a Wittgensteinian understanding of meaning. This third understanding of the literal sense gives to the community the role of the ultimate arbiter of the meaning of any and all biblical texts. That meaning is now indexed to the use of the text in the living out of the community's mission. It is here that we can see most clearly the influence of the later Wittgenstein as well as Frei's theological kinship with Lindbeck.

Frei continues his critique of liberal theology in its hermeneutical expression in "The 'Literal Reading' of Biblical Narrative in the Christian Tradition: Does It Stretch or Will It Break?"[42] Again, the viability of the literal reading of scripture will follow (or not) "from the actual, fruitful use religious people continue to make of it. . . ."[43] In hermeneutics, though, the literal reading is no longer primary because it has become dependent on a general hermeneutic theory. Whatever one thinks of Frei's summary of hermeneutics and its consequences,[44] it seems clear that his principal objection is that the reference of the biblical narratives (a mode of being-in-the-world) is established transcendentally—thus, independently of the community's actual use of the texts. Notice the parallel to Wittgenstein. On Frei's reading, Ricoeur and Tracy argue that the world of the text that is opened up can have meaning only if it is a *"possibly true* world."[45] It seems to me that Frei is reading Ricoeur and Tracy as deriving the meaning of the text by reference to the truth conditions of the text. Frei cites Kermode, Nietzsche, and Derrida here (and not Wittgenstein), and his language is Derridean. But the critique is thoroughly Wittgensteinian. The notion that such truth

41. The theory he has in mind is New Criticism, which gained prominence in British and American universities in the years following World War I. For an interesting account of similarities between New Criticism and neo-orthodox theology, see Lynn M. Poland, "The New Criticism, Neoorthodoxy, and the New Testament," *Journal of Religion* 65 (Oct. 1985): 459–77.

42. Hans W. Frei, "The 'Literal Reading' of Biblical Narrative in the Christian Tradition: Does It Stretch or Will It Break?" in *The Bible and the Narrative Tradition*, ed. Frank McConnell (New York: Oxford Univ. Press, 1986), 36–77; reprinted in Frei, *Theology and Narrative*, 117–152 (page references are to reprint edition).

43. Frei, "'Literal Reading' of Biblical Narrative," 119. The literal reading here is a way of expressing the meaning of biblical narratives. So he describes several different ways scripture has been read in the Christian community. There have been typological readings, figural readings, allegorical readings. But all these readings depend on, or are understandable because of, the literal reading of the texts (122).

44. Frei, "'Literal Reading' of Biblical Narrative," 125–29.

45. Frei, "'Literal Reading' of Biblical Narrative," 132 (emphasis in original).

conditions are accessible to a reader, considering a text in isolation from its use in a community, is indistinguishable (on my view) from what Frei means when he says that "'understanding' as self-presence is the indispensable and irreducible counterpart to textual 'meaning' as linguistic presence, and vice versa."[46] To be more specific, Frei takes phenomenological hermeneutics to be particularly susceptible to deconstructionist critique. In Ricoeur's hermeneutics, interpretation need not get behind the text to the intention of the author, but must inhabit the world that is opened up or disclosed in front of the text. On Frei's reading of Ricoeur, this disclosed world is what gives meaning to the language of the text. But for the language to be understandable, the reader or interpreter must also inhabit this disclosed world. Thus, meaning and understanding constitute a mutually referential conceptual pair that simply play off each other. Meaning is established by reference to a disclosed and thus understood world, while understanding is constituted by the meaning that depends on it. So meaning and understanding signify by mutually referring to each other, creating a circle that is never closed. Thus, the process of signification that is supposed to end in reference is endlessly deferred.[47] So far as I can see, this critique at least bears a strong family resemblance to the later Wittgenstein's claim that meaning cannot be established by reference to truth conditions. Indeed, in my view, it makes precisely the same point.

This parallel is reinforced by the similarity of their remedies. For Frei, the central problem of both phenomenological hermeneutics and arguments regarding the historical factuality (or lack of it) of the biblical narratives is that "'meaning' is identical with 'possible truth'. . . ."[48] Frei thinks a better alternative is "a theory confined to describing how and in what specific context a certain kind of reading functions. . . ."[49] The virtue of this theory is that it does not concern itself with possible truth (i.e., with truth conditions) but with the role the interpretation of texts plays in the life of the community (the Christian form of life). It is this role that gives the texts their meaning. Similarly, Wittgenstein's remedy for philosophical analysis is to foreswear explanation and to limit its therapeutic task to description.

It is helpful here to recall Wittgenstein's three central notions. First, the *agreement* of the community is absolutely essential to ascribing a

46. Frei, "'Literal Reading' of Biblical Narrative," 135. Although Frei is sometimes regarded as an antirealist in his later writings, it is worth noting that his objection to hermeneutics can be construed as an agreement with deconstructionists that hermeneutics itself cannot escape antirealism. See "'Literal Reading' of Biblical Narrative," 136.

47. Frei, "'Literal Reading' of Biblical Narrative," 134–37.

48. Frei, "'Literal Reading' of Biblical Narrative," 139.

49. Frei, "'Literal Reading' of Biblical Narrative," 139.

meaning to the biblical texts, and indeed to our theological language. Quoting Lindbeck, Frei is persuaded that "'[m]eaning is constituted by the uses of a specific language rather than being distinguished from it.'"[50] That is, meaning is not derivable from transcendentally established truth conditions, but only from the use—the agreed use—of the community. Second, the notion of *forms of life* also plays a critical role in Frei's method. Christians have a distinctive form of life, and the meanings of their religious language, of theological language, and of the biblical texts, all derive from the role such language plays in their form of life. Third, there must be *criteria* by which members of the community can judge whether a person is correctly following the rules for use of language about God, and of religious language more broadly. That criteria is the literal sense of the biblical texts.[51] This is why Frei can make two claims that may at first seem inconsistent. First, the *sensus literalis* "governs, and bends to its own ends whatever general categories it shares—as indeed it has to share—with other kinds of reading. . . ." Second, "it is not only case-specific but as such belongs first and foremost into the context of a sociolinguistic community, that is, of the specific religion of which it is part, rather than into a literary ambience."[52] He can make both these claims because the community has established the *sensus literalis* as its criteria by which to determine whether the rules for playing its language game have been followed. In short, in my view, Frei's critique of liberal theology, his analysis of theological claims, and his own method are thoroughly suffused with, if not dependent on, the later Wittgenstein's views on linguistic meaning. We can see this affinity again in Frei's final work, which I will discuss in the next section.

III. FREI'S COMPARATIVE ANALYSIS OF THEOLOGICAL METHOD

At the end of his life, Frei was working on a thematic history of Christianity in England, Germany, and North America since 1700.[53] The material in this last project presupposes Frei's move toward the later Wittgenstein in his understanding of linguistic meaning and illustrates the crucial role played by linguistic considerations in his analysis of theological method.

50. Frei, "'Literal Reading' of Biblical Narrative," 147 (quoting Lindbeck, *The Nature of Doctrine*, 114).
51. For Lindbeck, doctrines play this criteriological role.
52. Frei, "'Literal Reading' of Biblical Narrative," 143–44.
53. Unfortunately he died before the project could be completed. The material outlining the typology, along with other helpful material, was published posthumously as Hans W. Frei, *Types of Christian Theology*, ed. George Hunsinger and William C. Placher (New Haven, Conn.: Yale Univ. Press, 1992).

He developed a typology of Christian theology to organize the material, and his assessment of the various types demonstrates his continuing commitment to advancing the Barthian project he identified in his dissertation. It is therefore fitting to conclude this chapter with a discussion of this remarkable analytical work.

Frei's typology is structured around the relations between two different ways of doing theology. On the first way, theology is so closely related to philosophy that its method of proceeding is given through philosophical analysis. For this way of doing theology,

> philosophy may be regarded as being a foundational discipline which, rather than giving us information, provides us with the criteria of meaning and certainty, coherence as well as truth, in any arena of human reflection. In other words, the rules of correct thought are invariant and all-fields-encompassing.[54]

The second way of doing theology limits theological method to Christian self-description. Here the cognate discipline is not philosophy but sociology or cultural anthropology, or both. On this view, theology takes more seriously the fact that religion is a culture and proceeds primarily by way of "thick description."[55] Frei organizes his typology by asking how theologians relate these two ways of doing theology.[56] For each general type, the answer to this basic question is a function of two relations: first, between external descriptions of Christianity and internal self-description; second, between specific description of Christianity and "general criteria for meaningful description."[57] Frei articulates five general types of theology and judges their adequacy by asking how well they deal with the literal sense of scripture. By setting up the criteria for individuation and assessment in this way, Frei gives an important methodological role to the linguistic meaning of theological claims, and discussions of linguistic meaning figure prominently in Frei's descriptions of the five types.[58]

> Frei states that the first type is exemplified by Gordon Kaufman. For this type, *Theology as a philosophical discipline* in the academy takes complete priority over Christian self-description within the religious community called the Church,

---

54. Frei, *Types of Christian Theology*, 20.
55. Frei, *Types of Christian Theology*, 13. The term is borrowed from Clifford Geertz, *The Interpretation of Cultures* (New York: Basic Books, 1973), 12–13.
56. Frei, *Types of Christian Theology*, 23. The typology, he says, is broadly empirical rather than logically exhaustive.
57. Frei, *Types of Christian Theology*, 27.
58. See Frei, *Types of Christian Theology*, 18.

and Christian self-description, in its subordinate place, tends to emulate the philosophical character of academic theology by being as general as possible or as little specific about Christianity as it can be, and the distinction between external and internal description is basically unimportant.[59]

In fact, Christian self-description so emulates academic theology (which Frei considers external description) that "properly speaking, there is no specific self-description of Christianity. . . ."[60] The criteria for meaningful description are set by philosophical reflection, and any specific description of Christianity must conform to those general criteria. The task of theology is to specify these criteria for the subject matter of theological discourse and for the articulation of the concept of God. This concept, "God," is a metaphysical concept, and theology must articulate the rules for conceiving and using it coherently. Therefore, the concept of God as culturally constructed by any specific religion, insofar as it is meaningful at all, is ultimately indistinguishable from "the general, metaphysical construct of the concept that is grounded presumably in the very structure of human nature and experience."[61] In type 1, therefore, theology is a purely philosophical discipline exhaustively characterized as "not only subordinate to, but undertaken as part of, a general intellectual-cultural inquiry."[62]

The second type Frei takes to be exemplified by David Tracy. Here also theology is a philosophical enterprise, but it is distinguished from the first type by its attempt to take the specificity of the Christian religion more seriously by insisting that Christian theological claims are more than imaginative metaphorical constructions, but are indeed specific assertions about reality. Nonetheless, in type 2, Frei again takes theology as Christian self-description to be subordinate to theology as a philosophical discipline because theological method consists in philosophical reflection.[63] Theology must adhere to universally applicable criteria of meaning and truth that are determined through philosophical reflection.[64] Consequently, "external

---

59. Frei, *Types of Christian Theology*, 28 (emphasis in original).
60. Frei, *Types of Christian Theology*, 28.
61. Frei, *Types of Christian Theology*, 29.
62. Frei, *Types of Christian Theology*, 30.
63. "'Contemporary Christian theology is best understood as philosophical reflection upon the meanings present in common human experience and the meanings presenting the Christian tradition'" (Frei, *Types of Christian Theology*, 30, quoting David Tracy, *Blessed Rage for Order* [New York: Seabury Press, 1975], 34).
64. "There are separately statable, general, and fields-encompassing criteria for meaning (internal conceptual coherence), meaningfulness (language that discloses actual experience), and truth (transcendental or metaphysical explication of the condition of possibility of common human experience)" (Frei, *Types of Christian Theology*, 30).

description and self-description merge into one, and the joint product is justified by a foundational philosophical scheme."[65] This foundational scheme is phenomenology, on Frei's reading, and theology proceeds by way of critical correlation between the truly specific Christian "fact" and common human experience.

On Frei's interpretation, Christian self-description, therefore, is a mode of a more general external description of religion, and this description proceeds according to a method articulated by phenomenology. This method is a philosophical (phenomenological) analysis of the structure of human consciousness itself—that is, an analysis of what is common to any and all human experience. Thus it is a transcendental method, even as it also analyzes the specific cultural forms through which human experience is expressed.[66] On Frei's reading, then, the meaning of religious claims is understood referentially in this second type, and the referent of such claims is a mode-of-being-in-the-world.[67] "'Meanings' then are modes-of-being-in-the-world that are essences, or constant and identifiable characteristics, of the experiencing self."[68] In the second type, hermeneutics is concerned both with the art of interpreting texts and with the act of understanding itself.[69] "There is a general structure presupposed in all intelligent exegesis, a kind of prescriptive rule that explains how it is possible for us to understand any and all discourse, especially texts."[70] For this type, first-order religious language is expressive, and what it expresses is the "limit experience," a notion that both Tracy and Ogden borrow from Stephen Toulmin.[71] This limit experience is the religious dimension of human existence. Religious language gets its meaning by describing or referring to a mode-of-being-in-the-world that is disclosed by the limit language of the New Testament.[72]

This second type takes theology as Christian self-description and theology as a philosophical enterprise to be fundamentally related. On this type, Frei argues, Christian self-description is a regional instantiation of

65. Frei, *Types of Christian Theology*, 30.
66. Frei, *Types of Christian Theology*, 31–32.
67. "Religious language is the indirect self-articulation of the prelinguistic, immediately experienced self" (Frei, *Types of Christian Theology*, 31).
68. Frei, *Types of Christian Theology*, 32.
69. For Frei's own definition of hermeneutics, see Frei, *Identity*, 61.
70. Frei, *Types of Christian Theology*, 32.
71. Frei, *Types of Christian Theology*, 32. Tracy and Ogden seem to rely primarily on Stephen Toulmin, *An Examination of the Place of Reason in Ethics* (Cambridge: Cambridge Univ. Press, 1950); *The Philosophy of Science: An Introduction* (London: Hutchinson & Co., 1953); *Foresight and Understanding: An Enquiry into the Aims of Science* (London: Hutchinson & Co., 1961); and *The Uses of Argument* (Cambridge: Cambridge Univ. Press, 1958).
72. Frei, *Types of Christian Theology*, 33.

a more general procedure of phenomenological analysis. This relationship implies that Christian self-description must follow the methodological rules set out by the more general procedure. Consequently, Christian self-description cannot in principle be different from external description, and theology must be fundamentally a context-invariant philosophical enterprise.[73] Precisely because theology is context invariant, external and internal description are related in that the claims made by each acquire meaning in the same way—by their reference to the religious dimension of common human experience. Thus Frei calls *meaning* the "glue" that unites external and internal description as fundamentally the same type of discourse.[74] And the reason for this is that the language of both internal and external description acquires meaning through truth conditions rather than any use in a particular form of life. Consequently, on Frei's reading, the church as a historically particular institution cannot play any crucial role in specifying the meaning of theological claims or their assessment.[75] The differences between the first two types are subtle but real. Still, for both types, theology as Christian self-description is subordinate to theology as academic philosophical analysis, and in Frei's view neither provide the most adequate way of rendering the literal sense of the biblical texts.[76]

In the third type, exemplified (ambiguously) by Schleiermacher, theology is an academic discipline, but equally and independently, a self-descriptive discipline within the church.[77] The independence of Christian self-description from academic theology is ambiguous in this type, reflecting the ambiguity in the relationship between internal Christian self-description and external description. For Schleiermacher, religion, or the feeling of absolute dependence, is a universal human condition, but can be present only in a

73. Frei, *Types of Christian Theology*, 33–34.
74. "Meaning, as the internal experience of selves, and religious experience in particular, is the glue that allows external and internal description to be one, and Christian description or self-description is one instance of the general class 'religious meaningfulness'" (Frei, *Types of Christian Theology*, 33).
75. "It is interesting that the Church as the necessary context for the use of Christian concepts and language plays no part at all in Tracy's layout of his method. *Experience* is its substitute" (Frei, *Types of Christian Theology*, 33 [emphasis in original]). It is, of course, perfectly appropriate for Frei to articulate this second type in any manner he wishes for his own constructive purposes. Nonetheless, in my own view, Frei's reading fails to accord adequate weight to Tracy's indebtedness to Gadamer (especially Gadamer's articulation of historically effected consciousness in part 2 of Hans-Georg Gadamer, *Truth and Method*, 2nd rev. ed., trans. Joel Weinsheimer and Donald G. Marshall [New York: Continuum, 1994]).
76. See Frei, *Types of Christian Theology*, 33–34.
77. Frei, *Types of Christian Theology*, 34–35.

"positive" cultural form. The "wedding" of this universal condition and its cultural form is expressed through first-order statements, and theology is reflection on these first-order statements. This reflection constitutes theology as Christian self-description, which must then be correlated with theology as an academic discipline, though both remain autonomous. Theology is thus likewise independent of philosophy, though Frei makes the following curious statement: "The issue of philosophy is secondary, because Schleiermacher treats it as important only to the extent that philosophy plays a role in defining the criteria to which the 'cultural sciences' must be subject."[78] This raises the question whether theology itself is a cultural science. If so, then its autonomous standing vis-à-vis philosophy seems to me to be much more precarious, though Frei does not elaborate the issues arising out of this statement regarding criteria.

In this third type, Christian self-description and external description are correlated, but this correlation is located in experience, which itself is culturally located (in the church).[79] Although this correlation in experience seems similar to type 2, Frei differentiates them on the basis of the linguistic meaning of their claims. He argues that here, unlike the first two types, "Christian use of language always remains distinctive and irreducible to any other, even if its home lies in experience."[80] On Frei's reading, the church as a cultural phenomenon has its own criteria of meaning that may be correlated with those of the discourse of external description, but that are nonetheless independently derived. Thus, although there is a method of correlation in type 3, philosophy and dogmatics remain independent, and in Frei's view this independence distinguishes type 3 from type 2.[81] Theology and philosophy in type 3 therefore have an autonomous but reciprocal relationship. Like Kant, Schleiermacher believes that philosophy can point to a transcendental ground of all being, but can say no more about it. Religion, on the other hand, is the feeling of absolute dependence on this very ground. So theology and philosophy are autonomous and reciprocally related, and must be correlated, but philosophy does not serve as a foundational discipline for theology.[82]

For Frei's fourth type, exemplified by Barth, theology as Christian self-description takes priority over theology as philosophical analysis or

78. Frei, *Types of Christian Theology*, 35.
79. Frei, *Types of Christian Theology*, 36.
80. Frei, *Types of Christian Theology*, 36–37.
81. Frei, *Types of Christian Theology*, 37.
82. In other words, Frei says, their "reciprocity and mutual autonomy is not explained by any more basic structure of thought under which the two factors would be included" (Frei, *Types of Christian Theology*, 38).

as an academic enterprise. This priority takes two forms. "First, theology is not philosophically founded. . . ."[83] That is, it is not dependent on universal philosophical concepts (whether those of metaphysics or of a transcendentally derived philosophical anthropology) either for its assertions to have meaning or for its criteria of truth or rational assent. Second, the rules with which theology must comply in order to qualify as *Wissenschaft* are derived from the context and subject matter of theology itself, rather than from universal, context-invariant principles. As Frei puts it,

> what makes theology an orderly and systematic procedure . . . is for Barth not a set of universal, formal criteria which are certain and all-fields-encompassing and can therefore be stated apart from the context of specific application. . . . theology has its own rules of what makes it a science—a set of rules that are usually implicit and developed only as the context of theology itself develops— in that sense also Christian self-description is quite independent of every external endeavor to describe Christianity as a specific religion: for example, every historical account.[84]

For Barth, philosophical theology is not a meta-theory or meta-language to which dogmatics is beholden, but instead is part of the dogmatic enterprise of the church.[85] As a consequence, Barth does not distinguish first-order from second-order statements as sharply as others do, including Lindbeck and Frei, on the one hand, and Tracy and Ogden, on the other.[86] Barth recognizes the need for using metaphysical schemes. But such schemes, like criteria of meaning, must remain "highly formal, in the sense that the use of the conceptual scheme must be firmly governed by the specific Christian descriptions that such schemes are asked to render in second-order re-descriptions."[87] Not only must such schemes remain highly formal, their use must be subordinate to the dogmatic context in which they are used. Consequently, their use must remain ad hoc, and cannot be controlled by any "supertheory, say, like that of David Tracy, for assigning Christian meaning to a more general context, and therefore assigning it its place

83. Frei, *Types of Christian Theology*, 38–39.
84. Frei, *Types of Christian Theology*, 39.
85. Frei, *Types of Christian Theology*, 39. "Philosophy as conceptual system describing and referring to 'reality' is not a basis on which to build theology, and even philosophy as a set of formal, universal rules or criteria for what may count as coherent and true in Christian discourse as in every other kind of conceptual practice is not basic to or foundational of Christian theology" (Frei, *Types of Christian Theology*, 40).
86. Frei, *Types of Christian Theology*, 39–40.
87. Frei, *Types of Christian Theology*, 41.

within that context."[88] In sum, all criteria of meaning and truth must arise within specific theological contexts, and cannot be imposed universally, either by theology or from "outside" theology. Barth "claims that for theology there is no such thing as a general context-invariant criteriology. . . ."[89] Barth remains adamant about this claim, in Frei's view, even for that most basic of such criteria, the law of noncontradiction.[90]

One of Frei's overriding concerns is whether and how such a project can justify itself without, on the one hand, its basic theses becoming a matter of mere assertion or, on the other, resorting to universal criteria of meaning or rational assessment. Frei, of course, thinks he can provide justification for the project, and his avenue for doing so is simultaneously the most salient feature distinguishing it from the first three types—namely, its understanding of Christianity as having its own language distinct from every other form of discourse. For type 4, "Christianity has its own distinctive language, which is not to be interpreted without residue into other ways of thinking and speaking."[91] The crucially distinct feature of Christian discourse is that its criteria of meaning are not descriptivist or referential. On Frei's reading, "Barth is absolutely certain that the meaning of Christian statements is not their reference. . . ."[92] In Frei's view, one of the things that distinguished Barth from Schleiermacher and makes his method superior is that Barth rejects a descriptivist understanding of the meaning of theological statements, an understanding that it is plausible to read Schleiermacher as adopting: Barth "would chide Schleiermacher if Schleiermacher made his description of that [Christian] self-description subject to an invariant, formal, universal criterion: *the* test for the meaningfulness and coherence of dogmatic assertions is their referring only by way of a co-reference to the experience of absolute dependence."[93] Barth rejects any general theory of the meaningfulness of Christian language as a condition of understanding it. Yet Barth understands that some criterion of meaningfulness is required. Nonetheless, no such criterion can be imposed from "outside" theology via a general theory of meaning. Instead, such criteria must somehow arise from the context of a specific theological issue under discussion. Criteria of meaningfulness must arise from the

88. Frei, *Types of Christian Theology*, 41.
89. Frei, *Types of Christian Theology*, 45.
90. Frei, *Types of Christian Theology*, 45.
91. Frei, *Types of Christian Theology*, 38.
92. Frei, *Types of Christian Theology*, 38.
93. Frei, *Types of Christian Theology*, 40.

"inside" or intracontextually because of the "self-involving, existential" nature of the language of Christian theological discourse.[94]

> To learn, for example, to explicate Christian scripture about faith, hope, and love, is not only to master these concepts, but to be able to apply them pertinently and propose the same to others. On the one hand, justification by faith is a doctrine that functions as a rule in, let us say, orthodox Christian discourse. Not only does it function as a rule but it looks as though it were asserting something about how God deals with human beings, and to that extent is a statement that holds true regardless of the attitude of the person or persons articulating it. On the other hand, it is equally true that the assertion works as a concept that is meaningless apart from the appropriate attitude of gratitude, and obedience subsequent to gratitude, which is the condition for understanding it—indeed, the manner in which it is understood.[95]

In other words, as Christian self-description, theological statements must be practiced as well as uttered as a necessary condition for their acquiring meaning. Furthermore, such practice is also a necessary condition of understanding such statements. Yet neither of these points implies any rejection of a correspondence understanding of truth in theological discourse. Christian theological statements have two "aspects" necessary for their meaning, for understanding them, and for assessing them. They have a use- or praxis-oriented aspect as well as a normative aspect. The latter, normative, aspect is necessary in order to apply Christian discourse to other linguistic contexts (an application necessary in some unspecified sense). These two aspects, however, cannot be systematically correlated. Barth's rejection of such correlation in turn implies that although Christian discourse overlaps other linguistic contexts, Christian language (and thus Christian self-description) is not reducible to any other, or more universal, language. Further, the rules for the use of Christian language can never be absolute, but are always subject to modification by the actual use of the community.[96]

In sum, for type 4, theology proceeds both as Christian self-description and as a philosophical discipline, but the latter task is subordinate to the former. Christian self-description does not await the results of philosophical theology, but governs such results. The two tasks cannot be systematically

94. Frei, *Types of Christian Theology*, 41–42.
95. Frei, *Types of Christian Theology*, 42.
96. Frei, *Types of Christian Theology*, 42–43. "There can be for Barth no single, articulable, super-rule for the way in which Christian language is used" (42).

correlated but maintain only ad hoc relations. Likewise, though Christian self-description can and should overlap with various external descriptions of Christianity, there cannot in principle be any correlation between the two. What makes Barth's method superior to the other types in Frei's view is that it makes possible a distinct literary approach to the Bible. The superiority of Barth's approach consists in its rejection of a referential or descriptivist understanding of the meaning of biblical texts in favor of an understanding that locates the meaning of the texts in the texts themselves. This understanding in turn yields an understanding of the literal sense more faithful to the tyrannical nature of the biblical texts.[97]

The fifth and final type is exemplified in the work of D. Z. Phillips, who explicitly attempts to follow the later work of Wittgenstein. This type is "Christian self-description with no holds barred. There is not even a subordinated place for philosophy, neither in adducing criteria for coherence, adequacy, or appropriateness, nor most certainly in the employment, either materially or formally, of any metaphysical scheme by the theologian."[98] Frei differentiates type 5 from Barth's method in terms of the criteria for the meaning and truth of theological claims. For Phillips, the meaning of many words or concepts is different in religious contexts than in nonreligious contexts. Words such as "exists" and love" signify something different in religious discourse than in nonreligious discourse. To say that *my desk exists* is to say something very different than to say that *God exists*, and not only because "desk" and "God" have different referents. The two sentences have two different grammars: "[W]hen we say that something is a fact we indicate not a description of that something but its context: that is, what it would and would not be sensible to say or do in connection with it. But this is not the grammar of the concept of divine reality."[99] For Phillips, the criteria for deciding which sentences are meaningful in religious contexts (and what meaning they have) are completely internal to religious discourse. Religious language gets its meaning from the way it is *used* in religious discourse. Thus, "even conflicts over the reality of God are conflicts between differing religions' use of the word. It would be a conflict over the functioning of 'Yahweh' and 'Allah,' not over the factuality of someone designated by either term."[100]

In contrast, Frei argues, Barth holds that distinctions between the use of language or criteria within Christian discourse and the use of language

97. Frei, *Types of Christian Theology*, 44–46.
98. Frei, *Types of Christian Theology*, 46.
99. Frei, *Types of Christian Theology*, 47.
100. Frei, *Types of Christian Theology*, 47.

or criteria outside such discourse "are not absolute rules but essential guides or signposts for orientation."[101] For Barth, philosophy is subordinate within theology and cannot make absolute rules for the relations between internal and external description. Theological and religious contexts or forms of life can and do overlap with other forms of life, allowing for a limited ad hoc borrowing of criteria of meaning or rational belief. The possibility of ad hoc borrowing in turn implies that there *may* in fact be universal criteria of meaning or truth though we do not have access to the universality of such criteria.[102]

For Phillips, on the other hand, the inside/outside distinction is "absolute, and theology is strictly inside talk. . . ."[103] Philosophy is "wholly external" to theology, a different form of life with different criteria of meaning and rational belief.[104] Frei does not read Phillips as holding that there can never be, in principle, any overlap between the two. Such a prescriptive philosophical principle would ironically make theology subordinate to philosophy. Given this reading, it is not difficult to see why Frei struggles to differentiate Phillips from Barth. If both allow overlap, why does Frei read Phillips as keeping philosophy "out of bounds for theology,"[105] and Barth as making it subordinate within theology? The crucial differentiating feature seems to be that the task or goal of theology is far more limited in Phillips's view than it is in Barth's. For Phillips, it is not part of the task of theology to propound universal theories about human nature, the nature of reality, the nature of God, etc., because theology is a part of religious discourse; and the point of religious discourse is not to describe the world, but to actualize the goal of religion, which is to orient and guide religious persons in the living of their lives. This goal, in turn, guides the community in establishing the meaning of its concepts and language. The concept of God is not, therefore, intended to signify or describe some reality, but to function in this regulatory manner.[106] This relationship between the goal of religion and the meaning of religious assertions is also the salient feature by which Frei distinguishes Phillips from Tracy (and from Schleiermacher): For Tracy, "the meaning of Christian concepts is the specifically Christian way in which they shape religious consciousness. For Phillips, it is the way

101. Frei, *Types of Christian Theology*, 48. Barth, Frei says, "would say that we must be prepared in actual practice to make transitions, to slide from one mode to another in connective ways, but for this operation our distinctions don't make provision" (48).
102. Frei, *Types of Christian Theology*, 51.
103. Frei, *Types of Christian Theology*, 48.
104. Frei, *Types of Christian Theology*, 51.
105. Frei, *Types of Christian Theology*, 52.
106. See Frei, *Types of Christian Theology*, 52.

in which they help us dispose ourselves Christianly and affectively toward the important matters of life."[107] Thus, the reason that, in type 5, theology excludes philosophy is not that as forms of life, each with its own language game, they do not overlap.[108] Instead, whatever the goal of philosophy might be, it differs from the regulatory goal of religion. Religion is therefore not unrelated to other forms of life, but it does not depend on other forms of life to justify its claims, nor to specify criteria of justification. The criteria for assessment of religious claims and the criteria for specifying the meaning of such claims are different from such criteria in other forms of life. This difference in criteria implies a corresponding difference between the nature of religious claims and of other kinds of claims. In contrast to other forms of life, Phillips maintains that statements of religious beliefs are not assertions, "since he thinks assertions belong to a class with identifiable criteria for their assessment, and religion isn't like that."[109]

Thus, on Frei's reading, Phillips makes the boundary between Christian self-description and external description absolute. He maintains this division through his articulation of the differing ways in which religious language and other kinds of language acquire meaning. Yet Frei argues that this refusal of any overlap with other kinds of discourse prevents Phillips from any significant redescription of traditional Christian claims.[110] On my reading, Frei is arguing that the overlap between religious and other forms of discourse is what allows for the development of religious traditions. Without such overlap, our only options when faced with traditional claims are arbitrary departure from them, simple repetition of them, or silence.[111] Paradoxically, Frei argues, Phillips's confinement of theology

107. Frei, *Types of Christian Theology*, 55.
108. "Phillips is concerned that what he said might be taken as a plea for self-contained language games, and he doesn't want to be guilty of that" (Frei, *Types of Christian Theology*, 52). Frei's use of "language games" is confusing here. He says that Phillips allows overlap in language games, but not between internal and external description. As for overlap between "modes of discourse," Frei says, "we find not so much that [Phillips] objects as that he has simply dematerialized" (55). Consequently, I read Frei as here using "language games" as interchangeable with "forms of life."
109. Frei, *Types of Christian Theology*, 53. This construal of religious beliefs makes it difficult for Phillips to differentiate himself from the view that religious assertions are reducible to assertions of attitudes (54).
110. Phillips admits overlap with other forms of life. "But when we ask about any kind of overlap with other modes of discourse that would help us both to render and make accessible a responsible redescription of biblical and traditional beliefs, both in order to understand them and to appraise them critically in the light of that which—Him or Her who is the ultimate Ruler of Scripture, tradition, and Christian conscience—when we try to get help from Phillips on these matters we find not so much that he objects as that he has simply dematerialized" (Frei, *Types of Christian Theology*, 55).
111. Frei, *Types of Christian Theology*, 55.

to pure Christian self-description is a function of the dominance of (later Wittgensteinian) philosophical theory. He states the paradoxical result succinctly: "In matters of doctrinal statement, pure self-confinement to Christian self-description means no self-description."[112]

IV. CONCLUDING REMARKS AND A LOOK FORWARD

In Frei's analysis of different types of theological method, he clearly identifies an essential area in which he wants to distance his own method from that of Phillips. This distancing is made more difficult by his move away from an emphasis on the narrative form and toward an emphasis on a particular understanding of the literal sense of the narratives. This is because, as I argued above, Frei's move toward a new understanding of the literal sense is a move toward the later Wittgenstein, or at least toward making his reliance on Wittgenstein more apparent. On my reading, Frei distinguishes type 4 (his and Barth's view) from type 5 (Phillips) by distinguishing Barth's understanding of the goal of religion from that of Phillips. Yet this very differentiation presupposes the same Wittgensteinian concepts (forms of life, language games, meaning-as-use) as those used by Phillips. Irrespective of whether he succeeded in differentiating himself methodologically from Phillips, both have been accused of fideism. Frei (along with Lindbeck) has been accused, that is, of eliminating the methodological resources needed to account adequately for the fact that Christian theological claims are claims to *truth*. Consideration of this charge must await the next chapter.

Though Frei's positions on theological method and linguistic meaning deepened and gained nuance, and even shifted a bit over the years, he and Lindbeck both attempt to remain true to the methodological insights Frei gained from his dissertation on Barth. Most importantly, throughout his career Frei did his best to follow Barth's insistence on the primacy of the Word of God as given through the Bible. In my view, most important in this process—that is, most important in his pursuit of Barth's vision and in his Barthian critique of modern liberal Protestant theology as well as contemporary hermeneutics—was his use of the later Wittgenstein's central insights regarding the way language means what it does and Auerbach's understanding of the tyrannical nature of the biblical narratives. These linguistic insights are closely related to postliberal commitments regarding theological method, as we will see in the next chapter. The central

112. Frei, *Types of Christian Theology*, 55.

postliberal conviction—that descriptivist or referential views of linguistic meaning are fundamentally flawed and therefore should not be used in theology or biblical interpretation—was correct. Yet the strength of this conviction led Frei and Lindbeck to prohibit reference from playing any role at all in determinations of meaning. This prohibition, in turn, prevented Frei from distinguishing adequately between semantics and speech acts and from coherently distinguishing his own theological method from that of D. Z. Phillips. It has also made both Frei and Lindbeck vulnerable to charges of fideism.

PART THREE

Problems and Prospects

CHAPTER NINE

A Tale of Two Dead Ends

The Linguistic Problems of
Liberal and Postliberal Theology

L ater in his career, Wittgenstein became disenchanted with the essentially descriptivist nature of his earlier views. In his later period, he
developed a distinctly different approach to philosophy that had several
features: the notion that the meaning of sentences and subsentential units
is constituted entirely by their use in a form of life or language game; the
view that the notion of reference should be abandoned altogether; and a
distinct antitheoretical bias. What his later approach shared with his earlier views was a tendency to see all philosophical problems as confusions
about the use of language. Wittgenstein and the ordinary language philosophers who followed him had a powerful influence on Frei, Lindbeck, and
postliberal theology more generally. At the bottom of Lindbeck's critique
of what he calls "experiential-expressivist" and "cognitive-propositional"
approaches to doctrine is a thesis about the meaning of doctrinal and religious language. Similarly, however one construes the relationship between
Frei's earlier and later work, underlying his critique of liberal theology and
hermeneutics is a thesis about the nature of theological language and how
it acquires meaning. Whatever their differences, what Lindbeck and Frei
have in common is a commitment to a Wittgensteinian understanding of
linguistic meaning. They believe that the approach of Wittgenstein and
ordinary language philosophy is preferable to the descriptivist approach,
which they take to be closely associated with liberal theology.

Despite the flowering of ordinary language philosophy in the middle of
the century, descriptivism remained the dominant approach to language

in Anglo-American analytic philosophy. In the middle of the century, however, problems with both approaches began to become apparent. Ironically, liberal theologians began to respond seriously to the descriptivist questions associated with the falsification challenge just when descriptivism was itself coming under increasing scrutiny from Anglo-American philosophers. Similarly, Frei and other theologians began their enchantment with Wittgenstein and ordinary language philosophy just when problems with this approach were becoming apparent to many Anglo-American philosophers. It will be helpful to describe these developments very briefly, and then examine what these problems imply for both liberal and postliberal theology. In the last half of the century, several prominent criticisms of descriptivist reference were put forward. They show that there is a fatal flaw endemic to any descriptivist or truth-conditional approach to linguistic meaning. It will advance my analysis here to discuss these criticisms.

But there are also serious problems with the later Wittgenstein and ordinary language philosophy. A number of criticisms have been leveled against it, and some of its more difficult problems should suffice to indicate why it eventually lost its influence within Anglo-American philosophy. The middle and third quarter of the century also saw developments in the theory of reference that undermined the dominance of descriptivist theories of reference. These developments culminated in the publication of Saul Kripke's *Naming and Necessity,* an extraordinarily influential book based on lectures Kripke gave in 1970. In my view, there are reasons for thinking that the philosophical problems with descriptivism and ordinary language philosophy also spell problems for liberal and postliberal theology as they were practiced in the latter part of the twentieth century. Fortunately, as we will see in the next chapter, developments in analytic philosophy that moved it beyond both descriptivism and ordinary language philosophy also make possible a way forward, beyond the divide between liberal and postliberal theology.

I. LIBERAL THEOLOGY AND DESCRIPTIVISM IN RELIGIOUS LANGUAGE

Descriptivist theories are usually said to be truth-conditional theories, and here's why. As we saw in chapter 2, for descriptivist theories, each meaningful sentence (if it is not a tautology) *describes* a corresponding possible fact. If this possible fact is actual, the sentence is true; if not, it is false. In other words, a sentence acquires its meanings by virtue of its *truth conditions.* To ask what a sentence means, you must ask what facts must obtain for the sentence to be true. For sentence parts (other than logical terms), their meaning is also acquired descriptively, and this meaning is closely related to their reference. For example, the meaning of a singular term is a descriptive sense that uniquely describes the singular object to which the term refers. Reference, that is, proceeds by description. Similarly, the meaning of a sentence predicate is a description that describes the subject S of the sentence just in case the predicate is true of S.

A. Problems with Descriptivist Views of Meaning

The first problem with descriptivist or truth-conditional theories of meaning is that most of the referring expressions of a natural language can have multiple referents (i.e., their extensions consist of more than one member). For most sentences of a language, therefore, there can be multiple sets of truth conditions. This problem can be fairly easily remedied, however, by introducing variables that index the truth conditions to a particular speaker and time of utterance.[1] Other difficulties, however, are not so easily remedied.

Unfortunately, describing these other difficulties requires some rather technical considerations. The most important and influential truth-conditional theorist is Donald Davidson, and because of his immense influence, criticism of truth-conditional theories of meaning have centered around his work.[2] Davidson attempts to derive a theory of meaning from Alfred Tarski's theory of truth. In a groundbreaking article, Tarski provided a definition of truth for the languages of symbolic logic, which can be used to express sentences in mathematical sciences.[3] Tarski's definition was quickly

1. This convenience is utilized by Donald Davidson, "Truth and Meaning," *Synthese* (1967): 304–23; reprinted in Donald Davidson, *Inquiries into Truth and Interpretation* (Oxford: Clarendon Press, 2001), 17–36 (page references are to reprint edition). Thus "'I am tired' as (potentially) spoken by *p* at *t* is true if and only if *p* is tired at *t*" (Davidson, *Inquiries into Truth and Interpretation,* 34).
2. Almost all of the literature critical of Davidson is highly technical in nature. It is interesting to note that although Davidson has been highly influential in religious studies at least since the publication of Terry F. Godlove, Jr., *Religion, Interpretation, and Diversity of Belief: The Framework Model from Kant to Durkheim to Davidson* (Cambridge: Cambridge Univ. Press, 1989), the philosophical literature critical of Davidson seems to have had very little influence; indeed, it is hardly even acknowledged. For a critique of this reliance on Davidson, based in part on the critique of Davidson that follows in this chapter, see my "Why Not Davidson? Neopragmatism in Religious Studies and the Coherence of Alternative Conceptual Schemes," *Journal of Religion* 88 (April 2008): 159–89.
3. See Alfred Tarski, "The Concept of Truth in Formalized Languages," in *Logic, Semantics, Meta-Mathematics,* trans. J. H. Woodger, 2d ed. (Indianapolis: Hacket, 1983). For a more detailed explanation of Tarski's theory and some of the purposes to which it can (and cannot) be put, see Scott Soames, *Understanding Truth* (New York: Oxford Univ. Press, 1999), and William P. Alston, *A Realist Conception of Truth* (Ithaca, N.Y.: Cornell Univ. Press, 1996).

put to work providing interpretations of various formal languages.[4] Such interpretations perform several tasks: they specify the domain of objects about which the language makes claims and the name(s) that refer(s) to each object in the domain; they assign to each function sign in the language a mapping from one or more objects to (an)other object(s) in the domain; and they assign to each predicate in the language a set of objects (or pairs or multiples of objects) of which the predicate is true. These tasks provide an interpretation of the vocabulary of the language, and this interpretation of the vocabulary combines with Tarski's definition of truth to provide an interpretation of the sentences of the language.[5] This interpretation of sentences yields at least one so-called T-sentence for each sentence of the language being interpreted. Such T-sentences have the following form:

"S" is true in language L if and only if (iff) P.

In T-sentences of this form, S is replaced by a sentence of the interpreted language, and P is replaced by a paraphrase of that sentence.[6] An interpretation of an entire language is a finite set of statements that allows the derivation of one or more T-sentences for each sentence in the language. What Davidson did was to extend Tarski-style interpretations of formalized languages to natural languages, so that a Tarski-style theory of truth for a language that provides truth conditions for the sentences of that language counts as a theory of meaning for the language. On Davidson's view, a Tarski-style theory of truth for a language (adapted for natural languages through variables indexing a sentence to a particular speaker and time of utterance)

> works by giving necessary and sufficient conditions of the truth of every sentence, and to give truth conditions is a way of giving the meaning of a sentence.
> To know the semantic concept of truth for a language is to know what it is for

4. Here I am following the discussion of Scott Soames, *Philosophical Analysis in the Twentieth Century*, vol. 2: *The Age of Meaning* (Princeton, N.J.: Princeton Univ. Press, 2003), 291–95 (hereafter *Age of Meaning*).
5. Soames notes that when Tarski's work is used to provide an interpretation of a language, what it provides is not actually a definition of truth. Instead, it provides a theory that assigns truth conditions for every sentence of the language if and only if that sentence is true, where truth is understood antecedently and without definition (*Age of Meaning*, 293). Note that because of the formal nature of the languages interpreted, the problem of multiplicity of reference that arises in natural languages can be eliminated. See Alston, *A Realist Conception of Truth*, 30.
6. Note that a T-sentence of this form will be true when the sentences on either side of the biconditional have the same truth value—that is, whenever both are true or both are false.

a sentence—any sentence—to be true, and this amounts, in one good sense we can give to the phrase, to understanding the language.[7]

Davidson takes his theory to be holistic in the following sense. The truth conditions, and thus the meaning, of a sentence is derived from the semantically significant structure of the sentence, including the reference of each of its parts. And the reference of each part, in turn, is simply the contributions it makes to the truth conditions of each sentence of which it is a part. Thus what a theory of meaning for a language is supposed to do, in Davidson's view, is to specify the complex network of linguistic relationships whose mastery endows a speaker with competence in speaking that language.

Davidson acknowledges that a theory of truth (and meaning) for a language set up the way he suggested would generate T-sentences not only like (1), but also like (2):

(1) "Snow is white" is true in English iff snow is white.
(2) "Snow is white" is true in English iff grass is green.

But Davidson seems initially to have believed that the fact that his account is a holistic one would render T-sentences like (2) harmless.[8] A properly structured truth theory would still pair truths with truths and falsehoods with falsehoods, and would provide all that needed to be known about the meaning of the sentences of the language. Yet not long after Davidson proposed his theory it became clear, even to Davidson himself, that his theory could generate alternate sets of T-sentences for any language, one of which would be translational, such as (3), and the other of which would be nontranslational, such as (4).

(3) "Snow is white" is true in English iff snow is white.
(4) "Snow is white" is true in English iff snow is white and arithmetic is incomplete.

T-sentences such as (4) meet Davidson's requirements in every respect, but clearly a truth theory that generates such T-sentences cannot be regarded as a theory of meaning.[9] For a while, Davidson and others attempted various constraints that would yield only truth theories that entailed translational

7. Davidson, "Truth and Meaning," 24.
8. See Davidson, "Truth and Meaning," 26.
9. On this point see J. A. Foster, "Meaning and Truth Theory," in *Truth and Meaning: Essays in Semantics,* ed. Gareth Evans and John McDowell (Oxford: Clarendon Press, 1976; repr., 1999), 1–32 (page references are to reprint edition).

T-sentences like (3). Yet soon it became clear that whatever success such constraints might have, knowledge of that which is stated by the truth theories would not suffice for understanding the language. This is because one might know what is stated by a translational T-sentence without knowing that the T-sentence is translational. Consequently, one might know a truth theory that entails (3) as one of its T-sentences and still believe a sentence like (5).

(5) "Snow is white" means in English that snow is white and arithmetic is incomplete.

In other words, the same person could have true beliefs about truth conditions and false beliefs about meaning. One of Davidson's critics therefore proposed that Davidson amend his theory to say that *a truth theory for a language L, meeting proper constraints, entails that* . . . The dots in the sentence are then to be filled in with a conjunction of all the T-sentences of the theory. What the "proper constraints" do is to ensure that the truth theory entails translational T-sentences for each sentence of the object language. Therefore, if one knows the truth theory, one will know that it yields translational T-sentences. One therefore knows that the sentence on the right side of the biconditional expresses the same proposition as the sentence on the left side. This proposed revision was intended to rule out the possibility that sentences like (5) could be derived from a T-sentence like (3).[10]

Yet so far as I can see, as Scott Soames and others have argued, Davidson's proposal remains fundamentally flawed. Soames analyzes Davidson's argument as proceeding through six steps:

1. A truth theory for a language L, meeting proper constraints (i.e., a translational truth theory), entails that. . . . (the dots in the sentence are then to be filled in with a conjunction of all the T-sentences of the theory).
2. Thus, a translational truth theory for L states something that entails that "Snow is white" is true in L iff snow is white.
3. Thus, a translational truth theory for L has as a logical consequence a T-sentence that states that "Snow is white" is true in L iff snow is white.
4. Since the truth theory is translational, the T-sentence mentioned in step 3 above is one whose right-hand side means the same as the object-language sentence "Snow is white" mentioned on its left-hand side.

10. This proposal was made by Foster in "Meaning and Truth Theory." Davidson endorsed it in "Reply to Foster," in Evans and McDowell, *Truth and Meaning*, 33–41.

5. Since the T-sentence states that "Snow is white" is true in L iff snow is white, both the right-hand side of that T-sentence and the object-language sentence mentioned on the left-hand side must state that snow is white.

6. Thus, "Snow is white" means in L that snow is white. [Let's call this the M-sentence.] [11]

If the argument embodied in these six steps succeeds, it allows us to derive the meaning of the sentences of a language from a Tarski-style truth theory for that language. But Soames notes several important difficulties. First, neither the compositional character of the truth theories nor the truth of the claims made by the T-sentences themselves play any direct role in the derivation. So long as the moves from one step to another are warranted, all we would need in order to reach step 6 is to be provided with sentences "S" is F iff p, and a guarantee that p is a translation of S. Once we have sentences of this form and a translational guarantee, it does not matter what predicate F stands for, how the sentences are derived, or whether they are true or false. Thus the role of truth theories in providing information about meaning is in principle dispensable.

A more fundamental difficulty concerns step 4.[12] By step 3 the argument is supposed to have established that some translational truth theory entails a T-sentence that states that "Snow is white" is true in L iff snow is white. In order to get to step 4, however, we need to know that *this particular T-sentence* is translational. But the proposal does not guarantee this. If we knew in advance that a truth theory for our object language provided exactly one T-sentence for each sentence of the language, then we would know that the T-sentence for the sentence under consideration is translational. But in general, a truth theory will generate many T-sentences for each sentence in the object language, and Davidson's proposal only tells us

---

11. See Scott Soames, "Truth, Meaning and Understanding," *Philosophical Studies* 65 (1992): 17–35, esp. 26–27.

12. Soames also mentions a problem with steps 2 and 3. He notes that the entailment mentioned in step two is understood as a relation between propositions. But the logical consequence mentioned in step 3 is a relation between sentences. Therefore, in order to move from step two to step three, one must accept a hidden premise that goes something like this: "*If a sentence s expresses a proposition p, which entails a proposition q, then some sentence s′ that expresses q is a logical consequence of s*" (Soames, "Truth, Meaning and Understanding," 28). But it is not clear that we should accept this hidden premise. The biggest problem seems to concern the substitution of coreferential proper names in an extensional sentence that preserves the proposition that the original sentence expresses. See Soames, "Truth, Meaning and Understanding," 27–28, 34 n.10. In a subsequent discussion, however, Soames simply omits this point without mentioning it. See Soames, *Age of Meaning*, 306–309.

that one of them will be translational. It does not tell us *which* T-sentence is translational. But because on Davidson's proposal we do not know the meaning of the object-language sentence in advance (it is the truth theory that is supposed to tell us this), we cannot tell which T-sentence is translational for the object-language sentence under consideration.[13] As a result, Davidson's theory, and indeed any truth-conditional theory of meaning, cannot rule out a sentence like (5) above after all. To see why this is so, suppose that a truth theory entails some T-sentence *"S" is true iff p*. Suppose further that *q* is a logical consequence of either *p* or of the truth theory itself. In this case the truth theory will also entail the T-sentence *"S" is true iff p&q*. So far as I can see, something like this result will obtain for any truth theory that purports to act as a theory of meaning. Consequently, we cannot be sure that the T-sentence *"Snow is white" is true in L iff snow is white* is translational. Consequently, the move from step 3 to step 4 is unwarranted, and the "M-sentence" cannot be derived from the truth theory.[14] Again, so far as I can see, this difficulty will be endemic to any attempt to derive an understanding of meaning from a specification of truth conditions.

As will see in the final chapter, this critique of truth-conditional theories of meaning has significant implications for the kind of transcendental theological method practiced by liberal theologians such as Schubert Ogden and others. But there are also reasons for thinking that there are

13. On my reading, Davidson recognized this problem in "Radical Interpretation" (*Dialectica* 27 [1973]: 313–28; reprinted in *Inquiries into Truth and Interpretation*, 125–39), but he thought that his "holistic constraint" or "principle of charity" (the principle that, in order to adequately interpret the statements of anyone at all, we must assume that the vast majority of their statements are true) somehow supplied something that could stand in for Tarski's assurance of the translational nature of the T-sentence (139). Yet he is remarkably vague about just how this works: According to this holistic constraint, "[T]he totality of T-sentences should . . . optimally fit evidence about sentences held true by native speakers. The present idea is that what Tarski assumed outright for each T-sentence can be indirectly elicited by a holistic constraint. If that constraint is adequate, each T-sentence will in fact yield an acceptable interpretation" (139). He seems to realizes that significant indeterminacy will remain. Nonetheless, he remains confident that "the resulting indeterminacy cannot be so great but that any theory that passes the tests will serve to yield interpretations" (139). Unfortunately, there is no argument in either "Radical Interpretation" or "On the Very Idea of a Conceptual Scheme" (*Proceedings and Addresses of the American Philosophical Association* 47 [1974]: 5–20; reprinted in *Inquiries into Truth and Interpretation*, 183–98 [page references are to the reprint edition]) that establishes this, and it seems to me to depend on whether his truth-conditional theory of meaning can succeed on its own.

14. See Soames, "Truth, Meaning and Understanding," 28–29. For further discussions, see Soames, *Age of Meaning*, 306–11; Soames, "Semantics and Semantic Competence," *Philosophical Perspectives* 3 (1989): 575–96; and Soames, "Direct Reference, Propositional Attitudes, and Semantic Content," *Philosophical Topics* 15 (1987): 47–87, reprinted in *Readings in the Philosophy of Language*, ed. Peter Ludlow (Cambridge, Mass.: MIT Press, 1997; repr., 1998), 921–62 (page references are to reprint edition).

serious problems with the descriptivist view of reference that postliberal theologians take liberal theology to have assumed.

B. Criticisms of Descriptivist Reference

Bertrand Russell's understanding of reference was dominant until the middle of the twentieth century, when it came under attack from a number of quarters. In 1950, Peter Strawson published an influential article arguing that Russell's theory was formulated as an attempt to address statements in which the subject is a vacuous definite description.[15] Specifically, it was a response to one view of how sentences with vacuous definite descriptions can be significant. The view Russell thought incorrect was as follows: A sentence such as "The present king of France is wise" is significant, even though there be no present king of France. Since it is significant, the description "present king of France" must refer to something that exists (or subsists) in some possible world. On Russell's view, such an analysis is mistaken in that it confuses the grammatical subject of the sentence with the logical subject. Since there is no "present king of France," the sentence is not, logically, a typical subject-predicate sentence at all. Instead, it is a complex "existential proposition" that turns out to be false.[16] So sentences with vacuous names, on Russell's account, are false.

In Strawson's 1950 article, he argues that Russell's view produces some odd consequences. Suppose Jones were to say, "The king of France is wise," and Smith answered, "There is no king of France." On Russell's view, Smith is contradicting or denying Jones's statement. But Strawson takes this to be an odd use of "contradicting" or "denying"—indeed, not only odd but *absurd*. What produces this absurd result, in Strawson's view, is that Russell takes an *implication* of Jones's statement (i.e., that there is a king of France) to be an *entailment*. And the reason that Russell confuses implication and entailment here is that he also confuses the *meaning* of a name or a sentence with the *use* of the name or sentence or expression.

15. P. F. Strawson, "On Referring," *Mind* 59 (1950): 320–44; reprinted in *The Philosophy of Language*, ed. A. P. Martinich, 4th ed. (New York: Oxford Univ. Press, 2001) (page references are to reprint edition). Strawson's is the received reading of Russell. A better reading, however, takes Russell to be responding not only to vacuous definite descriptions, but to the more general problem raised by sentences that have as their subject things with which we are not acquainted. This is a much more serious problem because the vast majority of names in our language refer to things with which we are not acquainted, but which we know only by description.

16. More specifically, Russell would say that that "the present king of France is wise" means "There exists at least one present king of France (x); and for any y, if y is the present king of France, y is identical to x, and x is wise. Thus, let P represent "the present king of France" and W represent "wise"; $(\exists x)(Px \ \& \ (y)(\text{if } Py, \text{ then } y=x) \ \& \ Wx)$.

Strawson insisted (as did most of the Oxford ordinary language philosophers of the 1950s and 1960s) that it is important to distinguish between sentences and propositions. Speakers use sentences to make assertions (i.e., to assert propositions). The meaning of an expression is constituted by the general directions for its use; the meaning of a sentence is likewise constituted by the general directions for its use in making assertions.[17] So meanings, for Strawson, are not truth conditions because words themselves do not refer; people refer, using words to do so.[18]

It is important to see that the context of utterance becomes much more important in Strawson's view of reference. For Russell, the paradigmatic expression is a logically proper name, which falls within a very narrow class of definite descriptions. Strawson, in contrast, is sensitive to the fact that most definite descriptions fail to pick out a unique object. On Russell's account, any sentence containing such (indefinite) descriptions must be false. On Strawson's account, such sentences can be true, because the context can save the reference.[19]

The next contribution to this story of reference comes from Keith Donnellan,[20] who argued that Russell and Strawson make two common assumptions he takes to be unwarranted. First, they both assume "that we can ask how a definite description functions in some sentence independently of a particular occasion upon which it is used."[21] The second assumption is that the truth value of a sentence is affected if nothing exists that is described by a definite description used in the sentence.[22] To make sense of this, Donnellan offers a distinction between two different uses of definite descriptions: an "attributive" and a "referential" use. A definite description

17. To be more complete here, I should distinguish between meaning as directions governing possible uses and meaning governing the actual use to which people put words and sentences to make assertions. This distinction maps easily onto the distinction between semantic meaning and speaker meaning.

18. For some interpreters, Strawson's view implies that meaning and truth are functions of an account of language use that is a pragmatics, not a semantics. Thus, on this reading of Strawson, behind the dispute between Russell and Strawson is a larger dispute between a descriptive account of language use and a general theory of semantics. I do not take this characterization to be entirely accurate, but I do not have space to pursue it here.

19. Russell published a polemical reply in Bertrand Russell, "Mr Strawson on Referring," *Mind* 66 (1957): 385–89.

20. Keith Donnellan, "Reference and Definite Descriptions," *Philosophical Review* 75 (1966): 281–304; reprinted in *The Philosophy of Language*, ed. A. P. Martinich, 4th ed. (New York: Oxford Univ. Press, 2001), 247–59 (page references are to reprint edition).

21. Donnellan, "Reference and Definite Descriptions,"248.

22. Donnellan, "Reference and Definite Descriptions,"248. Russell considers the statement made by the sentence to be false; Strawson considers it to lack any truth value.

is *attributive* in an assertion if and only if the speaker states something about whatever or whoever may fit the description. But the description is *referential* in an assertion if and only if the speaker uses the description to enable her audience to pick out whoever or whatever she is talking about, and then states something about that person or thing.[23] Consider two examples, both of which occur as I am a spectator at a trial in which Jones has been accused of murdering Smith. In the first example, upon seeing Jones in the defendant's chair, I recall having previously seen him entering a psychiatric hospital in a straightjacket. So I say, "Smith's murderer is crazy." Here I am using the description "Smith's murderer" referentially to pick out Jones. Even if Jones is not the murderer and is acquitted, he is still the referent of my statement. Given the context, my listener sitting next to me in the courtroom will know I am talking about Jones. The context saves the reference. In the second example, I have never seen Jones before. I say, "Smith's murderer is crazy," upon seeing pictures of a particularly grisly murder scene. In this second example, I am using the description "Smith's murderer" attributively. Whether I think Jones is guilty or innocent, I am using the description to refer to *Smith's murderer, whoever that may be.*

Donnellan says that the attributive/referential distinction is a pragmatic, not a semantic distinction. This in turn leads Saul Kripke to offer a distinction between semantic reference and speaker's reference.[24] The semantic referent of a name or description is that thing or person or idea or concept (or whatever) to which the words themselves refer. Ordinarily this will be a set of multiple referents to which a speaker may *possibly* refer using the words (properly). The speaker's referent is that person or thing to which a speaker *in fact* refers on a given occasion using the words.[25]

These distinctions lay the groundwork for Kripke's more far-reaching critique of descriptivist theories of reference, and his own skeletal proposal or picture of reference in *Naming and Necessity*.[26] Descriptivist theories have

23. When a speaker is using a definite description attributively, that is, the speaker does not know who or what the referent is, or whether one exists; or the speaker may believe no referent exists.

24. Saul Kripke, "Speaker's Reference and Semantic Reference," in *Contemporary Perspectives in the Philosophy of Language*, ed. Peter A. French, Theodore E. Uehling, Jr., and Howard K. Wettstein (Minneapolis: Univ. of Minn. Press, 1979), 6–27.

25. Note that there is an intentional element in both kinds of reference. Kripke distinguishes between the speaker's general and specific intention. A speaker generally intends or means what the words semantically mean and specifically means or intends to refer to the referent.

26. Saul A. Kripke, *Naming and Necessity* (Cambridge, Mass.: Harvard Univ. Press, 1972; repr., 1999). This work was given as a series of lectures and originally published in *Semantics of Natural Language*, ed. Donald Davidson and Gilbert Harman (Dordrecht: Reidel, 1972).

in common the notion that a name is successful in referring to an object insofar as it stands for one or more definite descriptions that (either singly or together) uniquely describe the referent object.[27] That is, of the descriptions that a speaker takes to be satisfied by an object, the speaker takes one or some to belong uniquely to that object. If, however, no object uniquely satisfies the most important description(s), then the purported name does not refer. More specifically, this way of understanding reference was part of what Scott Soames calls the "reigning conception of language."[28]

In the years surrounding 1970, a group of philosophers began to attack the reigning consensus on meaning and reference. This group was led by Saul Kripke, Hilary Putnam, and Keith Donnellan. The most influential publication in this enterprise was Saul Kripke's *Naming and Necessity*, in which Kripke attacked the traditional descriptivist analyses of the reference of proper names, and suggested an alternative picture. Several objections are possible to such descriptivist theories, but two will suffice to show why Kripke (among others) thinks they will not do.[29] The first has to do with referential circularity. Descriptivist theories typically require that the descriptions associated with a referent pick out the referent in a way that is ultimately noncircular. Suppose, for example, that a person uses the name "Einstein" to refer to Einstein, but the only description of which he is aware that applies to Einstein is "the discoverer of relativity theory." Suppose further that the only thing the person can say about relativity theory is that it was discovered by Einstein. Descriptivist theorists, such as William Christian, will typically hold that reference has failed in such an instance.[30] Kripke insists, however, that such a person *does* refer to Einstein. If such a

27. On some such views, the constitutive description(s) just are the meaning of the name.

28. Scott Soames, *Reference and Description: The Case Against Two-Dimensionalism* (Princeton, N.J.: Princeton Univ. Press, 2005), 1–2.

29. It is possible to exaggerate Kripke's role in the attack on descriptivism. A number of philosophers have argued that Ruth Barcan Marcus, in fact, originated many of the ideas commonly attributed to Kripke. See, for example, Quentin Smith, "Marcus, Kripke and the Origin of the New Theory of Reference," *Synthese* 104:2 (Aug. 1995; ed. James H. Fetzer and Paul W. Humphreys): 179–89. See also James H. Fetzer and Paul W. Humphreys, eds., *The New Theory of Reference: Kripke, Marcus and Its Origins*, (Dordrecht: Kluwer Academic Publishers, 1998). For an example of Marcus's work, see Ruth Barcan Marcus, "Modalities and Intensional Languages," *Synthese* 13 (1961): 303–22; and *Modalities* (New York: Oxford Univ. Press, 1993). Without taking sides in this debate, I discuss Kripke's work here simply because I take it to be more widely known than that of the other critics of descriptivism, such as Marcus. Others were raising questions about descriptivism as well, including Peter Geach, Michael Dummett, Hilary Putnam, Paul Grice, Keith Donnellan, David Kaplan, Donald Davidson, and others.

30. See William A. Christian, *Meaning and Truth in Religion* (Princeton, N.J.: Princeton Univ. Press, 1964), 28–31.

person is asked who Einstein is and replies, "Einstein is the discoverer of relativity theory," his reference will succeed on Kripke's view, and his assertion will have meaning. The second objection involves a person who knows only a small number of descriptions of a person x, none of which *uniquely* pick out x. Suppose, for example, I say, "Dr. Busby is a reputable dermatologist," when the only things I know about Dr. Busby are that she practices in Chicago, she is a dermatologist, and she is reputable. Descriptivist theorists would typically say that reference has failed because such descriptions apply to a number of individuals. Again, however, Kripke insists that I have indeed referred to Dr. Busby. If I do not meet the requirement of any descriptivist theory, so much the worse for the theory.

Kripke does not deny that names or descriptions that satisfy the requirements of descriptivist theories—of unique, noncircular definite descriptions—can in fact refer. Yet names can refer, as the preceding paragraph points out, even when they don't meet such requirements. Kripke consequently provides an alternative for such cases. Kripke's alternative "picture"—often called a "causal theory of reference"—holds that a name picks out a person or object in something like the following way:

> A rough statement of a theory might be the following: An initial 'baptism' takes place. Here the object may be named by ostension, or the reference of the name may be fixed by a description. When the name is 'passed from link to link', the receiver of the name must, I think, intend when he learns it to use it with the same reference as the man from whom he heard it.[31]

More can be said about the limitations of descriptivist reference. But these comments by Kripke should suffice to indicate a few reasons why it is preferable to adopt a view that allows referring expressions to refer directly to their referents.[32]

Therefore, both of the major aspects of descriptivist understandings of language are, in my view, seriously flawed. In 1970, however, the only other

31. Kripke, *Naming and Necessity*, 96 (citations omitted).
32. This is the option preferred by William Alston. See William P. Alston, "Referring to God," *International Journal for the Philosophy of Religion* 24 (Nov. 1988): 113–28; reprinted in William P. Alston, *Divine Nature and Human Language* (Ithaca, N.Y.: Cornell Univ. Press, 1989), 103–17. Recently, several theorists have attempted to revive descriptivism. Among other things, these theorists believe that Kripke's direct reference or "causal" theory of reference does not deal adequately with Russell's puzzle over vacuous definite descriptions. See, for example, Frank Jackson, "Reference and Descriptions Revisited," *Nous-Supplement: Philosophical Perspectives*, vol. 12, *Language, Mind and Ontology* (1998), 201–18. For a description and extended critique of this revival, see Scott Soames, *Reference and Description: The Case Against Two-Dimensionalism* (Princeton, N.J.: Princeton Univ. Press, 2005).

major option known to most theologians was the approach of ordinary language philosophy. This was the approach chosen by postliberals such as Frei and Lindbeck. Yet this approach has serious flaws as well, both on its own and as it is appropriated by postliberals like Frei. So let's now turn to a discussion of these problems.

II. PROBLEMS WITH POSTLIBERAL THEOLOGY ON LANGUAGE

To review, Frei attempted to carry out the Barthian project, deriving his methodological commitments from his ontological or doctrinal statements about God. Frei never worked out any full-blown doctrinal statements about God the way Barth did, but he did follow Barth's insistence that such statements must be explications of God's self-revelation in Jesus Christ. Frei then sought to follow Barth in deriving his methodological commitments from this divine self-revelation rather than letting an independently formulated methodological scheme determine in advance the limits of what theology could and should say about God. This led him to the position that Christian theology should not concern itself with apologetics, except perhaps on an ad hoc basis, but should be content with self-description. In the view of William Placher, Frei and Lindbeck carry out this self-limitation of theology through three important theses.[33] First, narrative is the most important interpretive category for reading the Bible.[34] Second, the biblical narrative world has primacy over the reader's quotidian world. Thus the biblical world is to "absorb" our world, and interpretation places the reader in the world of the text rather than taking claims from the text and placing them in the reader's everyday world. Third, language is the condition of the possibility of fully human experience rather than being an instrument through which prelinguistic

33. William C. Placher, "Paul Ricoeur and Postliberal Theology: A Conflict of Interpretations?" *Modern Theology* 4 (Oct. 1987): 35–52.

34. Other commentators acknowledge something similar. Maurice Wiles, for example, views narrative theology as seeking to have "narrative," as both a literary and a theological category, play the role often played by theological anthropology in liberal theologies. Maurice Wiles, "Scriptural Authority and Theological Construction: The Limitations of Narrative Interpretation," in *Scriptural Authority and Narrative Interpretation*, ed. Garrett Green (Philadelphia: Fortress Press, 1987), 42–58. This priority attributed to narrative is defensible in the view of Paul Schwartzentruber because human beings become transparent to themselves only in the presence of Christ. Thus, Schwartzentruber argues, Frei's theological "modesty" is not a retreat but a substantive "post-post-modern" alternative. Paul Schwartzentruber, "The Modesty of Hermeneutics: The Theological Reserves of Hans Frei," *Modern Theology* 8:2 (April 1992): 181–95.

experience is expressed. Frei might have been uncomfortable with the transcendental sound of Placher's third thesis, but there is no doubt that language is a central theme in Frei's theological project.

Language assumes such a central role in Frei's thought because his historical work on the history of modern hermeneutics convinced him that one of the principal underlying causes of modern theology's "wrong turn" was a mistaken view about the meaning of the language used in the biblical narratives. The mistaken view, as we have seen, was that the meaning of this language was determined by its referential function. Theological-hermeneutical disputes during the period Frei studied became in his view largely disputes over the referent(s) of the language. Spurred by an apologetic impulse, this descriptivist or referential understanding of linguistic meaning led modern theology to become subservient, in Frei's view, to philosophy, so that philosophical concepts and schemes both set the methodological rules of theological hermeneutics and determined the limits of the content of Christian theological self description. If a referential view of meaning had led modern theology into its wrong turn, then what Frei needed in order to correct this wrong turn was an alternative understanding of linguistic meaning. The principle alternative to a referential view of meaning is an understanding of meaning-as-use, and Frei's reading of Wittgenstein and Ryle made him aware of such a view. When Frei argues for the literal reading of biblical texts as given by the Christian community's rule for reading them, he is arguing that their meaning is given by their use in the Christian community's form of life. And doctrines, on Lindbeck's view, are (part of) the Christian community's rules for reading them (and for other uses of Christian religious language). To put it in language Frei used earlier in his career, the meaning of the texts is "located" in the community practices of reading.

Wittgenstein comes to the assistance of postliberal theology in the following way. On a postliberal view, theology must be engaged solely in Christian self-description, using philosophical concepts only on an ad hoc basis to assist it in describing Christian beliefs and form of life. This seems to imply that theology can engage in neither apologetics nor external critique, at least not in the way that liberals from Schleiermacher to Ogden insist it must. This prohibition follows from Frei's appropriation of the later Wittgenstein's view of meaning-as-use in a form of life. On this view, the meaning of crucial criteriological terms, like "reasons," "truth," or "meaning," are unique within the Christian form of life. They may bear family resemblances to the way they are used in other forms of life, but their meaning within the Christian form of life is constituted by the way they are used in it. This will be different, in some sense or other, from the way such terms are used in other forms of life. So apologetics can occur, if at all, only within the area of overlap. Even then, it can occur only insofar as Christian theology's conversation partners share its construal of crucial criteriological terms such as "reasons," "truth," and "meaning." If such construals are given by their use in a community's form of life, this would seem to imply that theological differences could be resolved only to the extent that the conversation partners share a common form of life. If they do not, the most that can be hoped for is that differences can be understood, and this understanding is possible to whatever extent their differing forms of life can be understood by outsiders. But no means exist to resolve such differences, and therefore apologetics as it has been traditionally understood seems to be ruled out. This in turn implies that if differences can only be resolved within shared forms of life (or areas of overlap) then debates over theological differences can be restated without remainder as debates over the best description of the Christian form of life. And this is the way Frei says it should be. Just as Wittgenstein held that philosophy must limit itself to description and must eschew explanation, Frei holds that theology must limit itself to self-description and eschew apologetics. Likewise, Lindbeck disfavors apologetics because he takes it to be deleterious to ecumenical and interreligious dialogue and because it involves a misguided view of religious and doctrinal language. Consequently, if theology can proceed only in the way Frei and Lindbeck spell out, this will entail that Christian theological or religious claims must acquire their meaning through their use in the Christian form of life.

This is somewhat evident in Lindbeck's most influential work. But another indication that this is so is that Frei's understandings of meaning and of theological method can be derived from each other. On the one hand, he argues that the task and method of theology must be limited to Christian self-description, with philosophical concepts borrowed only on an ad hoc basis, and even then they must be "bent" to the ends of the community's use of the literal sense.[35] To say that the *sensus literalis* "governs and bends to its own ends" any philosophical concepts it uses just is to say that such concepts get their meaning by their use in the community's form of life. As Frei states, "The theoretical task compatible with the literal reading of the Gospel narratives is that of describing how and in what context

35. Hans W. Frei, "The 'Literal Reading' of Biblical Narrative in the Christian Tradition: Does It Stretch or Will It Break?" in *The Bible and the Narrative Tradition*, ed. Frank McConnell (New York: Oxford Univ. Press, 1986), 36–77; reprinted in Frei, *Theology and Narrative*, 117–152, esp. 143 (page references are to reprint edition).

it functions."[36] So far as I can see, to describe how and in what context the literal reading of the Gospel narratives *functions* is to describe how the literal reading is *used* in some particular form of life. Thus, a "use theory" of meaning can, it seems, be derived from a postliberal conception of the task and method of theology.

On the other hand, Frei argues that the meaning of the biblical narratives must be determined independently of any question of their reference. Yet he says that reference remains important, as does the church's commitment to the truth of the Gospel narratives. But it is not at all clear what "the truth of the Gospel narratives" means on a postliberal account. If the notion of truth must be bent to the ends of the literal sense, and if we have no epistemic access to (at least some of) the referents of the Gospel narratives (indeed, the most important referents), then somehow or other the meaning of the claim *that (at least some of) the Gospel's claims about Jesus are true* can only be a function of the community's use of those claims in its form of life—the life of faith. If so, and if the referents of those narratives are important to their truth, then it seems that George Hunsinger is correct in attributing to Frei the view that we have no independent epistemic access to (at least the most important of) the referents of the biblical narratives outside the community's form of life—the life of faith.[37] From this last statement it follows that theology has no means of properly engaging in apologetics (as traditionally understood), and that theology can only be description.

The view I am advancing here, that postliberal theological method is closely related to a Wittgensteinian understanding of meaning-as-use and more generally to Wittgenstein's antitheoretical orientation to philosophy, is supported by sympathetic interpreters of Frei and Lindbeck. For example, William Placher has argued that Frei's shift from the narrative structure to the literal sense is warranted because however one articulates criteria of meaning and truth for theology, the meaning of such articulations are indexed to the role they play in a particular form of life. It is not possible, on the postliberal view, to formulate such criteria that will be univocal across all forms of life.[38] Placher's argument implies that postliberal theology in the postliberal style must follow the admonitions of the later Wittgenstein. Indeed, Mark Ellingson argues that theology must follow such admonitions

36. Frei, *Theology and Narrative*, 144.
37. George Hunsinger, "Afterword," in Frei, *Theology and Narrative*, 266 n.13.
38. William C. Placher, "Revisionist and Postliberal Theologies and the Public Character of Theology," *The Thomist* 49 (1985): 392–416, esp. 408–409. For this reason, Placher believes that theology cannot be "public" in Ogden's sense.

if it is not to be susceptible to Feuerbach.[39] The only way to avoid Feuerbach, he argues, is through "a commitment to locating the meaning of Christian concepts and practices in themselves."[40] This requires a cultural-linguistic understanding of religion, such as that articulated by Lindbeck, and the kind of literal interpretation of scripture advocated by Frei. What Frei's and Lindbeck's project requires is a new category of religious assertions, and this new category will involve an appropriation of the later Wittgenstein.[41] Yet this Wittgensteinian understanding of religious claims must be free from the perspectivalism that Frei discerns in D. Z. Phillips. That is, Christian claims must be understandable to those not involved in the Christian form of life. Ellingson believes a literary model for understanding Christian claims is precisely what is required: a Wittgensteinian understanding of religious claims that avoids the perspectivalism of Phillips.[42] Kathryn Tanner can also be read as defending a version of the notion of meaning-as-use in an article describing the "plain sense." In her view it is only because the plain sense of scripture is constituted by the community's interpretive practices of using the texts that any distinction can arise between the text itself and its interpretation. That is, the understanding of the meaning of the text as its use in the community is itself a precondition for the text's gaining normative status in the community.[43]

39. Mark Ellingson, "Philosophical Reflections on the Task of Christian Proclamation," *Dialogue* 20 (Fall 1981): 306–13. Ellingson argues that the fatal difficulty of experiential-expressive models is that they are vulnerable to Feuerbach's critique: they offer "no basis upon which to assert unequivocally that religion is anything more than anthropology" (308). Expanding his criticism, he argues that "an endeavor to translate Christian concepts systematically into other anthropocentric patterns of meaning runs afoul of Feuerbach's critique" (308). Specifically, Ellingson argues that Ricoeur's method of interpretation, when applied to religious texts, is vulnerable to Feuerbach (310).

40. Ellingson, "Philosophical Reflections," 308.

41. The most noteworthy efforts as of 1981, he says, were made by Anders Nygren and Gustav Aulén. Ellingson, "Philosophical Reflections," 309; cf. Anders Nygren Please note the year discrepancy "Anders (1972)" in cross-reference and "Anders (972)" in reference, *Meaning and Method*, trans. Philip Watson (Philadelphia: Fortress Press, 1972); Gustav Aulén, *The Faith of the Christian Church*, trans. Eric Wahlstrom (Philadelphia: Fortress Press, 1973); Gustav Aulén, *The Drama and the Symbols*, trans. Sydney Linton (Philadelphia: Fortress Press, 1970). Ellingson faults Nygren and Aulén, however, for precluding any "point of contact" or overlap between the Christian form of life and others. This results in a kind of perspectivalism that Ellingson asserts must be avoided. Ellingson, "Philosophical Reflections," 309.

42. Unfortunately, Ellingson's description of this model is Delphic in its obscurity. He says only that his model is "looser" and "more formal" than those proposed by theorists like Ricoeur and that the model "construes religious assertions to embody the logical force of a literary claim." Ellingson, "Philosophical Reflections," 309.

43. Kathryn E. Tanner, "Theology and the Plain Sense," in in *Scriptural Authority and Narrative Interpretation*, ed. Garrett Green (Philadelphia: Fortress Press, 1987), 59–78.

There are difficulties, however, with the postliberal appropriation of Wittgenstein. These difficulties are of two kinds. First, there are problems with the argument Wittgenstein gives in the *Philosophical Investigations* for his understanding of meaning-as-use. Second, Frei's particular appropriation of Wittgenstein's later understanding of meaning carries two significant problems of its own. These latter problems have to do with the relationship of meaning and reference and with the role of what Alston (following Searle) calls "illocutionary force" in understanding meaning. Frei's failure to address these issues adequately leaves an ambiguity in his work over whether his understanding of the literal sense of the biblical texts is concerned with semantic meaning or speaker meaning.

A. Problems with Wittgenstein's Argument for Meaning-as-Use

In the *Philosophical Investigations*, Wittgenstein abandons the truth-conditional view of meaning he had previously advanced in the *Tractatus*.[44] In the *Investigations* he argues that understanding the meaning of a word cannot consist in the ability to follow a rule that the speaker knows and has internalized. This is because the rules themselves are made up of words or other signifiers that must themselves be understood before the speaker can use the rules. Wittgenstein's argument is that we cannot have an infinite regress; there must be a large set of words, phrases, or other signifiers that we can understand and use without having further internalized rules to govern their use. In genuinely new situations, he says, we just use words without thinking about whether our usage is correct. But there must be something that determines whether our usage is correct. And as we have seen, this something is a substantial agreement in our linguistic community that determines correct and incorrect usage.

But there seems to be a non sequitur in Wittgenstein's argument.[45] He tells us that distinguishing correct from incorrect usage of a term cannot be a matter of following an internalized rule. From this he takes it to follow that correct and incorrect usage of a word cannot be distinguished

---

44. See Ludwig Wittgenstein, *Philosophical Investigations*, 3d ed., trans. G. E. M. Anscombe (Englewood Cliffs, N.J.: Prentice-Hall, 1958), esp. §§143–55, 179–202.

45. Here I am following the analysis of Soames, *Age of Meaning*, 35–44; Soames, "Facts, Truth Conditions, and the Skeptical Solution to the Rule-Following Paradox," in *Philosophical Perspectives*, vol. 12: *Language, Mind and Ontology*, ed. James Tomberlin (Oxford: Blackwell, 1998), 313–48; Soames, "Skepticism About Meaning: Indeterminacy, Normativity, and the Rule Following Paradox," *The Canadian Journal of Philosophy*, supp. vol. 23 (1997): *Meaning and Reference*, ed. Ali A. Kazmi (1998), 211–49.

by *anything* internal to our minds at all—not by any of our past or present intentions, beliefs, or mental states. But this is a dubious inference. Suppose I am living alone on a desert island, having never before learned any language. I decide to establish my own language to aid my memory and to make a record of my sojourn. I see different flowers and other plants on the island and am able to distinguish a variety of different colors. I collect various samples and decide to use the word "blue" as a symbol for one color, "green" as a symbol for another, and so on. I form the intention thenceforth to use "green" to describe the color of new objects that are the same color as the objects I call "green" in my collection. For a brief period, when I encounter a new object, I must take it back to my collection to compare it to the originals in order to form a judgment about its color. Before long, though, I am able to apply the symbol "green" to new objects in conformity with my intention. After my disposition to use the color symbol according to my intention has become fairly strong, my original collection is lost in a storm. Yet I am still able to apply the word "green" in accordance with my intention and to distinguish blue objects from green ones, and green objects from yellow ones, etc. In this case, what makes my use of "green" to describe an object correct or incorrect is not an internalized rule, but whether my use accords with my original intention. Suppose I subsequently discover a certain root that when boiled produces fine-tasting broth. This broth has several effects on me, one of which is to cause me to use "blue" for objects that have the same color as those I previously had called "green." I make a chalk from flowers I now call "blue" and sketch a picture that seems to me to resemble a painting I had previously seen from Van Gogh's blue period. If I now say that my drawing is "blue," my statement is false, even if I currently have no way to discover my error. When I wake up the next morning, after the effects of the fine root have abated, I will again judge my drawing to be green and not blue and not to resemble (at least not in color) any paintings from Van Gogh's blue period.[46]

Such a situation illustrates that a solitary language user has no standard by which she can judge whether her use of a word, phrase, or sentence is correct other than her own memory. In this imaginary situation it is my past intention rather than an internalized rule that provides the

---

46. This example is derived from one mentioned in P. F. Strawson, "Review of *Philosophical Investigations*," *Mind* 63 (1954): 70–99, reprinted in *Wittgenstein: The Philosophical Investigations*, ed. George Pitcher (Garden City, N.Y.: Anchor Books, 1966), 22–64, esp. 42–43 (hereafter page references are to reprint edition). See also Soames, *Age of Meaning*, 35–36.

standard by which to judge my use of color words correct or incorrect. I do not think Wittgenstein would take this example to disprove his thesis.[47] Yet he does not demonstrate that I could not form the original intention to use "green" to stand for the color of objects that are green. This means that Wittgenstein in the *Philosophical Investigations* does not eliminate the possibility that my perceptions can provide content to my thoughts.[48] If they can, and if I can form an intention to act independently from any assistance from my linguistic community (which seems to me quite plausible), then it certainly seems plausible that I could form an intention to use some linguistic symbol to stand for the content that my perception provides. Finally, if I can form such a linguistic intention, then it also seems plausible that I could use language meaningfully, with standards of meaningful or correct usage, without community agreement. A. J. Ayer argues a point that is similar but more systematic. For Ayer, if we are not justified in relying on at least some of the outputs of our memory and sensory perceptual practices, others in our linguistic community will not be able to help us distinguish between correct and incorrect linguistic usage (or meaningful and meaningless linguistic behavior). In order for the linguistic behavior of others to assist us in the proper use of language, we must be able to perceive and interpret their linguistic behavior. And if we are able to perceive and interpret the linguistic behavior of others in our linguistic community, then it would seem that there is no reason why a solitary language user would not be justified in accepting her memory of her intention to use a word or symbol in a certain way as being accurate.[49]

Wittgenstein could respond that the above considerations still rely, at bottom, on factors external to the language user. Objects in the environment, relations among them, and the language user's perceptual

---

47. He would likely argue that my original intention to let particular words stand for particular bits of color presupposed some already understood language. And he would likely raise a similar objection about my later intention to use the color words in new cases in accordance with my earlier intention. On Kripke's interpretation, Wittgenstein would likely ask how I could know that my original intention was not an intention to use "green" to describe the color of all green objects *except plants with waxy leaves* (or some kind of object I had never encountered). See Saul A. Kripke, *Wittgenstein on Rules and Private Language* (Cambridge, Mass.: Harvard Univ. Press, 1982; repr., 2000) (page references are to reprint edition). Moreover, of course, Wittgenstein would likely deny that he had or needed a "theory," and maybe even that he had or needed a "thesis."

48. Prelinguistic persons such as infants can in fact distinguish different colors.

49. A. J. Ayer, "Can There Be a Private Language?" *Proceedings of the Aristotelian Society*, supp. vol. 28 (1954), 63–76; reprinted in *Wittgenstein: The Philosophical Investigations*, ed. George Pitcher (Notre Dame: Univ. of Notre Dame Press, 1968), part 1, esp. 256–57. See also Soames, *Age of Meaning*, 36–37 n.3.

apparatus play crucial roles in determining standards of linguistic correctness and, therefore, belief. Thus, he could argue, his position against internalized rule following has not been defeated. Nonetheless, to say that factors external to the mind of a language user are crucial to distinguishing between correct and incorrect linguistic usage is not yet to say that meaning is constituted by the agreement of a linguistic community. It is intuitively plausible that linguistic conventions play some role in determinations of correct usage and hence of meaning, but it is too large a leap to move from that conclusion to the conclusion that linguistic meaning *just* is a community agreement.

In fact it is not clear that this leap can be made. Strawson's example of the desert islander should make us skeptical of the notion that agreement among a linguistic community is necessary for meaningful language use. But it may not be sufficient either. Consider another example.[50] Suppose I am from a small, isolated community in Nova Scotia with a large number of small, furry animals with large ears, white tails, and twitchy noses. We agree that we will call all animals "rabbits" that are of the same species as our small, furry animals. After the 2010 U.S. midterm election, we are so baffled by the results that we decide to go to Texas to see if we can find a clue to help us understand the behavior of the American electorate. We have heard some frightening news stories about Texas, so we send two strong young men ahead of us to scout out the place for safety. They scout it out, and telephone back to us that so long as we are polite we are unlikely to be shot or executed. While in Texas, suppose we come across some jackrabbits and suppose further that jackrabbits are in fact of a different species than our Nova Scotian rabbits. Nonetheless, we all assume that these jackrabbits are of the same kind as our rabbits, but that their diet has made them larger and faster. Our scouts, however, do not agree. Unbeknownst to the rest of us, during their scouting mission the scouts had a discussion with a biologist from Texas A&M who explained that the jackrabbits were in fact of a different species than Nova Scotian rabbits. The biologist's slow drawl and large words kept the scouts from catching all of the explanation, but at the end they had a justifiable belief that jackrabbits are not "rabbits"; they're "jackrabbits." After we all go home, our scouts remain the lone holdouts, refusing to call the jackrabbits "rabbits." If community agreement were a sufficient standard for distinguishing correct from incorrect usage, then the scouts would be incorrect in their refusal, and they would be incorrect *by definition*. But surely the proper conclusion to draw is that the scouts are correct and the rest of the community incorrect in how they refer to

50. This example is adapted from Soames, *Age of Meaning*, 40–42.

jackrabbits.[51] And if so, then even if the biologist turns out to be wrong, and jackrabbits turn out to be a member of the same species as our Nova Scotian rabbits, our scouts are not *wrong by definition*.

What this example shows, I think, is that there must be at least some words whose meaning is not determined by community agreement. That is, for at least some words, community agreement is neither necessary nor sufficient to determine their meaning. But perhaps what Wittgenstein intended by "community agreement" is a more idealized kind of agreement—say, what most members of the community would agree to if they knew all the relevant facts. On this reading, if the community knew all the relevant facts about rabbits and jackrabbits, then the decision of most of them to use "rabbit" to refer to a jackrabbit would constitute incorrect usage. Unfortunately, it turns out to be extremely difficult to come up with a noncircular definition of what facts are "relevant" to a determination of correct and incorrect usages of "rabbit" (or any other word) without already understanding what the word means.[52] Further, if one objects that Wittgenstein's proposal about community agreement applies only to our "basic words," one encounters a similar problem. What does it mean for a word or phrase to be "basic?" Presumably, however one defined "basic," words like "under," "over," "and," "or," "after," etc., are more "basic" than "rabbit." Yet it is not at all clear which words or expressions Wittgenstein takes to be "basic" or what kind of criteria he would use to decide whether a word is or is not basic. If his response would be that a community would just agree on which words or expressions are basic and which ones are not, then this response again raises the issues discussed above regarding just what counts as community agreement and whether it is either necessary or sufficient.

The difficulties discussed above I take to be fairly serious problems for Wittgenstein's central thesis about linguistic meaning and community agreement. They may not be *in principle* irresolvable, but as far as I am aware, they have not yet been resolved by any of Wittgenstein's followers. Further, they are not the only problems, not even the only serious problems, with Wittgenstein's proposal.[53] But the above discussion should

51. On Kripke's interpretation, it seems to me that the scouts would be warranted or justified in asserting that *jackrabbits are not rabbits,* even if the community agreement to the contrary might also provide justification for their asserting that *jackrabbits are rabbits.*

52. For an illuminating discussion of these problems, see Kripke, *Wittgenstein on Rules and Private Language,* 22–37.

53. Wittgenstein's private-language argument is even more problematic, and these problems center around his comments regarding private sensations like pain. For a critique of Wittgenstein's private-language argument, see, for example, Soames, *Age of Meaning,* 44–59; see also Strawson, "Review of *Philosophical Investigations*," 41–49.

suffice to indicate why I cannot, at least not yet, be an enthusiastic sup-porter. Consequently, my own view is that, as Scott Soames has concluded, "the best that might be said of the thesis is that it is too vague either to be persuasively defended or to be conclusively refuted."[54]

B. Problems with Postliberal Appropriations of Wittgenstein on Meaning

The difficulties with Frei's appropriation of Wittgenstein's thesis regard-ing meaning, in addition to the problems discussed above with the the-sis itself, can be more specifically identified. In my view, these problems center around Frei's failure to distinguish semantics from speech acts (which in turn prevents him from addressing the role of illocutionary force) and his refusal to allow reference any role in determining mean-ing. Nicholas Wolterstorff, along with T. R. Wright, argues that the first step in Frei's method involves a genre decision about what kind of lit-erature the Gospel narratives are.[55] This decision requires a prior deci-sion about the meaning of the texts, a decision that is to some extent arbitrary in Frei's case just insofar as his understanding of meaning is incomplete. Frei understands that propositional content is constitu-tive of meaning, but by failing to distinguish semantics from speech acts he ignores the constitutive nature of illocutionary force. This is particularly important because illocutionary force is especially crucial for understandings of meaning-as-use of the kind Frei and Lindbeck advocate.

To clarify this objection, I need to introduce a few terms, including "sen-tential acts," "illocutionary acts," and "illocutionary force." In so doing, I shall follow the lead of William Alston.[56] Like J. L. Austin,[57] Alston articulates

54. Soames, *Age of Meaning*, 44.
55. Nicholas Wolterstorff, "Will Narrativity Work as Linchpin? Reflections on the Hermeneutic of Hans Frei," in *Relativism and Religion*, ed. Charles M. Lewis (New York: St. Martin's Press, 1995), 71–107; T. R. Wright, "Regenerating Narrative: The Gospels as Fiction," *Religious Studies* 20 (Spring 1984): 389–400, 395 (quoting Frank Kermode, *The Genesis of Secrecy* [Cambridge, Mass.: Harvard Univ. Press, 1979], 117–18).
56. William P. Alston, *Illocutionary Acts and Sentence Meaning* (Ithaca, N.Y.: Cornell Univ. Press, 2000). Despite the text's focus on sentence meaning, Alston does pro-vide arguments supporting ways he believes the meaning of subsentential units can be derived from sentence meaning.
57. See J. L. Austin, *How to Do Things with Words*, 2d ed., ed. J. O. Urmson and Marina Sbisà (Cambridge, Mass.: Harvard Univ. Press, 1975). Alston's "sentential acts" corre-spond roughly to Austin's "locutionary acts."

three kinds of speech acts.[58] A *sentential act* is "uttering a sentence or some sentence surrogate."[59] An *illocutionary act* is "uttering a sentence (or sentence surrogate) with a certain content, the sort of act paradigmatically reported by 'indirect discourse', as in 'Jones asked where the nearest newsstand is'."[60] A *perlocutionary act* is "producing an effect on some audience by an utterance."[61]

Note that the purpose of an illocutionary act is to communicate some content. One cannot do this, however, except by means of some communicative vehicle. A sentential act is a vehicle that can be used to communicate such content. A sentential act is simply the act of uttering a sentence. When one uses a sentential act to communicate some content, one is performing an illocutionary act. Because an illocutionary act is defined in terms of sentential acts, all illocutionary acts presuppose sentential acts.[62] But sentential acts do not presuppose illocutionary acts. One can perform a sentential act without communicating any content, or intending to do so. Practicing pronunciation alone in one's office, for example, is one way of performing a sentential act without performing an illocutionary act. Alston analyzes illocutionary acts into "propositional content" and "illocutionary force." The distinction between these notions is best brought out using an indirect discourse report. Thus, in "Mr. Powell admitted that diplomatic efforts to resolve the Iraq crisis had failed," the illocutionary force is that of admitting, and the propositional content is *that diplomatic efforts to resolve the*

---

58. In Alston's usage "speech" includes any employment of language, whether oral, written, or otherwise; a "speaker" includes any user of language, and "utterance" includes the production of any linguistic token. Alston, *Illocutionary Acts*, 11–12 n.1.

59. Alston, *Illocutionary Acts*, 2.

60. Alston, *Illocutionary Acts*, 2.

61. Alston, *Illocutionary Acts*, 2. These speech acts are related to each other hierarchically. "One performs an illocutionary act by (in) performing a sentential act. And one (normally) performs a perlocutionary act by (in) performing an illocutionary act. A typical speech act involves all three" (Alston, *Illocutionary Acts*, 2).

62. What about cases of communication that do not involve the utterance of any words, or less than a full sentence? For example, when asked if my father is still alive, I lower my eyes and shake my head negatively. Or, when asked which way to the Reynolds Club, I may simply say, "to the left." Or I may signal to my wife that I wish to leave a party by rubbing my earlobe. On Alston's view, such phenomena are derivative from sentential acts. In the first and third cases, I have used nonlinguistic devices as "sentence surrogates." Shaking my head is a surrogate for uttering "No, my father has passed away." Rubbing my earlobe is a surrogate, arranged with my wife in advance, for "I wish to leave the party." In the second case, uttering "to the left" is elliptical for "The Reynolds Club is located to the left of here." Alston's position seems to be that one might be able to take account of such communicative phenomena in a way other than his way, but that his provides a simpler and more complete account than its rivals. See Alston, *Illocutionary Acts*, 26–30.

Iraq crisis had failed.[63] Illocutionary acts involve both propositional content and illocutionary force.

To return to Frei, Wolterstorff argues that he ignores illocutionary force because he consistently blurs the distinction between speaker meaning (or author meaning) and semantic meaning (or text meaning). This causes Frei to construe narratives as sequences of propositions, Wolterstorff argues, rather than as sequences of speech acts.[64] It is this construal that allows Frei to insist that realistic narratives be interpreted in a way that is neutral as to whether they are history or fiction. But Wolterstorff points out that making a claim about an actual person named Jesus will express a different proposition from any that would be expressed by making a claim about a character named Jesus in a fictional story. The difference between the propositions is that in the former case the name "Jesus" is a singular referring expression, and the proposition is true if and only if the reference succeeds and the referent person exists (or did exist) and bears (or bore) the properties predicated of him in the proposition. If I am telling a fictional story in which Jesus appears as a character, the referent of "Jesus" will be different than if I were giving an historical account. This difference in reference will result in the story's expressing different propositions, and these different propositions expressed in the story will (or may) have different truth values (if they have truth values at all) than they would if the story were historical. Indeed, we are likely to conclude that criteria for assigning truth values will differ for propositions expressed in a fictional story than for those expressed in a historical story.[65] This indicates that the

63. Alston, *Illocutionary Acts*, 15. Here Alston is following John Searle, *Speech Acts* (Cambridge: Cambridge Univ. Press, 1969). Alston notes that this technique does not always provide obvious distinctions. In "Melody asked John to light the candles", the distinction is fairly obvious: the illocutionary force is that of asking and the propositional content is *that John light the candles*. Other cases are less clear. Thus 'A expressed enthusiasm for B's proposal' could be analyzed in either of the following two ways. *Expressing* could be seen as the illocutionary force and *that A is enthusiastic about B's proposal* as the propositional content. Alternatively, *expressing enthusiasm for* could be seen as the illocutionary force and *that B put forward a certain proposal* as the propositional content. Nonetheless, Alston believes that "in general the application is clear." Alston, *Illocutionary Acts*, 15.

64. As we will see below, what causes Wolterstorff to view Frei's construal of narratives as sequences of propositions rather than sequences of sentences is that he takes Frei to be concerned with speaker (or author) meaning rather than semantic (or text) meaning. On my view, however, as I will indicate below, whatever Frei's concerns may be, his articulation of the literal sense bears more resemblance to a description of semantic meaning than to speaker (or author) meaning.

65. Supporters of Frei such as William Placher have sought to devise truth criteria that would work for fictional stories as well as for the biblical narratives. See William C. Placher, "Scripture as Realistic Narrative: Some Preliminary Questions," *Perspectives in Religious Studies* 5 (Spring 1978): 32–41.

propositions expressed differ depending on whether the story is fictional or historical. And because a narrative is a sequence of propositions (on Wolterstorff's constual of Frei), determining which propositions are being expressed in the narrative depends on some prior, "extra-story" determination of whether the story is fictional or historical. On the other hand, if meaning is said to include illocutionary force, then part of interpreting the sense or meaning of the narrative will include a judgment about which parts are historical and which parts are not.[66]

As the above discussion illustrates, considerations of illocutionary force are related to considerations of the relation of reference to meaning. Among other things, and most pertinent for my purposes here, both illocutionary force and reference help differentiate speaker meaning from semantic meaning. The distinction between speaker and semantic meaning is consistently blurred by Frei. As we will see, the blurring of this distinction causes confusion when it comes to issues of reference. Indeed, the secondary literature displays a good deal of confusion regarding Frei's view of the relation of reference to meaning. In turn, this confusion regarding reference and meaning causes further confusion when it comes to Frei's view of whether and in what sense the Gospel narratives are true.

To illustrate this point it is useful to consider several conservative critics of Frei, including Carl F. H. Henry. These critics tend to fear that separating meaning from reference (or at least ostensive or ideal reference) will yield some kind of relativistic stance toward the truth of the biblical narratives. Frei himself admits that Christian theology needs to affirm that the Gospel narratives make some kind of historical reference to Jesus of Nazareth. But he says little about why this is so, and he continues to insist that the reference of the narratives is independent of a proper consideration of their meaning.

Most commentators, it seems, want to affirm the importance of the reference of the biblical narratives concerning Jesus. Amy Plantinga Pauw and others argue that the reference of the biblical narratives remains important, irrespective of its role in determining their meaning.[67] The question is whether Frei can adequately account for reference consistently with his

66. Wolterstorff, "Will Narrativity Work as Linchpin?" 103–104.

67. Amy Plantinga Pauw, review of *Types of Christian Theology* by Hans W. Frei, *Theology Today* 50 (April 1993): 124–26. Similarly, Henri Blocher argues against Frei and for a restoration of the referential meaning of the Gospel narratives. Henri Blocher, "Biblical Narrative and Historical Reference," in *Issues in Faith and History: Papers Presented at the Second Edinburgh Conference on Dogmatics, 1987*, ed. Nigel M. de S. Cameron (Edinburgh: Rutherford House Books, 1989), 102–22. In Blocher's view, if the Gospel narratives do not maintain the accuracy of their historical reference, Christianity is "the most perverse of illusions" (120). In my view, Blocher misinterprets Frei as holding that those narratives he takes to be "realistic narratives" do not refer to historical

understanding of the meaning of biblical texts. Carl Henry and Francis Watson, for example, argue that he cannot account for it. Henry judges Frei's failure to make an argument for the historical factuality of the resurrection to be a serious omission.[68] In his view, Frei's realistic interpretation not only brackets questions of historical reference, it at least implies that realistic narrative is incapable of conveying accurate historical data. Consequently, he takes it to be inappropriate to the New Testament's expressed concern for historical accuracy.[69] He judges postliberal theology's "epistemological hiatus" on the narratives' historical reference to offer inadequate grounds for assessing or defending theological claims.[70]

Watson advances a more subtle argument reaching a similar conclusion. He detects a peculiar dynamic that is apparent in *The Eclipse of Biblical Narrative*, but that is also a feature of Frei's other work. Although Frei's concerns are clearly theological, as are the issues he addresses, his analysis is literary-critical in nature.[71] This appears to leave Frei no means, at least within the framework of his narrative method, to address any historical question that might be put to the Gospel accounts, despite Frei's acknowledgment that Christian theology must affirm that Jesus' life, death, and resurrection really occurred. That is, Watson agrees that Frei's emphasis on narrative does a good job of handling the identification of meaning with reference that occurred in modern biblical hermeneutics and of specifying the problems this identification created. But Frei's focus on the difficulties of meaning-as-reference caused him to leave no room in his narrative method for dealing with questions of reference, even though he acknowledges that the accounts must have a "historical" dimension (in some sense or other of that term). Consequently, "when, at the end of *The Identity of Jesus Christ*, Frei suddenly asserts that the fundamental truthfulness of the resurrection narratives is actually very important, he has

---

events. On my reading, however, as I have tried to make clear in chapters 7 and 8, Frei simply holds that their meaning should not be indexed to the success or failure of their ostensive or ideal reference. Frei brackets questions of historical reference and of their accuracy or truth, for purposes of determining their meaning. He does not dismiss such questions, but holds that answering them is a separate inquiry than the inquiry into the meaning of the texts.

68. Carl F. H. Henry, "Narrative Theology: An Evangelical Appraisal," *Trinity Journal* 8 (Spring 1987): 3–19. "Surely the NT does not present the resurrection of the crucified Jesus without explicit historical claims to which it attaches first-order importance (1 Cor 15:3–8,17)" (11). Henry's article was originally delivered as a series of lectures at Yale in November 1985.

69. Henry, "Narrative Theology," 12–13. "The narrative approach unacceptably minimizes Luke's expressed concern for historically reliable sources and Paul's affirmation that our faith is vain unless Christ arose factually from the dead (1 Cor. 15:17)" (13).

70. Henry, "Narrative Theology," 19.

71. Francis Watson, *Text, Church and World: Biblical Interpretation in Theological Perspective* (Grand Rapids: Wm. B. Eerdmans Pub. Co., 1994), 23.

no conceptuality available for making this assertion plausible and is reduced to gnomic utterances about the mysteriousness of faith."[72]

Frei's clearest remarks on the issue of reference came in a reply to Henry, in which he clarifies that he never intended to say that the narratives are incapable of being used to make historical references.[73] He only intended to deny that their meaning is dependent on the nature or success of their referential functions.[74] He says in fact that we can use the narratives to refer in a double sense: "There is often a historical reference and often there is textual reference; that is, the text is witness to the Word of God, whether it is historical or not."[75] He does not unpack the notion of "textual reference" except to say that this occurs when a biblical text "refers to its divine original only by itself, textually."[76] This cryptic comment does not clarify matters much, but he goes on to say that referring to God is not like any other kind of reference. Nonetheless, however it happens, ordinary language is sufficient for the task of referring to God or to divine activity. He agrees that language about God is analogous, but the basis of such analogies is a literal reading of the Gospels (or other biblical texts) rather than a more nearly metaphorical reading.[77] Further, though he does not deny that the truth values of assertions about God are dependent on the success of their references, he maintains that such references are categorically different than referring to other, more mundane, events.[78]

---

72. Watson, *Text, Church and World*, 224 (citation omitted). Similarly, Colin Gunton argues that although Frei acknowledges the importance of the extratextual reference of the biblical narratives about Jesus, "it is not quite clear why and in what respect." Colin Gunton, review of *Types of Christian Theology* by Hans W. Frei, *Scottish Journal of Theology* 49:2 (1996): 234.

73. Frei's response was delivered orally at Yale following Henry's lectures in November 1985. It was published in the same issue as was Henry's article: Hans W. Frei, "Response to 'Narrative Theology: an Evangelical Appraisal,'" *Trinity Journal* 8 (Spring 1987): 21–24; reprinted in Hans W. Frei, *Theology and Narrative: Selected Essays*, ed. George Hunsinger and William C. Placher (New York: Oxford Univ. Press, 1993), 207–12 (page references are to reprint edition).

74. Frei repeats his adage that the texts "mean what they say" with such emphasis that it often seems as though he believes that the point cannot be further explicated (though he does spend several more pages attempting such an explication): "There really is an analogy between the Bible and a novel writer who says something like this: I mean what I say whether or not anything took place. I mean what I say. It's as simple as that: the text means what it says" (Frei, "Response," 208).

75. Frei, "Response," 209.

76. Frei, "Response," 209.

77. Frei, "Response," 209–10.

78. "For example, using the term 'God' Christianly is in some sense referential. But that doesn't mean that I have a theory of reference to be able to tell you *how* it refers. It is also true in some sense other than a referential one: It is true by being true to the way it works in one's life, and by holding the world, including the political, economic and social world, to account by the gauge of its truthfulness" (Frei, "Response," 210).

Despite his acceptance of a referential function for the biblical narratives, Frei takes Henry to task for his use of concepts like "historical" and "factuality." These concepts "are not privileged, theory-neutral, trans-cultural, an ingredient in the structure of the human mind and of reality always and everywhere for me, as I think they are for Dr. Henry."[79] This implies that, on Frei's view, there are two different kinds of reference going on in the biblical narratives and in our talk about the life, death, and resurrection of Jesus. The referential function of a text that tells about Jesus speaking in the synagogue would be the same as a text that told of St. Paul or Rabbi Hillel or anyone else speaking in the synagogue. But when a text speaks of the eternal Word of God made flesh in Jesus Christ, it uses a second kind of referential function. It is not metaphor, but neither is it ordinary historical reference. In Frei's view, however, Henry's use of the notions of factuality and historical reference implies that in all these cases the referential function, or the *modus significandi*, is the same. Frei rejects such a view, because he seems to believe that it somehow implies a diminution of the divine nature of the *res significata*. Indeed, the *modus significandi* must remain mysterious.[80] George Hunsinger's comment is worth repeating: "Frei is not claiming that the gospel narratives make no ostensive reference. He is rather claiming that they make no ostensive reference to an object to which we have independent epistemic access and whose factuality can be affirmed on any ground other than faith."[81]

For Frei, then, although he allows the texts to have a referring function, he insists that such reference has no role in determining the texts' meaning and that how such reference occurs (the *modus significandi*) must remain mysterious. In the view of William Placher, though, Frei's position remains ambiguous. Placher argues that both Frei and Lindbeck can be read in two different ways on the reference of the narratives. On the first reading

79. Frei, "Response," 211.
80. "Austin Farrer once said that people seem to think that if they could find an analogy to the notion of creation, they would secure that notion. He said that on the contrary, if there is an analogy to it, then the concept is lost. And that is in a different way true of Jesus Christ too. . . . 'Jesus' refers, as does any ordinary name, but 'Jesus Christ' in scriptural witness does not refer ordinarily; or rather, it refers ordinarily only by the miracle of grace. And that means that I do not know the manner in which it refers, only that the ordinary language in which it is cast will miraculously suffice" (Frei, "Response," 211–12).
81. George Hunsinger, "Afterword," in Frei, *Theology and Narrative*, 266 n.13. Frei says that the name "'Jesus' refers, as does any ordinary name, but 'Jesus Christ' in scriptural witness does not refer ordinarily; or rather, it refers ordinarily only by the miracle of grace. And that means that I do not know the manner in which it refers, only that the ordinary language in which it is cast will miraculously suffice. It is historical reference (to use our cultural category) but it is not historical reference in the ordinary way: nor of course is it metaphor" (Frei, "Response," 211–12).

(the strong version), religious language does not refer at all. Lindbeck's cultural-linguistic model follows the later Wittgenstein in insisting that the meaning of religious language just is its use in the religious community's form of life. Meaning is regulative on this understanding, and therefore "the question of reference simply never arises."[82] Similarly, in *The Eclipse of Biblical Narrative* Frei argues that the meaning of the narratives lies wholly within the narrative structure itself, and on Placher's reading this implies that "[t]he meaning of these texts sometimes does not seem to involve *any* reference to reality beyond themselves."[83] This seems to be the interpretation of Carl Henry. A second, less radical, reading (the weak version) limits Lindbeck's theory to doctrines and refrains from providing any general theory about the meaning of religious language. Doctrines, on this second view, have a regulative use, and this use constitutes their meaning, but nondoctrinal religious language can have other uses, such as making historical or ontological claims. Such other uses may involve a referential function.[84] Similarly, Frei argues in *The Identity of Jesus Christ* that although the meaning of the Gospel narratives is "located" in the narrative itself, the Passion-Crucifixion-Resurrection sequence forces the historical question. Consequently, the overall narrative portrayal of Jesus' identity does indeed refer to the historical figure, Jesus of Nazareth.[85] On this weaker version, the "translinguistic reference" question is not "obviated," like it is on the stronger version, but reference remains independent of and separable from meaning. Even on this weaker version, though, reference is relevant only to truth, not to meaning.

82. William C. Placher, "Paul Ricoeur and Postliberal Theology: A Conflict of Interpretations?," *Modern Theology* 4 (Oct. 1987): 35–52, at 46. Placher's article was published in the fall of 1987, roughly six months after the publication of Henry's critique and Frei's response, and nearly two years after the lectures and response were delivered at Yale. Placher views Frei and Ricoeur as closer than many have assumed. Nonetheless, Ricoeur's discussion of the reference of narrative opens up a crucial difference between himself and postliberal theology. Ricoeur, that is, insists that biblical narratives should be understood as having not only a meaning but also a reference. For texts such as parables, the referent is a new mode-of-being-in-the-world that the parable invites us to consider as a possibility for ourselves. Yet he also insists on a "hermeneutics of testimony" that will do justice to the importance of particular historical events as events (and not merely as symbols) in which God acts and to which many of the narrative texts refer. On Placher's reading, how to integrate these two emphases in Ricoeur's thought remains a puzzle, but both emphases assert the importance not only of the meaning of narrative texts, but of their reference as well ("Paul Ricoeur and Postliberal Theology," 42–46).

83. Placher, "Ricoeur and Postliberal Theology," 47–48. Though Frei's prose often seems to imply this reading, in my view the issue is complicated by Frei's comments in response to Carl Henry, discussed above.

84. Placher, "Ricoeur and Postliberal Theology," 46.

85. Placher, "Ricoeur and Postliberal Theology," 47.

This weaker view is, I think, a better interpretation, and it is the view of Frei's most sympathetic interpreters, including George Hunsinger.[86] Hunsinger notes that Henry misreads Frei on the importance of the historical reference of the Gospel narratives. Contrary to Henry's reading, Frei insists that Christian theology continue to assert the historicity of the Christ event. Yet Hunsinger notes that Frei considers only two assurances to be required from historical criticism: "first, that Christ's resurrection has not been historically disconfirmed; and second, 'that a man, Jesus of Nazareth, who proclaimed the Kingdom of God's nearness, did exist and was finally executed.'"[87] This second assurance is the only reference Frei requires from the Gospel narratives. Frei and Henry also differ on how the narratives refer. In Hunsinger's view, Henry insists on a literal or univocal reference, while for Frei it is analogical—that is, the texts often contain both a textual reference and a historical reference (though they may contain one or the other).[88] This means in Hunsinger's view that the narratives not only refer to the earthly or historical Jesus, "but also and at the same time to the risen Jesus Christ who lives to all eternity, and who attests himself to us through those narratives here and now."[89] In Hunsinger's view, this dual reference is what Frei means when he speaks of reference being used differently in Christian usage than elsewhere. Still, Frei's discussions of "dual reference" remain confusing. In the concluding chapter I shall suggest that greater attention to the distinction between speech acts and semantics, along with further attention to what William Alston calls "direct reference," can clarify the distinction Frei is (I think) trying to make with his discussion of dual reference. For now, let's turn to some of the reasons for Frei's confusion.

Frei's reading of Wittgenstein and Ryle was a double-edged sword. On the one hand, it showed him the problems with the view that the meaning of a statement is constituted by a descriptive sense that refers to a putative set of potential facts that would, if they were actual, make the statement

86. George Hunsinger, "Hans Frei as Theologian: The Quest for a Generous Orthodoxy," *Modern Theology* 8 (April 1992): 103–28, esp. 110 (emphasis in original).

87. George Hunsinger, "What Can Evangelicals and Postliberals Learn From Each Other? The Carl Henry/Hans Frei Exchange Revisited," *Pro Ecclesia* 5 (Spring 1996): 161–82, 173 (quoting Frei, *The Identity of Jesus Christ* [Philadelphia: Fortress Press, 1975], 51).

88. To the phrase "textual reference," Frei adds, "that is, the text is witness to the Word of God, whether it is historical or not" (Frei, "Response," 209). Presumably Frei is trying to differentiate actions of God from other kinds of historical facts, but I confess I don't find the phrase "textual reference" to be illuminating. The confusing nature of Frei's remarks, it seems to me, is partly a result of Frei's failure to distinguish speaker reference from semantic reference.

89. Hunsinger, "What Can Evangelicals," 176.

true. But on the other hand, Wittgenstein and Ryle tempted Frei to believe that reference could be done away with altogether. Frei never went quite that far, because he maintained the need to affirm the truth of the Gospel narratives, and he continued to believe that such an affirmation could only be made by utilizing the notion of reference in one way or another. But he continued to follow Wittgenstein and Ryle in his insistence that meaning be independent of reference. This was a mistake in my view. Reference is important in determining the meaning of any sentence in which singular (referring) expressions occur, and this is the case whether one understands meaning in a descriptivist or truth-conditional way or in some other way.

Frei's writings, however, obscure the role of reference in meaning due to two factors working in his thought. The first is his consistent rejection of any notion of "meaning-as-reference," a rejection in which he is largely justified, but which does not entail the stronger position that reference plays no role in meaning. The second is his failure to distinguish between speech acts and semantics. Consequently, he fails to distinguish between what we may call "speaker reference" and "semantic reference," on the one hand, and between "speaker meaning" and "semantic meaning," on the other. It may be helpful to discuss the second factor first. This latter distinction is analogous to Nicholas Wolterstorff's distinction between an *author's meaning* and a *text's meaning*. Wolterstorff notes that texts do not perform speech acts; instead, authors use them to perform speech acts.[90] Thus there is a distinction between a text's meaning and an author's meaning something by writing it. Frei never makes this distinction clear, and thus his use of "meaning" is consistently ambiguous. Nonetheless, Wolterstorff interprets Frei as being concerned with author-meaning rather than text-meaning.[91] If Frei is indeed concerned with author meaning, this raises a significant difficulty, because Frei consistently emphasizes that the accuracy of the texts—and indeed

---

90. Nicholas Wolterstorff, "Evidence, Entitled Belief, and the Gospels," *Faith and Philosophy* 6 (Oct. 1989): 429–59, 431. The language Frei uses in some of his later writings indicates that he is aware of this, at least with respect to reference. See, for example, Frei, "Response," 209. Yet he never makes use of the distinction in any constructive way.

91. Wolterstorff does not provide any interpretive argument for his reading of Frei at this point. He simply asserts: "Frei's concern throughout is clearly with author-meaning" ("Evidence, Entitled Belief," 436). Note that to say that Frei is concerned with author-meaning does not imply that he needs to seek the author's intention "behind" the text. If Frei is concerned with author-meaning, his concern is not necessarily with what the author intended to say, but what he did in fact say with the biblical texts. As I will indicate below, whatever Frei's *concern* may have been, his *articulation* of the literal sense resembles a description of text meaning (semantic meaning) more than author meaning (speaker meaning).

whether they were meant as fiction or history—has no bearing on the interpretation of the narratives. But an author's meaning will indeed be affected by whether she used the text to narrate actual events or to project a fictional world or story.[92] The nature of realistic narrative, Frei says, is that it can be used by an author to do either. But if hermeneutics is concerned with author-meaning, then it must also be concerned with whether the stories are history or fiction.[93] And Frei does indeed insist that, irrespective of whether all or many of their particulars are intended as historical reports or something else, and irrespective of whether all or many of those particulars that intended to report some event are historically accurate, the Gospel narratives are in fact about a historical person, Jesus of Nazareth. Further, Frei also insists in *The Identity of Jesus Christ* that a belief in the historicity of the Resurrection not only matters religiously, but is essential to understanding the identity of Jesus. Consequently, though Wolterstorff does not endorse any kind of referential or descriptivist theory of meaning such as those against which Frei argues in *The Eclipse of Biblical Narrative*, he argues that Frei would be better served by holding reference not to be irrelevant to the meaning of the narratives, at least if we are concerned with author-meaning.[94] Thus, Frei's failure to distinguish between semantics and speech acts is closely related to his resistance to allowing any role for reference in determinations of meaning.

William Placher finds the combination of Frei's refusal to offer a theory of reference, his repeated insistence that reference is irrelevant to the meaning of the biblical narratives, and his frequent use of language implying that the narratives do not refer to extratextual realities to be "a dangerous business." In Placher's view, this combination of positions risks the implication that the narratives witness to nothing beyond themselves.[95] This, again, was Henry's assessment. This unfortunate result, Placher says, may simply be the result of readers applying cultural assumptions regarding meaning, truth, and reference to Frei's view of narrative in the absence of any theory offered by Frei himself. On the other hand, the result may be implied by the cultural-linguistic model itself, at least if that model is given

---

92. This is because the meaning of a speech act is determined not only by its content but also what Wolterstorff calls its "mood" ("Evidence, Entitled Belief," 440–42). As I have discussed above, following William Alston, the meaning of a speech act is determined by both its "propositional content" and its "illocutionary force." Wolterstorff's "mood" corresponds to Alston's "illocutionary force."

93. Wolterstorff, "Evidence, Entitled Belief," 441.

94. Wolterstorff, "Evidence, Entitled Belief," 441–42.

95. Placher, "Paul Ricoeur and Postliberal Theology," 48 (citation omitted).

the "strong" reading described above. In Placher's view, Christian theology needs to maintain that Christian speech and action are in response to God's prior initiating gracious act. Therefore, Christian theology also needs to assert that the texts refer, in some way or another, to God's action in history. Simply to allow for the possibility of the texts' reference to God, while both insisting that the mode of such reference is in principle incomprehensible and refusing any general theory of reference is dangerous, in Placher's judgment. But Placher does not offer such a theory himself, so the problem of the reference of the biblical texts, he urges, remains "a central item on the agenda of postliberal theology. . . ."[96] So far as I'm aware, this problem remains on its agenda more than twenty-five years after Placher wrote these words.

Frei's desire to derive his theological method only from what he finds in the Gospel narratives displays a Barthian impulse. Yet there is a fundamental fissure in his thought between his acknowledgement that the reference of the narratives is important and his consistent resistance to any theoretical analysis of their reference. Two crucial insights from *The Eclipse of Biblical Narrative* turn against him at this point: his perception of the predominance of the assumption of "meaning-as-reference" in the hermeneutics of modern theologians, and his construal of narratives as essentially similar to realistic novels from the point of view of literary form. From Frei's point of view, realistic novels have meaning even though they do not refer to anything that "actually occurred" in the "real world." That is, they have meaning despite their failure to refer to any historical event or (in many cases) to any ideal religious, moral, political (etc.) teaching.[97] If the biblical narratives are similar to realistic novels, Frei believes that their meaning must be independent of their reference. As Hunsinger notes, for Frei, the question of their reference is not a question of their meaning.[98] But Frei does not explicate this position further, and this is unfortunate because the position is ambiguous. To hold meaning independent of reference can mean (more weakly) that meaning is not determined by reference, or it can mean (more strongly) that there is no relation whatsoever between the two. The first view I take to be defensible. On this view, it is possible that the two are related not in the sense that reference

---

96. Placher, "Paul Ricoeur and Postliberal Theology," 49.

97. On just this point, Wolterstorff disagrees, arguing that their referent is a projected plot or story. See Nicholas Wolterstorff, *Works and Worlds of Art* (New York: Oxford Univ. Press, 1980).

98. "The question of factual historicity, although directly posed by the narratives themselves, is simply *not* a question of their meaning. It is the question of their truth" (Hunsinger, "Hans Frei as Theologian," 110 [emphasis in original]).

determines meaning, but that meaning determines reference while at the same time reference contributes to, but does not determine, meaning.[99] But this is not possible on the second view. And it seems that Frei takes this second view, that meaning and reference bear no relation to one another, to be the only alternative to a notion of "meaning-as-reference" in which meaning is wholly determined by reference. This stronger view carries two consequences. First, it seems to leave no alternative to a fairly strict conformity to a later Wittgensteinian understanding of linguistic meaning as use in a language game. Any view that holds meaning and reference to be determined wholly independently will be very similar to such an understanding of linguistic meaning. And indeed, this is consistent with Frei's comments on the literal sense, in which he argues that the meaning of the biblical narratives is constituted by their use in the community's form of life.[100]

Second, the stronger view of the mutual independence of meaning and reference becomes even more problematic in light of Frei's failure to distinguish between semantics and speech acts—between semantic reference and speaker reference, and between semantic (or sentence) meaning and speaker-meaning. We can think of the semantic meaning of a sentence as the set of possible meanings a sentence can have—that is, the set of propositions it can properly be used to express. Speaker-meaning, on the other hand, is the meaning a sentence does in fact have on a given occasion of utterance—that is, the proposition a speaker in fact uses it to express on a given occasion.[101] Frei (similarly to Lindbeck) articulates the use of the literal sense in the Christian community in terms of following rules. That is, the community establishes a set of (more or less explicit) rules for reading its sacred texts. For any given narrative (or sentence within the narrative), there may be several possible readings that conform to the rules, but the rules establish the boundaries of permissible readings. Such a description certainly sounds as though Frei's understanding of the literal sense is articulated in terms of semantic meaning rather than speaker-meaning. Thus, if, by his articulation of the literal sense

99. Recall that for Frege, it is sense (*Sinn*) that fixes reference (*Bedeutung*), not vice versa. For Frege, though, the referent of a proposition is its truth value—either the True or the False.

100. See Hans W. Frei, "The 'Literal Reading' of Biblical Narrative in the Christian Tradition: Does It Stretch or Will It Break?" in *The Bible and the Narrative Tradition*, ed. Frank McConnell (New York: Oxford Univ. Press, 1986), 36–77; reprinted in Frei, *Theology and Narrative*, 117–152, esp. 144 (page references are to reprint edition).

101. Kripke describes the distinction (in general terms) as follows: "The notion of what words can mean, in the language, is semantical: it is given by the conventions of our language. What they mean, on a given occasion [i.e., speaker meaning], is determined, on a given occasion, by these conventions, together with the intentions of the speaker and various contextual features" (Saul Kripke, "Speaker's Reference and Semantic Reference," 14).

Frei intends to describe something like a notion of semantic meaning,[102] then the understanding of meaning expressed or implied by his description of the literal sense is independent of the notion of speech acts. This independence causes difficulty when we come to decide whether the narratives are true. The bearers of truth values are propositions, and propositions are expressed by utterances (sentences spoken or written at a particular time and place by a particular speaker or writer).[103] If the rules that constitute the literal reading yield semantic meaning rather than speaker-meaning (or, perhaps, rather than a subset of permissible speaker-meanings more restricted than the full range of semantic meaning but still broader than speaker-meaning), then the only sentences in the narratives whose expressed propositions can be analyzed for truth or falsity must be one of two kinds: (1) those that contain no indexicality and that express the same proposition on each occasion of utterance, or (2) those that may be used to express a set of propositions, all of which have the same truth value. But surely there are few if any sentences in the narratives that fit into one of these kinds. Interestingly, by way of contrast, a sentence that expresses a proposition that Schubert Ogden would count as a religious claim would fit into both kinds.

All this suggests that the postliberal project stands in need of a theory of truth. In my view, the way Frei articulates his notion of linguistic meaning in terms of the literal sense causes significant difficulties for the notion of truth. The way he speaks about reference causes even further difficulties. As I have suggested above, the stronger view of the mutual independence of meaning and reference leads Frei to adopt a later Wittgensteinian notion of meaning-as-use in a language game or form of life. But this stronger view

102. This is by no means the only possible reading of Frei, but it seems to me to be at least a reasonable reading of his comments on the literal sense. As I have noted, however, Wolterstorff disagrees, and believes that Frei intends to speak of author-meaning.

103. Saying this, of course, is not necessarily to say that propositions are some kind of independently existing Platonic entity. It is simply a way of expressing the fact that the same sentence uttered on different occasions or by different speakers may have different meanings—that is, they may express different propositions. "My bedroom has a window," when uttered by me, expresses something different (i.e., it has a different meaning; it expresses a different proposition) than it does when uttered by Lindbeck. Similarly, it expresses something different when I utter it in April 2003 than when I utter it in April 2012. But it is the speaker meaning that changes on these different occasions, while the semantic meaning of the sentence remains the same. Thus it is the independence from speech acts, which results from the mutual independence of meaning and reference, that causes the difficulties I am discussing here and that creates the twofold requirement I describe in the next sentence in the text. I should note here that the notion that it is propositions that are the bearers of truth values is a contested notion. For arguments in favor of the notion, see William P. Alston, *A Realist Conception of Truth* (Ithaca, N.Y.: Cornell Univ. Press, 1996), 15–22; Scott Soames, *Understanding Truth* (New York: Oxford Univ. Press, 1999), 13–19; Paul Horwich, *Truth*, 2d ed. (Oxford: Clarendon Press, 1998), 86–103.

seems to leave the status of reference unclear. With respect to meaning, it is most likely that Placher's early suggestion is correct, that "the translinguistic reference question" is "obviated."[104] If so, it is not clear just how to fix the reference of any referring expression in the narratives. Yet it seems that the reference of at least some names or expressions in the narratives must be fixed because Frei maintains that reference remains important. One might suppose that reference is fixed in the same way that the meaning of the sentences are determined—by the use of referring expressions in the community's form of life. Yet this would seem to be closely related to the determinations of the meaning of the sentences in which such expressions occur, when Frei has insisted that meaning and reference be independent. Further, there would seem to be no conceptual reason why the community could not decide to fix the references in the narratives the way many liberal theologians fix them—to treat (at least some of) them as largely mythological texts that refer to one or more transcendental propositions about authentic self-understanding. Whatever we may think of this result, it seems clear that Frei would not approve of it. If Hunsinger is correct that Frei takes reference to be relevant only to questions of truth, and not to questions of meaning, we are left in a quandary. For it is propositions that are the bearers of truth values, and if reference is irrelevant to the meaning of the sentences that express those propositions but relevant to questions of truth, then it is not at all clear just how questions of truth should be approached. Frei's insistence on the independence of meaning and reference, therefore, leave him no conceptual means to negotiate the fissure between meaning and reference in a way that renders the claims contained in the narratives amenable to any coherent analysis of their truth. Perhaps it is for this reason that Hunsinger reads Frei as holding that the truth of the narrative claims must be taken on faith.[105]

104. William C. Placher, "Scripture as Realistic Narrative: Some Preliminary Questions," *Perspectives in Religious Studies* 5 (Spring 1978): 32–41, esp. 33.

105. George Hunsinger, "Afterword," in Frei, *Theology and Narrative*, 266 n.13. I think that Frei would most likely respond that the question of truth itself must be "bent" to serve the ends of the community's use of the literal sense of scripture. For an attempt to "bend" truth in this manner, see Bruce Marshall, *Trinity and Truth* (Cambridge: Cambridge Univ. Press, 2000).

CHAPTER TEN

Conclusion

Navigating the Divide between Liberal and Postliberal Theology

This book is motivated by the conviction that greater attention to language can illuminate the nature of the differences between liberal and postliberal theology. In addition, it can also offer reasons for their intractability by illuminating common mistakes shared by liberal and postliberal theology in their views of language. Namely, neither makes an adequate place for the distinction between speech acts and semantics in linguistic meaning; neither has an adequate view of reference; and both assume that descriptivist and Wittgensteinian views on language are our primary, if not only, options. Fortunately, more adequate accounts of meaning and reference are available that allow the semantic meaning of the biblical texts to bear both the kind of demythologizing interpretation for which Ogden and other liberals argue and the more particularized literal reading for which postliberals argue. This allows the methodological differences between liberal and postliberal theology to be considered on more purely theological and hermeneutical bases, without distortion by a less adequate view of language that biases the consideration in favor of one or the other.

I. VALIDITY AND PARTICULARITY: THE MOTIVATING CONCERNS OF LIBERAL AND POSTLIBERAL THEOLOGY

A. The Liberal Concern for Validation

Characteristic of the liberal tradition in Protestant theology is a concern to assess the truth or falsity of theological claims and to revise or reject those one finds false or insupportable. It is indeed this concern for the assessment and validation of theological claims that drives theological method in most liberal theologians. In Schubert Ogden, this concern works together with a number of factors to give his theological method its peculiar shape. Important among these factors is a descriptivist view of language.

Liberal concern for the assessment and validation of theological claims takes shape in conjunction with an insistence on a secular understanding of the autonomy of human reason. This results in a view that the assessment of the credibility of theological claims can be accomplished adequately only by reference to criteria of truth that are genuinely public. And genuinely public criteria, liberals generally believe, must be (to use Frei's phrase) "all-fields encompassing." Or, as Ogden might put it, genuinely public criteria must be derived from the nature of human reason itself, and this will be the case for all areas of human intellectual investigation. This view of the public criteria of credibility motivates Ogden's only encounter with a Wittgensteinian understanding of language. In an article critical of D. Z. Phillips, Ogden argues that religious and theological assertions require "a general justification" because such assertions "tacitly or openly claim to be the kind of statements that need to be generally justified, i.e., they claim to be existential assertions or truth-claims."[1] Because they are *assertions*, religious and theological assertions claim to be true. Consequently, they presuppose some criteria of truth and therefore require a "general justification."[2] In other words, in Ogden's view, neither the truth value of assertions nor the criteria of their truth or credibility can be relative to a language game, or form of life, or field of discourse. Such truth values and criteria must be truly public. That is, the conditions that must obtain before an assertion can be judged true must be general, or "all-fields encompassing," conditions in order to support a "general justification." In turn, this implies that linguistic meaning—especially the meaning of criteriological terms such as "truth" or "credibility"—must be public in the same sense. Consequently, Ogden believes, the meaning

---

1. Schubert M. Ogden, "Linguistic Analysis and Theology," *Theologische Zeitschrift* 33 (Sept.–Oct. 1977): 318–25, quotation at 324.
2. Ogden, "Linguistic Analysis and Theology," 324.

of assertions, and in particular religious or theological assertions, must be constituted by their truth conditions.

Liberals generally pursue this concern for public criteria through a commitment to secularity, in one form or another, in theology. For Ogden, this commitment means that theological claims must be verified by common human experience. A state of affairs that is singular and universal and at the same time capable of being validated by common human experience must be a condition of the possibility of any human experience or act of thought. Religious assertions are therefore transcendental assertions in the sense that they can be validated only through a procedure that is ultimately transcendental. As we have seen, Ogden's transcendental method coheres nicely with a descriptivist or truth-conditional view of the meaning of religious assertions. To say that the meaning of religious assertions is constituted by their truth conditions is to say that they acquire their meaning referentially. If that is the case, and if one assumes a descriptivist view of reference, then religious assertions must have only one reference if they are to avoid a hopeless ambiguity. In order to have only one reference, that reference must be a singular and universal state of affairs. The meaning of a religious assertion, that is, must be constituted by its reference to a singular and universal state of affairs. And any transcendental condition of the possibility of human subjectivity will be just such a singular and universal state of affairs.

One mark that Ogden is appropriately situated within the liberal tradition in theology is the central place he gives to the recognition that religious and theological claims are always embedded in a cultural matrix that must change with cultural shifts. Yet the constitutive claims of a religion must be somehow retained if the religion is not to die out. Ogden's strategy for doing this in the case of the Christian religion is to adopt a demythologizing interpretive method whose inputs are the variously mythologized claims of the Christian scriptures and whose outputs are religious claims that are existential and transcendental. If claims are transcendental and true, they can never be coherently denied, irrespective of what kind of cultural shifts might occur.

As I have argued, a descriptivist or truth-conditional understanding of meaning cannot be sustained, but it is important to note that in liberal theology it is motivated by a concern to defend the truth of religious or theological assertions and to do so via criteria that are truly public. And indeed, the liberal fear regarding Frei and Lindbeck is that their proposals for theological method and narrative interpretation do not adequately vindicate this concern for public criteria of credibility. Consequently many liberals believe that under postliberal tutelage Christian claims will become ultimately arbitrary claims whose truth cannot be defended.[3] Any theological method that rejects a truth-conditional understanding of meaning will need an adequate way of vindicating the liberal concern for truth and public criteria.

B. Avoiding Feuerbach: Postliberal Concern for Particularity

Postliberals' equally legitimate concerns arise from the opposite end of the methodological spectrum. As we have seen, Frei's writings are motivated by his effort to carry forward Barth's neo-orthodox project. He seeks to derive his methodological claims from his positive affirmations about God, and in turn to draw such affirmations from God's self-revelation in Jesus, to which the Gospels are the most important witnesses. One way to characterize the difference between liberals and postliberals is to say that their largest fears differ from each other. Liberals like Ogden fear that an inadequate theological method will yield arbitrary theological claims whose truth cannot be defended. Postliberals, like Barth before them, fear that any theological method too concerned with apologetics will begin by propounding general anthropological or philosophical views as a way of showing that its claims can be sustained. Like Barth, postliberals take all theological claims so derived to distort the Christian kerygma and to be vulnerable to Feuerbach's critique. Thus, crucial to the postliberal project is a concern to vindicate the particularity of God's self-revelation in Jesus, as witnessed by the Gospels.

From Frei's point of view, the liberal understanding of religion and religious claims implies that the religious significance of God's self-revelation in Jesus can only be his disclosure or re-presentation of a universal possibility of authentic existence. In Frei's view, the method of liberals like Ogden, beginning anthropologically, will yield a generic (and distorted) Christ figure and make Christianity vulnerable to Feuerbach. Put thus starkly, and given Frei's fear of Feuerbach, it is not difficult to see why Frei would see Ogden's understanding of the theological task to be inadequate to preserve the particularity of Jesus' identity. It is also easy to understand their differences over Christology. Frei understands Jesus' life, death, and resurrection to be constitutive of the salvation offered by God through him. Indeed, in his view, if the particularity of Jesus' identity is to be maintained, such a constitutive Christology will be necessary. In contrast, liberals often argue against

---

3. As I have noted above, Frei's shift away from narrative structure and toward a full-blown understanding of meaning-as-use makes his reliance on Wittgenstein more evident in his later work. It also makes it more difficult for Frei to distinguish himself, methodologically, from overt "Wittgensteinian fideists" such as D. Z. Phillips.

constitutive Christologies and in favor of a re-presentative Christology. In so doing, Ogden argues that constitutive Christologies are inconsistent with a proper (demythologized) interpretation of God's self-revelation in Jesus. But he also argues that the truth or credibility of such constitutive Christological assertions cannot be sustained.[4] The differences between liberals and postliberals over Christology are fundamental, but here again it is important to see that both sides are motivated by legitimate concerns that must be addressed by any effort to mediate between them.

This respect for Feuerbach's critique also makes Frei reticent to articulate any general theories, such as a theory of reference or of meaning. But as we have seen, this reticence becomes an obstacle as well. He is much more forthcoming about the meaning of the Gospel narratives than he is about reference, because meaning is central to his critique of phenomenological hermeneutics and its methodological use in contemporary theology. He insists that Carl Henry and other conservative critics have misread him on the extratextual reference of the Gospel narratives. He insists that it is important to affirm the truth of the narratives, and that this requires a concomitant affirmation that the narratives do refer to extratextual realities, both creaturely and divine. Yet he steadfastly refuses to articulate any position on the linguistic mechanics of how such reference occurs. And when this refusal is read together with his shift on meaning away from the narrative structure and toward the later Wittgenstein, even his supporters acknowledge that he is left essentially in the position of holding that the Gospels must be affirmed to be true, but that their truth must be taken on faith. This critique, of course, is very similar to many liberals' view of Frei, and Ogden would consider it fatal to Frei's project. Again, however, Frei's wariness of Feuerbach is legitimate and important, and any attempt to depart from Frei's views on meaning and reference must show that it is immune to Feuerbach's critique.

II. LINGUISTIC ASSUMPTIONS OF LIBERALS AND POSTLIBERALS

A. Truth Conditions and Community Use: Liberals and Postliberals on the Meaning of Religious Language

In the 1960s and 1970s, before he turned his attention to liberation theology, Ogden was concerned to defend the truth-claims of Christian theology,

---

4. See Schubert M. Ogden, *Is There Only One True Religion or Are There Many?* (Dallas, Tex.: Southern Methodist Univ. Press, 1992).

which he took to be threatened from two fronts. On the one hand, falsifiability theorists like Antony Flew took John Wisdom's parable of the invisible gardener to imply an account of meaning that most theologians rightly took to be hostile to claims about God. On Flew's account, statements that could not be empirically falsified or verified (e.g., statements about God and normative statements about ethics) could not mean what they ostensibly mean. They had to be reinterpreted so that, for example, normative ethical statements actually stated nothing more than a personal preference. Against Flew and other falsification theorists, liberals argued that religious and ethical language is indeed *meaningful*. Religious and ethical language means what it purports to mean and is not merely an expression of some inner spiritual or psychological state of the speaker.

On the other hand, liberals like Ogden took later Wittgensteinian theorists like D. Z. Phillips to be a threat to Christian theological truth-claims as well. Phillips argued that Flew's falsifiability criterion of meaning was arbitrary in that it ignores the actual use of language, opting instead to legislate a normative use claimed to be valid irrespective of context. That is, Flew holds that the only way an assertion can acquire meaning is through its method of falsification, and that contextual factors, such as the language game in which it is used, are irrelevant to any determination of its meaning. Liberals like Ogden agreed that Flew's falsifiability requirement was arbitrary, but in Ogden's view this was not because of its failure to account for contextual factors or language games, but because of Flew's limitation of his account of experience to sensuous or empirical experience. Along with Whitehead and others, Ogden argues for a view of experience that includes nonsensuous experience. For Ogden, assertions can acquire meaning truth-conditionally, but such truth conditions must account for nonsensuous experience as well as empirical experience.

From Ogden's perspective, Phillips's criticism of Flew relied on a view of the meaning of religious claims that liberals take to be debilitating to any effort to defend the truth of Christian theological claims. Ogden rightly perceived that on Phillips's view, since language acquires meaning from its actual use in a community's form of life, assertions about the term or concept of "truth" or the property of "being true" would acquire their meaning in the same way. This position would imply the possibility that different communities engaging in different forms of life could disagree on the truth of a particular statement, and that each of these opposing positions could be correct. Such a position is fatal, on the liberal view, to any effort to defend the truth-claims of Christian theology, because logical rules that are relative to a particular language game do not provide for criteria that are truly public. In Ogden's view, if religious or theological assertions are to be interpreted as making claims to truth or "general validity," then such assertions presuppose criteria of truth that are truly "general" in the sense of being independent of language games or forms of life.[5] Contrary to Phillips's position, therefore, liberals like Ogden insist that the criteria for determining the meaning and truth of Christian claims must be "generally accessible"—in other words, normatively valid across language games and able to restrict the possible proper uses of language.

In his attempt to defend theology's ability to argue for the truth of its claims against what he took to be a threat from Phillips, two argumentative options were open to Ogden. The option he took was to insist on criteria for assessing religious claims that are publicly accessible or extracontextually normative. This insistence, he believed, requires a "realist" view of the meaning of religious claims such that religious language acquires its meaning through reference to extralinguistic "reality." Another option, however—one that no liberal theologian I am aware of did take—is to deny that a fully articulated "use theory" of meaning entails the relativization of truth to forms of life. I don't have space to pursue here the argument that such a theory of meaning is compatible with a realist view of truth, but note that it is a position that has been defended by philosophers such as William Alston.[6]

The option liberals pursued linked truth and meaning in a way that involved acceptance of a descriptivist or truth-conditional account of meaning. As I have argued, the currently most influential of such accounts, Donald Davidson's, suffers from fatal flaws I take to be endemic to any truth-conditional account of meaning. But meaning and truth conditions address different issues. Semantic meaning deals with the meaning of sentence types, and speaker-meaning deals with the meaning of sentence tokens—that is, particular utterances by speakers on particular occasions. Truth conditions and truth values, on the other hand, are used to analyze one of the things that speakers use sentences to produce—namely, assertions. Truth-conditional theorists have the relation between truth conditions and meaning reversed. It is the meaning of a sentence, together with contextual factors, that determine the truth conditions of a particular assertion—not vice versa (and not "holistically," whatever that might mean). More attention to the distinction between speech acts and semantics would

5. Ogden, "Linguistic Analysis and Theology," 323–24.
6. See William P. Alston, *A Realist Conception of Truth* (Ithaca, N.Y.: Cornell Univ. Press, 1996); Alston, *Illocutionary Acts and Sentence Meaning* (Ithaca, N.Y.: Cornell Univ. Press, 2000). See also Alston, *A Sensible Metaphysical Realism (Aquinas Lecture)* (Milwaukee: Marquette Univ. Press, 2001).

have permitted Ogden to argue against Phillips's relativization of truth to language games without opting for a descriptivist or truth-conditional account of the meaning of religious or theological assertions.

If Ogden's early engagements with Flew and others were formative of his views of language, certainly the same can be said about Frei's early engagements with language. From his earliest work, Frei's views on the meaning of religious and theological language were central to his work on theological method. The historical work that culminated in *The Eclipse of Biblical Narrative* convinced him that an improper understanding of how religious and theological claims acquired meaning had rendered modern liberal Protestant theology vulnerable to Feuerbach's critique. This improper understanding was a descriptivist or referential or truth-conditional view of linguistic meaning, and in Frei's view it has afflicted theology since the seventeenth century. The bulk of Protestant theology since then has interpreted the biblical narratives so that their true meaning lies elsewhere than in the narratives themselves. On this descriptivist view, the narratives get their meaning by referring either to some sequence of historical events or to some abstract religious or moral lesson. In either case the true meaning of the narratives was a product of human construction—either a sequence of reconstructed historical events or an abstract spiritual meaning.

Postliberals argued that this left theology with no means to respond to Feuerbach. Consequently, for postliberals no adequate theological method could presuppose such an understanding of meaning. Especially given the influence of Ryle and Wittgenstein, it was natural for postliberals to take the position that an adequate theological method must take account of the fact that the meaning of theological or religious assertions is constituted by their use in the Christian community's form of life. As I have argued in chapter 8, over the course of his career Frei moved closer to such a Wittgensteinian understanding of meaning (or at least to a position that made his Wittgensteinian proclivities more evident), and so also closer to Lindbeck. Note that this shift in Frei's understanding of meaning is a move to a more general understanding. In addition to biblical narratives, doctrines and religious assertions all acquire meaning in this way. Their meaning is constituted by their use in the form of life in which they are generated. Further, this understanding of meaning applies not only to religious assertions, but also to assertions regarding what counts as acceptable reasons for believing such assertions. And this move to a more general understanding in turn makes it more difficult for Frei to differentiate himself from Phillips regarding how to assess the truth of theological statements. As a result, Frei and Lindbeck endured a torrent of polemical criticism from conservative critics, and in response Frei attempted to differentiate himself from Phillips on the truth of Christian theological claims. This attempt involved some fairly vague assertions regarding the reference of the narratives, along with a determined refusal to articulate any theory of reference. Yet Frei retained his conviction that referential or truth-conditional theories of meaning were fatal to theology and that Wittgenstein offered the best alternative.

I have argued above that Wittgenstein's thesis on linguistic meaning, at least as it has been used in theology, has remained undeveloped, so that several of its central features are too vague to assess, and as a result also too vague to account for the way language acquires meaning. Nonetheless, whatever problems Wittgenstein's thesis on meaning may have, his central insights remain indisputably valuable. After Wittgenstein, it is difficult to deny the social nature of language and linguistic meaning. Further, he saw that much of our thought is conceptually dependent on linguistic competence. And if these insights are correct, it follows that we are dependent in part, in one way or another, on the contributions of our linguistic community for the content of much of our thought. What is needed is an approach that accounts for Wittgenstein's central insights through an appropriation of Searle's distinction between speech acts and semantics. This distinction is precisely what is lacking in both Ogden's and Frei's views of language. That is, despite the radical differences between Ogden and Frei, they share the assumption that the meaning of religious statements is independent of the notion of speech acts. This assumption combines with other elements of their theological projects to produce different results for liberals like Ogden and postliberals like Frei, respectively. Ogden limits religious statements to those that meet the twofold conditions of meaningfulness required by a truth-conditional theory of meaning, and his definition of religious claims as existential and transcendental does indeed meet these requirements nicely. Frei, on the other hand, seems to be left in the position described by Hunsinger—that the truth of the Gospel narratives must be taken on faith.[7]

The impasse between liberals and postliberals (or at least a large part of it) can be characterized as follows: From a liberal point of view, any

7. It is precisely to this situation that Bruce Marshall has addressed himself in *Trinity and Truth*, attempting to provide a sustained and defensible account of truth that is consistent with Frei's understanding of the task and method of theology. Bruce D. Marshall, *Trinity and Truth* (Cambridge: Cambridge Univ. Press, 2000). Curiously, however, in so doing, he rejects Frei's Wittgensteinian understanding of meaning-as-use in favor of the truth-conditional theory of Donald Davidson. He does not simply adopt Davidson's theory *tout court*, and it's at least arguable that he relies much more on Aquinas than on Davidson. Still, his use of Davidson is sufficient to make me, at any rate, uncomfortable.

Wittgensteinian understanding of the meaning of the biblical narratives implies that their criteria of truth will be specified by agreement within the Christian community. To liberals like Ogden, this relativization of the criteria of truth or validity to forms of life is fatal to the ability of Christian theology to defend its claims as true and renders the adjective "true" more or less equivalent to "characteristically or constitutively Christian." In Ogden's terms, it assimilates the criteria of credibility to that of appropriateness and cannot do justice to theology's claims to truth. From a postliberal point of view, any descriptivist view of reference and any truth-conditional or descriptivist view of meaning do not do justice to the particularity of the depictions of Jesus' identity in the Gospel narratives. Moreover, just because of this failure of particularity, they render the substantive claims of liberals like Ogden subject to Feuerbach's critique.

Fortunately, developments in philosophy of language have altered the situation so that we are no longer left with a Hobson's choice between descriptivism and Wittgenstein. William Alston, for example, has developed a theory of sentence meaning that is explicitly built on John Searle's theory of speech acts and can be understood in the spirit of Wittgenstein as a more complicated theory of meaning-as-use. As a result, it takes serious account of the sociality of language and thought, as well as Wittgenstein's insistence on the role of language use in any account of linguistic meaning. Alston also adopts Kripke's view of reference—a view that is also highly social in nature. Alston and others have shown how to incorporate the sociality of language within theories of meaning and reference so as to include contextual factors within the functioning of referring expressions and the constitution of sentence meaning. As I will suggest below, this theoretical incorporation of context allows for the kind of particularity in interpreting the meaning of sentences within the biblical narratives for which postliberals argue. Yet in building upon Searle's theory of speech acts, such a theory need not suffer from the kind of vagueness problems that Wittgenstein's informal and antitheoretical approach to philosophy prevented him from addressing adequately. Further, incorporating reference within a theory of sentence meaning permits the specification of truth conditions for assertions in a way that neither Phillips nor Frei can. In my view, then, a theory of meaning such as that of Alston serves as a corrective in that his theory of sentence meaning corrects the difficulties encountered both by Ogden's understanding of meaning in truth-conditional terms and by Frei's own particular appropriation of Wittgenstein. So let's now turn to the issue of reference to fill out this picture.

B. Descriptivism and a Refusal to Commit: Ogden and Frei on Reference

Ogden's argument for the existence of God (in opposition to Antony Flew and John Wisdom) implies his acceptance of a descriptivist view of reference. On this view, as we have seen, a referring expression is successful in referring to an object insofar as it stands for one or more definite descriptions that (either singly or together) uniquely describe the referent object. That is, of the descriptions that a speaker takes to be satisfied by an object, the speaker takes one or some to belong uniquely to that object. If, however, no object uniquely satisfies the most important description(s), then the purported name does not refer.

Wisdom's parable of the imaginary gardener and Flew's argument against theism on the basis of it both presuppose a descriptivist understanding of reference. The point of the falsification challenge is that theists cannot point to a description or a set of descriptions that is satisfied by God alone and not by an imaginary deity. In that case, theists' reference to God has failed. As we have seen, liberals responded to Flew and Wisdom in several different ways. But none tried to demonstrate that Flew's argument rested on a descriptivist view of reference and then argued that such an understanding of reference is mistaken. Ogden, for example, instead accepted the requirements imposed by descriptivists for successful reference, and then proceeded to argue that there is in fact a descriptive sense uniquely satisfied by God. That descriptive sense is that of unsurpassable love for all creation, which alone grounds human subjectivity and makes God's existence logically necessary, a set of descriptions possessed by nothing else.

Alston has commented that when a theologian's work adopts or assumes a descriptivist view of reference, her work is likely to begin by identifying a description or set of descriptions that are satisfied uniquely by God.[8] Such descriptions provide a basic set of concepts that become the primary subject matter of theology. I think we can see something like this at work in Ogden. His early work argues that the existence of God who boundlessly

---

8. William P. Alston, "Referring to God," *International Journal for the Philosophy of Religion* 24 (Nov. 1988): 113–28; reprinted in William P. Alston, *Divine Nature and Human Language* (Ithaca, N.Y.: Cornell Univ. Press, 1989), 103–17, esp. 116 (page references are to reprint edition). Recall that on a descriptivist view, a speaker must have in mind a description or set of descriptions that are uniquely satisfied by the referent or the reference will not succeed. In contrast, on a direct reference view, reference can proceed by description, but it need not. It can proceed by way of demonstration or other ways in which the referring expressions undergoes an "initial baptism," after which follows a kind of "chain" of reference.

loves all of creation is a necessary condition of the possibility of human subjectivity. For the most part, his subsequent essays include arguments whose theses are at least consistent with, if not necessitated by, the set of descriptions he believes uniquely to be satisfied by God.

From a postliberal point of view, however, this way of doing theology is profoundly mistaken, for at least two reasons. First, its positive statements about God are subject to methodological restrictions, rather than deriving the methodological procedures from positive affirmations about God. This, postliberals would say, makes any theological assertions that result from this way of doing theology unable to respond adequately to Feuerbach. Second, this way of doing theology does not do justice to the tyrannical nature of the biblical narratives. Similarly, it does not adequately respect the particularity of the identity of Jesus as depicted in the Gospel narratives.

In my view, the best way for postliberals to proceed would have been to argue that descriptivist views of reference are mistaken and that referring to God can be understood on a direct-reference view. When theology proceeds on the assumption of direct reference, postliberal concerns (the nature of the narratives, the particularity of Jesus' identity, the derivation of method from positive statements about God, etc.) can be more adequately addressed. But this is not the way Frei at any rate proceeds. Instead, he resolutely resists offering any view of reference at all. And as his supporters point out, this refusal creates some difficult problems.

Recall the dispute between Frei and Carl Henry over the reference of the Gospel narratives. As George Hunsinger characterizes their differences, Henry takes the narratives to refer to Jesus Christ in a literal or univocal way, while Frei takes them to use an analogical or dual reference—often containing both a "textual" reference and a "historical" reference (though sometimes only one or the other). The narratives (sometimes simultaneously) refer "historically" to the earthly or historical Jesus, and also to the risen, divine, living Jesus Christ.[9] Frei's obscure comments on reference imply that he takes reference to God or to divine acts to be *sui generis*. This in turn causes a good deal of confusion in deciding just what he means when he says Christians must affirm the truth of the Gospel narratives. If reference to divine *res significata* is *sui generis*, and if such references are relevant to the truth of claims containing them, then it would seem that determining or arguing for the truth of statements containing such

9. Hunsinger, George Hunsinger, "What Can Evangelicals and Postliberals Learn From Each Other? The Carl Henry/Hans Frei Exchange Revisited," *Pro Ecclesia* 5 (Spring 1996): 161–82, esp. 176.

references would also be *sui generis*. This is one of the reasons, I think, that Hunsinger interprets Frei as holding that the truth of the narratives must be taken on faith. If Hunsinger is correct in this interpretation, it is easy to see why liberals would consider Frei's method to be fideistic.

In my own view, one of the principal culprits opening Frei to such a charge is his inattention to the distinction between semantics and speech acts. This prevents him from distinguishing, on the one hand, between speaker-meaning and semantic meaning, and, on the other, between speaker-reference and semantic reference. More broadly, three aspects of Frei's work interact in problematic ways: his failure to distinguish between speech acts and semantics, his insistence that reference remains important to the truth of the narratives, and his Wittgensteinian understanding of the meaning of the narratives and of the church's statements about them. These positions led him, in my view, to treat both the reference and the truth of the narratives as effectively *sui generis*. In other words, he persistently maintained a separation between reference and meaning that prevented him from making coherent statements about the truth of the narratives.

Recent work by philosophers such as Alston can serve as an important corrective. They point out that reference can proceed by description, but it need not do so. Further, reference is an important contributing factor to the meaning of a number of speech acts, including assertions. Yet their meaning is not constituted by the reference of the whole utterance or sentence, nor by the constellation of the references of the utterance's referring expressions. On the contrary, it is the meaning of the utterance that fixes the utterance's references. More specifically, when a speaker (or author) utters a token of a particular sentence type, the semantic meaning of the sentence type interacts with contextual factors to yield the meaning of the utterance. There is a dynamic interplay between the reference of any referring expression in the utterance and the sense of the sentence so that the reference contributes to the meaning of the utterance while at the same time the meaning of the utterance fixes the reference. This dynamic interplay yields a determinate meaning for the utterance in many if not most cases. Often, of course, it will not be possible to tell which of the possible meanings a speaker intended her utterance to have, and often a speaker will intend an utterance to have several meanings. But when a determinate meaning is ascribed to the utterance in the way I have just indicated, the utterance (if it is an assertion) will become amenable to an analysis of its truth (or validity, or probable truth). This ascription of a determinate meaning to an utterance is, of course, an interpretation. And if reference is a part of the way in which the move from semantic meaning to utterance or speaker-meaning is accomplished, it must also be a part of interpretation. But this need not imply that the meaning of an uttered (or written) sentence or sequence of sentences is constituted by its reference to some extratextual entity. It makes more sense to talk about the reference of singular expressions than to talk about the reference of a sentence. And once the references of an assertive utterance have been fixed and a definite speaker-meaning assigned, the utterance will express a proposition that will have a truth value. Consequently, a more adequate theory of sentence meaning can make possible an analysis of the truth or validity of religious or theological assertions without insisting that the meaning of such assertions is constituted by their truth conditions.

III. LANGUAGE AND METHOD: NAVIGATING THE DIVIDE BETWEEN LIBERAL AND POSTLIBERAL THEOLOGY

Throughout this book I have been arguing that liberal and postliberal views on the meaning and reference of language are closely related to their differences over theological method. I have also suggested that recent work in analytic philosophy provides a helpful corrective to their views of language. If so, one might expect that more adequate views of meaning and reference would have analytical benefits for considering the kind of methodological differences we see in Ogden and Frei. And indeed, on my view there are at least three such benefits. First, to recall, descriptivists believe that the meaning of religious and theological assertions is constituted by their truth conditions and that the referents of referring expressions (and especially of "God") must be fixed by satisfaction of one or more descriptions. So if one is a descriptivist, it is at least natural also to believe that religious or theological claims should be argued for by appeal to transcendentally validated (and thus necessary) statements about human experience. This will also have the effect of limiting the class of claims that are candidates for being religious claims to those that are transcendental in the sense that they are validated by an argument that is, at least ultimately, transcendental. And on my reading, Ogden understands religious claims to be, among other things, transcendental.

But the converse is not necessarily the case. That is, one might believe that (at least some) religious claims are transcendental and that therefore validating (at least some) religious claims must involve a transcendental procedure without assuming either a descriptivist understanding of reference or a truth-conditional understanding of meaning. Consequently, if these ways of understanding meaning and reference are indeed invalid, this does not, at least on its own, entail that religious claims are not transcendental or that transcendental argument is not a proper way of arguing for (at least some) religious claims. What it does imply is that insofar as religious or theological claims are limited to transcendental claims in order to meet objections regarding their meaningfulness or regarding the failure of "God" to refer, the necessity of this limitation might be ripe for reconsideration.[10] It may be that the failure of descriptivist views of reference and meaning opens up space for more diversity in theological method.[11] Indeed, as William Alston points out, theology that assumes the possibility of direct reference to God is more likely to begin with the perception of God in individual and communal experience. Utilizing such an assumption is likely to result in a smaller role for natural theology and a larger role for tradition and religious experience than would be the case if one does theology assuming a descriptivist view of reference.[12] One can see this observation borne out in the work of liberals like Ogden and postliberals like Frei. The time is ripe for more adequate views of meaning and reference that can make possible a more diverse theological method that does a better job accounting for the central concerns of each theologian than either does on his own.

Second, as I have indicated above, vindication of a liberal concern for the truth or validation of Christian theological claims need not rule out the kind of particularity in interpretation of the Gospels that postliberals are concerned to preserve. For example, Alston's views of meaning and reference allow the ascription of meanings to statements that are amenable to analyses of their truth or validity. At the same time, Alston gives an important theoretical role to contextual factors, including reference, in his theory of sentence meaning as illocutionary act potential. This inclusion of contextual factors in ascribing meanings to the sequences of sentences in the biblical narratives is able to preserve the kind of particularity Frei

10. Any reconsideration of what counts as religious claims will involve a discussion of what constitutes religion. So far as I am aware, the most persuasive argument for an understanding of religious claims as transcendental is Franklin I. Gamwell, "A Forward to Comparative Philosophy of Religion," in *Religion and Practical Reason: New Essays in the Comparative Philosophy of Religion*, ed. Frank E. Reynolds and David Tracy (Albany: State Univ. of New York Press, 1994). My point in the text is simply that a proper understanding of language will allow this reconsideration without distortion by an unwarranted set of linguistic assumptions.

11. William Alston, for example allows reference to proceed by description, but insists that descriptivist requirements are not necessary. Alston, "Referring to God," 108–16. Thus by the "failure of descriptivist views" I mean the failure of the view that reference can succeed *only if* the intended referent uniquely satisfies a description or set of descriptions.

12. Alston, "Referring to God," 116.

is concerned to preserve. Moreover, his view of direct reference means that biblical narratives need not be interpreted *exclusively* as having an existential or transcendental meaning in order to make reference to God meaningful.

To illustrate the differences among liberals and postliberals regarding the meaning of biblical assertions regarding Jesus, let's look at two New Testament texts. First, the familiar empty-tomb story in Luke:

> But on the first day of the week, at early dawn, they came to the tomb, taking the spices that they had prepared. They found the stone rolled away from the tomb, but when they went in, they did not find the body. While they were perplexed about this, suddenly two men in dazzling clothes stood beside them. The women were terrified and bowed their faces to the ground, but the men said to them, "Why do you look for the living among the dead? He is not here, but has risen. Remember how he told you, while he was still in Galilee, that the Son of Man must be handed over to sinners, and be crucified, and on the third day rise again." (Luke 24:1–7)

Second, in the sermon reported in the tenth chapter of Acts, Peter declares:

> We are witnesses to all that he [Jesus] did both in Judea and in Jerusalem. They put him to death by hanging him on a tree; but God raised him on the third day and allowed him to appear, not to all the people, but to us who were chosen by God as witnesses, and who ate and drank with him after he rose from the dead. (Acts 10:39–41)

Of particular import for my purposes are the two statements "He is not here, but has risen" (by the sartorially dazzling duo) and "God raised him on the third day" (by Peter). Liberals like Bultmann and Ogden would interpret both statements mythologically. For Ogden, all talk of the Resurrection is talk of the decisive significance of Jesus as the re-presentation of boundless love of God. His understanding of language and his method work together to support this interpretation. Reference to God proceeds by description, so when the speakers in the texts refer to God, they must be interpreted as having in mind (at least implicitly) a description uniquely satisfied by God—for Ogden, as we have seen, it is something like *objective ground in reality of our existential faith*. And if God uniquely fits this description, it is because God unsurpassingly loves all of God's creation. This description then becomes part of the meanings of the two quoted statements, because, on Ogden's view, such meanings are constituted by their truth conditions.

I have discussed these truth conditions in more detail in chapter 1, but for now it should suffice to say, roughly, that Jesus' life and death re-presents or declares to us God's doing "all that could conceivably be done to save [us] from [our] sins."[13] Ogden's method then requires that this demythologized interpretation of the statements be validated (or invalidated) by common human experience and reason.[14]

In contrast, a postliberal like Lindbeck or Frei would insist on a more particularized interpretation of the statements.[15] Whatever happened when "God raised [Jesus] on the third day," Frei insists that it happened to the particular man Jesus, and that this particular event is indeed constitutive of his identity. Frei thinks any re-presentative or demythologizing interpretation will deprive Jesus of his unsubstitutable identity, and moreover will be vulnerable to Feuerbach's critique. On Frei's view, the meaning of each of the statements above is its literal sense, which is that the particular event of being raised happened to the particular man Jesus. Like Ogden, Frei would agree with Bultmann that the Resurrection is not an objective historical event like any other. Consequently, he takes the reference to God, who is said to have raised Jesus, to be some kind of *sui generis* reference. Yet when the scriptures speak of the Resurrection, Frei insists that they are not speaking mythologically or symbolically or re-presentatively, but at least in some sense factually. On Frei's interpretation, the Gospel accounts argue "that to grasp what this identity, Jesus of Nazareth (which has been made directly accessible to us), is is to believe that he has been, in *fact*, raised from the dead. . . . the argument holds good only in this one and absolutely unique case, where the described entity (who or what he is, i.e., Jesus Christ, the presence of God) is totally identical with his factual existence. He is the resurrection and the life. How can he be conceived as not resurrected?"[16] Earlier in his career, Frei would say that the structure of the narratives demands such an interpretation. Later, after modifying his understanding of the literal sense, he would insist that this literal reading

13. Schubert M. Ogden, *Is There Only One True Religion or Are There Many?* (Dallas, Tex.: Southern Methodist Univ. Press, 1992), 99.

14. See Schubert M. Ogden, *The Point of Christology* (San Francisco: Harper & Row, 1982; 2d ed., Dallas, Tex.: Southern Methodist Univ. Press, 1982), 128–40; Ogden, *Christ Without Myth: A Study Based on the Theology of Rudolf Bultmann* (New York: Harper, 1961; 2d ed, Dallas, Tex.: Southern Methodist Univ. Press, 1991), 83–88; 215–20 (page references are to 2d edition).

15. See Hans W. Frei, *The Identity of Jesus Christ: The Hermeneutical Bases of Dogmatic Theology* (Philadelphia: Fortress Press, 1975; repr., Eugene, Oreg.: Wipf & Stock, 1997), 176–83 (page references are to reprint edition).

16. Frei, *Identity of Jesus Christ,* 179.

was the proper one because it is the one the church has found useful in pursuing its form of life.

On the one hand, without a more adequate understanding of meaning, these would these would seem to be, utterly opposed interpretations: a postliberal insists that the language about the Resurrection *must* be interpreted literally or factually or else it will be distorted; a liberal (at least a consistent one) insists that such language *must* be interpreted mythologically or symbolically or else it cannot be validated and may not even be meaningful. A better view of meaning, on the other hand, allows us to say that both readings fall within the *semantic meaning* of the text. With liberals, we can say that the statements about the Resurrection are usable to perform the illocutionary act of asserting that Jesus is the decisive re-presentation of the boundless love of God. And with postliberals, we can say that the statements about the Resurrection are usable to assert that Jesus of Nazareth was raised from the dead. We don't need to be able to *imagine* what it would be like to be raised from the dead in order for the statement to have meaning, for we can certainly *conceive* that Jesus died and then was no longer dead but alive again. Further, we don't need to know just how to describe the difference between Jesus' resurrected body and our physical body in order for the statement that *Jesus' resurrected physical existence somehow differs from ours* to make sense. All we need is to understand the concept of difference in order to understand that Jesus' existence after the Resurrection is different from ours in one or more ways that we simply don't know enough about to describe.

Reference to God (who is said by Peter to have raised Jesus) for liberals like Ogden must proceed by description, and this descriptive sense must be validated by common human reason and experience. For postliberals like Frei, the reference is a kind of unanalyzable *sui generis* process. But on my view, the reference to God can proceed either by description or simply by direct reference. If Ogden is correct in his argument that God uniquely satisfies the description *objective ground in reality of our existential faith,* then the references to God in the quoted statements can quite properly proceed by description, and the description then becomes a part of the meaning of the statements. But reference can also proceed directly. Peter's experiential encounter with Jesus permits him simply to refer to Jesus directly.[17] Similarly, if Peter or his community has some experiential encounter with

17. In fact, on a direct reference view, Peter himself need not have such experiential contact. Such experiential contact *by someone* would constitute what Kripke (and Alston) call an initial baptism, and Peter could be simply someone in the referential chain of transmission.

God, he (or they) can simply refer to God directly as well. Nothing more is needed, at least for the reference to succeed. Thus, the language in the New Testament about the Resurrection will certainly bear the kind of particular, literal, factual interpretation for which postliberals argue. But it will also bear the kind of demythologizing interpretation that liberals like Ogden prefer. Indeed, neither Ogden's nor Frei's interpretation is demanded in order for the texts to have meaning, or for the references to God's gracious act in Jesus' resurrection to succeed.

What this means is that the argument about which "speaker-meaning" or "author-meaning" is to be preferred can proceed on more strictly theological and hermeneutical grounds without being biased one way or another by an inadequate view of language. In the end, the best course may be to refrain from deciding on one kind of reading to the exclusion of all others. What a more adequate view of language makes possible is the recognition that such texts bear an excess of meaning. More can be said about these points, but it does seem to me that discarding unworkable views on meaning and reference is helpful in clarifying the issues that need to be addressed.

The third implication concerns the issue of apologetics. As we have seen, postliberals like Frei and Lindbeck consistently argue that the task of Christian theology cannot include apologetics, because apologetic argument inevitably distorts the distinctive Christian message. Instead, just as Wittgenstein had argued that philosophy must foreswear explanation and limit itself to description, Frei argues that Christian theology must limit its task to Christian self-description and its method to the kind of "thick description" articulated by Clifford Geertz. Frei's argument against apologetics is an explicit argument in favor of the view that there are no "all-fields-encompassing" criteria that can serve to justify or validate claims in all forms of life or discourse. Implicit in the postliberal program, though, at least as I read Frei and Lindbeck, is the assertion that no other form of life or field of discourse sufficiently overlaps with the Christian form of life to permit shared or public criteria for what counts as reasonable assertions. Consequently, whatever the nature of religious or theological assertions may be, they cannot be transcendental or universal. They must, at least in some sense, be *sui generis*.

Leaving aside the apparent self-referential issues, from my own point of view, it is important to keep in mind two considerations on this subject. First, it is not at all clear to me that Christian theological discourse could not or should not overlap with other forms of life or fields of discourse sufficiently to permit shared criteria of credibility or reasonableness. Certainly, there may be forms of life with which Christian theological discourse does not so overlap. Yet this by no means implies that such overlap should be ruled out in advance for *all* other fields of discourse. I don't take this to be Frei's explicit position, for if it were, his comments on reference would be difficult to integrate into it. Further, his endorsement of ad hoc borrowing from other disciplines seems to imply the possibility of some shared criteria of reasonableness. Second, if my comments above are correct regarding the implication of meaning and reference for analysis of the truth of Christian theological assertions or of assertions in the biblical texts, then there seems to be no reason to hold that the meaning of such assertions is *sui generis*. Nor can I see any reason to hold that reference to God in the biblical texts must remain mysterious or unanalyzable or *sui generis*. Certainly some modes of referring are not available to the biblical writers simply because their communicative medium is written, not oral (for example, demonstration). But such modes are not available to writers of other texts, either. Further, some modes of referring are not available to any speaker (or writer) who wishes to refer to God rather than a corporeal person (for example, again, demonstration). But, again, such modes of referring are not available to speakers who wish to refer to any incorporeal reality (for example, numbers, sets, or concepts), and there is no reason to suppose that these more mundane cases of reference should remain mysterious or unanalyzable.

Perhaps, however, the motivating force behind Frei's opaque statements about "textual reference" is the idea asserted by many Christians that the biblical texts are not only records of biblical writers speaking about God; in addition, it is actually God who speaks to us through them. If we are to make sense of such an idea, then surely Calvin is correct when he says that God accommodates Godself to our modes of communication much like a nurse or mother accommodates herself to an infant's "lisping" mode of communication.[18] And if Calvin is correct about this, there seems to me to be no reason why the interpretive move from semantic meaning to speaker-meaning when God is the speaker could not proceed in a manner similar to when the speaker is a human writer. If this interpretive suggestion is correct, then God refers when speaking to us. It would be quite an involved task to reflect on how God speaks (and refers) or what we mean

18. The notion of accommodation, of course, goes back much further than Calvin. See Stephen Benin, *The Footprints of God: Divine Accommodation in Jewish and Christian Thought* (Albany, N.Y.: State Univ. of New York Press, 1993). Further, Calvin uses the notion in a large number of ways, all, it seems, in some way related to God's supreme accommodation in the Incarnation. See Ford Lewis Battles, "God Was Accommodating Himself to Human Capacity," in *Interpreting John Calvin*, ed. Robert Benedetto (Grand Rapids, Mich.: Baker Books, 1996). Unfortunately, I cannot pursue this suggestion here.

when we say God does so.[19] Such a reflection is beyond the scope of this book, but I see no reason to hold that this kind of reflection is inherently misleading.[20] And if in fact God makes assertions via the biblical texts, it seems to me that such assertions as are ascribed to God can be analyzed for truth or credibility or reasonableness without sacrificing the particularity of their meanings or distorting the meaning that the church ascribes to them. For myself, at a minimum I would need some argument explaining why such distortion is inevitable.

IV. A LOOK FORWARD

If the arguments I have advanced regarding the relation between language and method in liberal and postliberal theology are successful, then such arguments bring into view several related projects worth pursuing in future work. First, I have given some hints of a view of sentence meaning that can serve as a corrective to those often assumed by liberal and postliberal theologians. There is, of course, no shortage of proposals regarding linguistic meaning currently on offer by analytic philosophers, but one worth considering is that of William Alston.[21] Further, I have indicated what I take to be serious shortcomings inherent in the kind of proposal still currently dominant—namely, Donald Davidson's descriptivist view. And I have tried to indicate what I take to be some benefits of a theory like Alston's. In addition, both Alston's and Kripke's view of reference remains little more than a rough outline. There remains a need for a full-blown theory of reference

19. For a sustained reflection on this very question of God speaking to us, utilizing the distinction between semantics and speech acts that I am advocating here, see Nicholas Wolterstorff, *Divine Discourse: Philosophical Reflections on the Claim that God Speaks* (Cambridge: Cambridge Univ. Press, 1995).

20. In my own view, philosophical or theological reflection on the notion of God speaking or communicating to humans is not inconsistent with the notion that the mysteriousness of God is echoed in all creation, so that God becomes the preeminent case of the unknowability of all being, including ourselves. Indeed, language itself is an illustration of such unknowability. Nonetheless, we may insist that reflection on, and knowledge about, God, being and language may still be achieved without also asserting that such knowledge is exhaustive, even in principle. Alas, I cannot pursue this investigation here; I simply want to emphasize that I don't mean to imply any rejection of the tradition of negative theology.

21. Alston, *Illocutionary Acts and Sentence Meaning* (Ithaca, N.Y.: Cornell Univ. Press, 2000). Alston's view will of course need to be revisited in the light of criticisms, but few have been put forward to date. See, for example, Edwin Koster, "Een Filosofie van Tall en Tekst," *Philosophia Reformata* 68 (2003): 148–61; Stephen Barker, review of *Illocutionary Acts and Sentence Meaning* by William P. Alston, *Mind* 111 (July 2002): 633–39; Mark Siebel, review of *Illocutionary Acts and Sentence Meaning* by William P. Alston, *Grazer Philosophische Studien* 62 (2001): 48–61.

that will be suitable both for Christian theological assertions and biblical interpretation.

Second, further work is necessary in the area of interpretation. Notions of meaning, reference, truth, and interpretation are closely related, and the discussions here need supplementing by fuller articulations of truth and interpretation. But a couple of comments are in order. As may be clear by now, my own view is that deconstruction poses significantly less of a threat to the kind of hermeneutics practiced by Tracy and Ricoeur than Frei believes. Though Tracy and Ricoeur have taken some account of speech-act theory, it is Nicholas Wolterstorff who has been most explicit about incorporating speech-act theory, as well as insights more generally from analytical philosophy, into theological and biblical hermeneutics. These two approaches are preferable both to a more purely demythologizing approach, such as can be seen in Ogden, and to the Wittgensteinian approach of Frei and Lindbeck. Yet significant differences remain between Wolterstorff and hermeneutic theorists such as Tracy and Ricoeur. Nonetheless, Bultmann and Ogden, on the one hand, and Wittgenstein and Frei, on the other, achieved crucial insights regarding important issues in hermeneutics. Christian theological hermeneutics must be concerned with how to preserve constitutive Christian claims that are embedded in an overall web of cultural assumptions, many of which are quite properly discarded. This, I take it, is a central concern of Bultmann's demythologizing interpretation. So construed, this is also a concern of feminist theologians and liberation theologians, who have frequently utilized ideology critique in addressing this concern.[22] As we have seen, Ogden's own broadening of Bultmann's demythologizing to include de-ideologizing reflects the continuity of this concern.[23] On the other hand, these developments in theology can also be seen in the working out of Wittgenstein's and Frei's insights into the social nature of language.[24] And this in turn points to the need more generally for utilizing the work of social theorists in theology.[25] In my view attention to

22. For classic examples, see James M. Cone, *A Black Theology of Liberation* (1970; Maryknoll, N.Y.: Orbis Books, 1990); Gustavo Gutierrez, *A Theology of Liberation: History, Politics, and Salvation*, trans. and ed., Caridad Inda and John Eagleson (Maryknoll, N.Y.: Orbis, 1973); and Rosemary Radford Ruether, *Sexism and God-Talk: Toward a Feminist Theology* (Boston: Beacon Press, 1983).

23. See Schubert M. Ogden, *The Point of Christology* (San Francisco: Harper & Row, 1982; 2d ed., Dallas, Tex.: Southern Methodist Univ. Press, 1982).

24. Such a Wittgensteinian reading is supported by Habermas's defining ideology in terms of systemic distortion of a *communicative* environment. See Jürgen Habermas, *Knowledge and Human Interests*, trans. Jeremy J. Shapiro (Boston: Beacon Press, 1971).

25. See, for example, Kathryn Tanner, *Theories of Culture: A New Agenda for Theology* (Minneapolis, Minn.: Fortress Press, 1997).

considerations regarding reference, meaning, and the distinction between speech acts and semantics makes these interpretive issues more clear.

For example, many liberals and postliberals agree that the empirical-historical Jesus is not accessible, but this implies different consequences for different theologians. In Ogden's view, the inaccessibility of the empirical-historical Jesus means that questions about Jesus must be existential-historical questions. For Frei, on the other hand, though most of our questions about the empirical-historical Jesus may lack historically supportable answers, we can still ask about the identity of Jesus as depicted in the Gospels. And for Frei, interpreting the meaning of these depictions must remain independent of the question of whether the depictions are true. In my own view, however, Nicholas Wolterstorff's view of the relation of meaning and truth is more plausible than Frei's, because, as Wolterstorff argues, judgments about truth do and should intrude on judgments about meaning.[26] This is most obvious in the case of metaphors. In many cases, we judge a term to be used metaphorically precisely because it would otherwise yield an obvious falsehood.[27] But the principle is apparent in more mundane cases as well. When I say that *Susan works in the university's business office*, I may be referring to one of several persons named Susan. But because only one of them works at the business office, a judgment about truth will properly intrude to determine which Susan I am referring to and thus which proposition I am uttering. Among other things, this implies that even when theology is concerning itself only with self-description, it must also concern itself with determining which theological claims are rationally supportable or at least plausible.

These hermeneutical considerations raise the issue of how best to view the notion of a text's becoming independent of its author. To me, the best way to interpret this independence thesis is as follows. Semantic meaning sets a range of possible meanings that a sentence will bear. To say that a text (and its sentential parts) are independent of its author is just to say that readers will face a certain inevitable uncertainty about which possible

---

26. Nicholas Wolterstorff, "Will Narrativity Work as Linchpin? Reflections on the Hermeneutic of Hans Frei," in *Relativism and Religion*, ed. Charles M. Lewis (New York: St. Martin's Press, 1995), 71–107.

27. Wolterstorff, "Will Narrativity Work as Linchpin?" 102–103. Further, Wolterstorff notes that allowing "pressures of canonicity" or judgments about truth and falsity to intrude upon interpretative judgments is as old as the Christian community itself. Much of the difference between modern and ancient interpretation has to do with differences over which statements about God we take to be plausible or implausible. "A lot of what makes scriptural interpretation in the modern world different from what it was in the ancient world is that we more readily concede that

meaning was in fact the speaker's (or author's) intended meaning. Any act of interpretation will involve assigning a speaker meaning to the text, as I have mentioned above.[28] The question then becomes whether this assignment is purely an ideological construction, how it occurs, whether it is the most plausible or useful, etc. These examples illustrate that further work in hermeneutics will benefit from more extensive consideration of discussions regarding meaning and reference in philosophy of language.

Third, there is a need for a theory of truth consistent with the considerations discussed in this book. In *Trinity and Truth*, Bruce Marshall has advanced a detailed account of truth that he takes to be consistent with a postliberal understanding of the task and method of theology. Curiously, however, in so doing, he rejects Frei's Wittgensteinian understanding of meaning-as-use in favor of the truth-conditional theory of Donald Davidson (though arguably Aquinas is equally or more important to Marshall than Davidson). Further, important to his account of truth is Davidson's principle of charity in radical interpretation. It is beyond the scope of this book to address Marshall's proposal, but I will just note my discussion in chapter 9 of Davidson's descriptivist or truth-conditional account of linguistic meaning. In addition, though there clearly is something to Davidson's principle of charity, in my own view it is much less broadly useful than Davidson believes.[29] Others have offered detailed accounts of truth as well.[30] Discussion of subsidiary issues have become widespread in analytic philosophy as many philosophers have become disenchanted with Davidson's treatment of truth as primitive. Such issues include the nature of primary truth bearers. Are they propositions? Sentences? Or can Christian theologians properly say that Jesus Christ is *the* primary truth bearer? Marshall thinks so, and at this important point obviously departs from Davidson. If he is right, in what relation does Jesus Christ stand to true propositions or sentences? Consideration of these proposals and their

---

God suffers than that God works 'wonders'" ("Will Narrativity Work as Linchpin?" 104).

28. "Assigning a speaker meaning" is just the act of interpretation that results in a sentence (or text) being read as performing a particular illocutionary act (or sequence of illocutionary acts). It may, but need not involve any consideration of authorial intent.

29. See John Allan Knight, "Why Not Davidson? Neopragmatism in Religious Studies and the Coherence of Alternative Conceptual Schemes," *Journal of Religion* 88 (April 2008): 159–89.

30. See, for example, William P. Alston, *A Realist Conception of Truth* (Ithaca, N.Y.: Cornell Univ. Press, 1996); Scott Soames, *Understanding Truth* (New York: Oxford Univ. Press, 1999); Paul Horwich, *Truth*, 2nd ed. (New York: Oxford Univ. Press, 1998); Michael Lynch, *Truth in Context: An Essay on Pluralism and Objectivity* (Cambridge,

relation to the methodological issues I have discussed is an important project closely related to the project of this book.

Finally, there remains a need for a theory of epistemic warrant or justification consistent with the considerations discussed here regarding theological method. Both William Alston and Alvin Plantinga have advanced detailed proposals regarding epistemic justification or warrant, and these proposals have by now occasioned critical literature.[31] And since their proposals were published, analytic philosophers have put forward others. Review of these proposals and their critics are beyond the scope of this book, but as I have mentioned previously, whether a particular assertion can be rationally accepted (epistemically justified) is often a proper and necessary part of determining how that assertion is to be construed. Consequently, a theory of epistemic justification is an important part of any theological method.

In my view, then, there is a close relationship between liberal and postliberal theological methods and their respective views on the meaning and reference of language—specifically as these relations are played out in prominent representatives of these traditions in theology. Further, their views on meaning and reference face daunting or fatal obstacles. But developments in analytic philosophy of language and philosophy of religion represent an important improvement on those assumed or adopted by postliberals like Frei and liberals like Ogden. At a minimum, I hope that the discussions of meaning and reference in this study have helped to clarify the differences between liberal and postliberal theology. More generally, I would like to suggest that paying attention to analytic philosophy, and analytic philosophy of language in particular, is crucial for further work in theological method.

Mass.: MIT Press, 1998); Michael Lynch, *True to Life: Why Truth Matters* (Cambridge, Mass.: MIT Press, 2005).

31. William P. Alston, *Perceiving God: The Epistemology of Religious Experience* (Ithaca, N.Y.: Cornell Univ. Press, 1993); Alvin Plantinga, *Warrant: The Current Debate* (New York: Oxford Univ. Press, 1993); Alvin Plantinga, *Warrant and Proper Function* (New York: Oxford Univ. Press, 1993); Alvin Plantinga, *Warranted Christian Belief* (New York: Oxford Univ. Press, 2000). Michael Ruse, "Methodological Naturalism Under Attack," *South African Journal of Philosophy* 24 (2005): 44–60; John Bishop and Imran Aijaz, "How to Answer the *De Jure* Question About Christian Belief," *Int'l Journal for Philosophy of Religion* 56 (2004): 109–29; *Does Religious Experience Justify Religious Belief?: Do Mystics See God?* ed. Michael L. Peterson (Malden, Mass.: Blackwell Publishing, 2004); Michael J. Shaffer, "A Defeater of the Claim that Belief in God's Existence is Properly Basic," *Philo* 7 (2004): 57–70; Kevin Meeker, "Truth, Justification and the Epistemic Way," *Journal of Philosophical Research* 28 (2003): 287–309.

BIBLIOGRAPHY

Allen, Diogenes. Review of *Falsification and Belief* by Alastair McKinnon. *Princeton Seminary Bulletin* 64 (1971): 102–103.

Alston, William P. "Referring to God." *International Journal for Philosophy of Religion* 24 (Nov. 1988): 113–28.

———. *Divine Nature and Human Language: Essays in Philosophical Theology.* Ithaca, N.Y.: Cornell Univ. Press, 1989.

———. *Perceiving God: The Epistemology of Religious Experience.* Ithaca, N.Y.: Cornell Univ. Press, 1993.

———. *A Realist Conception of Truth.* Ithaca, N.Y.: Cornell Univ. Press, 1996.

———. *Illocutionary Acts and Sentence Meaning.* Ithaca, N.Y.: Cornell Univ. Press, 2000.

———. *A Sensible Metaphysical Realism (Aquinas Lecture).* Milwaukee, Wis.: Marquette Univ. Press, 2001.

Atkins, Anselm, O.C.S.O. "Religious Assertions and Doctrinal Development." *Theological Studies* 27:4 (1966): 523–52.

Auerbach, Erich. *Mimesis: The Representation of Reality in Western Literature.* Translated by Willard R. Trask. Princeton, N.J.: Princeton Univ. Press, 1953. Reprint, 1991.

———. *Dante: Poet of the Secular World.* Chicago: Univ. of Chicago Press, 1961.

———. "Scenes from the Drama of European Literature." In *From Time to Eternity: Essays on Dante's Divine Comedy.* Edited by Thomas G. Berger. New Haven, Conn.: Yale Univ. Press, 1967.

Aulén, Gustav. *The Drama and the Symbols.* Translated by Sydney Linton. Philadelphia: Fortress Press, 1970.

———. *The Faith of the Christian Church.* Translated by Eric Wahlstrom. Philadelphia: Fortress Press, 1973.

Austin, John L. *How to Do Things With Words.* Edited by J. O. Urmson and Marina Sbisà. 2d ed. Cambridge, Mass.: Harvard Univ. Press, 1975.

Ayer, A. J. "Can There Be a Private Language?" *Proceedings of the Aristotelian Society,* supp. vol. 28 (1954): 63–76. Reprinted in *Wittgenstein: The Philosophical Investigations.* Edited by George Pitcher. Notre Dame, Ind.: Univ. of Notre Dame Press, 1968.

Ayers, Robert H., and William T. Blackstone, eds. *Religious Language and Knowledge.* Athens: Univ. of Georgia Press, 1972.

Barker, Stephen. *Review of Illocutionary Acts and Sentence Meaning* by William P. Alston. *Mind* 111 (July 2002): 633–39.

Barth, Karl. *Fides Quaarens Intellectum: Anselm's Proof of the Existence of God in the Context of his Theological Scheme.* Translated by Ian W. Robertson. 2d ed. London: SCM Press, 1960.

———. *Protestant Thought in the Nineteenth Century.* Translated by Brian Cozens and John Bowden. Grand Rapids, Mich.: Wm. B. Eerdmans, 2002. Originally published as *Die protestantische Theologie im 19. Jahrhundert.* Zurich: Theoligischer Verlag, 1947; reprint, 1952.

Battles, Ford Lewis. "God Was Accommodating Himself to Human Capacity." In *Interpreting John Calvin.* Edited by Robert Benedetto. Grand Rapids, Mich.: Baker Books, 1996.

Benin, Stephen. *The Footprints of God: Divine Accommodation in Jewish and Christian Thought.* Albany, N.Y.: State Univ. of New York Press, 1993.

Bishop, John, and Imran Aijaz. "How to Answer the De Jure Question About Christian Belief." *International Journal for Philosophy of Religion* 56 (2004): 109–29.

Blaisdell, Charles R. "The Christian Norm: In Response to Williamson and Ogden." *Process Studies* 16 (Fall 1987): 169–73.

Blocher, Henri. "Biblical Narrative and Historical Reference." Pages 102–22 in *Issues in Faith and History.* Edited by Nigel M. de S. Cameron. Edinburgh: Rutherford House, 1989.

Braithwaite, R. B. *An Empiricist's View of the Nature of Religious Belief.* Cambridge: Cambridge Univ. Press, 1955.

Bultmann, Rudolf. *Theology of the New Testament.* Vol. 1. Translated by Kendrick Grobel. New York: Charles Scribner's Sons, 1951. Reprint, 1955.

———. *Kerygma und Mythos.* 2 vols. 2d ed. Edited by H. W. Bartsch. Hamburg: Herbert Reich-Evangelischer Verlag, 1952.

———. *Theologie des Neuen Testaments.* 2 vols. Tübingen: J. C. B. Mohr, 1948–1953.

———. *Existence and Faith: The Shorter Writings of Rudolf Bultmann.* Edited by Schubert M. Ogden. New York: Meridian Books, 1960.

Burkle, Howard R. "Counting Against and Counting Decisively Against." *Journal of Religion* 44 (1964): 223–29.

Cady, Linell Elizabeth. "Identity, Feminist Theory, and Theology." *Horizons in Feminist Theology: Identity, Tradition, and Norms.* Edited by Rebecca S. Chopp and Sheila Greeve Davaney. Minneapolis: Fortress Press, 1997.

Carlson, Jeffrey. "Ogden's 'Appropriateness' and Religious Plurality." *Modern Theology* 6 (Oct. 1989): 15–28.

Christian, William A. "Truth-Claims in Religion." *Journal of Religion* 42 (1962): 52–62. Reprinted in *Religious Language and the Problem of Religious Knowledge.* Edited by Ronald E. Santoni. Bloomington: Indiana Univ. Press, 1968.

———. *Meaning and Truth in Religion.* Princeton, N.J.: Princeton Univ. Press, 1964.

Cone, James. Review of *Faith and Freedom* by Schubert Ogden. *Union Seminary Quarterly Review* 35 (Spring-Summer 1980): 296–300.

Cone, James M. *A Black Theology of Liberation.* Maryknoll, N.Y.: Orbis Books, 1990.

Copleston, Frederick C. "God and Philosophy." *Journal of Theological Studies* 18 (1967): 303–308.

Cotton, James Harry. "Questions, Interest, and Theological Inquiry." *McCormick Quarterly* 22:2 (Jan. 1969): 121–33.

Crombie, I. M. "Theology and Falsification." *New Essays in Philosophical Theology.* Edited by Antony Flew and Alasdair MacIntyre. London: SCM Press, 1955. Reprint, 1958, 109–30.

———. "The Possibility of Theological Statements." *The Philosophy of Religion*, Edited by Basil Mitchell. New York: Oxford Univ. Press, 1971.

Cupitt, Don. *Taking Leave of God.* London: SCM Press, 1980.

Davidson, Donald. "Truth and Meaning." *Synthese* 17 (1967): 304–23.

———. "Reply to Foster." *Truth and Meaning: Essays in Semantics.* Edited by Gareth Evans and John McDowell. Oxford: Clarendon Press, 1976. Reprint, 1999.

———. *Inquiries into Truth and Interpretation.* Oxford: Clarendon Press, 2001.

Dawson, John David. "Figural Reading and the Fashioning of Christian Identity in Boyarin, Auerbach and Frei." *Modern Theology* 14 (April 1998): 181–96.

Devenish, Philip E. "Postliberal Process Theology: A Rejoinder to Burrell." *Theological Studies* 43 (Summer 1982): 504–13.

Devenish, Philip E, and George L. Goodwin, ed. *Witness and Existence: Essays in Honor of Schubert M Ogden.* Chicago: Univ. of Chicago Press, 1989.

Donnellan, Keith. "Reference and Definite Descriptions." *Philosophical Review* 75 (1966): 281–304. Reprinted in *The Philosophy of Language.* Edited by A. P. Martinich, 4th ed. New York: Oxford Univ. Press, 2001.

Dummett, Michael. *Frege: Philosophy of Language.* 2d ed. Cambridge, Mass.: Harvard Univ. Press, 1981.

———. *The Logical Basis of Metaphysics.* Cambridge, Mass.: Harvard Univ. Press, 1991.

Ellingson, Mark. "Philosophical Reflections on the Task of Christian Proclamation." *Dialogue* 20 (Fall 1981): 306–13.

Evans, Donald D. "Falsification and Belief." *Studies in Religion/Sciences Religieuses* 1 (1971): 249–50.

Feigl, Herbert, and Wilfred Sellars, eds. *Readings in Philosophical Analysis.* New York: Appleton-Century-Crofts, 1949.

Ferré, Frederick P. "God and the Verification Principle: Verification, Faith, and Credulity." *Religion in Life* 32:1 (1963): 46–57.

Fetzer, James H., and Paul W. Humphreys, eds. *The New Theory of Reference: Kripke, Marcus and Its Origins.* Dordrecht: Kluwer Academic Publishers, 1998.

Flew, Antony. "The University Discussion." Pages 96–99, 106–108 in *New Essays in Philosophical Theology.* Edited by Antony Flew and Alasdair MacIntyre. London: SCM Press, 1955. Reprint, 1958.

———. *God and Philosophy.* New York: Harcourt, Brace and World, 1966.

Flew, Antony, and Alasdair MacIntyre, eds. *New Essays in Philosophical Theology.* London: SCM Press, 1955. Reprint, 1958.

Foster, J. A. "Meaning and Truth in Theory." *Truth and Meaning: Essays in Semantics.* Edited by Gareth Evans and John McDowell. Oxford: Clarendon Press, 1976. Reprint, 1999.

Fraser, J. W. Review of *Christ Without Myth*, by Schubert Ogden. *Scottish Journal of Theology* 16 (March 1963): 97–101.

Frege, Gottlob. "On Sense [Sinn] and Reference [Bedeutung]." Translated by Max Black. *The Philosophical Review* 57 (1948): 207–30.

Frei, Hans W. "The Doctrine of Revelation in the Thought of Karl Barth, 1909–1922: The Nature of Barth's Break with Liberalism." Ph.D. diss., Yale Univ., 1956.

———. "Theological Reflections on the Accounts of Jesus' Death and Resurrection." *Christian Scholar* 49 (Winter 1966): 263–306.

———. "Feuerbach and Theology." *Journal of the American Academy of Religion* 35 (Summer 1967): 250–56.

———. "Karl Barth—Theologian." Pages 1–14, 28–29, 45–64 in *Karl Barth and the Future of Theology: A Memorial Colloquium Held at the Yale Divinity School, January 28, 1969.* Edited by David L. Dickerman. Yale Divinity School Association. Reprinted in *Reflection* 66:4 (May 1969): 5–9. Also reprinted in Hans W. Frei, *Theology and Narrative: Selected Essays.* Edited by George Hunsinger and William C. Placher. New York: Oxford Univ. Press, 1993.

———. *Eclipse of Biblical Narrative: A Study in Eighteenth and Nineteenth Century Hermeneutics.* New Haven, Conn.: Yale Univ. Press, 1974.

———. "An Afterword: Eberhard Busch's Biography of Karl Barth." Pages 95–116 in *Karl Barth in Review: Posthumous Works Reviewed and Assessed.* Edited by H.-Martin Rumscheidt. Pittsburgh, Pa.: Pickwick Press, 1981.

———. "The 'Literal Reading' of Biblical Narrative in the Christian Tradition: Does it Stretch or Will it Break?" Pages 36–77 in *The Bible and the Narrative Tradition.* Edited by Frank McConnell. New York: Oxford Univ. Press, 1986.

———. "Response to [C. F. H. Henry] 'Narrative Theology, An Evangelical Appraisal'" *Trinity Journal* 8 (Spring 1987): 21–24.

———. "Barth and Schleiermacher: Divergence and Convergence." Pages 65–87 in *Barth and Schleiermacher: Beyond the Impasse?* Edited by James O. Duke and Robert F. Streetman. Philadelphia: Fortress Press, 1988.

———. "How it all Began: On the Resurrection of Christ." *Anglican and Episcopal History* 58 (June 1989): 139–45.

———. "Epilogue: George Lindbeck and the Nature of Doctrine." Pages 275–82 in *Theology and Dialogue: Essays in Conversation with George Lindbeck.* Edited by Bruce D. Marshall. Notre Dame, Ind: Univ. of Notre Dame Press, 1990.

———. "'Narrative' in Christian and Modern Reading." Pages 149–63 in *Theology and Dialogue.* Edited by Bruce D. Marshall. Notre Dame, Ind: Univ. of Notre Dame Press, 1990.

———. "H. Richard Niebuhr on History, Church and Nation." Pages 1–23 in *The Legacy of H. Richard Niebuhr.* Edited by Ronald F. Thiemann. Minneapolis: Fortress Press, 1991.

———. "Conflicts in Interpretation." *Theology Today* 49 (Oct. 1992): 344–56.

———. *Types of Christian Theology.* Edited by George Hunsinger and William C. Placher. New Haven, Conn.: Yale Univ. Press, 1992.

———. "Remarks in Connection with a Theological Proposal." Pages 26–44 in Hans W. Frei, *Theology and Narrative: Selected Essays.* Edited by George Hunsinger and William C. Placher. New York: Oxford Univ. Press, 1993.

———. *Theology and Narrative.* Edited by George Hunsinger and William C. Placher. New York: Oxford Univ. Press, 1993.

———. *The Identity of Jesus Christ: The Hermeneutical Bases of Dogmatic Theology.* Philadelphia: Fortress Press, 1975. Reprint, Eugene, Oreg.: Wipf & Stock, 1997.

———. "The Doctrine of Revelation in Karl Barth." Pages 103–87 in *Ten Year Commemoration of the Life of Hans Frei (1922–1988).* Edited by Giorgy Olegovich. New York: Semenenko Foundation, 1999.

Frei, Hans W., and Robert Off. "Karl Barth—Theologian." Pages 5–14 in *Karl Barth and the Future of Theology.* New Haven, Conn.: Yale Divinity School Association, 1969.

Gadamer, Hans-Georg. *Truth and Method*. 2d rev. ed. Translated by Joel
Weinsheimer and Donald G. Marshall. New York: Continuum, 1994.

Gamwell, Franklin I. "A Forward to Comparative Philosophy of Religion." Pages
21–57 in *Religion and Practical Reason: New Essays in the Comparative Philosophy
of Religion*. Edited by Frank E. Reynolds and David Tracy. Albany: State Univ.
of New York Press, 1994.

———. "On the Theology of Schubert M. Ogden." *Religious Studies Review* 23:4 (Oct.
1997): 333–37.

Geertz, Clifford. *The Interpretation of Cultures*. New York: Basic Books, 1973.

Gerrish, Brian. *Tradition and the Modern World: Reformed Theology in the Nineteenth
Century*. Chicago: Univ. of Chicago Press, 1977.

———. *The Old Protestantism and the New*. Chicago: Univ. of Chicago Press, 1982.

———. *Continuing the Reformation: Essays on Modern Religious Thought*. Chicago:
Univ. of Chicago Press, 1993.

Gilkey, Langdon. "A Theology in Process: Schubert Ogden's Developing Theology."
Interpretation 21 (Oct. 1967): 447–59.

Godlove, Terry F., Jr. *Religion, Interpretation, and Diversity of Belief: The Framework
Model from Kant to Durkheim to Davidson*. Cambridge: Cambridge Univ. Press,
1989.

Green, Garrett, ed. *Scriptural Authority and Narrative Interpretation*. Philadelphia:
Fortress Press, 1987.

Griffiths, Paul J. "How Epistemology Matters to Theology." *Journal of Religion* 79
(Jan. 1999): 1–18.

Gunton, Colin E. Review of *Types of Christian Theology*, by Hans Frei. *Scottish Journal
of Theology* 49:2 (1996): 233–34.

Gutierrez, Gustavo. *A Theology of Liberation: History, Politics, and Salvation*.
Translated and edited by Caridad Inda and John Eagleson. Maryknoll, N.Y.:
Orbis, 1973.

Habermas, Jürgen. *Knowledge and Human Interests*. Translated by Jeremy J. Shapiro.
Boston: Beacon Press, 1971.

Hacker, P. M. S. *Wittgenstein: Connections and Controversies*. Oxford: Clarendon
Press, 2001.

Hare, R. M. "Theology and Falsification." Pages 99–103 in *New Essays in Philosophical
Theology*. Edited by Antony Flew and Alasdair MacIntyre. London: SCM Press,
1955. Reprint, 1958.

Harnack, Adolf von. *What is Christianity?* London, 1901. Reprint, New York: Harper
& Brothers, 1957; 2d reprint, Minneapolis: Fortress Press, 1986.

———. *Das Wesen des Christentums*. Stuttgart: Ehrenfried Klotz Verlag, 1950.

Hartshorne, Charles. *Man's Vision of God and the Logic of Theism*. New York: Harper &
Brothers, 1941.

———. *The Divine Relativity*. New Haven, Conn.: Yale Univ. Press, 1948.

———. *The Logic of Perfection and Other Essays in Neoclassical Metaphysics*. La Salle,
Ill.: Open Court Publishing, 1962.

Hartshorne, Charles, and William L. Reese, eds. *Philosophers Speak of God*. Chicago:
Univ. of Chicago Press, 1953.

Heidegger, Martin. *Sein und Zeit*. Tübingen: Max Niemeyer, 1927. Reprint, 1993.

———. *Being and Time*. Translated by John Macquarrie and Edward Robinson. New
York: Harper & Row, 1962.

Henry, Carl F. H. "Narrative Theology: An Evangelical Appraisal." *Trinity Journal* 8
(Spring 1987): 3–19.

Hick, John. *Faith and Knowledge*. Ithaca, N.Y.: Cornell Univ. Press, 1957.

———. "Theology and Verification." *Theology Today* 17:1 (April 1960): 12–31.

———. Review of *The Point of Christology*, by Schubert Ogden. *Journal of Religion* 64 (July 1984): 363–69.

High, Dallas M. "Belief, Falsification, and Wittgenstein." *International Journal for Philosophy of Religion* 3 (1972): 239–50.

Higton, M. A. "Frei's Christology and Linbeck's Cultural-Linguistic Theory." *Scottish Journal of Theology* 50:1 (1997): 83–95.

———. *Christ, Providence and History: Hans W. Frei's Public Theology*. London: T & T Clark, 2004.

Hill, William J. "The Historicity of God." *Theological Studies* 45 (June 1984): 320–33.

Horwich, Paul. *Truth*. 2d ed. Oxford: Clarendon Press, 1998.

Howe, Leroy T. "Theology and its Philosophical Commitments." *Scottish Journal of Theology* 24 (1971): 385–406.

Hunsinger, George. "Hans Frei as Theologian: The Quest for a Generous Orthodoxy." *Modern Theology* 8 (April 1992): 103–28.

———. "Afterword." Pages 235–70 in Hans W. Frei, *Theology and Narrative*. Edited by George Hunsinger and William C. Placher. New York: Oxford Univ. Press, 1993.

———. "What Can Evangelicals and Postliberals Learn from Each Other? The Carl Henry/Hans Frei Exchange Reconsidered." *Pro Ecclesia* 5 (Spring 1996): 161–82.

Jackson, Frank. "Reference and Descriptions Revisited." Pages 201–18 in *Language, Mind and Ontology*. Vol. 12: *Nous-Supplement: Philosophical Perspectives*. Edited by James Tomberlin. Oxford: Blackwell, 1998.

Kant, Immanuel. *Religion Within the Limits of Reason Alone*. Translated by Theodore M. Greene and Hoyt H. Hudson. New York: Harper & Row, 1960.

———. *Die Religion innerhalb der Grenzen der blossen Vernunft*, in *Werke in sechs Bänden*. Band 5. Köln: Könemann, 1995.

King, Robert H. "The Concept of Personal Agency as a Theological Model." Ph.D. diss., Yale Univ., 1965.

———. *The Meaning of God*. Philadelphia: Fortress Press, 1973.

King-Farlow, John, and William N. Christensen. "Faith—and Faith in Hypothesis." *Religious Studies* 7 (1971): 113–24.

Knight, John Allan. "Truth, Justified Belief, and the Nature of Religious Claims: Schubert Ogden's Transcendental Criterion of Credibility." *American Journal of Theology and Philosophy* 27 (Jan. 2006): 55–83.

———. "Why Not Davidson? Neopragmatism in Religious Studies and the Coherence of Alternative Conceptual Schemes." *Journal of Religion* 88 (April 2008): 159–89.

———. "The Barthian Heritage of Hans Frei." *Scottish Journal of Theology* 61:3 (Aug. 2008): 307–26.

———. "Descriptivist Reference and the Return of Classical Theism." In *Models of God and Other Ultimate Realities*. Edited by Jeanine Diller and Asa Kasher. Dordrecht: Springer, forthcoming 2012.

———. "Wittgenstein's Web: Hans Frei and the Meaning of Biblical Narratives," *Journal of Religion* (forthcoming).

Koster, Edwin. "Een Filosofie van Tall ed Tekst." *Philosophia Reformata* 68 (2003): 148–61.

Kripke, Saul. "Speaker's Reference and Semantic Reference." Pages 6–27 in *Contemporary Perspectives in the Philosophy of Language*. Edited by Peter A.

French, Theodore E. Uehling, Jr., and Howard K. Wettstein. Minneapolis: Univ. of Minnesota Press, 1979.

———. *Wittgenstein on Rules and Private Language*. Cambridge, Mass.: Harvard Univ. Press, 1982. Reprint, 2000.

———. *Naming and Necessity*. Cambridge, Mass.: Harvard Univ. Press, 1972. Reprint, 1999.

Lessing, G. E. "Gegensätze des Herausgebers." Page 813 in *Gesammelte Werke*. Vol 7. Edited by Paul Rilla. Berlin: Aufbau-Verlag, 1954–58.

Lewis, Charles M., ed. *Relativism and Religion*. London: Macmillan, 1995.

Lindbeck, George A. *The Nature of Doctrine: Religion and Theology in a Postliberal Age*. Philadelphia: Westminster Press, 1984.

Livingston, James C. *Modern Christian Thought*. Vol. 1: *The Enlightenment and the Nineteenth Century*. 2d ed. Upper Saddle River, N.J.: Prentice Hall, 1997.

Locke, John. *The Reasonableness of Christianity*. Edited by John C. Higgins-Biddle. Oxford: Clarendon Press, 1999.

Lonergan, Bernard. *Insight*. New York: Philosophical Library, 1970.

Loughlin, Gerard. "On Telling the Story of Jesus." *Theology* 87 (Summer 1984): 323–29.

Ludlow, Peter, ed. *Readings in the Philosophy of Language*. Cambridge, Mass.: MIT Press, 1997.

Lynch, Michael. *Truth in Context: An Essay on Pluralism and Objectivity*. Cambridge, Mass.: MIT Press, 1998.

———. *True to Life: Why Truth Matters*. Cambridge, Mass.: MIT Press, 2005.

Marcus, Ruth Barcan. "Modalities and Intensional Languages." *Synthese* 13 (1961): 303–22.

———. *Modalities*. New York: Oxford Univ. Press, 1993.

Marshall, Bruce. *Trinity and Truth*. Cambridge: Cambridge Univ. Press, 2000.

Martinich, A. P., ed. *The Philosophy of Language*, 4th ed. New York: Oxford Univ. Press, 2001.

Marxsen, Willi. *Das Neue Testament als Buch der Kirche*. Gütersloh: Gütersloher Verlagshaus Gerd Mohn, 1968.

Mason, David R. "Selfhood, Transcendence and the Experience of God." *Modern Theology* 3 (July 1987): 293–314.

Mavrodes, George. "God and Verification." *Canadian Journal of Theology* 10 (1964): 187–91.

McKinnon, Alistair. "Unfalsifiability and Religious Belief." *Canadian Journal of Theology* 12 (1966): 118–125.

———. *Falsification and Belief*. The Hague: Mouton, 1970.

McLeod, Mark S. "Schubert Ogden on Truth, Meaningfulness and Religious Language." *American Journal of Theology and Philosophy* 9 (Summer 1988): 195–207.

McPherson, Thomas. "The Falsification Challenge." *Religious Studies* 5:1 (Oct. 1969): 81–84.

Meeker, Kevin. "Truth, Justification and the Epistemic Way." *Journal of Philosophical Research* 28 (2003): 287–309.

Miller, John Franklin III. "First Order Principles in Science and Religion." *Iliff Review* 28:1 (Dec. 1971): 47–58.

Min, Anselm K. "Praxis and Theology in Recent Debates." *Scottish Journal of Theology* 39 (1986): 529–49.

Mitchell, Basil. "Theology and Falsification." Pages 103–105 in *New Essays in Philosophical Theology*. Edited by Antony Flew and Alasdair MacIntyre. London: SCM Press, 1955. Reprint, 1958.

———., ed. *Faith and Logic*. London: George Allen and Unwin, 1958.

———., ed. *Philosophy of Religion*. Oxford: Oxford Univ. Press, 1971.

Mourad, Ronney B. "Credibility and Warrant in Theology: An Epistemological Synthesis." *American Journal of Philosophy and Theology* 21.2 (May 2000): 118–45.

Nielsen, Kai. "Eschatological Verification." *Canadian Journal of Theology* 9 (1963): 271–81.

———. "God and Verification Again." *Canadian Journal of Theology* 11 (1965): 135–41.

Nygren, Anders. *Meaning and Method*. Translated by Philip Watson. Philadelphia: Fortress Press, 1972.

Ogden, Schubert M. "Bultmann's Project of Demythologization and the Problem of Theology and Philosophy." *Journal of Religion* 37 (1957): 156–73.

———. "The Debate on 'Demythologizing'." *Journal of Bible and Religion* 27 (Jan. 1959): 17–27.

———. "The Lordship of Jesus Christ: The Meaning of Our Affirmation." *Encounter* 21 (Autumn 1960): 408–22.

———. *Christ Without Myth: A Study Based on the Theology of Rudolf Bultmann*. New York: Harper, 1961. 2d ed, Dallas, Tex.: Southern Methodist Univ. Press, 1991.

———. "Theology and Philosophy: A New Phase of the Discussion." *Journal of Religion* 44 (Jan. 1964): 1–16.

———. *The Reality of God and Other Essays*. New York: Harper & Row, 1966. 2d ed., Dallas, Tex.: Southern Univ. Press, 1992.

———. "How Does God Function in Human Life?" *Christianity and Crisis* 27 (May 15, 1967): 105–108.

———. "God and Philosophy: A Discussion with Antony Flew." *Journal of Religion* 48 (April 1968): 161–81.

———. "Present Prospects for Empirical Theology." Pages 65–88 in *The Future of Empirical Theology*. Edited by Bernard Meland. Chicago: Univ. of Chicago Press, 1969.

———. "The Reality of God." Pages 119–35 in *Process Theology*. New York: Newman Press, 1971.

———. "Truth, Truthfulness and Secularity." *Christianity and Crisis* 31 (April 5, 1971): 56–60.

———. "Lonergan and the Subjectivist Principle." *Journal of Religion* 51 (July 1971): 155–72.

———. "The Task of Philosophical Theology." Pages 55–84 in *The Future of Philosophical Theology*. Edited by Robert A. Evans. Philadelphia: Westminster Press, 1971.

———. "What is Theology?" *Journal of Religion* 52 (Jan. 1972): 22–40.

———. "The Reformation that We Want." *Anglican Theological Review* 54 (Oct. 1972): 260–73.

———. "Lonergan and the Subjectivist Principle." Pages 218–25 in *Language, Truth and Meaning: Papers from the International Lonergan Congress 1970*. Edited by Philip McShane. Notre Dame, Ind.: Univ. of Notre Dame Press, 1972.

———. "Response." *The Perkins School of Theology Journal* 26 (Winter 1973): 45–57.

———. "Faith and Secularity." Pages 26–43 in *God, Secularization, and History: Essays in Memory of Ronald Gregor Smith*. Edited by Eugene Thomas Long. Columbia: Univ. of South Carolina Press, 1974.

———. "Falsification and Belief." *Religious Studies* 10 (March 1974): 21–43.

———. "'"Theology and Falsification" in Retrospect': A Reply." Pages 290–96 in *The Logic of God: Theology and Verification*. Edited by Malcolm L. Diamond and Thomas V. Litzenburg. Indianapolis: Bobbs-Merrill, 1975.

———. "The Authority of Scripture for Theology." *Interpretation* 30 (July 1976): 242–61. Reprinted in *On Theology*. San Francisco: Harper & Row, 1986. 2d ed., Dallas, Tex.: Southern Methodist Univ. Press, 1992.

———. "Sources of Religious Authority in Liberal Protestantism." *Journal of the American Academy of Religion* 44 (Sept. 1976): 403–16.

———. "Linguistic Analysis and Theology." *Theologische Zeitschrift* 33 (Sept.–Oct. 1977): 318–25.

———. "Faith and Freedom: How My Mind has Changed." *Christian Century* 97 (Dec. 17, 1980): 1241–44.

———. *The Point of Christology*. San Francisco: Harper & Row, 1982. 2d ed., Dallas, Tex.: Southern Methodist Univ. Press, 1982.

———. "The Experience of God: Critical Reflections on Hartshorne's Theory of Analogy." Pages 16–37 in *Existence and Actuality: Conversations with Charles Hartschorne*. Edited by John B. Cobb, Jr. and Franklin I. Gamwell. Chicago: Univ. of Chicago Press, 1984.

———. *On Theology*. San Francisco: Harper & Row, 1986.

———. "The Nature and State of Theological Scholarship and Research." *Theological Education* 24 (Autumn 1987): 120–31.

———. *Faith and Freedom: Toward a Theology of Liberation*. Rev. ed. Nashville, Tenn.: Abingdon Press, 1989. First published in 1979 by Abingdon Press.

———. *Is There Only One True Religion or Are There Many?* Dallas, Tex.: Southern Methodist Univ. Press, 1992.

———. "The Enlightenment is Not Over." Pages 321–27 in *Knowledge and Belief in America*. Edited by William M. Shea and Peter A. Huff. Cambridge: Cambridge Univ. Press, 1995.

———. *Doing Theology Today*. Valley Forge, Pa.: Trinity Press, 1996.

———. "Toward Bearing Witness." *Religious Studies Review* 23 (Oct. 1997): 333–40.

O'Regan, Cyril. "*De Doctrina Christiana* and Modern Hermeneutics." Pages 217–43 in De Doctrina Christiana: *A Classic of Western Culture*. Edited by Duane W. H. Arnold and Pamela Bright. Notre Dame, Ind: Univ. of Notre Dame Press, 1995.

Pauw, Amy Plantinga. Review of *Types of Christian Theology*, by Hans Frei. *Theology Today* 50 (April 1993): 124–26.

Peters, Ted. Review of *Faith and Freedom* by Schubert Ogden. *Interpretation* 35 (Jan. 1981): 78–82.

———. "The Theological Method of Schubert Ogden." *Dialog* 29 (Spring 1990): 125–34.

Peterson, Michael L., ed. *Does Religious Experience Justify Religious Belief? Do Mystics See God?* Malden, Mass.: Blackwell Publishing, 2004.

Phillips, D. Z. *Faith and Philosophical Inquiry*. London: Routledge & Keegan Paul, 1970.

———. *The Concept of Prayer*. New York: Seabury, 1981.

Pitcher, George, ed. *Wittgenstein: The Philosophical Investigations*. Notre Dame, Ind.: Univ. of Notre Dame Press, 1968.

Placher, William C. "Scripture as Realistic Narrative: Some Preliminary Questions." *Perspectives in Religious Studies* 5 (Spring 1978): 32–41.

———. "Revisionist and Postliberal Theologies and the Public Character of Theology." *The Thomist* 49 (1985): 392–416.

———. "Paul Ricoeur and Postliberal Theology: A Conflict of Interpretations?" *Modern Theology* 4 (Oct. 1987): 35–52.

———. "Introduction." Pages 3–25 in Hans W. Frei, *Theology and Narrative: Selected Essays*. Edited by George Hunsinger and William C. Placher. New York: Oxford Univ. Press, 1993.

Plantinga, Alvin. *Warrant: The Current Debate*. New York: Oxford Univ. Press, 1993.

———. *Warrant and Proper Function*. New York: Oxford Univ. Press, 1993.

———. *Warranted Christian Belief*. New York: Oxford Univ. Press, 2000.

Poland, Lynn M. "The New Criticism, Neoorthodoxy, and the New Testament." *Journal of Religion* 65 (Oct. 1985): 459–77.

Ramsey, Ian T. *Religious Language*. London: SCM-Canterbury Press, 1967.

Ritschl, Albrecht. *The Christian Doctrine of Justification and Reconciliation*. Vol. 3. Translated by H. R. Mackintosh and A. B. Macauley. Edinburgh: T & T Clark, 1900.

Ross, William Gordon. "God and the Verification Principle: The Question of Verification." *Religion in Life* 32:1 (1963): 8–18.

Ruether, Rosemary Radford. *Sexism and God-Talk: Toward a Feminist Theology*. Boston: Beacon Press, 1983.

Ruse, Michael. "Methodological Naturalism Under Attack." *South African Journal of Philosophy* 24 (2005): 44–60.

Russell, Bertrand. *The Principles of Mathematics*. 1903. 2d ed. New York: Norton & Co., 1938.

———. "On Denoting." *Mind* 14 (1905): 479–93. Reprinted in *The Philosophy of Language*. 4th ed. Edited by A. P. Martinich. New York: Oxford Univ. Press, 2001.

———. "Knowledge by Acquaintance and Knowledge by Description." *Proceedings of the Aristotelian Society* 11 (1910–11): 108–28.

———. "Mr Strawson on Referring." *Mind* 66 (1957): 385–89.

Ryle, Gilbert. *The Concept of Mind*. London: Hutchinson, 1949. Reprint, Chicago: Univ. of Chicago Press, 1984.

———. "Systematically Misleading Expressions." Pages 11–36 in *Logic and Language* (first series). Edited by Antony Flew. Oxford: Basil Blackwell, 1963.

———. "The Theory of Meaning." Pages 239–64 in *British Philosophy in the Mid-Century*, 2d ed. Edited by C. A. Mace. London: George Allen and Unwin, 1966.

Salmon, Nathan. "Existence." Pages 49–108 in *Philosophical Perspectives*. Vol. 1, *Metaphysics*. Atascadero, Calif.: Ridgeview, 1987.

———. "Nonexistence." *Noûs* 32 (1998): 277–319

Santoni, Ronald E. ed. *Religious Language and the Problem of Religious Knowledge*. Bloomington: Indiana Univ. Press, 1968.

Schleiermacher, Friedrich. *On Religion: Speeches to its Cultured Despisers*. Translated by Richard Crouter. Cambridge: Cambridge Univ. Press, 1988. Reprint, 1994.

———. *The Christian Faith*. 2d ed. Edited and translated by H. R. Mackintosh and J. S. Stewart. Edinburgh: T & T Clark, 1989.

Schner, George P. "*The Eclipse of Biblical Narrative*: Analysis and Critique." *Modern Theology* 8:2 (April 1992): 149–72.

Schwartzentruber, Paul. "The Modesty of Hermeneutics: The Theological Reserves of Hans Frei." *Modern Theology* 8:2 (April 1992): 181–95.

Searle, John. "Proper Names." *Mind* 67 (1958): 166–73.

———. *Speech Acts*. Cambridge: Cambridge Univ. Press, 1969.

Shaffer, Michael J. "A Defeater of the Claim that Belief in God's Existence is Properly Basic." *Philo* 7 (2004): 57–70.

Siebel, Mark. Review of *Illocutionary Acts and Sentence Meaning* by William P. Alston. *Grazer Philosophische Studien* 62 (2001): 48–61.

Smith, John MacDonald. "Philosophy and God." *Church Quarterly Review* 168: 366 (Jan. 1967): 75–83.

Smith, Quentin. "Marcus, Kripke and the Origin of the New Theory of Reference." *Synthese* 104:2 (Aug. 1995; edited by James H. Fetzer and Paul W. Humphreys): 179–89.

Soames, Scott. "Direct Reference, Propositional Attitudes, and Semantic Content." *Philosophical Topics* 15 (1987): 47–87. Reprinted in *Readings in the Philosophy of Language*. Edited by Peter Ludlow. Cambridge, Mass.: MIT Press, 1997. Reprint, 1998.

———. "Semantics and Semantic Competence." *Philosophical Perspectives* 3 (1989): 575–96.

———. "Truth, Meaning and Understanding." *Philosophical Studies* 65 (1992): 17–35.

———. "Skepticism About Meaning: Indeterminacy, Normativity, and the Rule Following Paradox." *The Canadian Journal of Philosophy*, supp. vol. 23 (1997): 211–49.

———. "Facts, Truth Conditions, and the Skeptical Solution to the Rule-Following Paradox." Pages 313–48 in *Language, Mind and Ontology*. Nous-Supplement: Philosophical Perspectives. Edited by James Tomberlin. Vol. 12. Oxford: Blackwell, 1998.

———. *Understanding Truth*. New York: Oxford Univ. Press, 1999.

———. *Beyond Rigidity: The Unfinished Semantic Agenda of Naming and Necessity*. New York: Oxford Univ. Press, 2002.

———. *Philosophical Analysis in the Twentieth Century*. 2 vols. Princeton, N.J.: Princeton Univ. Press, 2003.

———. *Reference and Description: The Case Against Two-Dimensionalism*. Princeton, N.J.: Princeton Univ. Press, 2005.

Springs, Jason A. *Toward a Generous Orthodoxy: Prospects for Hans Frei's Postliberal Theology*. New York: Oxford Univ. Press, 2010.

Strawson, P. F. *Review of Philosophical Investigations* by Ludwig Wittgenstein. *Mind* 63 (1954): 70–99. Reprinted in *Wittgenstein: The Philosophical Investigations*. Edited by George Pitcher. Garden City, N.Y.: Anchor Books, 1966.

———. "On Referring." *Mind* 59 (1950): 320–44. Reprinted in *The Philosophy of Language*. Edited by A. P. Martinich. 4th ed. New York: Oxford Univ. Press, 2001.

Surin, Kenneth. *The Turnings of Darkness and Light: Essays in Philosophical and Systematic Theology*. Cambridge: Cambridge Univ. Press, 1989.

Sykes, John. "Narrative Accounts of Biblical Authority: The Need for a Doctrine of Revelation." *Modern Theology* 5 (July 1989): 327–42.

Tanner, Kathryn E. "Theology and the Plain Sense." Pages 59–78 in *Scriptural Authority and Narrative Interpretation*. Edited by Garrett Green. Philadelphia: Fortress Press, 1987.

———. *Theories of Culture: A New Agenda for Theology*. Minneapolis: Fortress Press, 1997.

Tarski, Alfred. "The Concept of Truth in Formalized Languages." *Logic, Semantics, Meta-Mathematics*. Translated by J. H. Woodger. 2d ed. Indianapolis: Hackett, 1983.

TeSelle, Eugene. Review of *The Point of Christology* by Schubert M. Ogden. *Religious Studies Review* 9 (July 1983): 227–33.

Thomas, Owen C. "Theology and Experience." *Harvard Theological Review* 78:1–2 (1985): 179–201.

Tillich, Paul. "Religious Symbols and Our Knowledge of God." Pages 479–88 in *Philosophy of Religion*. Edited by W. L. Rowe and W. J. Wainwright. New York: Harcourt Brace Jovanovich, 1973.

Torrance, Thomas F. "Article Review of *Falsification and Belief* by Alastair McKinnon." *Scottish Journal of Theology* 25 (1972): 435–53.

Toulmin, Stephen. *An Examination of the Place of Reason in Ethics*. Cambridge: Cambridge Univ. Press, 1950.

———. *The Philosophy of Science: An Introduction*. London: Hutchinson & Co., 1953.

———. *The Uses of Argument*. Cambridge: Cambridge Univ. Press, 1958.

———. *Foresight and Understanding: An Enquiry into the Aims of Science*. London: Hutchinson & Co., 1961.

Townes, Emilie. *Womanist Ethics and the Cultural Production of Evil*. New York: Palgrave Macmillan, 2006.

Tracy, David W. *Blessed Rage for Order*. New York: Seabury Press, 1975.

———. "Lindbeck's New Program for Theology: A Reflection." *The Thomist* 49:3 (July 1985): 460–72

van Buren, Paul M. *The Secular Meaning of the Gospel*. New York: Macmillan, 1963. Reprint, 1965.

———. "On Doing Theology." Pages 52–71 in *Talk of God*. Edited by G. N. A. Vesey. London: Macmillan.

Wainwright, William J. "Religious Statements and the World." *Religious Studies* 2 (1966): 49–60.

Watson, Francis. *Text, Church and World: Biblical Interpretation in Theological Perspective*. Grand Rapids, Mich.: Wm. B. Eerdmans, 1994.

Welch, Claude. *Protestant Thought in the Nineteenth Century*. Vol. 1: *1799–1870*. New Haven, Conn.: Yale Univ. Press, 1972.

Wernham, James C. S. "Eschatological Verification and Parontological Obfuscation." *Canadian Journal of Theology* 13 (1967): 50–56.

Whitehead, Alfred North. *Process and Reality: An Essay in Cosmology*. New York: Macmillan, 1929.

———. *Modes of Thought*. New York: Macmillan, 1936.

———. *Process and Reality: An Essay in Cosmology*. Edited by David Ray Griffin and Donald W. Sherburne. Corrected ed. New York: Macmillan, 1978.

Wilburn, Ralph G. "The Problem of Verification in Faith-Knowledge." *Lexington Theological Quarterly* 4:2 (1969): 33–45.

Wiles, Maurice. "Scriptural Authority and Theological Construction: The Limitations of Narrative Interpretation." Pages 42–58 in *Scriptural Authority and Narrative Interpretation*. Edited by Garrett Green. Philadelphia: Fortress Press, 1987.

Winston, Trevor. "God and the Verification Principle: Faith versus Verification." *Religion in Life* 32:1 (1963): 29–35.

Wisdom, John. "Gods." *Proceedings of the Aristotelian Society* 45 (1944–45): 185–206.

Wittgenstein, Ludwig. *Lectures and Conversations on Aesthetics, Psychology and Religious Belief.* Edited by Cyril Barrett. Berkeley and Los Angeles: Univ. of California Press, n.d.

———. *Philosophical Investigations.* Translated by G. E. M. Anscombe. 3rd ed. Englewood Cliffs, N.J.: Prentice-Hall, 1958.

———. *Tractatus Logico-Philosophicus.* Translated by C. K. Ogden. London: Routledge & Keegan Paul, 1922. Reprint, London: Routledge, 1990.

Wolterstorff, Nicholas. "Evidence, Entitled Belief, and the Gospels." *Faith and Philosophy* 6 (Oct. 1989): 429–59.

———. *Divine Discourse: Philosophical Reflections on the Claim that God Speaks.* Cambridge: Cambridge Univ. Press, 1995.

———. "Will Narrativity Work as Linchpin? Reflections on the Hermeneutic of Hans Frei." Pages 71–107 in *Relativism and Religion.* Edited by Charles M. Lewis. London: Macmillan, 1995.

———. *Works and Worlds of Art.* New York: Oxford Univ. Press, 1984.

Wood, Charles M. *The Formation of Christian Understanding.* Philadelphia: Westminster Press, 1981.

Woolverton, John F. Review of *Types of Christian Theology,* by Hans Frei. *Anglican Theological Review* 75 (Winter 1993): 143–45.

———. "Hans W. Frei in Context: A Theological and Historical Memoir." *Anglican Theological Review* 79 (Summer 1997): 369–93.

Wright, T. R. "Regenerating Narrative: The Gospels as Fiction." *Religious Studies* 20 (Spring 1984): 389–400.

INDEX

Abstract objects, 44, 60, 148, 150–151, 169, 170, 284

Accommodation, 284

Acquaintance, 46–47, 59–60, 64, 101, 112, 120, 125

Allegorical interpretation, 209 n.43

Allen, Diogenes, 6 n.9

Alston, William P., 13, 15, 229 n.3, 239 n.32, 245, 250–252, 260 n.92, 263 n.103, 271, 274–275, 277, 279, 282 n.17, 285, 288–289

Altizer, Thomas, 62

Analytic philosophy, 13, 16, 38, 228, 278, 288–289

Antirealism, 210 n.46

Apologetics, 10, 15, 96–97, 138, 161–163, 171–174, 177–181, 195, 240–243, 268, 283

Aquinas, Thomas, 61, 91, 92 n.43, 273, 288

Assertions, 4, 7, 10, 38, 47–51, 53–77, 88, 97, 105–111, 115, 147, 194, 199, 204, 213, 217–222, 236–239, 240, 255, 266–289

Auerbach, Erich, 9–11, 138, 157–160, 162, 180, 183

Augustine, 208 n.40

Aulén, Gustav, 244 n.41

Austin, J. L., 12, 13, 201 n.9, 250

Authenticity, 71 n.66, 84–87, 99–100, 109–111, 113 nn.129 & 131, 116, 118, 204, 264, 268

Author meaning *See* Meaning, author's meaning

Authorial intention, 136, 167, 169–170, 175–176, 207, 210, 259 n.91, 287–288. *See also* Meaning, author's meaning

Ayer, A. J., 247

Barth, Karl, 125–138
  analogy of faith, 130, 132, 135
  Anselm and, 8, 128, 132–133, 183, 195
  biblical interpretation, 127, 129 n.12, 135–138, 161
  biblical realists, 129–131
  epistemology, 8, 127–130, 135, 137, 148
  experience, 125, 127–132, 218
  Feuerbach, 37–38, 125–128, 268
  grace and nature, 129, n.14, 132 n.33
  Holy Spirit, 129, 136
  Jesus Christ, 2, 127, 131–133, 137, 149
  knowledge of God, 127, 129–136
  ontology, 8–9, 127–130, 135–137, 161, 180, 182, 197, 240
  relational theology; relationalism, 128–129, 131–132, 134–135
  Schleiermacher and, 2, 21, 28, 31, 34, 132, 218
  systematizing, 9, 12, 127, 132, 134–137
  theological method, 130–135
  Word of God, 129, 132–136, 162, 208–209, 223

Belief, 22–23, 38, 45, 47–51, 54–57, 77 n.87, 92, 130, 133, 163, 195, 197, 203–204, 206, 221–222, 232, 241, 246, 248, 260

Bengel, Johann Albrecht, 164

Biblical narratives
    absorbing the world, 205, 240
    figural interpretation, 158, 163–165
    genre, 107, 156, 160, 174, 201, 250
    historical-critical interpretation, 28,
        30, 82, 104, 106, 161, 167–170,
        173, 205
    historical reference, 165, 167,
        175–176, 253–258, 276
    realistic interpretation, 9, 156, 163,
        165–166, 173–174, 176–177,
        179, 184, 200, 252, 253 n.67, 254,
        260–261
    tyrannical nature, 138, 158–160,
        162–163, 179, 181, 183–184, 220,
        223, 276
Blaisdell, Charles, 112 n.127, 108 n.108
Bliks, 7, 53, 56
Blocher, Henri, 253 n.67
Braithwaite, R. B., 54, 61 nn.27 & 28
Bultmann, Rudolf, 7, 8, 20, 80–87, 98,
        101, 106, 107 n.101, 110 n.115,
        117, 120 n.158, 187 n.130, 280,
        281, 286
    Heidegger and, 84–86, 98
    myth, 80–84
    New Testament interpretation, 80–87
    science, 81–83, 85

Cady, Linell Elizabeth, 3 nn.3 & 4
Calvin, John, 21, 204 n.21, 284
Carlson, Jeffrey, 109
Categorial adequacy, 203–204
Causal theory of reference, 239
Christian, William A., 69 n.60, 75–77,
        238
Christianity, essence of, 5, 20, 25, 32–35,
        78, 182–184
Christology, 74 n.80, 76 n.84, 104–112,
        119–121, 132, 237, 182, 194,
        268–269
Classical theism, 91–93
Cocceius, Johannes, 164
Coherence. See Truth, coherence
Collins, Anthony, 166–170, 180–181
Cone, James M., 116 n.141, 286 n.22
Consciousness
    Christian, of church, 29–30
    historical, of author, 175–177, 179,
        215

human consciousness, 23, 88–91, 92
        n.47, 98, 214
    of Jesus, 109, 179, 181
    religious, 24, 221
    self-consciousness, 22, 25–26, 68, 110
Crombie, I. M., 53, 58–61, 64
Culture, 113 n.131, 202, 212
Cupitt, Don, 54

Davidson, Donald, 12, 13, 14, 229–235,
        238 n.29, 273 n.7, 288
Dawson, John David, 158 n.6
Deism, 22, 24, 270 n.55, 171, 172
Demythologization, 8, 71 n.66, 80–87,
        91, 101–102, 105, 119, 194, 265,
        267, 269, 281, 283, 286
Derrida, Jacques, 56, 209
Descartes, Rene, 85, 88, 89, 90 n.36, 117
        n.146
Devenish, Philip E., 92 n.43, 113 n.129
Doctrines, 10, 11, 19, 23, 28, 137–138,
        157, 198, 201, 211 n.51, 219, 227,
        241, 257, 272
    cognitive-propositional view,
        201–202, 227
    cultural-linguistic view, 156, 202–205
    doctrinal development, change, 201
        n.11, 202 n.13, 203–204
    experiential-expressivist view,
        201–204
    rule theory, 201–205
Donnellan, Keith, 12, 236–238
Dummett, Michael, 39 n.1, 40 n.4, 238
        n.29

Ellingson, Mark, 243–244
Enlightenment, 20–21, 81, 114–115,
        171
Epistemic justification or warrant, 4, 15,
        16, 38, 51, 61, 66, 71 n.66, 106,
        117 n.144, 125, 248, 249 n.51,
        283, 289
Epistemology, 8–9, 36, 38, 41, 45–46,
        127–130, 134–135, 137, 148, 161,
        168–170, 172–173, 180–182, 184,
        197, 254
Essence of Christianity. See Christianity,
        essence of
Evidence, 7, 19–20, 38, 51, 53–58, 61,
        107 n.104, 164, 166